Teacher's Edition

SRA Open Court Reading

Level 3 • Unit 2
City Wildlife

— PROGRAM AUTHORS —

Carl Bereiter
Ann Brown
Joe Campione
Iva Carruthers
Robbie Case
Jan Hirshberg
Marilyn Jager Adams
Anne McKeough
Michael Pressley
Marsha Roit
Marlene Scardamalia
Marcy Stein
Gerald H. Treadway, Jr.

SRA
A Division of The McGraw-Hill Companies
Columbus, Ohio

Acknowledgments

Grateful acknowledgment is given to the following publishers and copyright owners for permissions granted to reprint selections from their publications. Al possible care has been taken to trace ownership and secure permission for each selection included. In case of any errors or omissions, the Publisher will be pleased to make suitable acknowledgments in future editions.

Copyright © 1970 by Phyllis Busch. First appeared in CITY LOTS: LIVING THINGS IN VACANT SPOTS, published by The World Publishing Co. Reprinte by permssion of Curtis Brown, Ltd.

From THE BOY WHO DIDN'T BELIEVE IN SPRING by Lucille Clifton, copyright © 1973 by Lucille Clifton, text. Used by permission of Dutton's Children's Books, an imprint of Penguin Putnam Books for Young Readers, a division of Penguin Putnam Inc.

"City Critters: Wild Animals Live in Cities, Too" from 3-2-1 CONTACT Magazine, Sept. 1988. Copyright 1988 Sesame Workshop (New York, New York). Al rights reserved.

"Raccoon" from THE LLAMA WHO HAD NO PAJAMA: 100 FAVORITE POEMS, copyright © 1973 by Mary Ann Hoberman, reprinted by permission of Harcourt, Inc.

From MAKE WAY FOR DUCKLINGS by Robert McCloskey, copyright 1941, renewed © 1969 by Robert McCloskey. Used by permission of Viking Pengui an imprint of Penguin Putnam Books for Young Readers, a division of Penguin Putnam Inc.

From URBAN ROOSTS by Barbara Bash. Copyright © 1990 by Barbara Bash. By permission of Little, Brown and Company.

"The Worm" by Raymond Souster is reprinted from COLLECTED POEMS OF RAYMOND SOUSTER by permission of Oberon Press.

"Pigeons" from I THOUGHT I HEARD THE CITY by Lilian Moore. Copyright © 1969 Lilian Moore. © renewed 1997 Lilian Moore Reavin. Reprinted by permission of Marian Reiner for the author.

TWO DAYS IN MAY by Harriet Peck Taylor, pictures by Leyla Torres. Copyright © 1999 by Harriet Peck Taylor, illustrations copyright © 1999 by Leyla Torres. Reprinted by permission of Farrar, Straus & Giroux, LLC.

SECRET PLACE by Eve Bunting, illustrated by Ted Rand. Text copyright © 1996 by Eve Bunting. Illustrations copyright © 1996 by Ted Rand. Reprinted b permission of Clarion Books/Houghton Mifflin Co. All rights reserved.

www.sra4kids.com

SRA/McGraw-Hill

A Division of The **McGraw-Hill** *Companies*

Send all inquiries to:
SRA/McGraw-Hill
8787 Orion Place
Columbus, OH 43240-4027

Printed in the United States of America.

ISBN 0-07-602754-6

3 4 5 6 7 8 9 WEB 10 09 08 07 06 05

Making the Difference

Welcome to

SRA OPEN COURT READING

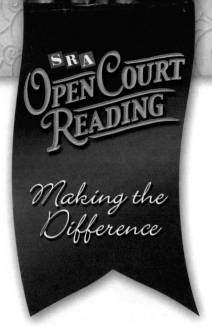

SRA Open Court Reading

Making the Difference

Proven Results

Inspire a lifetime love of learning by using research-based instruction.

Open Court Reading is an instructional leader for three key reasons.

1. Research-based instruction that works
2. Teacher-tested lessons that are effective in classrooms like yours
3. Unparalleled support to help you do what you do best—Teach

Achieve your classroom goals with ***Open Court Reading's*** proven approach.

Students attending schools using ***Open Court Reading*** score higher in basic reading skills than students attending schools that do not use ***Open Court Reading*** materials.

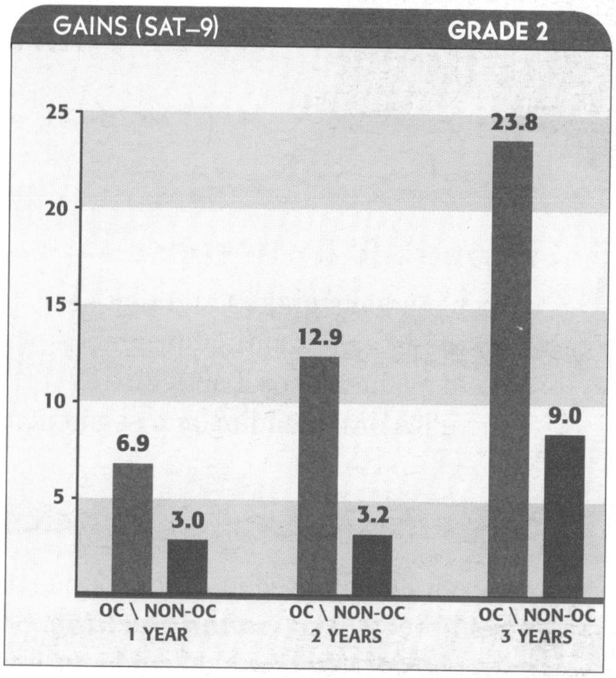

In California schools serving large concentrations of Low Socioeconomic Status students, differences over three years were most impressive.

"Since using ***Open Court Reading,*** our students have gone beyond even my expectations. ***Open Court Reading*** is by far the best systematic approach to instruction of reading skills that I have taught in my thirty years as an instructor or administrator."

— **Gerald Judd,** 6th Grade Language Arts
Dunbar 6th Grade Center,
Fort Worth, TX

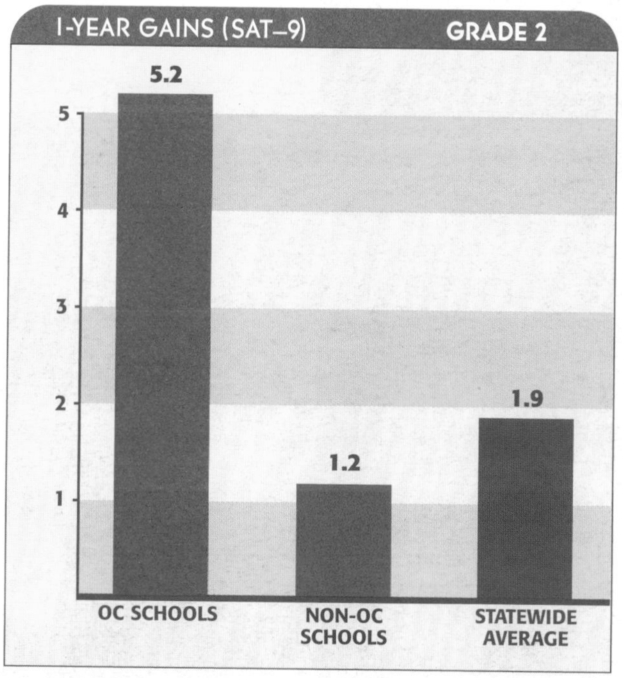

One-year gains for students in more than 700 California schools show that ***Open Court Reading*** schools outgain non-***Open Court Reading*** schools by a factor of four.

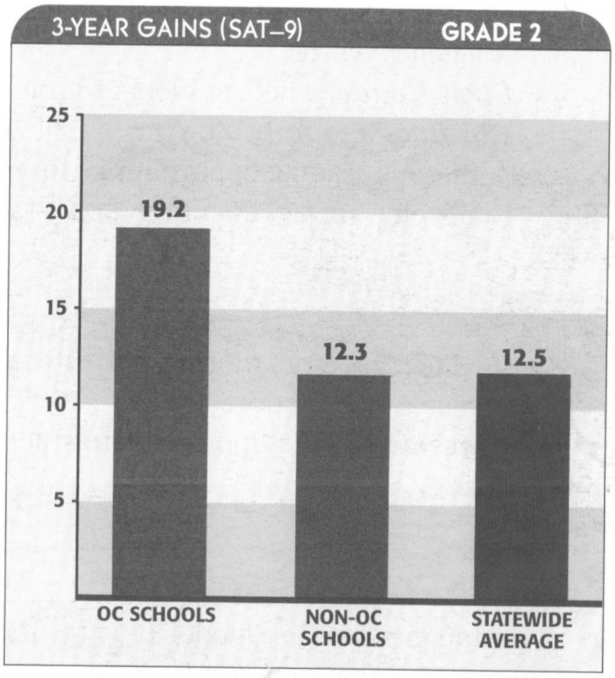

Open Court Reading schools outgain demographically similar non-***Open Court Reading*** schools as well as the statewide average by 50 to 75 percent.

For a copy of the detailed ***Open Court Reading*** **Research Report** and **Results Report**, visit SRAonline.com, or contact SRA at 1-888-SRA-4543.

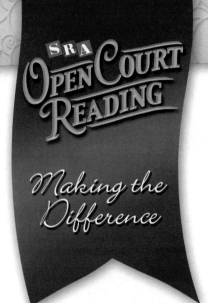

SRA Open Court Reading

Making the Difference

Effective Instruction

Lead the way in research-based instruction with ***Open Court Reading.***

40+ YEARS OF RESEARCH-VALIDATED RESULTS

1 Phonemic Awareness

- help students understand that speech is made up of distinct, identifiable sounds
- quick, gamelike oral activities
- includes oral blending and segmentation

discriminating the sounds that make up words

2 Systematic, Explicit Phonics

- developmental sequence of sound spellings
- reinforced using ***Sound/Spelling Cards***
- ***Decodable Books*** help students apply, review, and reinforce sound/spelling correspondences

applying the links between letters and sounds to printed words

3 Fluency

- explicit teaching of blending and high-frequency words
- ***First Readers*** help students transition from ***Big Books*** to ***Anthologies***
- numerous reading opportunities for students to become strong, fluent readers

reading effortlessly with speed, accuracy, and expression

4 Vocabulary

- instruction before, during, and after reading
- research-based strategies
- reviewed and incorporated into students' writing

learning word meanings to build comprehension

5 Text Comprehension

- strategies are first modeled by the teacher
- graphic organizers can be used to categorize information
- skills are explicitly taught and reviewed

thinking actively before, during, and after reading

Manage instructional time to make the most of your day.

Beginning with a strong foundation in Pre-Kindergarten, ***Open Court Reading*** effectively builds skills and strategies throughout all grade levels.

Comprehensive Program

Pre-K	Letter Recognition	Print/Book Awareness	Phonological and Phonemic Awarenes	Phonics	Comprehension and Fluency	Writing
K	Letter Recognition	Print/Book Awareness	Phonological and Phonemic Awareness	Phonics	Comprehension and Fluency	Writing
1	Letter/Book/Print Awareness	Phonemic Awareness	Phonics	Comprehension and Fluency	Writing	Language Arts and Vocabulary
2	Phonics/Word Knowledge	Comprehension and Fluency	Inquiry Learning	Writing	Language Arts and Vocabulary	
3	Phonics/Word Knowledge	Comprehension and Fluency	Inquiry Learning	Writing	Language Arts and Vocabulary	
4	Word Knowledge	Comprehension and Fluency	Inquiry Learning	Writing	Language Arts and Vocabulary	
5	Word Knowledge	Comprehension and Fluency	Inquiry Learning	Writing	Language Arts and Vocabulary	
6	Word Knowledge	Comprehension and Fluency	Inquiry Learning	Writing	Language Arts and Vocabulary	

This chart shows the time allocated for skill instruction at each grade level.

SRA Open Court Reading

Making the Difference

Award-Winning Literature

Engage students with great literature to help them become independent readers.

The literature in each theme was thoughtfully selected with the following goals in mind:

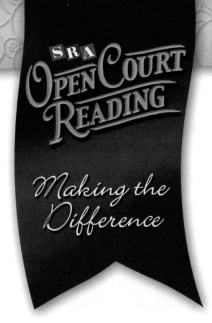

- **A variety of literature** provides a full spectrum of fiction and nonfiction.
- **Excellent literature** provides models for student writing and helps students develop their expertise as writers.
- **Award-winning authors** and different styles of writing encourage students to develop a cultural literacy.

Literature in ***Open Court Reading*** is available in a variety of formats, depending on the grade level.

- Big and Little Books
- Anthologies
- Teacher Read Alouds
- Story Time Selections (Kindergarten)
- Leveled Classroom Libraries
- First Readers

Thought-provoking themes in ***Open Court Reading*** span grade levels.

	Pre-K	K	1	2	3	4	5	6
	BIG BOOKS	BIG BOOKS	BIG BOOKS	STUDENT ANTHOLOGIES	STUDENT ANTHOLOGIES	STUDENT ANTHOLOGIES	STUDENT ANTHOLOGIES	STUDENT ANTHOLOGIES
Unit 1	I'm Special	School	Let's Read!	Sharing Stories	Friendship	Risks and Consequences	Cooperation and Competition	Perseverance
Unit 2	Families Everywhere	Shadows	Animals	Kindness	City Wildlife	Dollars and Sense	Astronomy	Ancient Civilizations
Unit 3	All Kinds of Friends	Finding Friends	Things That Go	Look Again	Imagination	From Mystery to Medicine	Heritage	Taking a Stand
Unit 4	Helping Hands	The Wind	Our Neighborhood at Work	Fossils	Money	Survival	Making a New Nation	Beyond the Notes
Unit 5	Let's Go!	Stick to It	Weather	Courage	Storytelling	Communication	Going West	Ecology
Unit 6	Senses	Red, White, and Blue	Journeys	Our Country and Its People	Country Life	A Changing America	Journeys and Quests	A Question of Value
			STUDENT ANTHOLOGIES					
Unit 7	At the Farm	Teamwork	Keep Trying					
Unit 8	Changes	By the Sea	Games					
Unit 9			Being Afraid					
Unit 10			Homes					

"Reading is the basis for all learning. I applaud ***Open Court Reading*** for allowing teachers to spend so much time on reading and yet not miss out on some of the other areas of learning. So much science and social studies is built into the program that it really makes my job as a teacher easier."

— **Deanna Sinift**, Grade 1 Teacher
Woodville Elementary School,
Porterville, CA

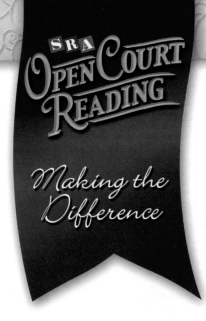

Making the Difference

Comprehensive Resources

Open Court Reading **materials will help your students expand their knowledge by exploring, discussing, and researching ideas.**

Student Materials

Big and Little Books
- Award-winning authors and illustrators
- Variety of cultures and genres represented

Anthologies
- Award-winning authors and illustrators
- Wide variety of cultures and genres represented
- Concept Connections include vocabulary practice

First and Second Readers
- Transitions Level 1 students from ***Big Books*** to ***Anthologies***
- Reviews skills in Level 2

Decodable Text
- Pre-Decodable and Decodable stories in either book or takehome format
- Practice blending strategies and high-frequency words

Story Time Selections
- Trade books to support Kindergarten unit themes

Leveled Classroom Libraries
- Leveled trade books that support unit themes

Desk Strips
- Miniature pictures of ***Alphabet Sound Cards*** or ***Sound/Spelling Cards***

Language Arts Big Books
- Language arts skills for students in Kindergarten and Level 1

Language Arts Handbooks
- Language Arts conventions and examples for students in Levels 2–6

Practice Books
- Activities to practice and reinforce skills found in all parts of the lesson

Science/Social Studies Connection Centers
- Reinforce reading across the curriculum

Online

Online Phonics
- Interactive multimedia lessons to practice phonics skills
- Includes an assessment tool to monitor student progress

Literacy Launcher
- ***Online Phonics*** and vocabulary instruction
- Assessment and management tools included

CD-ROMs

Alphabet Book Activities
- Interactive activities to accompany ***Alphabet Big Book***

Decodable Book Activities
- Includes interactive activities to practice and review sound/spellings

Spelling Software
- Features a variety of interactive activities to review spelling patterns

Ultimate Writing and Creativity Center
- Activities to reinforce writing process skills

Research Assistant
- Provides forms to help students plan, organize, present, and assess research projects

TechKnowledge
- Technology skills and applications to help students research, write, calculate, and present topics more effectively
- Step-by-step instruction made easy

Leap Into™ Phonics
- Phonemic awareness and phonics activities

Power Vocabulary
- Vocabulary practice for ***Leveled Classroom Libraries*** in Levels 3–6

Audiocassettes/CDs

Listening Library
- ***Big Book*** and ***Anthology*** selections available on audiocassette or compact disc

Alphabet Sound Card Stories
- Appropriate grade-level jingles set to music

Sound/Spelling Card Stories
- Appropriate grade-level jingles set to music

Teacher materials help you make the most of your day.

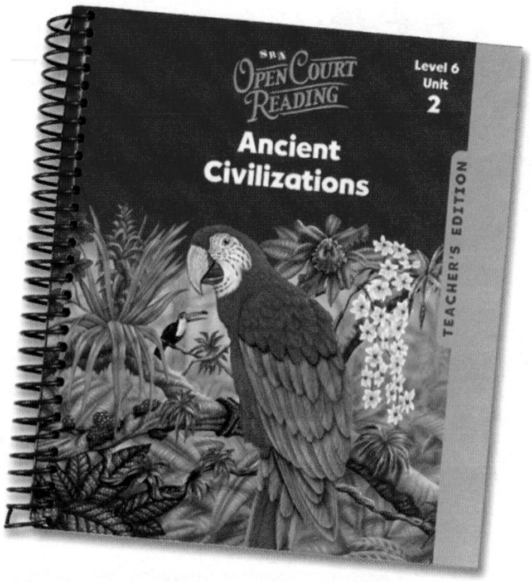

Teacher's Editions
- Separate books for each unit theme
- Three-part lessons, each containing phonics, reading comprehension, and language arts
- Plans to help differentiate instruction
- Tips to accommodate students learning English

Teacher Read Alouds
- Available in every unit for each grade level

Phonics Packages
- Contain manipulatives necessary for phonics instruction

Home Connection
- Blackline masters to inform and support ***Open Court Reading*** lessons

Part 1 Lesson Cards
- Easy-to-use aid to use while teaching the phonics portion of each lesson (Levels K–3)

Teacher Management
- Printable blackline masters of all practice, ***Reteach,*** and ***Challenge*** books

Assessments to track and meet the needs of all students

Program Assessment
- Includes Pretests, Midyear Tests, and Posttests

Unit Assessments
- Assess skills introduced or reviewed in each lesson
- Include charts to monitor student progress

Test Preparation and Practice
- Prepares students for taking standardized tests

Assessment CD-ROM
- Printable blackline masters of all assessments
- Interactive record charts

Online Assessment
- Helps differentiate instruction
- Correlated to state standards
- Charts progress and monitors instruction
- Reports available at student, class, building, and district level

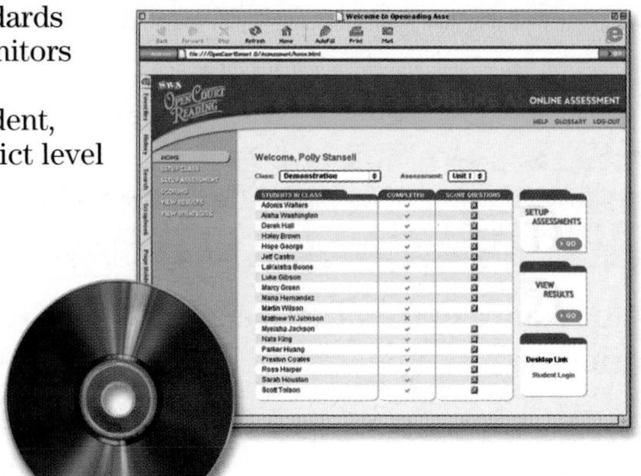

Materials to Differentiate Instruction

English Learner Support Guides and Activities
- Preteach and review ***Open Court Reading*** lessons

Intervention Guides and Workbooks
- Support students who need remediation

Reteach
- Activities for students who need a skill review during the lesson

Challenge
- Activities for students who would benefit from a skill challenge during the lesson

Differentiating Instruction Support Activities
- Quick activities available at the end of the unit to address students who need an additional review before moving to the next unit
- Activities are also available for those students who would benefit from extending a skill lesson

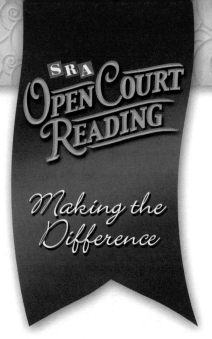

Open Court Reading

Making the Difference

Differentiating Instruction

Meet students' individual needs during Open Court Workshop.

The ***Open Court Reading Teacher's Editions*** provide easy-to-use references to ensure that you have the tools you need to help every student succeed in reading.

English Learner Support

Lessons using English Learner routines to preteach skills and concepts critical to understanding each ***Open Court Reading*** lesson

Reteach lessons

For those students who need extra practice on any of the lesson's skills

Intervention lessons

More intensive support, with controlled vocabulary selections and specific skills lessons to bring students up to grade level

Challenge activities

Continued stimulation for students working at or above grade level

Science/Social Studies Connection Centers

Additional cross curricular support

Differentiating Instruction Support Activities

For students who require extra practice activities to help bolster skills and extend unit instruction

:nvestigation Goals

he goal of Unit 2: City Wildlife is for students to develop an awareness nd understanding of the many forms of wildlife that exist in and around n urban environment. Many students may be unaware of the wildlife that nhabits our cities. More importantly, students may be unaware of how the resence of urban wildlife affects them, and how they affect the well-being f the wildlife. This unit has many significant environmental lessons to each the students. Students will gain knowledge of the various forms of ity wildlife, as well as become aware of how they can be instrumental in naintaining a healthy environment and coexistence for humans and the vildlife that inhabit the cities. The investigation goals for this unit are to:

- understand that wildlife does not just have to be in a jungle or a rural environment; it can be in a city, too.
- understand that plants as well as animals are wildlife.
- understand how wildlife survives in the city.
- learn how wildlife survives in the city and the difference between wildlife and pets.
- gain an appreciation for city wildlife.
- understand that people have a responsibility to protect the wildlife that surrounds them.

.earning Goals

Vildlife surrounds humans, yet we often do not realize it and even take it or granted. However, we are all part of interdependent relationships with ach other, whether or not we realize it. Throughout this unit, some specific earning goals will lead students to an awareness of wildlife in cities and a eeper understanding of the relationships between human communities nd wildlife. In this unit, students will:

- **listen, write, and speak** on the topic of city wildlife.
- **participate in small and large group discussions and lead discussions** about city wildlife.
- **ask and answer questions** relevant to city wildlife.
- **relate the ideas and experiences of the texts** to their own ideas and experiences.
- **develop** a vocabulary about city wildlife.
- **make cultural connections** by reading the selections.
- **identify different types of literature.**
- **use reference materials,** including interviews, to gain information.
- learn the importance of **note taking and organizing information.**
- learn how to use **indexes and charts.**
- **work through the research cycle** to learn more about city wildlife.

Teacher Tip To stimulate your own thinking about city wildlife, you might ask yourself questions like the following:

- ✔ What makes wildlife wild? (How are domesticated animals such as dogs and cats different from wild animals such as wolves and mountain lions?)
- ✔ What do wildlife species need to survive? How can wild plants and animals find these things in a city?
- ✔ What wild animals are able to live in cities? Do they have anything in common? Their size? How they move about? When they move about?
- ✔ How can humans help create and maintain a healthy relationship with wildlife in the city?

Exploring the Theme

Supporting Student Investigations

Students are encouraged to deepen their knowledge of each of the themes presented throughout ***Open Court Reading.*** In learning more about city wildlife, students will need to talk to people about it, as well as read stories and articles that revolve around the theme of city wildlife.

City wildlife is a subject for which there is abundant factual material, and one that may naturally pose intellectual questions or arouse curiosity. Students' initial browsing will provide them with many investigation ideas. It is best for students to generate problems or questions for investigation before they have had an opportunity to consult encyclopedias or other reference books. In this way, students' ideas are more likely to be driven by their natural interests than by what they think will be easy to investigate.

Encourage students to use their personal experiences to interpret the literature they read on city wildlife. Because it is also important for students to extend their thinking and for their views to be challenged and developed, encourage them to use this literature to reinterpret their personal experiences.

Explain to students that they will gain a better understanding of city wildlife as they progress through the unit's selections and as they work on the unit investigation.

Following are some formats students may want to use for the presentation of their investigations. Be sure to tell students that this is just a list of suggestions and they are encouraged to propose their own ideas.

- A miniplay or puppet show about city wildlife
- A role-playing game to work out a problem about city wildlife
- A panel discussion about city wildlife-related issues
- A debate on an issue related to city wildlife
- A newspaper column dealing with city wildlife-related problems
- A personal experience story about city wildlife

Unit Investigations

Throughout this unit, students will engage in activities of their own choosing that allow them to investigate city wildlife and to use the questions they have raised to do so. These investigations may relate to the selection that students are reading or to other source materials, but they must revolve around the theme concepts.

Suggested Activities

The activities suggested below are intended to support the unit investigation.

- Students may want to find out what about the city makes it possible for wildlife to survive there.
- Students may decide to survey their own neighborhoods and catalog the wildlife they find.
- Students may want to find out why some wildlife species are considered pests (such as rats and ragweed) and other species are not (such as sparrows and sycamore trees).
- Students may want to find out why some species move into human-populated areas.
- Students may want to keep logs about observation of wildlife.
- Students may want to debate relevant issues.
- Students may want to do a library search on disappearing habitats.

	OVERVIEW OF SELECTION	LINK TO THE THEME	UNIT INVESTIGATIONS	SUPPORTING STUDENT INVESTIGATIONS
esson 1 *The Boy Who Didn't Believe n Spring*	■ King Shabazz, with the aid of his faithful friend, Tony Polito, hits the streets in search of the mysterious spring.	■ Wildlife can be found in any city neighborhood, no matter how crowded.	■ Students create a Wildlife Observation Log.	■ Introduce investigation possibilities. Groups form and brainstorm initial plans.
esson 2 *ity Critters*	■ A variety of "wild" animals are found in cities, in unusual places. These "critters" may be able to tell us about the effects of urban living on human city-dwellers.	■ What's the difference between a wild animal and a pet? Scientists study city animals to find out about the effects of pollution and other city phenomena.	■ Students may invite a wildlife expert to be a guest speaker in class.	■ Groups refine problems and form conjectures.
esson 3 *ake Way for ucklings*	■ Mrs. Mallard and her eight ducklings are due at the Public Garden, where they are to meet Mr. Mallard. But first they have to cross a busy Boston street.	■ Some animals have a natural ability to seek and adapt to environments that meet their needs. People also have a responsibility to nurture and protect wildlife.	■ Students record information about potential dangers for city wildlife.	■ Groups create investigation plans, assign tasks, and begin investigation.
esson 4 *rban Roosts*	■ This selection will guide city naturalists to birds' nests hidden in different places throughout the nation's cities.	■ Birds have learned to adapt to city living in a variety of ways.	■ Students compare natural habitats to urban habitats.	■ Revise plans and continue investigation.
esson 5 *wo Days n May*	■ When a family of deer end up in the city looking for food, a community must decide how to help them.	■ As natural habitats disappear, wildlife enters cities and towns. People have a desire to protect wildlife.	■ Students investigate disappearing wildlife habitats.	■ Groups present informal presentations, make necessary revisions, and continue investigation.
esson 6 *ecret Place*	■ A hidden spot by the river right in the middle of the city is home to many species. But what would happen to their home if people found out about it?	■ Wildlife can thrive in cities but must be protected.	■ Students hold discussions about disappearing wildlife habitats and create proposals for protecting wildlife in urban areas.	■ Final preparations and presentation of results.

Student Materials

Student Anthology
Pages 112–195

Inquiry Journal
Pages 28–54

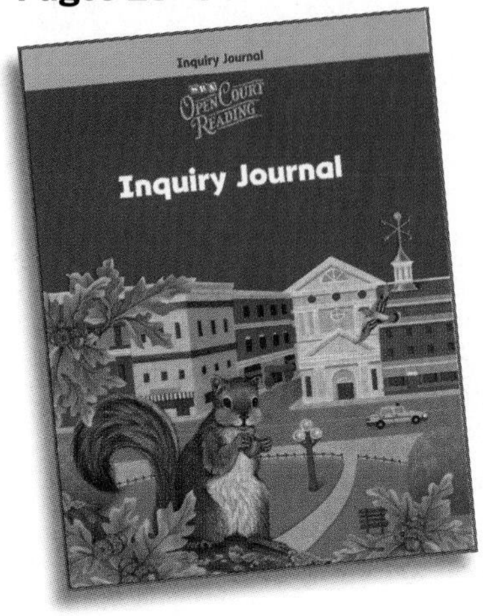

Writer's Workbook
Pages 6–29

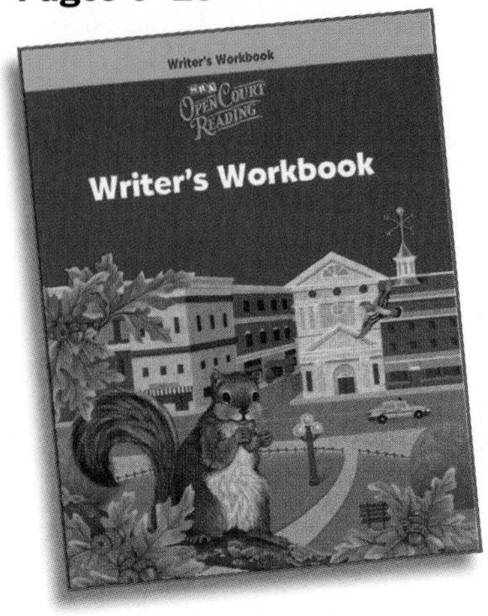

Comprehension and Language Arts Skills
Pages 26–57

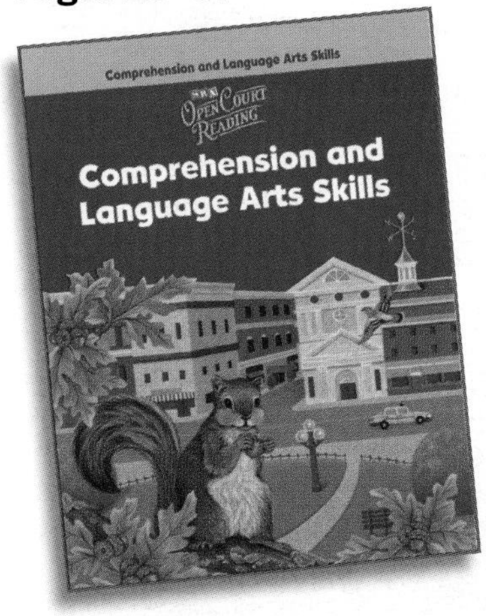

Spelling and Vocabulary Skills
Pages 26–49

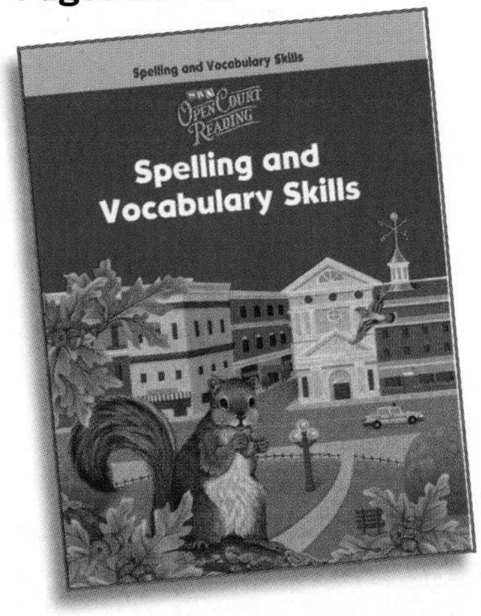

Language Arts Handbook

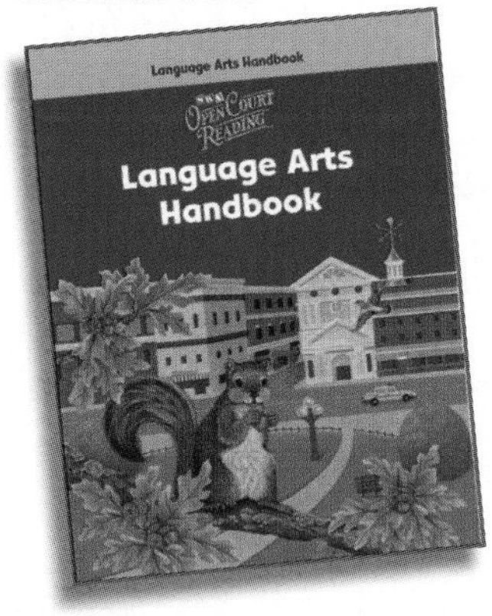

Additional Materials

- Listening Library Audiocassettes/CDs
- Unit 2 Assessment
- Writing Folder
- Student Research Assistant
- Science/Social Studies Connection Center

Differentiating Instruction

- English Learner Support Activities
- Intervention Workbook
- Reteach
- Challenge
- Decodable Books
- Decodable Takehome Books
- Decodable Book Activities CD-ROM
- Leveled Classroom Library

Teacher Materials

eacher's Edition, Book 2
ages 112–195P

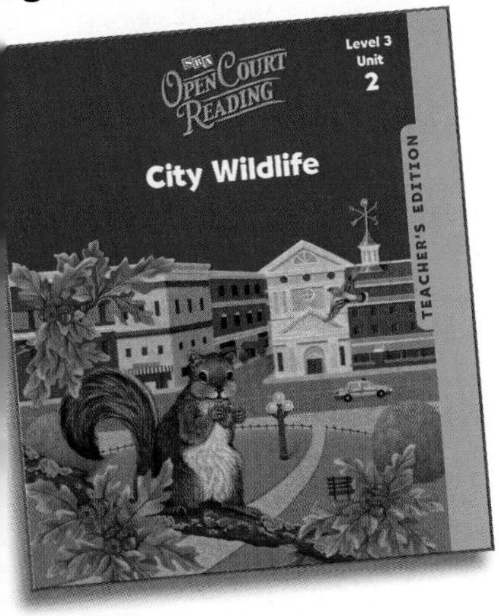

Read Aloud
City Lots: Living Things in Vacant Spots

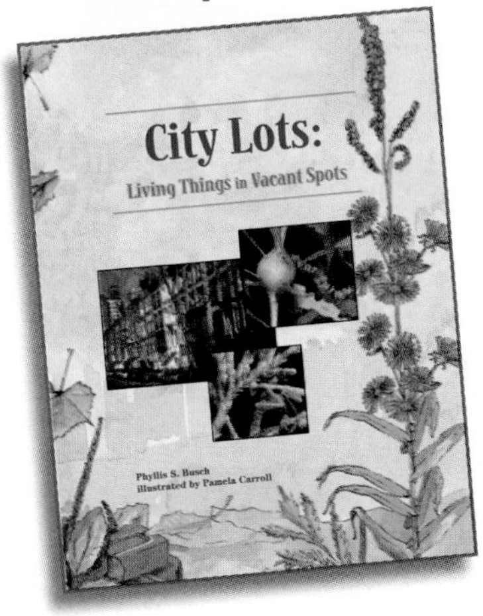

Home Connection
Pages 15–28

omprehension and
anguage Arts Skills
eacher's Edition
ages 26–57

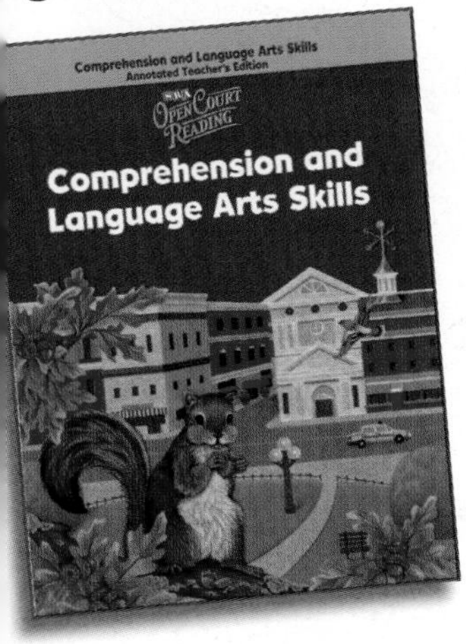

Spelling and Vocabulary
Skills Teacher's Edition
Pages 26–49

Writer's Workbook
Teacher's Edition
Pages 6–29

verhead Transparencies
eading Numbers 10–15
anguage Arts Numbers 4, 10, 11, 13,
7, 20, 23, 25–27, 29, 31, 35

Additional Materials

- Teacher's Professional Guides
- Phonics Lesson Cards
- Manipulative Package
- Read Alouds
- Online Professional Development
- Teacher Resource Library
- Online Phonics
- Online Assessment

Differentiating Instruction

- English Learner Support Guide
- Intervention Guide
- Intervention Annotated Bibliography
- Reteach Teacher's Edition
- Challenge Teacher's Edition

Leveled Classroom Library*

Easy

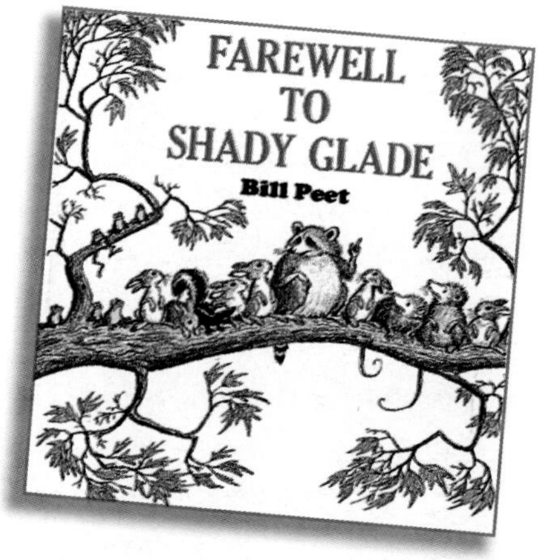

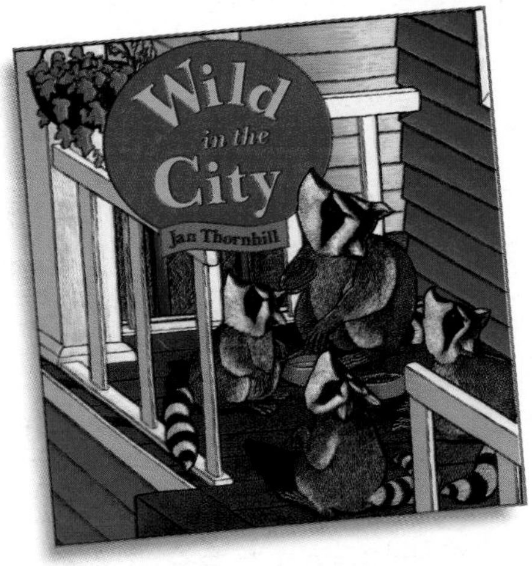

Average

Advanced

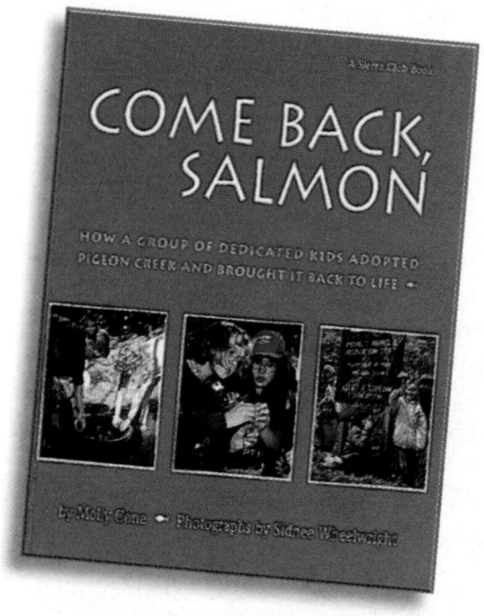

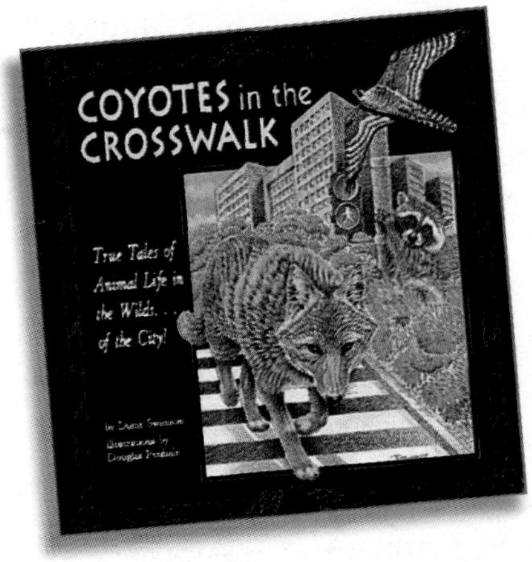

Bibliography**

Nature in Your Backyard: Simple Activities for Children **by Susan S. Lang**

The Gardener **by Sarah Stewart**

City Green **by DyAnne DiSalvo-Ryan**

Down to Earth **by Michael J. Rosen**

The Empty Lot **by Dale H. Fife**

The City Kid's Field Guide **by Ethan Herberman**

Backyard Safaris: 52 Year-Round Science Adventures **by Phyllis S. Busch**

Sunflowers for Tina **by Anne Norris Baldwin**

Note: Teachers should preview any trade books and videos for appropriateness in their classrooms before recommending them to students.

* These books, which all support the unit theme City Wildlife, are part of a 36-book ***Leveled Classroom Library*** available for purchase from SRA/McGraw-Hi

** Check libraries or bookstores for availability.

TECHNOLOGY

Web Connections

City Wildlife Web Sites

Information and links to sites concerning City Wildlife can be found at **www.sra4kids.com.**

Online Assessment

Online Assessment offers automated delivery and scoring of End of Unit and Program Assessments. Data is analyzed and compiled into reports that help teachers make classroom instruction decisions and guide individualized instruction. Available at **www.SRAonline.com.**

Online Phonics

Online Phonics offers Internet-based activities that provide students with additional phonics practice to support ***Open Court Reading*** lessons. In addition, the management tool collects students' data and notifies the teacher of their progress. Available at **www.SRAonline.com.**

Online Professional Development

Online Professional Development delivers 20 courses with full-motion video teaching examples for grades K–6. In addition, teachers can participate in Learning Communities and Discussion Boards available exclusively through the site. Available at **www.SRAonline.com.**

CD-ROMs

* Decodable Book Activities

Use the ***Decodable Book Activities CD-ROM*** activities to support the phonics review in this unit.

* Research Assistant

As students continue their investigation of City Wildlife, the ***Research Assistant CD-ROM*** program will help them organize and share their findings.

* OCR Spelling

Use this software for extra spelling review in this unit.

* The Ultimate Writing and Creativity Center

THE LEARNING COMPANY, 2002

Students can use this word processing software to get ideas, draft, revise, edit, and publish their Writing Process Strategies activities in this unit.

* Teacher Resource Library

Teacher Resource Library covers subjects such as classroom management, English Learners, assessment, and more. Included are videos of real teachers and students in their classrooms and a wealth of text-based resources for teachers of grades K–6.

Videocassettes

A Little Duck Tale

DISCOVERY COMMUNICATIONS INC., 1993

The true story of how a mother duck and her twelve ducklings live and survive in the middle of Tokyo. 56 min.

* *Mama Don't Allow*

Possums, gators, and other swamp creatures populate this neighborhood where Mama don't allow no music playin'. Available in English and Spanish. 9 min.

* *Mr. Popper's Penguins*

Mr. Popper's love of penguins is put to the test when he receives a surprise package. 42 min.

Audiocassettes/CDs

* Listening Library: City Wildlife

Students will enjoy listening to the selections they have read. Encourage them to listen during Workshop.

* *Sound/Spelling Card Stories*

Students can listen to and practice the ***Sound/Spelling Card Stories*** during Workshop.

Computer Skills

* TechKnowledge

SRA TechKnowledge program can be used to help students develop computer skills within the context of the unit theme.

Titles preceded by an asterisk (*) are available through SRA/McGraw-Hill. Other titles can be obtained by contacting the publisher listed with the title.

UNIT 2 OVERVIEW

UNIT SKILLS OVERVIEW

Lesson	WORD KNOWLEDGE/ PHONICS & FLUENCY	COMPREHENSION	LITERARY ELEMENTS
Lesson 1 *The Boy Who Didn't Believe in Spring* **Genre: Realistic Fiction** 	■ Set 1: antonyms; compound words; suffix *-y;* prefix *un-;* /ar/ spelled *ar;* /âr/ spelled *air* ■ Set 2: review /ū/ spelled *u, u_e, _ue, _ew*	**Strategies** ■ Asking Questions ■ Monitoring and Clarifying ■ Visualizing ■ Predicting **Skills** ■ Classify and Categorize	■ Characterization
Lesson 2 *City Critters* **Genre: Expository Text** 	■ Set 1: compound words; homophones; suffixes *-tion, -ly;* /er/ spelled *ur* and *ir;* /or/ spelled *or* and *ore* ■ Set 2: open syllables with long vowels	**Strategies** ■ Asking Questions ■ Monitoring and Clarifying ■ Summarizing **Skills** ■ Drawing Conclusions	■ Fiction vs. Nonfiction
Lesson 3 *Make Way for Ducklings* **Genre: Fantasy** 	■ Set 1: word families; synonyms; /əl/ spelled *-le* ■ Set 2: open syllables with vowel digraphs	**Strategies** ■ Asking Questions ■ Predicting **Skills** ■ Fantasy and Reality	■ Fiction vs. Nonfiction
Lesson 4 *Urban Roosts* **Genre: Expository Text** 	■ Set 1: compound words; related words; vivid verbs; /ow/ spelled *ou_* and *ow* ■ Set 2: long vowels found in open syllables with vowel-consonant-vowel structure; /s/ spelled *sc*	**Strategies** ■ Monitoring and Clarifying ■ Summarizing ■ Asking Questions **Skills** ■ Cause and Effect	■ Details
Lesson 5 *Two Days in May* **Genre: Realistic Fiction** 	■ Set 1: contractions; suffixes *-ing, -ly;* prefix *un-;* /oi/ spelled *oi* and *_oy* ■ Set 2: words ending in *-le* with long and short vowels	**Strategies** ■ Asking Questions ■ Making Connections ■ Summarizing **Skills** ■ Cause and Effect	■ Setting
Lesson 6 *Secret Place* **Genre: Realistic Fiction** 	■ Set 1: compound words; inflectional ending *-ed;* antonyms; vivid verbs; review /âr/, /or/, /er/, /əl/, /ow/, /oi/ ■ Set 2: review multisyllabic words with long and short vowels; review /ə/	**Strategies** ■ Monitoring and Adjusting Reading Speed ■ Summarizing ■ Visualizing **Skills** ■ Author's Purpose	■ Onomatopoeia

INQUIRY	WORD ANALYSIS	WRITING PROCESS STRATEGIES	ENGLISH LANGUAGE CONVENTIONS
■ Interviewing	**Spelling** ■ The /âr/ and /ar/ Sounds **Vocabulary** ■ Antonyms	**Expository Writing** ■ Responding to Fiction **Writer's Craft** ■ Time and Order Words	**Mechanics** ■ Quotation Marks in Dialogue **Listening, Speaking, Viewing** ■ Listening: Remembering What We Hear **Penmanship** ■ Cursive Letters *n* and *m*
■ Choosing Appropriate Sources	**Spelling** ■ The /er/ and /or/ Sounds **Vocabulary** ■ Levels of Specificity	**Expository Writing** ■ Summary Paragraph **Writer's Craft** ■ Organization of Expository Writing	**Mechanics** ■ Commas in a Series **Listening, Speaking, Viewing** ■ Speaking: Speaking Clearly **Penmanship** ■ Cursive Letters *m* and *x*
■ Tables and Charts	**Spelling** ■ The Final /əl/ Sound **Vocabulary** ■ Synonyms	**Expository Writing** ■ Fiction Book Review **Writer's Craft** ■ Paragraph Form	**Mechanics** ■ Commas in Dialogue **Listening, Speaking, Viewing** ■ Language: Language Reflects Cultures **Penmanship** ■ Cursive Letters *y*, *z*, and *v*
■ Parts of a Book (Index)	**Spelling** ■ The /ow/ Sound **Vocabulary** ■ Word Concept	**Expository Writing** ■ Responding to Nonfiction **Writer's Craft** ■ Topic Sentences	**Mechanics** ■ Capitalization of Places **Listening, Speaking, Viewing** ■ Viewing: Using Visual Aids **Penmanship** ■ Cursive Letters *e* and *l*
■ Note Taking	**Spelling** ■ The /oi/ Sound **Vocabulary** ■ Homophones	**Expository Writing** ■ Explaining a Process **Writer's Craft** ■ Purpose and Audience	**Mechanics** ■ Question Marks and Exclamation Points **Listening, Speaking, Viewing** ■ Interacting: Asking Questions **Penmanship** ■ Cursive Letters *h* and *k*
■ Diagrams	**Spelling** ■ Unit 2 Review **Vocabulary** ■ Unit 2 Review	**Expository Writing** ■ Research Report **Writer's Craft** ■ Effective Beginnings	**Mechanics** ■ Review **Listening, Speaking, Viewing** ■ Presenting: Chronological Order **Penmanship** ■ Cursive Letters *f* and *b*

UNIT 2 OVERVIEW

Differentiating Instruction

DIFFERENTIATING INSTRUCTION

	Reteach	English Learner	Challenge	Intervention
Lesson 1 *The Boy Who Didn't Believe in Spring*	**Language Arts** ■ **Spelling:** The /âr/ and /ar/ Sounds ■ **Vocabulary:** Antonyms ■ **Mechanics:** Quotation Marks in Dialogue ■ **Writer's Craft:** Time-Order Words	**Reading and Responding** ■ Vocabulary ■ Comprehension: Classify and Categorize	**Language Arts** ■ **Spelling:** The /âr/ and /ar/ Sounds ■ **Vocabulary:** Antonyms ■ **Mechanics:** Quotation Marks in Dialogue ■ **Writer's Craft:** Time-Order Words	**Preparing to Read** ■ Word Knowledge **Reading and Responding** ■ Selection Vocabulary **Language Arts** ■ Vocabulary Strategies; Grammar, Usage, and Mechanics
Lesson 2 *City Critters*	**Reading and Responding** ■ Drawing Conclusions **Language Arts** ■ **Spelling:** The /er/ and /or/ Sounds ■ **Vocabulary:** Levels of Specificity ■ **Mechanics:** Commas in a Series ■ **Writer's Craft:** Organization of Expository Writing	**Reading and Responding** ■ Vocabulary ■ Comprehension: Drawing Conclusions	**Reading and Responding** ■ Drawing Conclusions **Language Arts** ■ **Spelling:** The /er/ and /or/ Sounds ■ **Vocabulary:** Levels of Specificity ■ **Mechanics:** Commas in a Series ■ **Writer's Craft:** Organization of Expository Writing	**Preparing to Read** ■ Word Knowledge **Reading and Responding** ■ Selection Vocabulary **Language Arts** ■ Vocabulary Strategies; Grammar, Usage, and Mechanics
Lesson 3 *Make Way for Ducklings*	**Reading and Responding** ■ Fantasy and Reality **Language Arts** ■ **Spelling:** The Final /əl/ Sound ■ **Vocabulary:** Synonyms ■ **Mechanics:** Commas in Dialogue ■ **Writer's Craft:** Paragraph Form	**Reading and Responding** ■ Vocabulary ■ Comprehension: Asking Questions	**Reading and Responding** ■ Fantasy and Reality **Language Arts** ■ **Spelling:** The Final /əl/ Sound ■ **Vocabulary:** Synonyms ■ **Mechanics:** Commas in Dialogue ■ **Writer's Craft:** Paragraph Form	**Preparing to Read** ■ Word Knowledge **Reading and Responding** ■ Selection Vocabulary **Language Arts** ■ Vocabulary Strategies; Grammar, Usage, and Mechanics
Lesson 4 *Urban Roosts*	**Language Arts** ■ **Spelling:** The /ow/ Sound ■ **Vocabulary:** Word Concept ■ **Mechanics:** Capitalization of Places ■ **Writer's Craft:** Topic Sentences	**Reading and Responding** ■ Vocabulary ■ Comprehension: Cause and Effect	**Language Arts** ■ **Spelling:** The /ow/ Sound ■ **Vocabulary:** Word Concept ■ **Mechanics:** Capitalization of Places ■ **Writer's Craft:** Topic Sentences	**Preparing to Read** ■ Word Knowledge **Reading and Responding** ■ Selection Vocabulary **Language Arts** ■ Vocabulary Strategies; Grammar, Usage, and Mechanics
Lesson 5 *Two Days in May*	**Reading and Responding** ■ Cause and Effect **Language Arts** ■ **Spelling:** The /oi/ Sound ■ **Vocabulary:** Homophones ■ **Mechanics:** Question Marks and Exclamation Points ■ **Writer's Craft:** Purpose and Audience	**Reading and Responding** ■ Vocabulary ■ Comprehension: Cause and Effect	**Reading and Responding** ■ Cause and Effect **Language Arts** ■ **Spelling:** The /oi/ Sound ■ **Vocabulary:** Homophones ■ **Mechanics:** Question Marks and Exclamation Points ■ **Writer's Craft:** Purpose and Audience	**Preparing to Read** ■ Word Knowledge **Reading and Responding** ■ Selection Vocabulary **Language Arts** ■ Vocabulary Strategies; Grammar, Usage, and Mechanics
Lesson 6 *Secret Place*	**Reading and Responding** ■ Author's Purpose **Language Arts** ■ **Spelling:** Unit 2 Review ■ **Vocabulary:** Unit 2 Review ■ **Mechanics:** Review ■ **Writer's Craft:** Effective Beginnings	**Reading and Responding** ■ Vocabulary ■ Comprehension: Summarizing	**Reading and Responding** ■ Author's Purpose **Language Arts** ■ **Spelling:** Unit 2 Review ■ **Vocabulary:** Unit 2 Review ■ **Mechanics:** Review ■ **Writer's Craft:** Effective Beginnings	**Preparing to Read** ■ Word Knowledge **Reading and Responding** ■ Selection Vocabulary **Language Arts** ■ Vocabulary Strategies; Grammar, Usage, and Mechanics

Above are suggestions for adapting instruction to meet the individual needs of students. These are the same skills shown on the Unit Skills Overview; however, these pages provide extra practice opportunities or enriching activities to meet the varied needs of students

ASSESSMENT

Informal Assessment	Progress Assessment	Formal Assessment
Comprehension Strategies, 114J, 114 **Concept Connections**, 124 **Mechanics**, 125H ***Listening, Speaking, Viewing**, 125I **Vocabulary**, 125J ***Penmanship**, 125J	**Comprehension and Language Arts Skills**, 26–29 **Reteach**, 29–32 **Challenge**, 27–29 **Writer's Workbook**, 6–9 **Spelling and Vocabulary Skills**, 26–29 **Inquiry Journal**, 29, 32–36	**Unit 2 Assessment** **Lesson 1** ■ Selection Assessment, 2–5 ■ Spelling Pretest, 26 ■ Spelling Final Test, 27 *Research Rubrics, 114J *Writing Process Assessment Rubrics, 125J
Comprehension Strategies, 126J, 126 **Concept Connections**, 132 **Mechanics**, 133H ***Listening, Speaking, Viewing**, 133I **Vocabulary**, 133J ***Penmanship**, 133J	**Comprehension and Language Arts Skills**, 30–35 **Reteach**, 33–38 **Challenge**, 30–34 **Writer's Workbook**, 10–13 **Spelling and Vocabulary Skills**, 30–33 **Inquiry Journal**, 29, 37–39	**Unit 2 Assessment** **Lesson 2** ■ Selection Assessment, 6–9 ■ Spelling Pretest, 28 ■ Spelling Final Test, 29 *Research Rubrics, 126J *Writing Process Assessment Rubrics, 133J
Comprehension Strategies, 136J, 136 **Concept Connections**, 144 **Mechanics**, 145H ***Listening, Speaking, Viewing**, 145I **Vocabulary**, 145J ***Penmanship**, 145J	**Comprehension and Language Arts Skills**, 36–41 **Reteach**, 39–44 **Challenge**, 35–39 **Writer's Workbook**, 14–17 **Spelling and Vocabulary Skills**, 34–37 **Inquiry Journal**, 30, 40–43	**Unit 2 Assessment** **Lesson 3** ■ Selection Assessment, 10–13 ■ Spelling Pretest, 30 ■ Spelling Final Test, 31 *Research Rubrics, 136J *Writing Process Assessment Rubrics, 145J
Comprehension Strategies, 148J, 148 **Concept Connections**, 162 **Mechanics**, 163H ***Listening, Speaking, Viewing**, 163I **Vocabulary**, 163J ***Penmanship**, 163J	**Comprehension and Language Arts Skills**, 42–45 **Reteach**, 45–48 **Challenge**, 40–43 **Writer's Workbook**, 18–21 **Spelling and Vocabulary Skills**, 38–41 **Inquiry Journal**, 30, 44–47	**Unit 2 Assessment** **Lesson 4** ■ Selection Assessment, 14–17 ■ Spelling Pretest, 32 ■ Spelling Final Test, 33 *Research Rubrics, 148J *Writing Process Assessment Rubrics, 163J
Comprehension Strategies, 166J, 166 **Concept Connections**, 180 **Mechanics**, 181H ***Listening, Speaking, Viewing**, 181I **Vocabulary**, 181J ***Penmanship**, 181J	**Comprehension and Language Arts Skills**, 46–51 **Reteach**, 49–50 **Challenge**, 44 **Writer's Workbook**, 22–25 **Spelling and Vocabulary Skills**, 42–45 **Inquiry Journal**, 31, 48–50	**Unit 2 Assessment** **Lesson 5** ■ Selection Assessment, 18–21 ■ Spelling Pretest, 34 ■ Spelling Final Test, 35 *Research Rubrics, 166J *Writing Process Assessment Rubrics, 181J
Comprehension Strategies, 182J, 182 **Concept Connections**, 194 **Investigation Presentation**, 195C **Mechanics**, 195H ***Listening, Speaking, Viewing**, 195I **Vocabulary**, 195J ***Penmanship**, 195J	**Comprehension and Language Arts Skills**, 52–57 **Reteach**, 55–56 **Challenge**, 49 **Writer's Workbook**, 26–29 **Spelling and Vocabulary Skills**, 46–49 **Inquiry Journal**, 31, 51–52	**Unit 2 Assessment** **Lesson 6** ■ Selection Assessment, 22–25 ■ Spelling Pretest, 36 ■ Spelling Final Test, 37 *Research Rubrics, 182J *Writing Process Assessment Rubrics, 195J **End of Unit 2 Assessment**

*_Teacher's Edition_ page reference

UNIT 2 OVERVIEW

PREVIEWING THE UNIT

Activating Prior Knowledge

Tell students that good readers relate what they know to what they are reading. Students should get into the habit of thinking about an upcoming theme and selections or activities relevant to that theme. As they read the upcoming selections, they should make certain to relate what they already know about city wildlife to what they are reading. Ask students questions such as the following:

- What do you know about city wildlife before we read these selections?
- What do you know about the kinds of animals and plants that live and grow in the city?
- Have you already read any books about city wildlife?

As students read the selections, they encounter some of these ideas, as well as new ideas. When they read something they already know, encourage them to make a note about this information. When they learn something new, have them to be sure to notice that, too. Encourage students to share any stories they have already read about city wildlife. For English Learners and others with limited language experience, exploring city wildlife on the Internet may be helpful.

When students have had some time to compose their thoughts and ideas, call on volunteers to speak. After each student expresses himself or herself, allow a few minutes for questions. As students present their ideas, add them to the Concept/Question Board.

Read Aloud

Read aloud to students the expository text "City Lots: Living Things in Vacant Spots" by Phyllis S. Busch. Prior to reading, provide students with the following background information.

- This is a nonfiction article that discusses *habitat*—the natural environment of living things.
- The author of the article has been a high school biology teacher, an associate professor of science, and assistant director of the Museum of Natural History in New York City.
- This article is part of an ecology series of articles she wrote that present environmental education using problem-solving methods.

It is important for you as the teacher to let your students know that you use the comprehension strategies being taught in the program when you read. Thus, before you read "City Lots: Living Things in Vacant Spots," make some predictions aloud as to what the selection might be about. As you read, let students know what questions occur to you, what images pop up in your mind as you read, and how points made in the reading relate to ideas you already know.

Toward the end of the reading, summarize for students. If you cannot summarize the selection well, let students see you go back and reread to fill in the gaps. Let students see you use comprehension strategies.

Below are some responses that you can model while you read aloud. Model two or three of these by "thinking aloud" as you read to students. Choose responses that fit the text you are reading. Invite students to offer their responses by thinking aloud as you do.

- React emotionally by showing joy, sadness, amusement, or surprise.
- Wonder about ideas in the text by posing questions that you really do wonder about.
- Relate the text to something that has happened to you or to something you already know.
- Clarify the meanings of words and ideas in the text.

About the Author

PHYLLIS S. BUSCH has taught students in elementary and high school as well as college. She teaches about biology and the environment. For many years she has been working on projects to teach elementary students and their parents about the environment through outdoor investigations and experiments. She is involved with nearly twenty different environmental groups and has received many awards for her work in science education. She has written dozens of educational books and guides that bring science to life for children.

About the Illustrator

PAMELA CARROLL is a well-known illustrator of children's books. *The Dolphins and Me*, *Nature's Living Lights*, and *Life in a Tidal Pool* are some of the books she has illustrated.

Focus Questions How important are open spaces in a city? What makes a city a good place to live for some wildlife?

City Lots: Living Things in Vacant Spots

Phyllis S. Busch
illustrated by Pamela Carroll

Cities are full of buildings—all kinds of buildings. There are big homes and small ones, where people live. There are factories and offices where people work. There are schools, libraries, museums, where people learn.

Cities are also full of people. There are homemakers, housepainters, streetcleaners, shopkeepers, factory workers, firefighters, carpenters, clerks, bankers, bakers, and all their children.

But among this mass of people and their dwellings you can find some vacant spots—large or small places where there are neither people nor buildings. These are known as city lots.

Is there a city lot near where you live? Perhaps you use it as a short cut to a friend's house, or to a store, or to a bus stop.

Some city lots are just narrow shaded passageways between two buildings. Others are bright and sunny. You can find these lots on street corners, or where there are large spaces between buildings.

Was the lot in your neighborhood always vacant? Or was there once a building which was torn down? You might search for evidence such as bricks or pieces of plaster. But first make sure that the lot is a safe place to play this game of exploration.

A vacant lot is really not vacant at all. It is a place where many plants and animals live all year round. A vacant lot contains all the things plants and animals need in order to live: soil, water, air, sunlight, food, space. Here you can watch the changes that take place in living things all through the year.

In the corner of an old city lot you may find a London plane tree, also known as a sycamore. This tree has surprises for every season. In the bright spring sunshine, the brown and tan trunk is a sparkling patchwork of colors. The bark peelings which cause this colorful pattern lie scattered on the ground.

READ ALOUD

Examine these before and after a rain. You will discover that the tight bark rolls are brittle in dry weather, and loose and softened when it is wet. In the summer it is pleasant to sit in the shade of a sycamore tree, under its spreading dark green leaves. Take the temperature of the air under the tree. How is it different from the temperature of the air in the sunlight?

With the coming of autumn the sycamore leaves turn brown and fall to the ground to form a crunchy carpet. Remove a leaf not yet fallen and find the little hollow at the end of the leaf stalk. Notice how this forms a cap over a new bud—a little bundle of energy ready to start next year's growth.

Winter is the time to see the sycamore balls hanging high in the tree. A strong wind dashes them to the ground, where you can collect some and observe their seeds. How many seeds does one of these balls of fruit contain? How many trees might develop from all the seeds of one parent tree? It is a wonder that the lot is not full of sycamores.

You can also follow the seasons with the ailanthus tree, the commonest city tree. In China, where it came from, it is known as the Tree-of-Heaven. Observe it after the leaves have fallen as it stands with its stout bare branches outstretched against the sky. Large heartshaped scars show where the leaves were attached. You might see bunches of fruit up in the tree, and hear them rattle in the breeze.

Ailanthus trees grow rapidly in the spring and can occupy a large portion of a city lot. If you play in a "jungle" in your lot in summer, it is probably a tangle of these trees.

A patch of spring sunshine in the corner of a lot may gleam with the gold of dandelions.

A shadier spot might be adorned with a little violet, a spot of purple beauty even among discarded garbage and its hovering flies. Wouldn't the violet be prettier without garbage that brings flies and rats?

You learn to avoid the tangles of prickly blackberry as you explore, but you should stop to admire the rich red color of the leaves in the fall. The fruits are quickly eaten by birds.

It is often from the fall fruits left uneaten by mice and birds that new plants arise in the spring. You yourself may have helped to scatter the seeds of burdock, also known as stickers.

Run your finger up the stalk of the common plantain when it is wet. Feel the sticky seeds. All who walk over the flat-leaved plantains carry with them some seeds which are later dropped to grow into next year's crop.

It is fun to spend a year watching any one plant, and milkweed is a happy choice. Milkweed pods are beautiful whether they are open or closed. Look inside a bright green pod in early autumn. See how the many brown seeds with their silvery parachutes fit neatly into a package.

Later in the season all the fruit pods, now in shades of tan, are open. Watch the seeds float in the air on a windy day. Which way do the beautiful wisps travel? How far do they go? Will they give rise to more milkweed plants next spring? What insects will be attracted to their fragrant lavender flowers in summer?

In autumn a city lot is bound to have some tall flourishing ragweed. Although the flowers are tiny, hayfever sufferers know when the plant is in bloom. Large amounts of pollen float in the air and disturb sensitive noses. Shake some flowers over a piece of glass which is covered with a thin layer of petroleum jelly. You can then observe this flower dust under a microscope. The flowers look like miniature sculptures.

Where ragweed grows you might find a corner made bright with purple asters and yellow goldenrod.

If city lots have plants they certainly must have animals. Some insects lay their eggs in the stems of goldenrod. This causes the plant to form a swelling known as a gall. Here the young develop, to hatch out the following spring. If you cut open a gall, you may find an immature insect.

Is there a wild black cherry tree on the lot? In the spring you might find a mass of tent caterpillars resting in a silken shelter which they have spun between supporting branches. These insects appear to have regular periods for feeding and for spinning. Observe a colony of tent caterpillars over the weeks in order to learn their routine.

Those caterpillars which are not gobbled up by hungry birds or destroyed by parasites change into brown moths. Look for their shiny dark brown bands of eggs on bare winter twigs.

Small green plant lice or aphids are frequently found feeding on the juices of stems or leaves. A praying mantis might stalk nearby, gobbling up these and other insects. The praying mantis is a large green and brown insect whose bent front legs make it appear as if it is praying. You can locate its hard brown egg mass among the winter shrubs. Over three hundred babies may hatch from one such egg case in the spring.

A city lot is a suitable habitat for many birds. They need a safe place to build a nest, as well as an adequate food supply and a source of water. Most common is the English sparrow. Observe it as it hops, flies, builds a nest, sits on its eggs, feeds spiders and flies to its young, bathes in rain pools and dusts in sandy spots.

READ ALOUD

Try to follow the habits of the pigeons which are sure to be there. Maybe there is also a robin, attracted to the cherries in the cherry tree. Are there some squawking starlings? They lead busy lives too.

Did you ever visit the lot during or after a light rainfall in spring or summer? It smells different from the rest of the city—cool and refreshing. How much cooler the air is over the lot than over the pavement. Feel the gentle raindrops on your face. Open your mouth and taste some fresh rainwater. Watch the rain strike the leaves, run down the stalks and onto the stems from where it slowly continues down into the soil. Here is where it is available to the plant roots which absorb it. Miniature streams and lakes form where there are depressions in the ground. Perhaps a puppy or a bird comes for a drink or a bath, leaving its footprints in the mud nearby.

People need places to live, to work, and to shop. But people also need open spaces. Every neighborhood should have a lot which is left without buildings—a place to rest and to play and to make new discoveries about its plants and animals.

Discussing the Read Aloud

After you have finished the Read Aloud, ask students the following questions.

- Why is this selection called "City Lots: Living Things in Vacant Spots"? *(It is about the plants, insects, and animals that live in city lots.)*
- Why do many plants and animals live in vacant lots all year round? *(They find everything they need to live there, such as food, water, sunlight, and space.)*
- How do the plants in city lots help insects to live? *(Some insects lay their eggs in the plants; others feed on the plants and use them for shelter.)*

Remind students of some of the questions you asked them to think about before you read the story.

- What do you know about city wildlife?
- What do you know about the kinds of animals and plants that live and grow in a city?

Discuss with the class how this Read Aloud is related to the theme City Wildlife. To stimulate discussion, ask students questions such as the following:

- What did you learn about city wildlife?
- How is the theme City Wildlife reflected in the Read Aloud?
- How did this selection change your ideas about city wildlife?
- What questions do you have or what do you wonder about the Read Aloud or the theme? *(Answers will vary.)*

Concept/Question Board

The Concept/Question Board is a place for students to ask questions and find answers in order to have a better understanding of the unit theme. It is also a place to publish the results of their investigations.

To get started in this unit, you could have students cut brown construction paper in the shape of a bird to represent the Read Aloud, "City Lots: Living Things in Vacant Spots." Students could write their questions, comments, or theme words on the cutout shape, which would easily identify the story in the unit.

To begin using your Concept/Question Board, ask the students to formulate statements about what they know about city wildlife or what they believe to be important about city wildlife after listening to the Read Aloud. Write these statements and attach them to the Concept side of the Board. Then, write any preliminary questions they have about city wildlife and attach those to the Question side of the Board.

Another idea to help get the students started is to put up a chart or web that they can add to throughout the unit. For example, you might put up two categories—Animal Wildlife and Plant Life—and as they read the selections in the City Wildlife unit, students can post examples of each concept.

As the students progress through the unit, they can refer to the Board to learn which of their classmates have interests similar to their own. This information can be used to form groups to investigate questions and ideas about the unit theme.

Throughout the unit, have the students reread and reflect on the contributions listed on the Concept/Question Board. Have them note, in their Writer's Notebooks, the contributions that mean the most to them. Suggest that they expand on the original contributions by adding their own thoughts, articles, pictures, and so on. Discuss whether the selection has provided information that might be added or that might revise existing postings.

Setting Reading Goals

Good readers regularly set goals when they are reading. Have students examine and share their thoughts on the unit opener in the ***Student Anthology,*** pages 112–113. Remind them that good readers are always thinking when they read. Also, remind students that good readers browse what they are going to read before reading. Guide their browsing by using the following procedure:

- Turn to the unit opener pages. First, look at the unit title. Ask what the title means and what kinds of selections may be in the unit.
- Look at the illustration on the opener pages. The illustration may answer questions about the title or prompt more questions. Post new questions on the Concept/Question Board.
- Ask students what they are thinking about as they read the unit opener.
- Invite students to browse the selections in the unit. Read the titles and quickly browse each one, looking briefly at the illustrations and the text. Encourage students to look not only at content but also at the genre: Is the selection a story? A poem? Expository text, such as an article? Encourage students to make any observations that interest them.

When students have had sufficient time to browse the unit, encourage them to share their observations. Return to the unit opener on pages 112–113 and use the illustration to help initiate a discussion. Allow them to share whatever comments they have about the illustration.

Tell students that good readers make predictions about what might be in the selections they are about to read. Ask them if they are making predictions about the selections or if they are asking themselves questions about the selections they are about to read. Model asking questions that might have occurred to you as you browsed the selections.

Inquiry Journal

- Have students complete page 28 in their ***Inquiry Journals*** and provide time for them to share their responses.
- Share ideas about city wildlife that students would like to investigate.

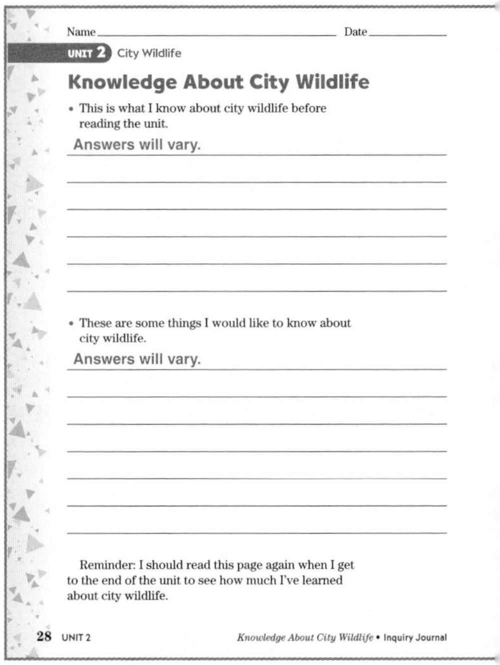
Name __________ Date ______

UNIT 2 City Wildlife

Knowledge About City Wildlife

- This is what I know about city wildlife before reading the unit.

Answers will vary.

- These are some things I would like to know about city wildlife.

Answers will vary.

Reminder: I should read this page again when I get to the end of the unit to see how much I've learned about city wildlife.

28 UNIT 2 *Knowledge About City Wildlife* • Inquiry Journal

Inquiry Journal p. 28

Professional Resources

Bereiter, C., and M. Scardamalia. *Surpassing Ourselves: An Inquiry into the Nature and Implications of Expertise.* Chicago: Open Court, 1993.

Bransford, J. D., A. L. Brown, and R. R. Cocking, eds. *How People Learn: Brain, Mind, Experience, and School.* Washington, DC: National Academy Press, 1999.

Dewey, J. *How We Think.* New York: Houghton-Mifflin College, 1997.

Schack, G. D., "Involving Students in Authentic Research," *Educational Leadership.* (April 1993): 29–31.

Vosniadou, S., "Children's Naïve Models and the Comprehension of Expository Text." M. Carretoero, M. Pope, R. J. Simons, and J. I. Pozo, eds., *Learning and Instruction: European Research in an International Context* 3 (1991): 325–336. Oxford: Pergamon Press.

Vosniadou, S., "Designing Curricula for Conceptual Restructuring: Lessons from the Study of Knowledge Acquisition in Astronomy, *Journal of Curriculum Studies* 23 (1991): 219–237.

Home Connection

Distribute page 15 of ***Home Connection.*** Students can read books and articles about city wildlife with their families. A few stories are listed to get started. This ***Home Connection*** is also available in Spanish on page 16. Remind parents and students to review and practice the vocabulary and spelling words in preparation for the upcoming week's lessons.

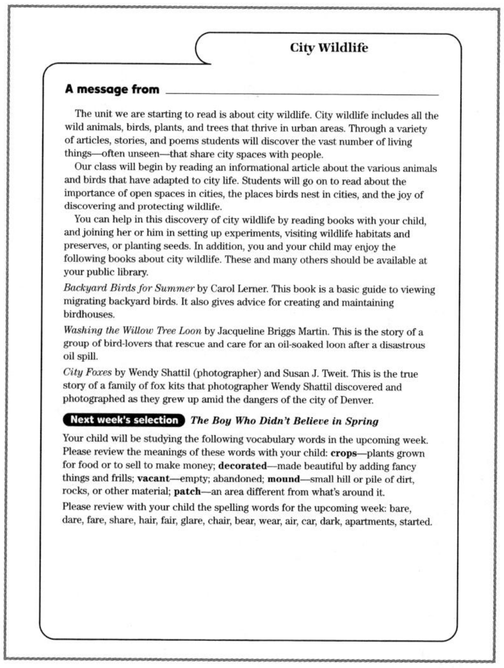

City Wildlife

A message from ______________________

The unit we are starting to read is about city wildlife. City wildlife includes all the wild animals, birds, plants, and trees that thrive in urban areas. Through a variety of articles, stories, and poems students will discover the vast number of living things—often unseen—that share city spaces with people.

Our class will begin by reading an informational article about the various animals and birds that have adapted to city life. Students will go on to read about the importance of open spaces in cities, the places birds nest in cities, and the joy of discovering and protecting wildlife.

You can help in this discovery of city wildlife by reading books with your child, and joining her or him in setting up experiments, visiting wildlife habitats and preserves, or planting seeds. In addition, you and your child may enjoy the following books about city wildlife. These and many others should be available at your public library.

Backyard Birds for Summer by Carol Lerner. This book is a basic guide to viewing migrating backyard birds. It also gives advice for creating and maintaining birdhouses.

Washing the Willow Tree Loon by Jacqueline Briggs Martin. This is the story of a group of bird-lovers that rescue and care for an oil-soaked loon after a disastrous oil spill.

City Foxes by Wendy Shattil (photographer) and Susan J. Tweit. This is the true story of a family of fox kits that photographer Wendy Shattil discovered and photographed as they grew up amid the dangers of the city of Denver.

Next week's selection ***The Boy Who Didn't Believe in Spring***

Your child will be studying the following vocabulary words in the upcoming week. Please review the meanings of these words with your child: **crops**—plants grown for food or to sell to make money; **decorated**—made beautiful by adding fancy things and frills; **vacant**—empty; abandoned; **mound**—small hill or pile of dirt, rocks, or other material; **patch**—an area different from what's around it.

Please review with your child the spelling words for the upcoming week: bare, dare, fare, share, hair, fair, glare, chair, bear, wear, air, car, dark, apartments, started.

Home Connection p. 15

Research in Reading

Ann Brown and Joseph Campione on Communities of Learners

Students in the third grade find the goal of "doing research" an exciting one. Once they begin "reading to learn" about some topic, they will often persist at the task for much longer than they did when they were just "learning to read." Even the weakest of readers can make important intellectual contributions to inquiry projects where the whole class (including the teacher) is involved, and their reading skills will make great strides in the process.

Science/Social Studies Connection Center

Refer to the ***Science/Social Studies Connection Center*** Card 8 for a science activity that students can investigate.

Science/Social Studies Connection Center

Refer to the ***Science/Social Studies Connection Center*** Card 9 for a science activity that students can investigate.

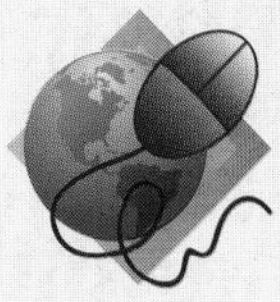

www.sra4kids.com
Web Connection

Check the Reading link of the SRA Web page for more information on Research in Reading.

Focus Questions What is city wildlife? What types of wildlife would you expect to find in a city?

The Boy Who Didn't Believe in Spring

Lucille Clifton
illustrated by Brinton Turkle

Once upon a time there was a little boy named King Shabazz who didn't believe in Spring. "No such thing!" he would whisper every time the teacher talked about Spring in school. "Where is it at?" he would holler every time his Mama talked about Spring at home.

114

SELECTION INTRODUCTION

Selection Summary

Genre: Realistic Fiction

At home and at school, King Shabazz keeps hearing that spring is "just around the corner." But King is doubtful. He surely hasn't seen any signs of its arrival. So, with the aid of his faithful friend Tony Polito, King hits the streets of his neighborhood in search of the mysterious spring.

Realistic fiction involves stories about people and events that are true to life and that could really happen.

Some elements of realistic fiction are:

- The characters behave as people do in real life.
- The setting of the story is a real place or could be a real place.
- The events in the story could happen in real life.

About the Author

"The Boy Who Didn't Believe in Spring" was written by **LUCILLE CLIFTON.** The author, poet laureate of Maryland from 1979 to 1982, won the Coretta Scott King Award for *Everett Anderson's Good-bye.*

Clifton, who has six children, says that children are her inspiration. The author uses words and expressions that reflect language spoken by children in informal situations.

Students can read more about Clifton on page 125 of the ***Student Anthology.***

About the Illustrator

BRINTON TURKLE has illustrated several award-winning books, including the Caldecott Honor Book *Thy Friend, Obadiah.*

Students can read more about Brinton Turkle on page 125 of the ***Student Anthology.***

Inquiry Connections

"The Boy Who Didn't Believe in Spring" illustrates that no matter how crowded a city neighborhood might be, wildlife can be found there if one looks hard enough. Key concepts explored in this selection are:

- Wild birds and plants survive in the city without anyone taking care of them.
- Care should be taken not to disturb the homes of wildlife.
- Wild plants and animals need sunlight, air, space, and soil to survive.

Before reading the selection:

- Point out that students may post a question, concept, word, illustration, or object on the Concept/Question Board at any time during the course of their unit investigations. Be sure that students include their names or initials on the items they post so that others will know whom to go to if they have an answer or if they wish to collaborate on a related activity.
- Students should feel free to write an answer or a note on someone else's question or to consult the Board for ideas for their own investigations throughout the unit.
- Encourage students to read about city wildlife at home and to bring in articles or pictures that are good examples to post on the Board.

Concept/Question Board

PROGRAM RESOURCES

Leveled Practice

Reteach
Pages 29–32

Challenge
Pages 26–29

English Learner Support Activities

Intervention Workbook

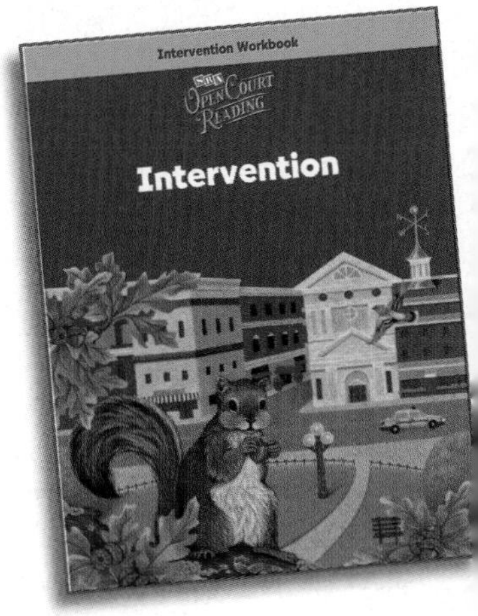

Decodable Book 17

Leveled Classroom Library*

Encourage students to read at least 30 minutes daily outside of class. Have them read books in the ***Leveled Classroom Library*** to support the unit theme and help students develop their vocabulary by reading independently.

Farewell to Shady Glade

BY BILL PEET. HOUGHTON, 1981.

A humorous and unique look at what happens to the wildlife in a place when the bulldozers and city life move in. (Southern California Council on Literature for Children and Young People Award) **(Easy)**

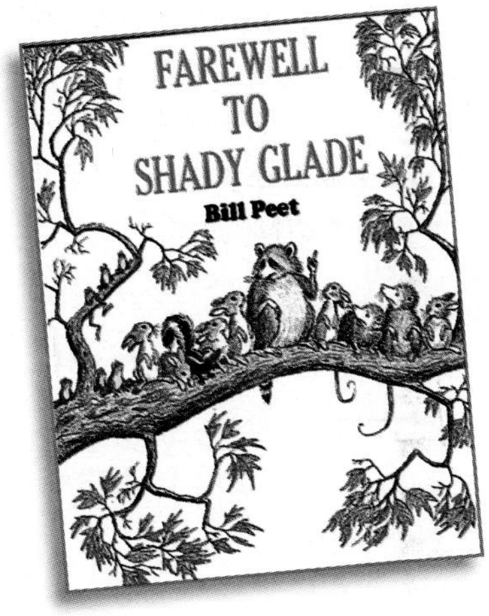

Birds, Nests and Eggs

BY MEL BORING. NORTHWORD, 1998.

Fourteen birds are introduced to young readers through color illustrations, simple descriptions of their songs and nesting habits, and simple facts. **(Average)**

Come Back Salmon: How a Group of Dedicated Kids Adopted Pigeon Creek and Brought It Back to Life

BY MOLLY CONE. SIERRA JUVENILE CLUB, 1994.

Students from Jackson Elementary School in Everett, Washington, adopt a polluted creek, bring it back to life, and preserve it as a place for salmon to spawn. (Outstanding Science Trade Book) **(Advanced)**

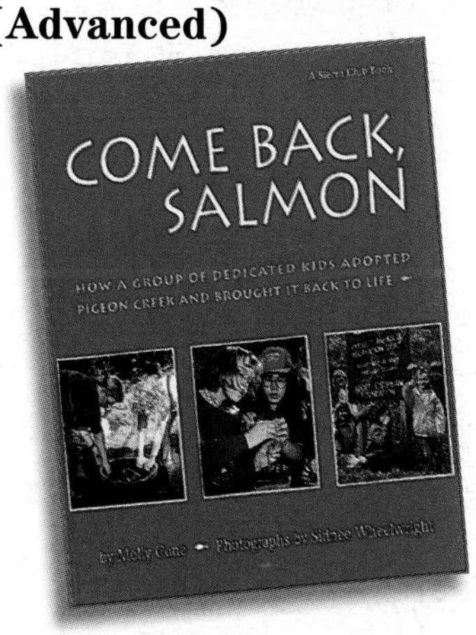

* These books, which all support the unit theme City Wildlife, are part of a 36-book ***Leveled Classroom Library*** available for purchase from SRA/McGraw-Hill. Note: Teachers should preview any trade books for appropriateness in their classrooms before recommending them to students.

SRA TECHNOLOGY

Web Connections

- City Wildlife Web Site
- Online Professional Development
- Online Phonics
- Online Assessment

CD-ROMs

- Research Assistant
- Decodable Book Activities
- Teacher Resource Library

Audiocassettes/CDs

- Listening Library: City Wildlife
- Sound/Spelling Card Stories

Computer Skills

TechKnowledge

Materials are available through SRA/McGraw-Hill.

LESSON PLANNER

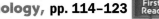

Suggested Pacing: 3–5 days	DAY 1	DAY 2
	DAY 1	DAY 2
1 Preparing to Read **Materials** ■ Student Anthology, Book 1, pp. 112–125 ■ Decodable Book Activities CD-ROM ■ Sound/Spelling Card 36 ■ Decodable Book 17 ■ Routine Cards 1, 3, Routines 1–2, 8–9	**Unit Overview** ■ Previewing the Unit, pp. 112–113R ■ Read Aloud, pp. 113L–113O **Word Knowledge,** p. 114K ■ antonyms ■ synonyms ■ compound words ■ suffix *-y* ■ prefix *un-* ■ *ar* and *air* spelling patterns **About the Words and Sentences,** pp. 114K–114L	**Word Knowledge** **Developing Oral Language,** p. 114L
2 Reading & Responding **Materials** ■ Student Anthology, Book 1, pp. 112–125 ■ Program Assessment ■ Reading Transparencies 10, 46, 50, 53 ■ Routine Cards 1–2, Routines 3–6 ■ Inquiry Journal, p. 29 ■ Home Connection, p. 17 ■ Unit 2 Assessment, pp. 2–5 ■ Writer's Notebook	**Build Background,** p. 114O **Preview and Prepare,** pp. 114O–114P **Selection Vocabulary,** p. 114P **Reading Recommendations,** pp. 114Q–114R	**Student Anthology,** pp. 114–123 First Read ✓**Comprehension Strategies** ■ Asking Questions, p. 114 ■ Monitoring and Clarifying, pp. 114, 118 ■ Visualizing, p. 116 ■ Predicting, pp. 120, 122 **Discussing Strategy Use,** p. 122 **Discussing the Selection,** p. 123A ■ Review Selection
Inquiry **Materials** ■ Student Anthology, Book 1, pp. 112–125 ■ Inquiry Journal, pp. 32–36 ■ Research Assistant CD-ROM	✓**Investigation** ■ Investigating Concepts Beyond the Text, p. 125A	**Investigation** ■ Concept/Question Board, p. 125B
3 Language Arts **Materials** ■ Student Anthology, Book 1, pp. 112–125 ■ Comprehension and Language Arts Skills, pp. 26–29 ■ Language Arts Handbook, pp. 78–79 ■ Language Arts Transparencies 4, 11, 26, 35 ■ Sound/Spelling Card 27 ■ Spelling and Vocabulary Skills, pp. 26–29 ■ Writer's Workbook, pp. 6–9 ■ The Ultimate Writing and Creativity Center ■ Routine Card 2, Routine 7	**Word Analysis** ✓■ Spelling: The /âr/ and /ar/ Sounds Pretest, p. 125F **Writing Process Strategies** ■ Expository Writing: Responding to Fiction, Getting Ideas, p. 125F **English Language Conventions** ■ Mechanics: Quotation Marks in Dialogue, p. 125F	**Word Analysis** ■ Spelling: Word Sorting, p. 125G ■ Vocabulary: Antonyms, p. 125G **Writing Process Strategies** ■ Expository Writing: Responding to Fiction, Prewriting, p. 125G **English Language Conventions** ■ Mechanics: Quotation Marks in Dialogue, p. 125G

P Phonics ✓Informal Assessment Available ✓Formal Assessment Available

DAY 2 continued	DAY 3	
DAY 3	**DAY 4**	**DAY 5**
Ⓟ **Phonics and Fluency,** p. 114M ■ Review /ū/ spelled *u, u_e, _ue, _ew* **About the Words and Sentences,** p. 114M	Ⓟ **Phonics and Fluency** **Developing Oral Language,** p. 114N **Dictation,** p. 114N	**General Review**
Student Anthology, pp. 114–123 Second Read **Comprehension Skills** ■ Classify and Categorize, pp. 115, 117, 119, 121, 123 **Checking Comprehension,** p. 123 **Supporting the Reading,** p. 123C ■ Visualizing	**Student Anthology** ✓■ Concept Connections, p. 124 ■ Meet the Author/Illustrator, p. 125 **Review Selection Vocabulary,** p. 123B **Literary Elements,** p. 123D ■ Characterization **Science Connection** ■ Wildlife Notebook, p. 123E	✓**Selection Assessment** ■ "The Boy Who Didn't Believe in Spring," pp. 2–5 **Home Connection,** p. 123B **Social Studies Connection** ■ Explorers, p. 123F
✓**Investigation** ■ Investigation Planning, p. 125C	**Supporting the Investigation** ■ Interviewing, p. 125D	**Investigation** ■ Unit Investigation Continued ■ Update Concept/Question Board
Word Analysis ■ Spelling: The /âr/ and /ar/ Sounds, p. 125H ■ Vocabulary: Antonyms, p. 125H **Writing Process Strategies** ■ Expository Writing: Responding to Fiction, Drafting, p. 125H **Writer's Craft** ■ Time-Order Words, p. 125H **English Language Conventions** ✓■ Mechanics: Quotation Marks in Dialogue, p. 125H	**Word Analysis** ■ Spelling: The /âr/ and /ar/ Sounds, p. 125I ■ Vocabulary: Antonyms, p. 125I **Writing Process Strategies** ■ Expository Writing: Responding to Fiction, Revising, p. 125I **English Language Conventions** ✓✓■ Listening, Speaking, Viewing Listening: Remembering What We Hear, p. 125I	**Word Analysis** ✓■ Spelling: The /âr/ and /ar/ Sounds Final Test ✓■ Vocabulary: Antonyms, p. 125J **Writing Process Strategies** ✓■ Expository Writing: Responding to Fiction, Editing/Proofreading and Publishing, p. 125J **English Language Conventions** ✓■ Penmanship: Cursive Letters *n* and *m*, p. 125J

Below are suggestions for differentiating instruction. These are the same skills shown in the Lesson Planner; however, these pages provide extra practice opportunities or enriching activities to meet the varied needs of students.

WORKSHOP

Differentiating Instruction

Teacher Directed: Individual and Small-Group Instruction

Spend time each day with individuals and small groups to individualize instruction. Each day:

- preteach students who need help with the next lesson.
- reteach students who need to solidify their understanding of content previously taught.
- listen to students read to check their fluency.
- hold writing and inquiry conferences.

Use the following program components to support instruction:

- ***Reteach*** with students who need a bit more practice
- ***Intervention*** for students who exhibit a lack of understanding of the lesson concepts
- ***English Learner Support*** with students who need language help

Student: Independent Activities

Students can work alone, with a partner, or in small groups on such activities as:

- Review sound/spellings
- Practice dictation words
- Partner reading
- Practice fluency
- Independent reading
- Reading Roundtable
- Concept vocabulary
- Selection vocabulary
- Writing in progress
- Conference
- Language Arts
- Challenge activities
- Inquiry and Investigation activities
- Listening Library
- Online Phonics

For Workshop Management Tips, see Appendix page 41.

	DAY 1
Decoding/ Word Knowledge	**Teacher Directed** ▪ Blending: Prefix *un-*, ***Intervention Guide,*** p. 61 **Independent Activities** ▪ ***Online Phonics***
Fluency	**Independent Activities** ▪ Self-test fluency rate ▪ Partner reading
Comprehension	**Teacher Directed** ▪ Preteach "The Boy Who Didn't Believe in Spring," ***Intervention Guide,*** pp. 63–64 ▪ Preteach Intervention Selection One, ***Intervention Guide,*** pp. 64–65 ▪ ***English Learner Support Guide*** • Vocabulary, pp. 92–93 • Comprehension Skill: Classify and Categorize, pp. 93–94 **Independent Activities** ▪ Record reaction to Read Aloud in Writer's Notebook ▪ Browse ***Leveled Classroom Library*** ▪ Add vocabulary in Writer's Notebook
Inquiry	**Independent Activities** ▪ Concept/Question Board ▪ Record ideas about City Wildlife in ***Inquiry Journal,*** p. 28 ▪ Explore OCR Web site for theme connections ▪ Wildlife Observation List, ***Inquiry Journal,*** p. 32
Language Arts	**Teacher Directed** ▪ Grammar, Usage, and Mechanics, ***Intervention Guide,*** pp. 67–68 **Independent Activities** ▪ Quotation Marks, ***Comprehension and Language Arts Skills,*** pp. 26–27

DAY 2	DAY 3	DAY 4	DAY 5
Teacher Directed ▪ Developing Oral Language, ***Intervention Guide,*** p. 61 **Independent Activities** ▪ ***Online Phonics***	**Teacher Directed** ▪ Dictation and Spelling: Prefix *un-*, ***Intervention Guide,*** p. 62 **Independent Activities** ▪ ***Online Phonics***	**Teacher Directed** ▪ Blending: /ū/ spelled *u_e, u,* and *_ew*, ***Intervention Guide,*** p. 62 **Independent Activities** ▪ Read ***Decodable Book 17,*** *Hugo Bugle*	**Teacher Directed** ▪ Developing Oral Language, ***Intervention Guide,*** p. 62 ▪ Dictation and Spelling: /ū/ spelled *u_e, u,* and *_ew*, ***Intervention Guide,*** p. 63
Independent Activities ▪ Orally read "The Boy Who Didn't Believe in Spring" ▪ Partner reading	**Independent Activities** ▪ Oral reading of selection for fluency ▪ Partner read	**Independent Activities** ▪ Partner reading of selection ▪ Partner read ***Decodable Book 17,*** *Hugo Bugle*	**Teacher Directed** ▪ Repeated Readings/Fluency Check, ***Intervention Guide,*** p. 67 **Independent Activities** ▪ Reread ***Decodable Book 17***
Teacher Directed ▪ Preteach "The Boy Who Didn't Believe in Spring," ***Intervention Guide,*** pp. 63–64 ▪ Comprehension Strategies, ***Intervention Guide,*** p. 65 ▪ Reread Intervention Selection One, ***Intervention Guide,*** pp. 64–65 ▪ ***English Learner Support Guide*** • Vocabulary, pp. 95–96 • Comprehension Skill: Classify and Categorize, pp. 95–97 **Independent Activities** ▪ Choose ***Leveled Classroom Library*** book for independent reading ▪ Record response to selection in Writer's Notebook ▪ ***Listening Library Audiocassette/CD*** ▪ ***English Learner Support Activities,*** p. 13	**Teacher Directed** ▪ Reread "The Boy Who Didn't Believe in Spring," ***Intervention Guide,*** pp. 63–64 ▪ Preteach Intervention Selection Two, ***Intervention Guide,*** pp. 65–66 ▪ ***English Learner Support Guide*** • Vocabulary, pp. 97–98 • Comprehension Skill: Classify and Categorize, pp. 98–99 **Independent Activities** ▪ Read ***Leveled Classroom Library*** book ▪ ***Listening Library Audiocassette/CD*** ▪ Complete Link to Writing in Supporting the Reading, p. 123C	**Teacher Directed** ▪ Discuss Concept Connections, p. 124 ▪ Reread "The Boy Who Didn't Believe in Spring," ***Intervention Guide,*** pp. 63–64 ▪ Comprehension Strategies, ***Intervention Guide,*** p. 66 ▪ Reread Intervention Selection Two, ***Intervention Guide,*** pp. 65–66 ▪ ***English Learner Support Guide*** • Vocabulary, pp. 100–101 • Comprehension Skill: Classify and Categorize, pp. 100–102 **Independent Activities** ▪ Independent reading ▪ Add words to Word Bank ▪ Complete Independent Practice in Literary Elements, p. 123D ▪ Science Connection, p. 123E	**Teacher Directed** ▪ ***English Learner Support Guide*** • Review Vocabulary, p. 102 • Comprehension Skill: Classify and Categorize, pp. 102–103 **Independent Activities** ▪ Read ***Leveled Classroom Library*** book as independent reading ▪ Reading Roundtable ▪ Social Studies Connection, p. 123F ▪ ***English Learner Support Activities,*** p. 14
Independent Activities ▪ Concept/Question Board ▪ Explore OCR Web site for theme connections ▪ Use ***Research Assistant CD-ROM*** to begin Investigation	**Independent Activities** ▪ Project Planning Calendar, ***Inquiry Journal,*** pp. 33–34 ▪ Concept/Question Board ▪ Explore OCR Web site for theme connections	**Independent Activities** ▪ Concept/Question Board ▪ Interviewing Guidelines and Questions, ***Inquiry Journal,*** pp. 35–36 ▪ Explore OCR Web site for theme connections	**Independent Activities** ▪ Concept/Question Board ▪ Continue research
Teacher Directed ▪ Grammar, Usage, and Mechanics, ***Intervention Guide,*** p. 68 ▪ Spelling: Word Sort, p. 125G ▪ Quotation Marks, ***Reteach,*** p. 31 **Independent Activities** ▪ Seminar: Plan a Response to Fiction, p. 125G ▪ Vocabulary: Antonyms, ***Spelling and Vocabulary Skills,*** pp. 26–27 ▪ Quotation Marks, ***Challenge,*** p. 28	**Teacher Directed** ▪ Writing Activity, ***Intervention Guide,*** pp. 68–69 ▪ Vocabulary: Antonyms, ***Reteach,*** p. 30 **Independent Activities** ▪ Spelling: The /âr/ and /ar/ Sounds, ***Spelling and Vocabulary Skills,*** p. 28 ▪ Vocabulary: Antonyms, ***Challenge,*** p. 27 ▪ Writer's Craft: Time and Order Words, ***Comprehension and Language Arts Skills,*** pp. 28–29	**Teacher Directed** ▪ Writer's Craft: Time and Order Words, ***Reteach,*** p. 32 ▪ Writing Activity, ***Intervention Guide,*** p. 69 ▪ Spelling: The /âr/ and /ar/ Sounds, ***Reteach,*** p. 29 **Independent Activities** ▪ Spelling: The /âr/ and /ar/ Sounds • ***Spelling and Vocabulary Skills,*** p. 29 • ***Challenge,*** p. 26	**Independent Activities** ▪ Seminar: Edit/Proofread and Publish a Response to Fiction, p. 125J ▪ Penmanship: Practice Cursive Letters *n* and *m*, p. 125J ▪ Writer's Craft: Time and Order Words, ***Challenge,*** p. 29

ASSESSMENT

Formal Assessment Options

Use these summative assessments along with your informal observations to assess student progress.

Name ____________ Date ________ Score ______

UNIT 2 City Wildlife • Lesson I

LESSON ASSESSMENT

The Boy Who Didn't Believe in Spring

Read the following questions carefully. Then completely fill in the bubble of each correct answer. You may look back at the story to find the answer to each of the questions.

1. Why doesn't King Shabazz believe in spring?
   - Ⓐ He hasn't seen it yet.
   - Ⓑ He thinks spring is over.
   - Ⓒ He likes winter best.
2. What do King Shabazz and Tony see in the vacant lot?
   - Ⓐ apple trees in bloom
   - Ⓑ a flock of robins
   - Ⓒ an old red car

Read the following questions carefully. Use complete sentences to answer the questions.

3. Why do King Shabazz and Tony go for a walk?
   King Shabazz wants to look for spring.
4. What places did King Shabazz and Tony pass on the first part of their walk?
   They passed the school playground, Weissman's bakery, and some apartments.
5. After King Shabazz and Tony find the car, why does King Shabazz hold Tony's hand?
   He holds his hand because they are both a little frightened of the noises coming from the car.

2 Unit 2 • Lesson I *The Boy Who Didn't Believe in Spring* • Unit 2 Assessment

Unit 2 Assessment p. 2

The Boy Who Didn't Believe in Spring *(continued)*

6. Why does Tony stop at the streetlight and pretend to tie his shoes?
   Tony stops because he and King Shabazz have not walked past the streetlight by themselves before.
7. After they walk past the streetlight, what places do King Shabazz and Tony pass?
   They pass the Church of the Solid Rock and a restaurant and some more apartments.
8. What are the strange noises that are coming out of the car?
   The strange noises are the sounds of birds going in and out of the car.

Read the following questions carefully. Then completely fill in the bubble of each correct answer.

9. What are the crops that are near the car?
   - Ⓐ flowers
   - Ⓑ buns
   - Ⓒ corn
10. Tony and King Shabazz find a bird's nest inside the car. Which of these is most like a bird's nest?
    - Ⓐ a herd of cows
    - Ⓑ a school of fish
    - Ⓒ a bee hive

Unit 2 Assessment • *The Boy Who Didn't Believe in Spring* Unit 2 • Lesson I 3

Unit 2 Assessment p. 3

The Boy Who Didn't Believe in Spring *(continued)*

Read the questions below. Use complete sentences in your answers.

Linking to the Concepts Have you ever seen signs of wildlife on the school playground or in your neighborhood? Tell about them.

Answers will vary. Accept all reasonable answers.

Personal Response What are the first signs of spring where you live?

Answers will vary. Accept all reasonable answers.

4 Unit 2 • Lesson I *The Boy Who Didn't Believe in Spring* • Unit 2 Assessment

Unit 2 Assessment p. 4

The Boy Who Didn't Believe in Spring *(continued)*

Vocabulary

Read the following questions carefully. Then completely fill in the bubble of each correct answer.

1. King Shabazz becomes curious about spring when his mama talks about the crops coming up. **Crops** are
   - Ⓐ plants you can eat
   - Ⓑ cousins who live far away
   - Ⓒ puddles of water
2. The boys find an old car in a vacant lot. What does the word **vacant** mean?
   - Ⓐ clean
   - Ⓑ junky
   - Ⓒ empty
3. The old car is on a mound of dirt. A **mound** is like a
   - Ⓐ city street
   - Ⓑ small hill
   - Ⓒ playground
4. Tony and King Shabazz find a patch of yellow pointy flowers. A **patch** is like a
   - Ⓐ deep valley
   - Ⓑ large field
   - Ⓒ small area
5. The windows of the church in this story are **decorated.** This means that the church windows look
   - Ⓐ fancy
   - Ⓑ broken
   - Ⓒ old

Unit 2 Assessment • *The Boy Who Didn't Believe in Spring* Unit 2 • Lesson I 5

Unit 2 Assessment p. 5

Name ____________ Date ________ Score ______

UNIT 2 City Wildlife • Lesson I *The Boy Who Didn't Believe in Spring*

Spelling Pretest: The /ar/ and /âr/ Sounds

Fold this page back on the dotted line. Take the Pretest. Then correct any word you misspelled by crossing out the word and rewriting it next to the incorrect spelling.

1. bare
2. dare
3. fare
4. share
5. hair
6. fair
7. glare
8. chair
9. bear
10. wear
11. air
12. car
13. dark
14. apartments
15. started

26 Unit 2 • Lesson I *Spelling Pretest: The /ar/ and /âr/ Sounds* • Unit 2 Assessment

Unit 2 Assessment p. 26

Name ____________ Date ________ Score ______

UNIT 2 City Wildlife • Lesson I *The Boy Who Didn't Believe in Spring*

Spelling Final Test: The /ar/ and /âr/ Sounds

Mark the letter next to the underlined word that is misspelled. Focus on the underlined word.

1. Ⓐ A bear catches fish in its paws.
   Ⓑ Football players waire helmets.
   Ⓒ Sisters share the same mother.
   Ⓓ Correct as is.
2. Ⓔ A dark sky is a sign of a storm.
   Ⓖ A person sits in a chair.
   Ⓗ The air we breathe consists of gas.
   Ⓘ Correct as is.
3. Ⓐ Walls with no pictures are bair.
   Ⓑ Some women wear high heels.
   Ⓒ Many states have an annual fair.
   Ⓓ Correct as is.
4. Ⓐ A lion's mane is haire.
   Ⓑ The cost of a ride is the fare.
   Ⓗ Reflections can cause a glare.
   Ⓙ Correct as is.
5. Ⓐ Matches have started forest fires.
   Ⓑ Swimmers wear swimsuits.
   Ⓒ A deark cave can seem scary.
   Ⓓ Correct as is.
6. Ⓔ Sea gulls fly in the air.
   Ⓕ It is kind to shair with others.
   Ⓗ A teddy bear is a stuffed animal.
   Ⓙ Correct as is.

Unit 2 Assessment • *Spelling Final Test: The /ar/ and /âr/ Sounds* Unit 2 • Lesson I 27

Unit 2 Assessment p. 27

Online Assessment for ***Open Court Reading*** helps teachers differentiate classroom instruction based on students' scores from the weekly and end-of-unit assessments. It provides exercises best suited to meet the needs of each student. For more information, visit SRAonline.com.

Informal Comprehension Strategies Rubrics

Asking Questions

- The student asks questions about ideas or facts presented in the text and attempts to answer these questions by reading the text.

Monitoring and Clarifying

- The student notes characteristics of the text, such as whether it is difficult to read or whether some sections are more challenging or more important than others.
- The student shows awareness of whether he or she understands the text and takes appropriate action, such as rereading, in order to understand the text better.
- The student rereads to reconsider something presented earlier in the text.
- The student recognizes problems during reading, such as a loss of concentration, unfamiliar vocabulary, or lack of sufficient background knowledge to comprehend the text.

Predicting

- The student makes predictions about the text.
- The student updates predictions during reading, based on information in the text.

Visualizing

- The student visualizes ideas or scenes described in the text.

Research Rubrics

During Workshop, assess students using the rubrics below. The rubrics range from 1–4 in most categories, with 1 being the lowest score. Record each student's score on the inside back cover of the ***Inquiry Journal***.

Formulating Research Questions and Problems

1 With help, identifies things he or she wonders about in relation to a topic.

2 Expresses curiosity about topics; with help, translates this into specific questions.

3 Poses an interesting problem or question for research; with help, refines it into a researchable question.

4 Identifies something he or she genuinely wonders about and translates it into a researchable question.

1 Preparing to Read

Objectives

- Students practice recognizing antonyms and synonyms.
- Students practice recognizing compound words.
- Students practice recognizing base words and the suffix *-y* and the prefix *un-*.
- Students practice recognizing the spelling patterns *ar* and *air.*
- Students practice recognizing /ū/ spelled *u, u_e, _ue, _ew.*

Materials

- Student Anthology, Book 1, pp. 112–125
- Decodable Book Activities CD-ROM
- Decodable Book 17
- Sound/Spelling Card 36
- Routine Cards 1, 3, Routines 1–2, 8–9

Teacher Tip SYLLABICATION To help students blend words and build fluency, use the syllabication below of the words in the word lines.

hol • lered	whis • pered	grinned
frowned	va • cant	emp • ty
bare	street • light	play • ground
tip • toe	spik • y	cot • ton • y
smel • ly	sil • ver • y	un • be • liev • a • ble
un • dec • o • rat • ed	un • tied	un • eat • en
un • oc • cu • pied	star • ted	a • part • ments
dark	car	air

Differentiating Instruction

If...	Then...
Students need extra help with synonyms or compound words	Use ***Online Phonics***
Students need extra help with the prefix *un-*	Use ***Intervention Guide*** pages 61–62

WORD KNOWLEDGE

Word Knowledge

Reading the Words and Sentences

Use the established procedure as you have students read each line of words and the sentences in this and in subsequent lessons. The words in **boldface** are from the selection.

Line 1:	hollered	whispered	grinned	frowned	
Line 2:	vacant	empty	bare		
Line 3:	streetlight	playground	tiptoe		
Line 4:	spiky	cottony	smelly	silvery	
Line 5:	unbelievable	undecorated	untied	uneaten	unoccupied
Line 6:	started	apartments	dark	car	air
Sentence 1:	Tony stopped and made believe his sneaker was untied to see what King was going to do.				
Sentence 2:	"Well, come on, man," King whispered, and they started down the street.				
Sentence 3:	Just after the friends passed some apartments, they came to a vacant lot.				
Sentence 4:	An indigo car is a dark blue color.				

About the Words and Sentences

- **Line 1:** The words in Line 1 are antonyms. Ask a student to tell what an antonym is *(opposite)*. Ask students to identify the antonyms *(hollered/whispered, grinned/frowned)*. Have students use each word in a sentence. Ask students to think of other antonyms *(hot/cold, hard/soft, up/down, left/right, day/night, all/none)*.
- **Line 2:** These words are synonyms. Have a student tell what a synonym is *(words that mean the same thing)*. Give a word and ask students to give a synonym or synonyms *(happy/joyful, tired/sleepy, large/huge/big, end/finish/complete, grow/mature/develop)*.
- **Line 3:** These words are compound words. Have students tell you the two words that make up the compound word. Ask if the two words help us understand the meaning of the word.
- **Line 4:** In this line, the suffix *-y* is added to base words. Have the students give a definition for each word and use the word in a sentence. Ask the class to identify the part of speech the word becomes in the sentence. The students should be able to generalize that by adding this suffix the word becomes an adjective *(describing word)*.
- **Line 5:** In this line, the prefix *un-* is added to words. Ask the class what the prefix *un-* means *(not)*. Have students give the base word and explain how the meaning changes when the prefix *un-* is added to the base word.

- **Line 6:** The words in the last line are spelling words found in "The Boy Who Didn't Believe in Spring" and review the spelling patterns *ar* and *air*.
- **Sentences 1–3:** These sentences are from the story students are about to read. Ask students to identify words that have either antonyms or synonyms and give examples *(Antonyms: stopped/started, untied/tied, whispered/shouted, down/up, after/before, friends/enemies, vacant/occupied; Synonyms: stopped/discontinued, untied/undone, started/began, some/several, vacant/bare/empty)*. Have students identify the word with a prefix or suffix and give its meaning *(untied—not tied)*.
- **Sentence 4:** Have students identify the words in the last sentence that contain the /âr/ sound spelled *ar (car, dark)*.

Developing Oral Language

Use direct teaching to review the words. Use one or both of the following activities to help students practice the words aloud.

- Have one student choose a line of words from the board and point to a word in that line. Then have the student choose a classmate to read the word and use the word in a sentence.
- Have students focus on one of the lines. Have a volunteer choose a word and use it in a sentence to begin a story. Have another volunteer continue the story by supplying a sentence that uses another word from the line. Continue until all the words are used.

WORD KNOWLEDGE

Teacher Tip FLUENCY Gaining a better understanding of the spellings of sounds and structure of words will help students as they encounter unfamiliar words in their reading. By this time in Grade 3, students should be reading approximately 107 words per minute with fluency and expression. As students read, you may notice that some need work in building fluency. During Workshop, have these students select a section of the text (a minimum of 160 words) to read several times in order to build fluency.

Spelling
See pages 125E–125J for the corresponding spelling lesson for the /ar/ and /âr/ sounds.

Routine Card
Refer to ***Routine 1*** for whole-word blending and ***Routine 2*** for sentence blending.

Teacher Tip REMINDER Set 1 provides instruction on word structure. Word structure activities will continue through Unit 6. Set 2 provides a review of phonics instruction. The phonics reviews will continue through Unit 3.

PHONICS

Teacher Tip SYLLABICATION To help students blend words and build fluency, use the syllabication below of the words in the word lines.

u•nit	used	men•u	U•tah
cue	hu•man	hu•mid	Jan•u•ar•y
pu•ny	fu•el	pu•pil	u•ni•corn
mew	few	u•ni•fy	u•ni•verse

Teacher Tip The Phonics and Fluency exercises provide review and maintenance for students who have used the ***Open Court Reading*** program in Grade 2 and will continue to use it in Grade 3. (It also serves as a general course of phonics instruction for students who have not been exposed to the ***Open Court Reading*** program.)

Teacher Tip Remind students that long vowels appear in a yellow box on the ***Sound/Spelling Cards.***

Online Phonics
SRA's ***Online Phonics*** program provides Web-based practice with the ***Open Court Reading*** sounds and spellings. For more information about this program, visit the SRA home page SRAonline.com

Differentiating Instruction

If...	Then...
Students need extra help with /ū/ spelled *u, u_e,* and *_ew*	Use ***Intervention Guide*** pages 62–63

Phonics and Fluency

Review the /ū/ sound spelled *u, u_e, _ue, _ew*

Blending

- Use direct teaching to teach the following words and sentences.
- Display ***Sound/Spelling Card 36,*** the /ū/ sound.
- Follow the established procedure to have students read the following words and sentences. **Boldface** words are found in the selection.

Line 1:	unit	used	menu	Utah
Line 2:	cue	human	humid	January
Line 3:	puny	fuel	pupil	unicorn
Line 4:	mew	few	unify	universe
Sentence 1:	My favorite month is January.			
Sentence 2:	I ate a few cookies after dinner.			
Sentence 3:	He used to sit with his friend Tony Polito on the bottom step when the days started getting longer and warmer and talk about it.			

About the Words and Sentences

- **Lines 1–4:** The words provide practice with the /ū/ sound. Have students identify the /ū/ spelling in each word.
- **Sentences 1–2:** Have students identify the words with the /ū/ sound and then use them in a different sentence. *(January, few)*
- **Sentence 3:** This sentence is from the selection. Have students identify the word with the /ū/ sound. *(used)*

Developing Oral Language

Use direct teaching to review the words. Use one or both of the following activities to help students practice words aloud.

- Say some sentences with missing words, and ask the students to point to and read words from Lines 1–4 to fill in the blanks. Possible sentences: A ______ is a mammal. *(human)* ______ is a cold month. *(January)*
- Have individual students touch a word on the board, say it, underline it, and then use it in a sentence. Have each student choose another student to extend the sentence by adding to the beginning or ending of the original sentence. Sentences can also be extended by adding adjectives or adverbs to the original sentence.

Dictation

Following the established procedure, erase the blending lines and sentences on the board and have students take out writing paper. Dictate the following words and sentence for students to write.

Line 1:	humor	utilize	unity
Line 2:	useful	mute	menu
Challenge Word:	community		
Sentence:	The band wants new bugles and uniforms in the future.		

Have students follow the proper steps for proofreading the dictated words and sentence.

Building Fluency

Decodable Books are used to help develop fluency for students who need extra practice. The only way to gain fluency is to read. Students will have many opportunities to read, including the ***Student Anthology,*** the ***Leveled Classroom Library,*** and their own reading. The ***Decodable Books*** can be used to practice the phonics and fluency elements being reviewed. Refer to the Appendix for the procedure on using these books. For this lesson, use ***Decodable Book 17,*** *Hugo Bugle.*

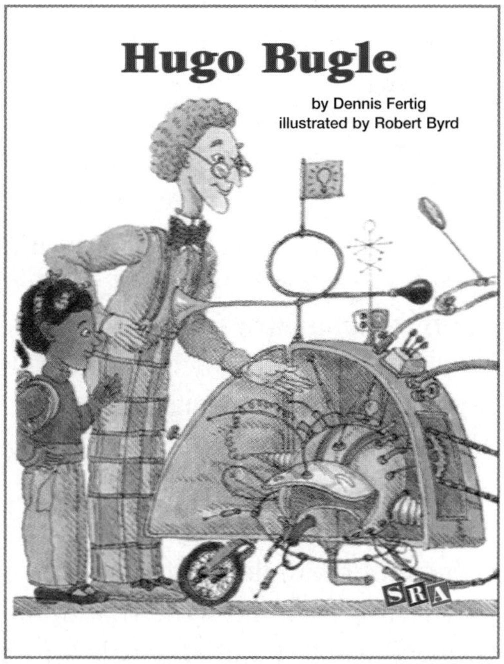

Decodable Book 17

PHONICS

Routine Card
Refer to ***Routine 8*** for whole-word dictation and ***Routine 9*** for sentence dictation.

Teacher Tip Encourage students to just read the words. Stop and blend only those words that give them problems.

Use the ***Decodable Book Activities CD-ROM*** for activities that support this Phonics lesson.

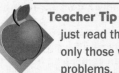

Objectives

- Students will understand the selection vocabulary before reading, using strategies such as suffixes and structural cues.
- Students will spell words with the affixes *-y* and *un-*, and recognize antonyms, synonyms, and compound words.
- Students will connect prior knowledge to subjects discussed in text.
- Students will use comprehension strategies such as Asking Questions, Clarifying, Visualizing, and Predicting to construct meaning from the text and monitor reading.
- Students will use the comprehension skill Classify and Categorize as they read the story the second time.
- Students will discuss personal reactions to the story to begin identifying their own personal reading preferences.

Materials

- Student Anthology, Book 1, pp. 112–125
- Program Assessment
- Reading Transparencies 10, 46, 50, 53
- Inquiry Journal, p. 29
- Home Connection, p. 17
- Unit 2 Assessment, pp. 2–5
- Routine Cards 1–2, Routines 3–6

Differentiating Instruction

If...	Then...
Students need extra help with selection vocabulary	Use ***Intervention Guide*** pages 63–64

Clues	Problems	Wonderings
Can a person "believe" in Spring?	Weissman's	How can you find Spring?

Reading Transparency 46

Build Background

Activate Prior Knowledge

Discuss the following with students to find out what they may already know about the selection and have already learned about city wildlife.

- Preteach "The Boy Who Didn't Believe in Spring" by first determining what students remember about what they learned about city wildlife from the Read Aloud.
- Discuss signs of spring and ask students to relate personal experiences noticing the first signs of spring.
- See if there are any questions on the Concept/Question Board that this story might answer.

Background Information

The following information may help students to better understand the selection they are about to read.

- "The Boy Who Didn't Believe in Spring" is realistic fiction. Realistic fiction may include descriptions of actual places and things, and also situations that are made up but could happen. The author invents the characters, then involves them in solving a problem.
- The author, Lucille Clifton, uses idiomatic spellings and phrases. Explain to students that some of the spellings used in the story were purposefully written to reflect natural speech and that they differ from the dictionary spellings *(bou* for *about* and *comin* for *coming).*

Preview and Prepare

Browse

- Have students read aloud the title and the author's and illustrator's names. This allows them to activate prior knowledge relevant to the story. Demonstrate and remind students how to browse. Because this is a fiction story, have students preview the selection by browsing through only the first page or two of the story in order not to prematurely disclose any surprises in the story. Discuss with students what they think this story might reveal about city wildlife.
- Display ***Reading Transparency 46,*** Clues, Problems, and Wonderings. Unde each heading, write in note form the observations that students generate as they browse. For example, students might question if someone could "believe" or "not believe" in spring and write that under Clues. They might note under Problems any questions, unfamiliar words, or long sentences that arise during reading. Under Wonderings students can note their questions, such as "How can you finc spring?" To save time and model note taking, write students' observations as brief notes rather than as complete sentences.

- As students prepare to read the selection, have them browse the Focus Questions on the first page of the selection. Tell them to keep these questions in mind as they read.

Set Purposes

Encourage students to set their own purposes for reading the selection. For example, they may seek to learn more about city wildlife, or about how the story exemplifies realistic fiction. If necessary, prompt students to look for examples of wildlife and where the wildlife is found. Invite students to set other reading goals for themselves.

Selection Vocabulary

As students study vocabulary, they will use a variety of skills to determine the meaning of a word. These include context clues, word structure, and apposition. Students will apply these same skills while reading to clarify additional unfamiliar words. Students can write their definitions in their Writer's Notebooks.

Display ***Reading Transparency 10*** before reading the selection to introduce and discuss the following words and their meanings.

crops: plants grown for food or to sell to make money (page 115)
decorated: made beautiful by adding fancy things and frills (page 119)
vacant: empty; abandoned (page 119)
mound: small hill or pile of dirt, rocks, or other material (page 120)
patch: an area different from what is around it (page 121)

Have students read the words in the word box, stopping to blend any words that they have trouble reading. Demonstrate how to decode multisyllabic words by breaking the words into syllables and blending the syllables. Then have the students try. If students still have trouble, refer them to the ***Sound/Spelling Cards*** to blend the words sound by sound. If the word is not decodable, give the students the pronunciation. Other words that may be unfamiliar to students should be clarified during reading, with each definition tied to the way that the word is used in the story *(examples: shades; bar-b-q)*.

Have students read the sentences on the transparency to determine the meaning of the underlined words. Each word has two sentences that students will read and from which they should be able to derive the meaning of the underlined word. Remind them to use one or more of the skills they have learned—context clues, word structure, or apposition—to figure out the meaning before using a dictionary. Be sure students explain which skills they are using and how they figured out the meanings of the words. Have students reread the sentence, substituting the definition to see if the sentence makes sense. Have a volunteer create a new sentence using the underlined word.

Routine Card
Refer to ***Routine 4*** for the Clues, Problems, and Wonderings procedure.

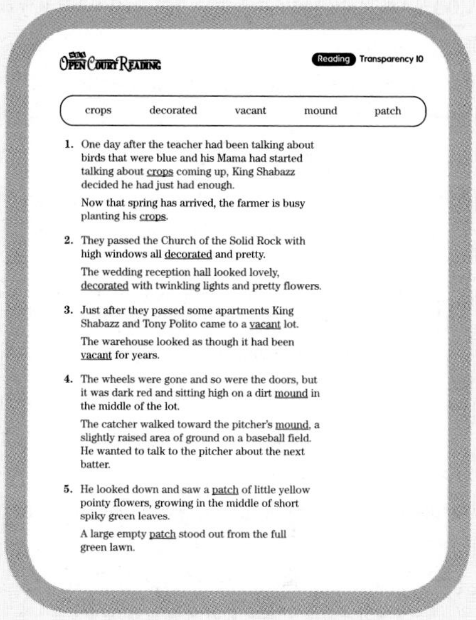
OPEN COURT READING   Reading Transparency 10

crops   decorated   vacant   mound   patch

1. One day after the teacher had been talking about birds that were blue and his Mama had started talking about crops coming up, King Shabazz decided he had just had enough.
   Now that spring has arrived, the farmer is busy planting his crops.
2. They passed the Church of the Solid Rock with high windows all decorated and pretty.
   The wedding reception hall looked lovely, decorated with twinkling lights and pretty flowers.
3. Just after they passed some apartments King Shabazz and Tony Polito came to a vacant lot.
   The warehouse looked as though it had been vacant for years.
4. The wheels were gone and so were the doors, but it was dark red and sitting high on a dirt mound in the middle of the lot.
   The catcher walked toward the pitcher's mound, a slightly raised area of ground on a baseball field. He wanted to talk to the pitcher about the next batter.
5. He looked down and saw a patch of little yellow pointy flowers, growing in the middle of short spiky green leaves.
   A large empty patch stood out from the full green lawn.

Reading Transparency 10

Teacher Tip SELECTION VOCABULARY To help students decode words, divide the words into syllables when you are saying them, as shown below. The information following each word tells how students can figure out the meaning of each word. When writing words on the board, do not divide them into syllables.

crops	context clues
dec • o • rat • ed	context clues
va • cant	context clues
mound	context clues
patch	context clues

Teacher Tip Students may recall learning in "City Lots: Living Things in Vacant Spots," that wild plants and animals need soil, water, sunlight, food, and space to survive. Ask students to discuss what kinds of plants and animals they may have seen in their neighborhoods and to explain how the wildlife meets these needs.

Routine Card
Refer to ***Routine 3*** for the vocabulary procedure.

Teacher Tip Dialect is a form of informal language. All cultures and ethnic groups use informal language at home and in other casual situations. In "The Boy Who Didn't Believe in Spring," Lucille Clifton purposefully used dialect as a way to help African-American children relate to literature. She often uses words and expressions that reflect language spoken by children in informal situations.

Teacher Tip ACTIVATE PRIOR KNOWLEDGE Inform students that good readers typically activate what they already know about a topic before reading something new about the topic. Tell students that they should get in the habit of thinking about the topic of an upcoming selection and activating relevant background knowledge.

During Workshop, and after the selection has been read at least once, have students listen to the recording of this lesson's selection on the ***Listening Library Audiocassette/CD.*** After students have listened, have them discuss their personal preferences of the selections read. Ask them what other things they have listened to and like to listen to on the radio, on audiocassettes, or on CDs.

Routine Card
Refer to ***Routine 5*** for the procedure on reading the selection.

DIFFERENTIATING INSTRUCTION

If...	Then...
Students need extra help with visualizing	Use ***Intervention Guide*** pages 64–65
Students need extra help with asking questions	Use ***Intervention Guide*** pages 65–66

Reading Recommendations

Oral Reading

This story is a natural for oral reading because of its conversational style. Students should read aloud fluently with appropriate expression, vocal patterns, and intonation. Make sure the students attend to punctuation and read in phrases. Tell students to add a sense of feeling or anticipation as they read.

Have students make use of the comprehension strategies listed below to help them understand the selection. Have them stop reading periodically or wait until they have completed the selection to discuss the reading strategies. After the students have finished reading the selection, use the Discussing the Selection questions on page 123A to see if they understand what they have read.

Using Comprehension Strategies First Read

Comprehension strategy instruction allows students to become aware of how good readers read. Good readers constantly check their understanding as they are reading and ask themselves questions. In addition, skilled readers recognize when they are having problems and stop to use various comprehension strategies to help them make sense of what they are reading.

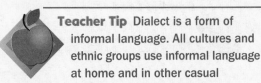

During the reading of "The Boy Who Didn't Believe in Spring," you will model the use of the following reading strategies.

- **Asking Questions** helps readers focus attention on what they are reading and engages them in deeper understanding of themes, concepts, and ideas.
- **Monitoring and Clarifying** takes different forms, including clarifying the meaning of words and clarifying difficult ideas or passages. In order to clarify meanings, students can use context, use structural analysis, use apposition, reread the text, use charts or graphic organizers, or use resources outside of the text.
- **Predicting** causes readers to analyze information given about story events and characters in the context of how it may logically connect to the story's conclusion.
- **Visualizing** requires readers to mentally picture the events or characters in the story, resulting in a more vivid and imaginative understanding of the story.

As students read, they should be using a variety of strategies to help them understand the selection. Encourage students to use the strategies listed on the previous page as the class reads the story aloud. Do this by stopping at the points indicated by the numbers in the magenta circles on the reduced student page and using a particular strategy. Students can also stop periodically to discuss what they have learned and what problems they may be having.

Starting in Unit 2, students should begin to assume more responsibility for the use of comprehension strategies. Prompting and Student Samples serve as the transition from the teacher modeling that was done in Unit 1. Prompting provides a springboard for students to think and respond using the strategy mentioned in the prompt. The Student Sample is written in the language that students might use in their actual responses.

The Student Sample may be one of many possible responses. Accept other responses that are reasonable and appropriate. If students' responses indicate that the students do not understand the strategy, be ready to discuss their responses and to provide additional instruction. As students proceed through the lessons, teacher modeling and prompting of strategy use should become less and less necessary as students assume more and more responsibility for using strategies.

Building Comprehension Skills Second Read

Revisiting or rereading a selection allows readers to apply skills that give them a more complete understanding of the text. Some follow-up comprehension skills help students organize information. Others lead to deeper understanding—to "reading between the lines," as mature readers do. In this selection, students will review the following comprehension skill:

- **Classify and Categorize:** Readers put like things or ideas together in order to understand new information.

Reading with a Purpose

Have students look for ways any of the story characters discover city wildlife throughout the selection.

Teacher Tip COMPREHENSION STRATEGIES Remind students as they read the story on the second day to summarize what they learned from the first day.

Research in Action

The discussion about the selection and its relation to the unit theme should add measurably to students' understanding of the concepts. Make sure that students feel free to offer their opinions and explain their ideas. Students should state their ideas clearly and give reasons for their thinking. At the same time, you should participate in the discussion, offering your own opinions and ideas.
(Ann Brown and Joe Campione)

Teacher Tip Keep your mind open for new or unexpected student comments.

COMPREHENSION

Read pages 114–123.

Comprehension Strategies

First Read

Read the story aloud, taking turns with the students. Start by modeling the use of strategies for the students.

Teacher Modeling

1 Asking and Answering Questions *Good readers ask questions while they read to make sure that they understand the story. Why doesn't the boy believe in spring? What could this mean? I know that it's the title of this story, so it must be important. King Shabazz says, "Where is it at?" I think he doesn't believe in spring because he can't see it or doesn't know where to look for it.*

Teacher Modeling

2 Monitoring and Clarifying *The words* "talkin bout" *look strange to me. I think I'll read the sentence again. Now I understand that the words mean* "talking about." *I think the writer spelled each word the way it sounds when it's pronounced quickly. Writing the words this way is closer to the way people sound when they talk quickly. This makes the story seem more real. Rereading a portion of the text can sometimes help clarify the text. Let's continue to clarify ideas and words as we read.*

Word Knowledge

SCAFFOLDING: The skills students are reviewing in Word Knowledge should help them in reading the story. This lesson focuses on antonyms, synonyms, compound words, and the affixes *un-* and *-y.* These words will be found in boxes similar to this one throughout the selection.

antonyms: whisper holler

First Reading Recommendation

ORAL • CHORAL

Focus Questions What is city wildlife? What types of wildlife would you expect to find in a city?

The Boy Who Didn't Believe in Spring

Lucille Clifton

illustrated by Brinton Turkle

Once upon a time there was a little boy named King Shabazz who didn't believe in Spring. 1 "No such thing!" he would whisper every time the teacher talked about Spring in school.

"Where is it at?" he would holler every time his Mama talked about Spring at home.

114

Informal Assessment

Observe individual students as they read and use the Teacher Observation Log, found in the ***Program Assessment Teacher's Edition,*** to record anecdotal information about each student's strengths and weaknesses.

He used to sit with his friend Tony Polito on the bottom step when the days started getting longer and warmer and talk about it.

"Everybody talkin bout Spring!" he would say to Tony. 2

"Big deal," Tony would say back.

"No such thing!" he would say to Tony.

"Right!" Tony would say back.

One day after the teacher had been talking about birds that were blue and his Mama had started talking about crops coming up, King Shabazz decided he had just had enough. He put his jacket on and his shades and went by for Tony Polito.

"Look here, man," King said when they got out to the bottom step, "I'm goin to get me some of this Spring."

115

Comprehension Skills

Second Read

Classify and Categorize

Ask students to tell what they know about classifying and categorizing. If necessary, remind them that it is sometimes useful to put story information into sections or categories. Putting things that are alike together in a group will help students understand and remember the information.

- Point to the reference to birds and crops on page 115. Write these words on the board under the heading *Signs of Spring. (appearance of blue birds; crops coming up)*
- Another category students might use with this story is *People in the Story.* Ask students to identify the people. *(the teacher, his mother, King Shabazz, and Tony Polito)*

Ask students to tell what other things might be classified under these categories or others.

Tell students to look for additional words or concepts in this story that can be grouped under different headings or categories.

Skills Trace

Classify and Categorize

Introduced in Grade 1.

Scaffolded throughout Grades 2 and 3.

REINTRODUCED:	Unit 1, Lesson 1
REINFORCED:	Unit 2, Lesson 1
	Unit 3, Lesson 5
	Unit 5, Lesson 4
	Unit 6, Lesson 5
TESTED:	Unit 2 Assessment

Second Reading Recommendation

ORAL • **SILENT**

COMPREHENSION

Differentiating Instruction

If...	Then...
English Learners need extra help with vocabulary	Use ***English Learner Support Guide*** pages 92–93
English Learners need extra help with classifying and categorizing	Use ***English Learner Support Guide*** pages 93–94

Word Knowledge

antonyms: **bottom** (top)
started (stopped)
longer (shorter)
warmer (colder)

COMPREHENSION

Comprehension Strategies

First Read

Teacher Modeling

3 Visualizing *Good readers form visual images in their minds as they read. This adds to their enjoyment and helps them to organize and remember the details of the story. When I read how the boys stopped at Weissman's Bakery, I pictured the bakery shop just as Tony and King Shabazz must have seen it—rows and rows of hot, freshly baked bread, a few cakes or pies, and probably some doughnuts or bagels. The author tells us that the boys can smell the aroma of the bread. Reading about the bakery and visualizing it makes me think that I can smell the hot bread too! What visual images did you picture? How do you think the boys' neighborhood looked? What kinds of people and places do you picture the boys passing as they walk down the street? Good readers are always getting images in their heads about what they read. If you get a good one, tell the class about it.*

Word Knowledge

compound words: everybody

Teacher Tip COMPREHENSION STRATEGIES Refer to the Comprehension Strategies poster as the class reads the selection. As students are reading, ask them, "Which of the strategies listed on the poster might be good to use at this point in the selection?"

"What you mean, man?" Tony asked him.

"Everybody talkin bout Spring comin, and Spring just round the corner. I'm goin to go round there and see what do I see."

Tony Polito watched King Shabazz get up and push his shades up tight on his nose.

"You comin with me, man?" he said while he was pushing.

Tony Polito thought about it for a minute. Then he got up and turned his cap around backwards.

"Right!" Tony Polito said back.

116

Differentiating Instruction

Intervention Tip

VISUALIZING Have students think of a movie based on a story they had read. Did they say afterward, "That's not the way I pictured it"? This is because they visualized something during reading. The people who made the movie read the same words but visualized something different.

King Shabazz and Tony Polito had been around the corner before, but only as far as the streetlight alone. They passed the school and the playground.

"Ain't no Spring in there," said King Shabazz with a laugh. "Sure ain't," agreed Tony Polito.

They passed Weissman's. They stopped for a minute by the side door at Weissman's and smelled the buns. 3

"Sure do smell good," whispered Tony.

"But it ain't Spring," King was quick to answer.

117

Comprehension Skills

Second Read

Classify and Categorize

Tell students that they will continue to put related words into groups as they read.

- Write the heading *Things in King and Tony's Neighborhood* on the board. On page 117 there are story words that could be put into this category. Ask students to identify these words and then write them under the heading. *(streetlight, school, playground, Weissman's)*
- Another category could be *Things King Does. (looks for Spring, wears shades, smells food from the bakery)*

COMPREHENSION

Word Knowledge

compound words: **streetlight**
playground

Teacher Tip Good readers constantly evaluate their understanding of what they read. Stop often to make sure students are doing this.

Differentiating Instruction

If...	Then...
Students are having difficulty classifying and categorizing	Help them sort concrete objects, such as different shapes and colors of blocks, and label the categories
English Learners need extra help with vocabulary	Use ***English Learner Support Guide*** pages 95–96
English Learners need extra help with classifying and categorizing	Use ***English Learner Support Guide*** pages 95–97

COMPREHENSION

Comprehension Strategies

First Read

Begin prompting students for responses. Praise answers that are appropriate, even if they do not match the Student Sample. This will encourage students to use strategies as they read.

Prompting

4 Monitoring and Clarifying

I'm confused. I wonder why Tony and King stop at the streetlight for so long. It seems as if they're both waiting to see what the other will do next. But why? I know that both boys had only gone as far as the streetlight alone before. I bet that's the reason it takes them a long time to decide to cross. Each boy is waiting to see if the other one is going to cross. What else can we clarify?

Student Sample

5 Monitoring and Clarifying

I don't know what King means when he says, "Well, if we find it, it ought to be now." What does he mean by "it"? I remember that King and Tony are looking for spring. So I guess that "it" means spring. Now I understand.

Word Knowledge

prefix *un-*: **untied**

Teacher Tip Encourage students to respond to questions with appropriate elaboration.

They passed the apartments and walked fast in case they met Junior Williams. He had said in school that he was going to beat them both up.

Then they were at the streetlight. Tony stopped and made believe his sneaker was untied to see what King was going to do. King stopped and blew on his shades to clean them and to see what Tony was going to do. They stood there for two light turns and then King
4 Shabazz grinned at Tony Polito, and he grinned back, and the two boys ran across the street.

"Well, if we find it, it ought to be now," said King. 5

Tony didn't say anything. He just stood looking around.

"Well, come on, man," King whispered, and they started down the street.

118

They passed the Church of the Solid Rock with high windows all decorated and pretty.

They passed a restaurant with little round tables near the window. They came to a take-out shop and stood by the door a minute to smell the bar-b-q.

"Sure would like to have some of that," whispered King.

"Me too," whispered Tony with his eyes closed. They walked slower down the street.

Just after they passed some apartments King Shabazz and Tony Polito came to a vacant lot. It was small and had high walls from apartments on three sides of it. Three walls around it and right in the middle—a car!

119

Differentiating Instruction

If...	Then...
Students are having difficulty classifying and categorizing	Provide them with category labels and then have students list things that would fit under each heading

COMPREHENSION

Comprehension Skills

Second Read

Classify and Categorize

Have students continue to look for words on this page that can be added to groups. You may want to divide the class into different groups and have them look for different things to classify and categorize.

- Under the heading *Things in King and Tony's Neighborhood*, students can add *Church of the Solid Rock, restaurant, take-out shop, apartments*, and *vacant lot.*
- Another group might be *Things Tony and King Smell. (Weissman's bakery, bar-b-q)*

Have students continue to add to other categories that you and your students have identified.

Word Knowledge

antonyms:
pretty (ugly)
closed (opened)
slower (faster)
after (before)
vacant (full)

Teacher Tip Ask students one or more of the following questions to make sure they understand what they are reading: Is anyone confused? Do you need clarification? Can you summarize what you have read so far? Does what you are reading make sense to you?

COMPREHENSION

Comprehension Strategies

First Read

Prompting

6 Predicting *Predicting helps us to think about what we have read and helps us to make sense of the story. I wonder what could be making the sounds in the car. What do you think it might be? Maybe the boys will investigate the noise. Let's all make a prediction about what is making the noise. After we read more in the story, we can check our predictions to see if it is confirmed or not.*

Student Sample

Predicting *I predict it is a stray cat making the noise because I know cats like hiding in empty things.*

Word Knowledge

antonyms:
beautiful (ugly)
whispered (shouted)
little (big)
smooth (rough)

Teacher Tip Watch to see if the students' application of a given strategy is becoming more effective over time.

Teacher Tip COMPREHENSION Good readers are active readers. They interact with the text as they read by emoting, reacting, responding, and problem solving in their efforts to construct and maintain meaning.

It was beautiful. The wheels were gone and so were the doors, but it was dark red and sitting high on a dirt mound in the middle of the lot.

"Oh man, oh man," whispered King.

"Oh man," whispered Tony.

Then they heard the noise.

It was a little long sound, like smooth things rubbing against rough, and it was coming from the car. It happened again. King looked at Tony and grabbed his hand. 6

120

"Let's see what it is, man," he whispered. He thought Tony would say no and let's go home. Tony looked at King and held his hand tightly.

"Right," he said very slowly.

The boys stood there a minute, then began tiptoeing over toward the car. They walked very slowly across the lot. When they were halfway to the car, Tony tripped and almost fell. He looked down and saw a patch of little yellow pointy flowers, growing in the middle of short spiky green leaves.

"Man, I think you tripped on these crops!" King laughed.

"They're comin up," Tony shouted. "Man, the crops are comin up!"

121

Comprehension Skills

Second Read

Classify and Categorize

Have students continue putting things that are alike together in groups and think about what they have read.

- Help students identify words on this page that could be grouped under the heading *Signs of Spring.* Write the heading and the words on the board. *(yellow, pointy flowers; short, spiky, green leaves; crops)*
- At this point, students may want to add a section to classify details about the vacant lot in the Read Aloud "City Lots." Encourage them to discuss the differences between the two.

Word Knowledge

suffix *-y*: **pointy** **spiky**

Teacher Tip GENERATING QUESTIONS TO EXPLORE Tell students that good readers often generate questions as they read, and then use these questions to guide their own writing.

COMPREHENSION

Differentiating Instruction

If...	Then...
English Learners need extra help with vocabulary	Use ***English Learner Support Guide*** pages 97–98
English Learners need extra help with classifying and categorizing	Use ***English Learner Support Guide*** pages 98–99

COMPREHENSION

Comprehension Strategies

First Read

Teacher Modeling

7 Confirming Predictions *Now that we've read a little further, let's take a moment to see if our predictions were correct. As we read, we discovered that the noise that the boys heard was made by birds that had built a nest in the car. Is that what you predicted? Even when our predictions are not confirmed, making predictions is useful and fun.*

Discussing Strategy Use

While students are reading the selection, encourage them to tell what strategies they used.

- How did they clarify confusing passages?
- What questions did they ask as they read?
- How did they make, confirm, and revise predictions as they read?
- What predictions did they make?
- What did they visualize as they were reading?

These are questions good readers ask after they read a text. After reading, the students should always be asking, "What did I find interesting? What is important here?" Later, remind the students again that whenever they conclude a reading, they should ask themselves questions about what was in the text.

Word Knowledge

antonyms:	**noise** (silence)
	out (in)
	long (short)
	light (dark)

And just as Tony was making all that noise, they heard another noise, like a lot of things waving in the air, and they looked over at the car and three birds flew out of one of the door holes and up to the wall of the apartment.

King and Tony ran over to the car to see where the birds had been. They had to climb up a little to get to the door and look in.

They stood there looking a long time without saying anything. There on the front seat down in a whole lot of cottony stuff was a nest. There in the nest were four light blue eggs. Blue. King took off his shades. 7

"Man, it's Spring," he said almost to himself.

"Anthony Polito!"

122

Teacher Tip Whenever possible, allow students to generate and direct discussion and to take over the process of instruction.

Informal Assessment

Use the Informal Comprehension Strategies Rubrics on page 114J to determine whether a student is using the strategies being taught.

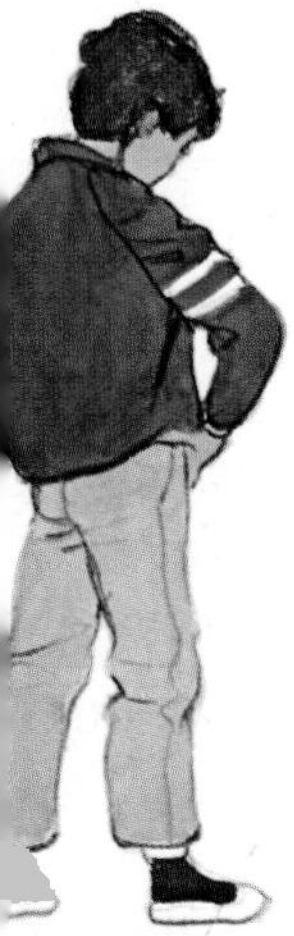

King and Tony jumped down off the mound. Somebody was shouting for Tony as loud as he could.

"Anthony Polito!"

The boys turned and started walking out of the vacant lot. Tony's brother Sam was standing at the edge of the lot looking mad.

"Ma's gonna kill you, after I get finished, you squirt!" he hollered.

King Shabazz looked at Tony Polito and took his hand.

"Spring is here," he whispered to Tony.

"Right," whispered Tony Polito back.

123

Differentiating Instruction

If...	Then...
:nglish Learners need extra help with ·ocabulary	Use ***English Learner Support Guide*** pages 100–101
:nglish Learners need extra help with ·lassifying and categorizing	Use ***English Learner Support Guide*** pages 100–102
:nglish Learners need extra help reviewing The Boy Who Didn't Believe in Spring"	Use ***English Learner Support Guide*** pages 102–103

COMPREHENSION

Comprehension Skills

Second Read

Classify and Categorize

Remind students to continue placing words from the story into groups.

- Under *Signs of Spring*, students can add *bluebird's eggs*.
- Under *Things in King and Tony's Neighborhood*, students can add *old car*.

Checking Comprehension

- What does this story have to do with city wildlife? *(Tony and King find plants beginning to grow and a bird's blue eggs in the car in a vacant lot.)*
- What do Tony and King realize when they find the flowers and the bird's eggs? *(They realize that spring has really arrived.)*
- How do you think they feel about their discovery? *(They feel happy and amazed at finding signs of spring in the city.)*

Teacher Tip FLUENCY By this time in third grade, good readers should be reading approximately 107 words per minute with fluency and expression. The only way to gain this fluency is through practice. Have students reread the selection to you and to each other during Workshop to help build fluency. As students read, you may notice that some need work in building fluency. During Workshop, have these students select a section of the text (a minimum of 160 words) to read several times in order to build fluency.

Formal Assessment

See pages 2–5 in ***Unit 2 Assessment*** to test students' comprehension of "The Boy Who Didn't Believe in Spring."

Routine Card
Refer to ***Routine 6*** for the *handing-off process.*

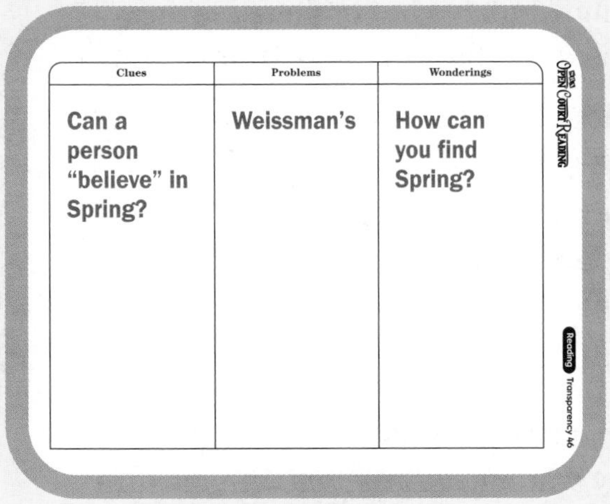

Clues	Problems	Wonderings
Can a person "believe" in Spring?	Weissman's	How can you find Spring?

Reading Transparency 46

www.sra4kids.com
Web Connection
Some students may choose to conduct a computer search for additional books or information about city wildlife. Invite them to make a list of these books and sources of information to share with classmates and the school librarian. Check the Reading link of the SRA Web page for additional links to the theme-related Web site.

Discussing the Selection

After the first read, the whole group discusses the selection and any personal thoughts, reactions, problems, or questions that it raises. To stimulate discussion, students can ask one another the kinds of questions that good readers ask themselves about a text: *How does it connect to City Wildlife? What have I learned that is new? What did I find interesting? What is important here? What was difficult to understand? Why would someone want to read this?* Throughout this discussion, make sure studen use specific information from the text to defend their interpretations.

Handing-Off Process Seeing you as a contributing member of the group set a strong example for students. However, to help students learn to keep the discussion student-centered, have each student choose the next speaker instead of handing the discussion back to you. Using the *handing-off process* will help students to take responsibility for the discussion.

Engage students in a discussion to determine whether they have grasped the following ideas:

- why King didn't believe in spring
- what he and Tony did to find spring
- what signs of spring they found
- what types of wildlife are common in cities

During this time, have students return to the clues, problems, and wonderings they noted during browsing to determine whether the clues were borne out by the selection, whether and how their problems were solved, and whether their wonderings were answered or deserve further discussion and investigation. Let the students decide which items deserve further discussion.

Also have students return to the Focus Questions on the first page of the selection. Select a student to read the questions aloud, and have volunteers answer the questions. If students do not know the answers to the questions, hav them return to the text to find the answers.

You may wish to review the elements of realistic fiction with the students at this time. Discuss with them how they can tell that "The Boy Who Didn't Believe in Spring" is realistic fiction.

Have students break into small groups to discuss what this story tells them about wildlife in urban areas or the relationship between peopl and wildlife in urban areas. Groups can discuss their ideas with the rest of the class.

Writer's Notebook

Students may wish to record their personal responses to the selection. If students have ever experienced wildlife in a city or discovered signs of spring on their own, encoura them to record these events.

Review Selection Vocabulary

Have students review the definitions of the selection vocabulary words that they wrote in the vocabulary section of their Writer's Notebooks. Remind them that they discussed the meanings of these words before reading the selection. Have students write sentences for each of the vocabulary words after the definitions in the same section of their Writer's Notebooks. They can use the definitions and the sentences to study for the vocabulary portion of their Lesson Assessments. Have them add any other interesting words that they clarified while reading to the Personal Dictionary section of their Writer's Notebooks. Encourage students to refer to the selection vocabulary words throughout the unit. The words from the selection are:

crops **decorated** **vacant** **mound** **patch**

Create a Word Bank for this unit, organizing words by lesson. Encourage students to find words from other resources, their investigations, and family discussions to add to the Word Bank.

Home Connection

Distribute ***Home Connection,*** page 17. Encourage students to discuss "The Boy Who Didn't Believe in Spring" with their families. Parents and caregivers are encouraged to discuss the signs of spring with their students. A Spanish version of this letter appears on page 18.

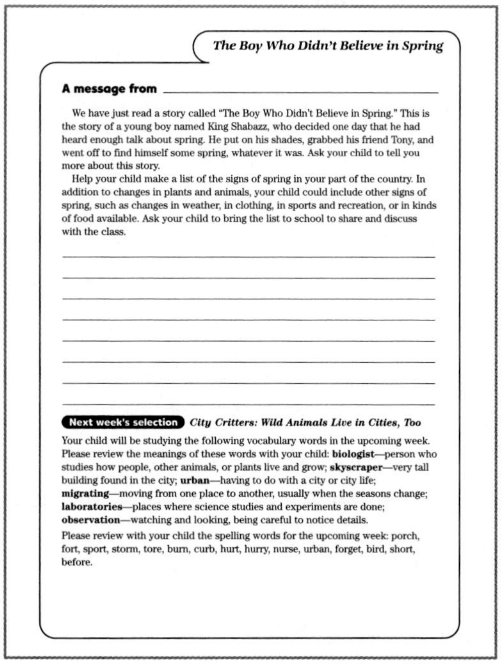

The Boy Who Didn't Believe in Spring

A message from ______________________

We have just read a story called "The Boy Who Didn't Believe in Spring." This is the story of a young boy named King Shabazz, who decided one day that he had heard enough talk about spring. He put on his shades, grabbed his friend Tony, and went off to find himself some spring, whatever it was. Ask your child to tell you more about this story.

Help your child make a list of the signs of spring in your part of the country. In addition to changes in plants and animals, your child could include other signs of spring, such as changes in weather, in clothing, in sports and recreation, or in kinds of food available. Ask your child to bring the list to school to share and discuss with the class.

Next week's selection ***City Critters: Wild Animals Live in Cities, Too***

Your child will be studying the following vocabulary words in the upcoming week. Please review the meanings of these words with your child: **biologist**—person who studies how people, other animals, or plants live and grow; **skyscraper**—very tall building found in the city; **urban**—having to do with a city or city life; **migrating**—moving from one place to another, usually when the seasons change; **laboratories**—places where science studies and experiments are done; **observation**—watching and looking, being careful to notice details.

Please review with your child the spelling words for the upcoming week: porch, fort, sport, storm, tore, burn, curb, hurt, hurry, nurse, urban, forget, bird, short, before.

Home Connection p. 17

Teacher Tip RESPONDING When you call on a student, allow him or her a few seconds to consider your question and arrive at an answer.

Teacher Tip Have the students choose a book to read from the library relating to the theme. This book should identify their preference in either literary or nonfiction texts. Encourage students to read often from their preferred genre.

- **Sentences 1–3:** These sentences are from the story students are about to read. Ask students to identify the word that has a homophone *(waste/waist, great/grate)*. Have students identify words with the suffixes *-tion* or *-ly* *(especially, pollution)*. Have students identify the plural nouns *(parks, places, scientists, falcons, laboratories)*.
- **Sentence 4:** Have students identify the words in the last sentence that contain the /er/ sound *(bird, urban)*.

Developing Oral Language

Use direct teaching to review the words. Use one or both of the following activities to help students practice the words aloud.

- To review homophones, have a volunteer choose one of the homophones from Lines 2 or 3 and use it in a sentence. Then ask a volunteer to identify the homophone in that sentence and erase it from the board.
- Have a student choose and point to a word. Then select another student to pronounce that word and use it in a sentence. The student who pronounces and uses the word correctly then goes to the board, chooses a new word, and selects a new student to pronounce it and use it in a sentence. Repeat the process.

WORD KNOWLEDGE

Teacher Tip FLUENCY Gaining a better understanding of the spellings of sounds and structure of words will help students as they encounter unfamiliar words in their reading. By this time in Grade 3 students should be reading approximately 107 words per minute with fluency and expression. As students read, you may notice that some need work in building fluency. During Workshop, have these students select a section of the text (a minimum of 160 words) to read several times in order to build fluency.

Differentiating Instruction

If...	Then...
Students need extra help with compound words, /er/ spelled *ur* and *ir*, or /or/ spelled *or* and *ore*	Use ***Online Phonics***
Students need extra help with the suffixes *-tion* and *-ly*	Use ***Intervention Guide*** pages 71–72

Spelling
See pages 133E–133J for the corresponding spelling lesson for the /er/ and /or/ sounds.

PHONICS

Teacher Tip SYLLABICATION To help students blend words and build fluency, use the syllabication below of the words in the word lines.

si • lent	ba • con	ri • val	to • tal
mu • sic	ho • tel	ar • e • a	Chi • na
pro • tect	ea • gle	o • mit	la • bel
pup • pet	ze • bra	bal • co • ny	

Teacher Tip Encourage students to just read the words. Stop and blend only those words that give them problems.

Teacher Tip Remind students when they see the Vowel-Consonant-Vowel pattern they need to try the long and short vowel sounds to see which makes sense. Does the word sound right?

Differentiating Instruction

If...	Then...
Students need help recognizing open syllables with long vowels	• Use ***Online Phonics*** • Use ***Intervention Guide*** pages 72–73

Phonics and Fluency

Open syllables with long vowels

Blending

- Use direct teaching to teach the following words and sentences.
- Follow the established procedure to have students read the following words and sentences. **Boldface** words are found in the selection.

Line 1:	silent	bacon	rival	**total**
Line 2:	music	hotel	**area**	China
Line 3:	**eagle**	omit	**protect**	
Line 4:	label	puppet	zebra	**balcony**
Sentence 1:	The piano player made beautiful music.			
Sentence 2:	We were silent while the teacher spoke.			
Sentence 3:	Our grasslands area is home to all these birds.			

About the Words and Sentences

- **Lines 1–3:** These words provide practice with open syllables, as well as a review of *long* vowels. After reading the words in Lines 1–3, have the students say each word clapping the syllables. Ask the students what vowel sound they heard at the end of the first syllable. Ask why the vowel had a long vowel sound. *(Open syllables end with a single vowel that usually has the long sound.)*
- **Line 4:** The words alternate between open and closed syllables as a review. In closed syllables, the single vowel is followed by a consonant. As each word is read, have the students clap the syllables. Discuss the vowel sound heard in each syllable and have the students tell why the vowel was long or short.
- **Sentences 1–2:** These sentences reinforce the open syllables. Have students identify and use the words with open syllables in a new sentence.
- **Sentence 3:** This sentence is from the selection. Have the students identify the words with long vowels.

Developing Oral Language

Use direct teaching to review the words. Use one or both of the following activities to help students practice words aloud.

- Invite students to choose any of the words from Lines 1–4 and give a riddle clue for it. For example, "I'm a large bird. What am I?" *(eagle)* Have another student find the word and underline it.
- Point to words on Lines 1–3. Have students say the words, use the words in a sentence, and then place a slash between the vowel and the consonant. Ask students to identify the long vowel. Have volunteers add words to the board that follow the same pattern.

Dictation

Following the established procedure, erase the blending lines and sentences on the board and have students take out writing paper. Dictate the following words and sentence for students to write.

Line 1:	hero	yoga	zero
Line 2:	baby	lady	prolong
Challenge Word:	piano		
Sentence:	We'll go ice skating when the lake is frozen.		

Have students follow the proper steps for proofreading the dictated words and sentence.

Building Fluency

Decodable Books are used to help develop fluency for students who need extra practice. The only way to gain fluency is to read. Students will have many opportunities to read, including the ***Student Anthology,*** the ***Leveled Classroom Library,*** and their own reading. The ***Decodable Books*** can be used to practice the phonics and fluency elements being reviewed. Refer to the Appendix for the procedure on using these books. For this lesson, use ***Decodable Book 18,*** *Queen Kit.*

Decodable Book 18

Research in Action

Oral Language Development

Because children who enter school without a strong foundation in oral language have difficulty learning to read, early reading instruction must engage children in numerous oral language activities. Such activities include interactive story reading, telling and retelling stories, dramatic play, and discussion.
(Richard C. Anderson, Elfrieda H. Hiebert, Judith A. Scott, and *Ian A. G. Wilkinson,* Becoming a Nation of Readers: The Report of the Commission on Reading)

Use the ***Decodable Book Activities CD-ROM*** for activities that support this Phonics lesson.

Routine Card

Refer to ***Routine 8*** for whole-word dictation and ***Routine 9*** for sentence dictation.

Objectives

- Students will understand the selection vocabulary before reading, using strategies such as suffixes and structural cues.
- Students will recognize compound words and homophones and spell words with the suffixes *-tion* and *-ly*.
- Students will connect prior knowledge to subjects discussed in the text.
- Students will use comprehension strategies such as Asking Questions, Clarifying, and Summarizing to construct meaning from the text and monitor reading.
- Students will use the comprehension skill Drawing Conclusions as they read the story the second time.
- Students will discuss personal reactions to the story to begin identifying their own personal reading preferences.

Materials

- Student Anthology, Book 1, pp. 126–135
- Program Assessment
- Reading Transparencies 11, 46, 53
- Inquiry Journal, p. 29
- Science/Social Studies Connection Center Cards 10, 11
- Home Connection, p. 19
- Comprehension and Language Arts Skills, pp. 30–31
- Unit 2 Assessment, pp. 6–9
- Routine Cards 1–2, Routines 3–6

Routine Card
Refer to ***Routine 4*** for the Clues, Problems, and Wonderings procedure.

Clues	Problems	Wonderings
headings = what story is about	peregrine	I wonder what the title "Scientists' Helpers" means?

Open Court Reading — Reading Transparency 46

Reading Transparency 46

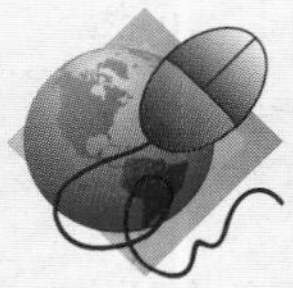

www.sra4kids.com
Web Connection
Students can use the connections to City Wildlife in the Reading link of the SRA Web page for more background information about city wildlife.

Build Background

Activate Prior Knowledge

Discuss the following with students to find out what they may already know about the selection and have already learned about city wildlife.

- Preteach the article by first inviting students to think of animals that they already know about that live in cites or towns. Remind them that animals include birds, fish, mammals, and insects. Encourage them to think of animals that are not pets and then write their ideas on the Concept/Question Board.
- Ask students to think of any articles or stories they may have read that were about wild animals that live in cities.

Background Information

The following information may help students to better understand the selection they are about to read.

- Explain to students that while large books are divided into sections called chapters, the nonfiction selections in a magazine are called articles or expository text.
- Explain to students that the article they will be reading is an expository text written by Richard Chevat, and that it was published in a magazine called *3-2-1 Contact.*
- Have students look at the title of this article. If they have never heard the term, help them to clarify that *critter* is a word that means "creature" or "animal."

Preview and Prepare

Browse

- Have students read the title, subtitles, and the author's name aloud. This allows them to activate prior knowledge relevant to the selection. Because "City Critters" is an informational article rather than a fictional story that might have a surprise ending, you may wish to have students preview the selection by browsing the entire selection before reading. Discuss with students what they think this article might reveal about city wildlife.
- Have students search for clues that tell them something about the selection and for any problems, unfamiliar words, or long sentences that they notice while reading, as well as any wonderings they might have. Use ***Reading Transparency 46*** to record their observations as they browse. For example, students will probably notice that this magazine article has a heading for each section of text. These headings alert readers to what they will be reading about before they read it. Students might not know what *peregrine* means. They might wonder what the title "Scientists' Helpers" means. To save time and to model note taking, write students' observations as brief notes rather than as complete sentences.

- As students prepare to read the selection, have them browse the Focus Questions on the first page of the selection. Tell them to keep these questions in mind as they read.

Set Purposes

Encourage students to set multiple purposes for reading the selection. Students should define their own purposes, but may need help defining the possibilities. Offer several possibilities, such as to learn more about how this story exemplifies the genre of expository text, or to gather information about city wildlife. What animals are considered to be wild? What kinds of things can people learn from city wildlife? Help students to define other reading goals.

Selection Vocabulary

As students study vocabulary, they will use a variety of skills to determine the meaning of a word. These include context clues, word structure, and apposition. Students will apply these same skills while reading to clarify additional unfamiliar words. Students can write their definitions in their Writer's Notebooks.

Display ***Reading Transparency 11*** before reading the selection to introduce and discuss the following words and their meanings.

biologist: person who studies how people, other animals, or plants live and grow (page 127)
skyscraper: very tall building found in the city (page 127)
urban: having to do with a city or city life (page 127)
migrating: moving from one place to another, usually when the seasons change (page 128)
laboratories: places where scientific studies and experiments are done (page 129)
observation: watching and looking, being careful to notice details (page 131)

Have students read the words in the word box, stopping to blend any words that they have trouble reading. Help students decode multisyllabic words by breaking the words into syllables and blending the syllables. If students still have trouble, refer them to the ***Sound/Spelling Cards.*** If the word is not decodable, give the students the pronunciation. Other words that may be unfamiliar to students should be clarified during reading, with each definition tied to the way that the word is used in the story. *(examples: habitat, pollution)*

Have students read the sentences on the transparency to determine the meanings of the underlined words. Each word has two sentences that students will read and from which they should be able to derive the meaning of the underlined word. Remind them to use one or more of the skills they have learned—context clues, word structure, or apposition—to figure out the meaning before using a dictionary. Be sure students explain which skills they are using and how they figured out the meanings of the words. Have students reread the sentence, substituting the definition to see if the sentence makes sense. Have a volunteer create a new sentence using the underlined word.

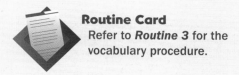

Routine Card
Refer to ***Routine 3*** for the vocabulary procedure.

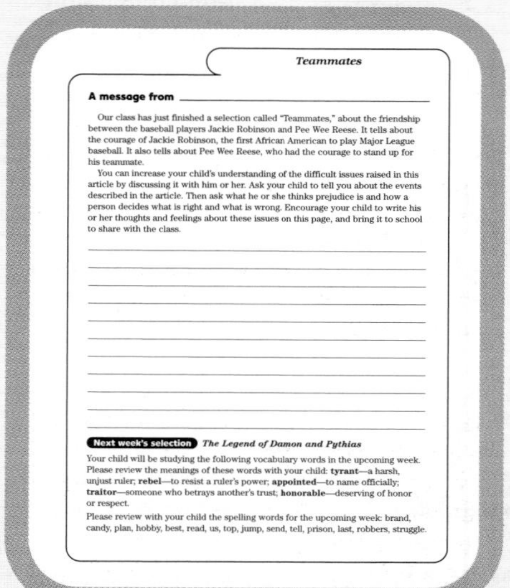
Teammates

A message from ____________

Our class has just finished a selection called "Teammates," about the friendship between the baseball players Jackie Robinson and Pee Wee Reese. It tells about the courage of Jackie Robinson, the first African American to play Major League baseball. It also tells about Pee Wee Reese, who had the courage to stand up for his teammate.

You can increase your child's understanding of the difficult issues raised in this article by discussing it with him or her. Ask your child to tell you about the events described in the article. Then ask what he or she thinks prejudice is and how a person decides what is right and what is wrong. Encourage your child to write his or her thoughts and feelings about these issues on this page, and bring it to school to share with the class.

Next week's selection ***The Legend of Damon and Pythias***

Your child will be studying the following vocabulary words in the upcoming week. Please review the meanings of these words with your child: **tyrant**—a harsh, unjust ruler; **rebel**—to resist a ruler's power; **appointed**—to name officially; **traitor**—someone who betrays another's trust; **honorable**—deserving of honor or respect.

Please review with your child the spelling words for the upcoming week: brand, candy, plan, hobby, best, read, us, top, jump, send, tell, prison, last, robbers, struggle.

Reading Transparency 11

Teacher Tip **SELECTION VOCABULARY** To help students decode words, divide the words into syllables when you are saying them, as shown below. The information following each word tells how students can figure out the meaning of each word. When writing words on the board, do not divide them into syllables.

bi • ol • o • gist	context clues
sky • scrap • er	context clues
ur • ban	context clues
mi • grat • ing	context clues
lab • o • ra • tor • ies	context clues
ob • ser • va • tion	context clues

Differentiating Instruction

If...	Then...
Students need extra help with selection vocabulary	Use ***Intervention Guide*** pages 73–74
English Learners are having difficulty with vocabulary	Use pictures, objects, board stick drawings, or pantomime to help them visualize

Differentiating Instruction

If...	Then...
Students need help building fluency	Help them read "City Critters" during Workshop before the whole-class reading

Routine Card
Refer to ***Routine 5*** for the procedure on reading the selection.

During Workshop, and after the selection has been read at least once, have students listen to the recording of this lesson's selection on the ***Listening Library Audiocassette/CD.*** After students have listened, have them discuss their personal preferences of the selections read. Ask them what other things they have listened to and like to listen to on the radio, on audiocassettes, or on CDs.

Teacher Tip For extra practice in oral fluency, have individual students read aloud to you a selection they have previously read, either from a ***Decodable Book*** or a passage from the ***Student Anthology.*** Time each student for one minute. If the student reads more than 107 words correctly, have the student retell the selection he or she has just read. Use one prompt if the student seems to be stuck, and allow a maximum of one minute for the student to retell the story. If the student does not read more than 107 words correctly, have the student try reading from an earlier ***Decodable Book*** to help you determine where the problem lies.

Reading Recommendations

It is suggested that your first reading of the selection focus on developing the reading strategies found to the left of the reduced student pages. The second reading should focus on the comprehension skills and should be done on another day.

Oral Reading

This is a good selection for students to read aloud. Encourage them to express their thoughts, ask questions, or give opinions as they read. Students should read aloud fluently with appropriate expression, vocal patterns, and intonation. Make sure that students attend to punctuation and read in phrases.

Help students make use of the comprehension strategies listed below to help them understand the selection. Have them stop reading periodically or wait until they have completed the selection to discuss the reading strategies. After the students have finished reading the selection, use the Discussing the Selection questions on page 131A to see if they understand what they have read.

Using Comprehension Strategies First Read

Comprehension strategy instruction allows students to become aware of how good readers read. Good readers constantly check their understanding as they are reading and ask themselves questions. In addition, skilled readers recognize when they are having problems and stop to use various reading strategies to help them make sense of what they are reading.

During the reading of "City Critters," you will model and prompt the use of the following reading strategies.

- **Asking Questions** helps readers focus attention on what they are reading and engages them in deeper understanding of themes, concepts, and ideas.

- **Monitoring and Clarifying** takes different forms, including clarifying the meaning of words and clarifying difficult ideas or passages. In order to clarify meanings, students can use context, use structural analysis, use apposition, reread the text, use charts or graphic organizers, or use resources outside of the text.
- **Summarizing** prompts readers to keep track of what they are reading and to focus their minds on important information.

As students read, they should be using a variety of strategies to help them understand the selection. Encourage students to use the strategies listed above as the class reads the story aloud. Do this by stopping at the points indicated by the numbers in the magenta circles on the reduced student pages and using a particular strategy.

Building Comprehension Skills Second Read

Revisiting or rereading a selection allows students to apply skills that give them a more complete understanding of the text. Some follow-up comprehension skills help students organize information. Others lead to deeper understanding—to "reading between the lines," as mature readers do.

An extended lesson on the comprehension skill, drawing conclusions, can be found in the Supporting the Reading section on pages 131C–131D. This lesson is intended to give students extra practice with drawing conclusions. However, it may be used at this time to introduce the comprehension skill to students.

- **Drawing Conclusions (Introduction):** Readers draw conclusions, using what they already know together with what they learn about characters and events, to understand the total picture in a story.

Reading with a Purpose

Have students keep track of the wildlife they read about in this selection. Have them track how and why they live in the city.

Teacher Tip SET PURPOSES Remind students that good readers have a purpose when they read. Let them know that they should know the purpose for reading whenever they read.

Research in Action
Comprehension Monitoring

Good readers are aware of how their reading is going and why. They know, for example, when a text is difficult to read because it contains many new ideas, and when it is difficult to read because it is poorly written. They are adept at using their prior knowledge as they read to make predictions about what might happen next and to understand ideas as they encounter them. (*S. C. Paris, B. A. Wasik,* and *J. C. Turner,* Handbook of Reading Research (vol. 2))

Differentiating Instruction

If...	Then...
Students need extra help with summarizing	Use ***Intervention Guide*** pages 74–75
Students need extra help with asking questions	Use ***Intervention Guide*** pages 75–76

Science Connection

Life Structure of Wildlife

In "City Critters," students learned about the habitats of various types of urban wildlife. The creatures thrive in habitats that meet their needs for survival.

Have groups of students choose one type of plant or animal out of the many they have observed in an urban setting. Then, have them conduct research to learn about the different growth, survival, and reproductive structures of the plant or animal they have chosen and present an informative presentation for the class. Students should be able to explain how the habitat of the species meets its needs for survival and how changes to that habitat might affect the species.

Encourage students to use visual aids, such as charts, diagrams, maps, or photographs, to enhance their presentations. If time allows, students might enjoy creating a model of a habitat.

After each group has finished its presentation, allow students in the audience to ask questions about what they have seen and learned. Tell the presenters to respond to the questions, clarify ideas, and paraphrase ideas as necessary for their audience.

Teacher Tip MATERIALS
- ✔ notebook
- ✔ wildlife in urban setting
- ✔ poster boards
- ✔ colored pencils or markers

Teacher Tip PURPOSE To learn the different structures responsible for growth, survival, and reproduction in one type of plant or animal.

Teacher Tip A good way to ensure that students have comprehended a presentation is to have them retell or explain what the speaker said.

Science/Social Studies Connection Center

Refer to the ***Science/Social Studies Connection Center*** Card 10 for a science activity that students can investigate.

Differentiating Instruction

If...	Then...
English Learners are having difficulty writing captions for their photographs	Help them write the captions by having them prompt you with drawings, words, or gestures

Concept Connections

Linking the Selection

- Birds make their nests on tall buildings, and raccoons live in sewers.
- Wild animals need food and water to survive in the city.

Exploring Concept Vocabulary

The concept word for this lesson is ***adapt.*** Write the word on the board. Work with students to develop a definition that clearly links to the unit theme. Have students copy the word and definition into the Vocabulary section of their Writer's Notebooks.

Adapt: to make changes to fit in a new surrounding or situation. For example, the geese adapt to the city by nesting on a balcony.

- Wild animals find homes in the city that are similar to their natural surroundings.
- Wildlife must adapt to its surroundings to survive.

Make sure the sentences students create show an understanding of the concept word and the selection vocabulary word. For example, the sentence *A biologist watches animals adapt* does not show the meaning of the word ***adapt.***

Expanding the Concept

You may want to do a whole-group discussion to help students continue to develop their ability to engage in meaningful dialogue. However, students may conduct these dialogues in small groups. If students work in small groups, bring the groups together and have them share their ideas with the whole class.

As students complete their discussions, have them record their ideas and impressions about the selection on page 29 of their ***Inquiry Journals.***

City Critters:

Wild Animals Live in Cities, Too

Concept Connections

Linking the Selection

Writer's Notebook

Think about the following questions, and then record your responses in the Response Journal section of your Writer's Notebook.

- Where are some of the places that wild animals live in the city?
- What do wild animals need to survive in the city?

Exploring Concept Vocabulary

The concept word for this lesson is ***adapt.*** If you do not know what this word means, look it up in a dictionary. Answer these questions:

- How do wild animals ***adapt*** to living in the city?
- Why is it important for wildlife to ***adapt*** to its surroundings?

Think about the word ***adapt*** and the selection vocabulary words. Then make up an oral sentence using the concept word and one of the selection vocabulary words.

132

Informal Assessment

This may be a good time to observe students working in small groups and to mark your observations in the Teacher Observation Log found in the ***Program Assessment Teacher's Edition.***

Teacher Tip CONCEPT VOCABULARY Developing a repertoire of concept-related vocabulary will help students deepen their understanding of theme concepts, help facilitate class discussions, and help students formulate ideas, problems, and questions for inquiry.

Expanding the Concept

Think about the selection "City Critters" and the story "The Boy Who Didn't Believe in Spring." Where else could King and Tony have looked for spring in the city?

Try to include the word ***adapt*** in your discussion.

Add new ideas about city wildlife to the Concept/Question Board.

Meet the Author

Richard Chevat loved to read and make up stories of his own as a child in New York City. Today he lives in New Jersey with his wife, two children, and a pet bird named Madonna. He writes at home while his children are at school and his wife is at work. *"I play the guitar, I like to cook, and spend a lot of time with my kids,"* says Mr. Chevat.

133

Meet the Author

After students read the information about Richard Chevat, discuss the following questions with them.

- Richard Chevat writes while his wife is at work and his children are at school. Why do you think it would be a good idea for a writer to create while no one else is around? *(Possible answer: There aren't any distractions. He can put his undivided attention into what he is trying to create.)*
- After growing up in New York City, why do you think Richard Chevat would want to write a story called "City Critters"? *(Possible answer: He loves animals and is very interested in the world around him. He loves the fact that there is wildlife even in a bustling city, and he wants others to be aware also.)*

Teacher Tip You may wish to direct students' attention to the photo credits in "City Critters." Explain to students that the photographs that illustrate the story were taken by several different photographers.

Objectives

- Students learn about the different types of wildlife that live in cities.
- Student groups form conjectures.
- Students learn to choose appropriate resources.

Materials

- Student Anthology, Book 1, pp. 126–135
- Inquiry Journal, pp. 14, 37–39
- Research Assistant CD-ROM

Teacher Tip Remind students that they can use any of the activities performed during the unit to help them come up with their investigation questions, problems, and conjectures. The various activities, readings, and writing projects should generate ideas. Also remind students that the investigation they choose should be one that really interests them. They should be excited about seeking the answers to their questions.

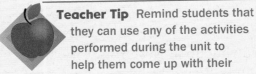

Formal Assessment

Use the Research Rubrics on page 126J to assess students' ability to formulate research questions and problems.

INVESTIGATION

Investigating Concepts Beyond the Text: Questions and Problems

By this point students have formed groups, explored investigation possibilities, and charted important dates. Throughout the reading of this selection, students should refine problems or questions and form conjectures. At the beginning of this selection, have students present their proposed problems and the reasons for choosing them, allowing open discussion of how promising and interesting various proposed problems are. Have students complete ***Inquiry Journal,*** page 37, in their groups. Remind the students that a good problem cannot be answered by examining one encyclopedia entry and that the question or problem must add to the group's understanding of the investigation. This constant emphasis on group knowledge building will help set a clear purpose for the students' investigation. As students define their problems and questions and form their conjectures, remind them that they are not to reproduce information aimlessly, but are to find information that will help them and their classmates increase their understanding of city wildlife.

After reading "City Critters," have students complete ***Inquiry Journal,*** page 38. By this time, students should have developed their investigations within their groups. Completing this page will help them define the purpose of their investigations. Students might want to arrange for an expert on wildlife in your part of the country to talk to the class. They can do so by contacting the local humane society or the state's department of forestry or parks and recreation. Local universities and colleges are other possibilities. Before the expert visits, review with students the task of interviewing and how it can be a research tool. Discuss ahead of time what questions students would like to ask the expert; keep track of their questions for later use. Discuss with students how they will keep a record of the things the expert tells them.

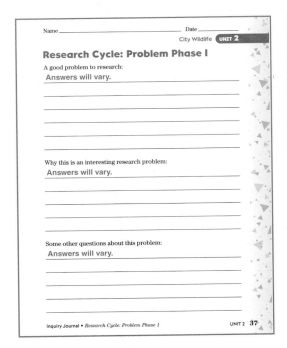

Name ______ Date ______

City Wildlife UNIT 2

Research Cycle: Problem Phase I

A good problem to research:

Answers will vary.

Why this is an interesting research problem:

Answers will vary.

Some other questions about this problem:

Answers will vary.

Inquiry Journal • *Research Cycle: Problem Phase 1* UNIT 2 37

Name ______ Date ______

UNIT 2 City Wildlife

Research Cycle: Problem Phase 2

My group's problem:

Answers will vary.

What our research will contribute to our investigation and to the rest of the class:

Answers will vary.

Some other questions about this problem:

Answers will vary.

38 UNIT 2 *Research Cycle: Problem Phase 2* • Inquiry Journal

Inquiry Journal pp. 37–38

Concept/Question Board

After reading each selection, students should use the Concept/Question Board to:

- Post any questions they asked about a selection before reading that have not been answered yet.
- Refer to as they formulate statements about concepts that apply to their investigations.
- Post general statements formulated by each collaborative group.
- Continue to post news articles or other items that they find during the unit investigation.
- Read and think about posted questions, articles, or concepts that interest them and provide answers to the questions.

Concept/Question Board

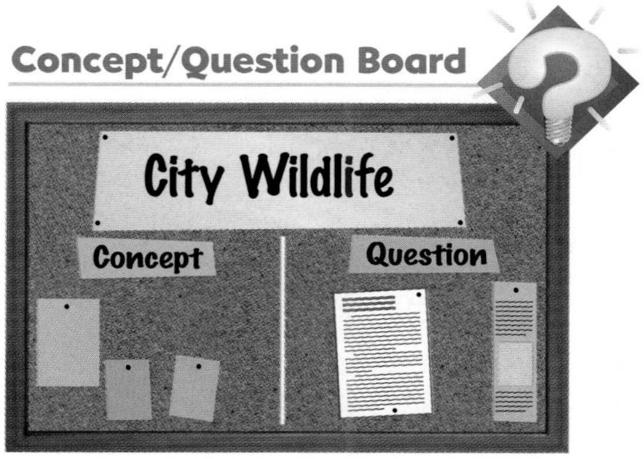

Unit 2 Investigation Management

Lesson 1	Introduce investigation possibilities. Groups form and brainstorm initial plans. Plans are presented to the whole class and discussed. Groups can take a neighborhood tour to identify city wildlife.
Lesson 2	Collaborative Investigation **Groups refine problems and form conjectures.** Supplementary Activity **Students can invite an expert to class.**
Lesson 3	Groups create investigation plans, assign tasks, and begin investigation. Groups can hold a discussion about the benefits and dangers of city living.
Lesson 4	Groups revise plans and continue investigation. Groups can compare urban and natural animal habitats.
Lesson 5	Groups present informal presentations, make necessary revisions, and continue investigation. Groups can investigate and lead a panel discussion on the issue of disappearing natural habitats and how wildlife is affected.
Lesson 6	Groups make final preparations and presentations of findings. Groups can create a proposal for protecting wildlife in urban areas.

INVESTIGATION

Teacher Tip Encourage students to use the Concept/Question Board by noticing who is using it and pointing out contributions to the rest of the class.

Research Assistant

The *Research Assistant CD-ROM* can assist students in their investigations.

Teacher Tip For information regarding humane and environmental issues, contact the National Association for Humane and Environmental Education, the Youth Education Division of The Humane Society of the United States. This association offers resources for classroom teachers and educators to teach the value of, and respect for, animals and our natural environment.

Teacher Tip Ensure that students understand that conjectures can and should change over the course of the investigation.

Formal Assessment

Use the Research Rubrics on page 126J to assess students' ability to make conjectures.

Differentiating Instruction

If...	Then...
Students are having difficulty forming conjectures	Work with them on ***Inquiry Journal*** page 39 during Workshop

INVESTIGATION

Forming Conjectures

Remind students that a conjecture is a hypothesis without proof or evidence, or an explanation of something that we suggest before we have a great deal of evidence. Conjectures may be confirmed, or proved wrong, or modified in some way by the evidence. Have the students work on the Conjecture Phase of the Research Cycle on page 39 in their ***Inquiry Journals.*** You might consider modeling a conjecture by choosing a problem that has already been suggested for investigation, but that has not been chosen by any group. In that way, the whole class can engage in conjecturing without anything being taken away from an individual group's work on a problem. As students share their conjectures, record them on the board. If students are comfortable with the Conjecture Phase of the Research Cycle, they can go directly to work on their initial plans.

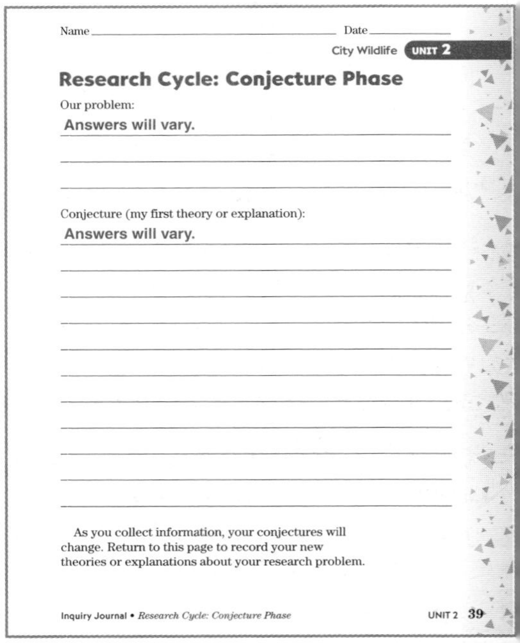
Name ____ Date ____

City Wildlife UNIT 2

Research Cycle: Conjecture Phase

Our problem:

Answers will vary.

Conjecture (my first theory or explanation):

Answers will vary.

As you collect information, your conjectures will change. Return to this page to record your new theories or explanations about your research problem.

Inquiry Journal • *Research Cycle: Conjecture Phase* UNIT 2 39

***Inquiry Journal* p. 39**

SUPPORTING THE INVESTIGATION

Choosing Appropriate Sources

Teach Tell students that a good way to get facts for an informational article is to interview experts. Richard Chevat interviewed at least six people for "City Critters." Not every expert will know about a particular topic, and even when they do, it is a good idea to get more than one opinion. Writers should ask themselves two questions before they interview:

What do I want to know?
Who will know the most about what I want to know?

Guided Practice Ask students what Richard Chevat wanted to know before he wrote his article. *(He wanted to know about the wild animals that live in cities.)* Then have students find the names and job titles of the people that he interviewed for "City Critters." Write the list on the board:

Mike Matthews, scientist (page 126)
Dave Tylka, urban biologist (page 127)
Charles Nilon, biologist (page 127)
Don Reipe, scientist (page 130)
Laura Jackson, biologist (page 130)
Stephen Petland, biologist (page 131)

Ask students why they think Richard Chevat chose these people to interview. *(All of them are biologists and scientists who study city wildlife.)* Point out that, according to the article, these experts live in five different states. One way to interview them would be to travel to where they live. Ask students to name other ways a writer might interview them.

Ask students to name other sources the author might have used for his article *(encyclopedia, Internet, nonfiction book, magazine or newspaper, almanac, maps, photographs, charts)*. Tell students that they can always use multiple sources to gain information. In this instance, the interview would have been the primary source (or the major source) and perhaps an encyclopedia entry or magazine article could have been a secondary source (or supporting source).

Independent Practice Have students create a preliminary list of people they might interview or sources they might consult for their investigations. Encourage students to make use of the Internet to contact wildlife agencies that might provide them with resources to investigate answers for their questions about city wildlife.

Ask students which other resources besides experts might be helpful in their investigations. Remind them of sources, such as maps and charts, that can serve as primary sources for their research. Have students refer to ***Inquiry Journal,*** page 14, for a list of possible sources.

TECH KNOWLEDGE

Encourage students to use ***TechKnowledge*** to learn more about how to use a computer for various tasks.

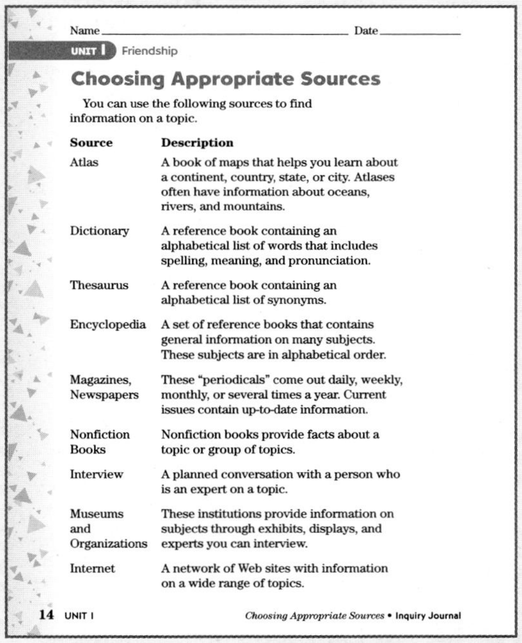
Name ______________ Date ________

UNIT 1 Friendship

Choosing Appropriate Sources

You can use the following sources to find information on a topic.

Source	Description
Atlas	A book of maps that helps you learn about a continent, country, state, or city. Atlases often have information about oceans, rivers, and mountains.
Dictionary	A reference book containing an alphabetical list of words that includes spelling, meaning, and pronunciation.
Thesaurus	A reference book containing an alphabetical list of synonyms.
Encyclopedia	A set of reference books that contains general information on many subjects. These subjects are in alphabetical order.
Magazines, Newspapers	These "periodicals" come out daily, weekly, monthly, or several times a year. Current issues contain up-to-date information.
Nonfiction Books	Nonfiction books provide facts about a topic or group of topics.
Interview	A planned conversation with a person who is an expert on a topic.
Museums and Organizations	These institutions provide information on subjects through exhibits, displays, and experts you can interview.
Internet	A network of Web sites with information on a wide range of topics.

14 UNIT 1 *Choosing Appropriate Sources* • Inquiry Journal

Inquiry Journal p. 14

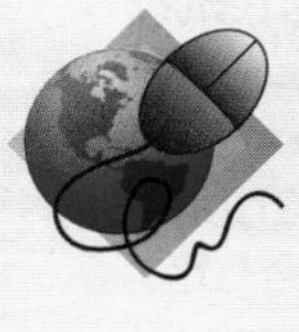

www.sra4kids.com
Web Connection
More information about City Wildlife and links to Web sites concerning city wildlife can be found at www.sra4kids.com.

Objectives

Word Analysis

Spelling

- **The /er/ and /or/ Sounds.** Develop understanding of the /er/ sound spelled *ur* or *ir* and /or/ sound spelled *or* or *ore*.

Vocabulary

- **Levels of Specificity and Categories.** Using words from "City Critters," learn to recognize levels of specificity when discovering the meaning or meanings of an unknown word.

Writing Process Strategies

- **Expository Writing: Summary Paragraph.** Identify the components of a summary paragraph to learn the form and function of writing a summary.

English Language Conventions

Grammar, Usage, and Mechanics

- **Commas in a Series.** This lesson teaches the correct use of commas in a series.

Listening, Speaking, Viewing

- **Speaking: Speaking Clearly.** Practice effective oral speaking skills.

Penmanship

- **Cursive Letters *m* and *x*.** Develop handwriting skills by practicing formation of cursive *m* and *x*.

Materials

- Language Arts Handbook
- Comprehension and Language Arts Skills, pp. 30–35
- Writer's Workbook, pp. 10–13
- Language Arts Transparencies 13, 23
- Spelling and Vocabulary Skills, pp. 30–33
- Sound/Spelling Card 29
- Student Anthology

DIFFERENTIATING INSTRUCTION

Reteach, Challenge, and ***Intervention*** lessons are available to support the language arts instruction in this lesson.

Research in Action

Holding a regular pencil is different from using a crayon, chalk, or felt pen; children holding a pencil too close to the point or too tightly find writing fatiguing. Pencils should be held comfortably (not gripped) at the bottom of the painted portion. (*Charles Temple* and *Jean Wallace Gillet*, Language Arts: Learning Processes and Teaching Practices)

OVERVIEW

Language Arts Overview

Word Analysis

Spelling The Spelling activities on the following pages introduce the /er/ sound spelled *ur* and *ir*, and the /or/ sound spelled *or* and *ore* by developing spelling skills through various strategies.

Selection Spelling Words

These words from "City Critters" contain the /er/ or /or/ sound.

before **short** **bird** **forget** **urban**

Vocabulary The Vocabulary activities introduce the levels of specificity that can help a student categorize an unfamiliar word, and therefore understand its specific meaning. Magazine pictures will be needed for the Category Guessing Game on Day 2. *(animals with wings, car models, things that make noises)*

Vocabulary Skill Words

scientist **biologist*** **skyscraper*** **exhaust** **habitats**

**Also Selection Vocabulary*

Additional Materials: dictionary, magazine

Writing Process Strategies

The Writing Process Strategies lesson involves instruction in writing a summary paragraph by restating the main idea of the longer piece in the student's own words, showing comprehension of the longer work.

TECH KNOWLEDGE: To learn basic computer skills for writing, have students practice keying **H** and **E**, **I** and **R**, **O** and **T**, and **N** and **G** keys; show students how to use the left **Shift** and **Period** keys. ***TechKnowledge,*** Level 3, Lessons 9–13, teach these keyboarding skills.

English Language Conventions

Grammar, Usage, and Mechanics **Commas in a Series.** Learn the correct use of commas in a series. Find instances of commas in a series in "City Critters: Wild Animals Live in the City, Too."

Listening, Speaking, Viewing **Speaking: Speaking Clearly.** In this Speaking lesson, students will practice speaking clearly with appropriate rate, volume, and pitch.

Penmanship **Cursive Letters *m* and *x*.** This lesson develops cursive handwriting skills by having students learn correct formation of cursive *m* and *x*. Students then practice writing words from the literature selection that contain those letters.

DAY 1

Word Analysis

Spelling

Assessment: Pretest

The /er/ and /or/ Sounds

Teach

Give the Pretest on page 28 of ***Unit 2 Assessment.*** Have them proofread and correct any misspelled words.

Pretest Sentences

1. **porch** A **porch** is the area in front of a door.
2. **fort** A historic **fort** in South Carolina is Fort Sumter.
3. **sport** Baseball is a **sport** played in a series of innings.
4. **storm** The sound of thunder can be a sign of a **storm**.
5. **tore** The playful dog **tore** the coat.
6. **burn** An oven can **burn** you.
7. **curb** Park next to the **curb**.
8. **hurt** Shoes can **hurt** your feet.
9. **hurry** Emergency room doctors **hurry** to help patients.
10. **nurse** A **nurse** checks your pulse.
11. **urban** A city is an **urban** area.
12. **forget** Some people **forget** where they park.
13. **bird** The cardinal is the state **bird** of Ohio.
14. **short** The opposite of tall is **short.**
15. **before** You should brush your teeth **before** bedtime.

Diagnose any misspellings by determining whether students misspelled the /er/ and /or/ sounds or some other part of the word. Then use the Pretest as a take-home list to study the spellings of words with the /er/ and /or/ sounds.

Writing Process Strategies

Getting Ideas

Summary Paragraph

Teach

Introduce Summaries

- Read ***Language Arts Handbook,*** pages 80–83, to introduce summaries.
- Share the formal assessment rubrics with the students (see Day 5 of this lesson).

Inspiration

Teacher Model: *"I liked the article 'City Critters: Wild Animals Live in Cities, Too,' and I'd like to tell friends what the article is about. I will tell the main idea and a couple of other important ideas I remember."*

Brainstorming

Encourage students to suggest stories and articles for summary paragraphs. Make a list of students' suggestions on the board.

Guided Practice

Getting Ideas

Direct students to write the ideas they have for a summary paragraph in their Writer's Notebooks.

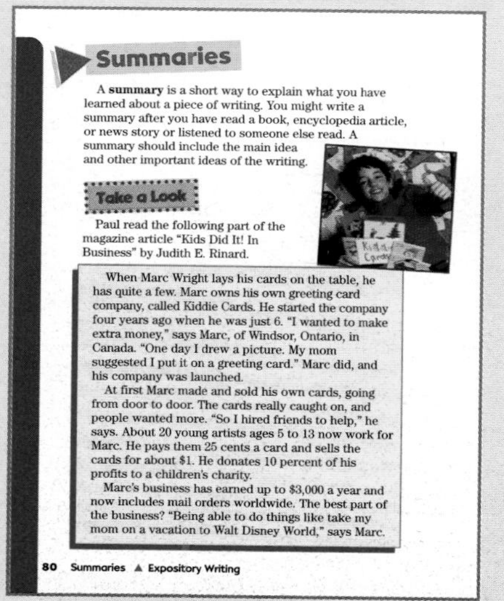

Summaries

A **summary** is a short way to explain what you have learned about a piece of writing. You might write a summary after you have read a book, encyclopedia article, or news story or listened to someone else read. A summary should include the main idea and other important ideas of the writing.

Take a Look

Paul read the following part of the magazine article "Kids Did It! In Business" by Judith E. Rinard.

When Marc Wright lays his cards on the table, he has quite a few. Marc owns his own greeting card company, called Kiddie Cards. He started the company four years ago when he was just 6. "I wanted to make extra money," says Marc, of Windsor, Ontario, in Canada. "One day I drew a picture. My mom suggested I put it on a greeting card." Marc did, and his company was launched.

At first Marc made and sold his own cards, going from door to door. The cards really caught on, and people wanted more. "So I hired friends to help," he says. About 20 young artists ages 5 to 13 now work for Marc. He pays them 25 cents a card and sells the cards for about $1. He donates 10 percent of his profits to a children's charity.

Marc's business has earned up to $3,000 a year and now includes mail orders worldwide. The best part of the business? "Being able to do things like take my mom on a vacation to Walt Disney World," says Marc.

80 Summaries ▲ Expository Writing

Language Arts Handbook p. 80

English Language Conventions

Grammar, Usage, and Mechanics

Mechanics: Commas in a Series

Teach

- **Review** the comma as a way to create pauses within sentences.
- Explain that commas are used in a list of more than two items—a series. Write these sentences on the board as examples.
  - *I like peas, broccoli, and spinach.*
  - *You can go Monday, Wednesday, Friday, or Saturday.*
  - *We have to clean our rooms, return our library books, and eat dinner.*
- Use ***Language Arts Handbook,*** page 271, for examples of proper usage of commas in a series.

Independent Practice

Use ***Comprehension and Language Arts Skills,*** pages 32–33, to proofread for the correct use of commas in a series.

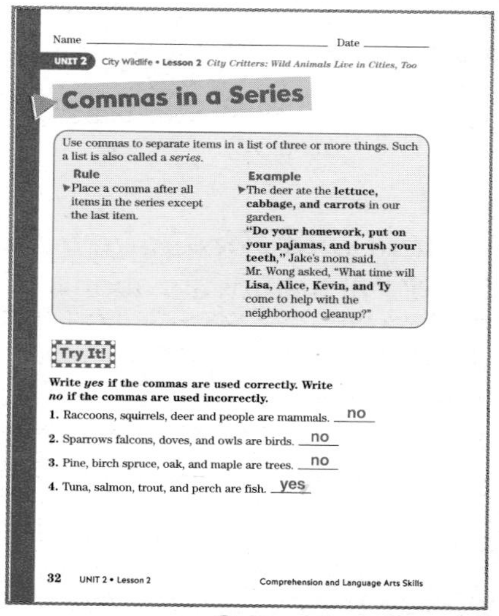

Name ______________________ Date __________

UNIT 2 City Wildlife • Lesson 2 *City Critters: Wild Animals Live in Cities, Too*

Commas in a Series

Use commas to separate items in a list of three or more things. Such a list is also called a *series.*

Rule	Example
▸Place a comma after all items in the series except the last item.	▸The deer ate the **lettuce, cabbage, and carrots** in our garden. **"Do your homework, put on your pajamas, and brush your teeth,"** Jake's mom said. Mr. Wong asked, "What time will **Lisa, Alice, Kevin, and Ty** come to help with the neighborhood cleanup?"

Try It!

Write *yes* if the commas are used correctly. Write *no* if the commas are used incorrectly.

1. Raccoons, squirrels, deer and people are mammals. no
2. Sparrows falcons, doves, and owls are birds. no
3. Pine, birch spruce, oak, and maple are trees. no
4. Tuna, salmon, trout, and perch are fish. yes

32 UNIT 2 • Lesson 2 Comprehension and Language Arts Skills

Comprehension and Language Arts Skills p. 32

DAY 2

Word Analysis

Spelling

Word Sorting

- Hold up ***Sound/Spelling Card 29*** and ask the class to say *bird*, listening to the /er/ sound. Have the class say *sort* and listen to the /or/ sound.
- Write *corner, door, murmur, forest, horn, return, store, first, surprise,* and *story* on the board. Have students sort the words under *The /er/ Sound* or *The /or/ Sound.*

Vocabulary

Levels of Specificity and Categories

Teach

- Write *scientist* on the board. Explain that words become clearer when divided into specific categories. There are different types of scientists in "City Critters."
- Category Guessing Game: Get pictures of things from categories. Without naming the category, have a student hold up pictures until someone has guessed the category.

Guided Practice

Use ***Spelling and Vocabulary Skills,*** page 30, to teach students about categories. Ask students to complete page 31 as independent practice.

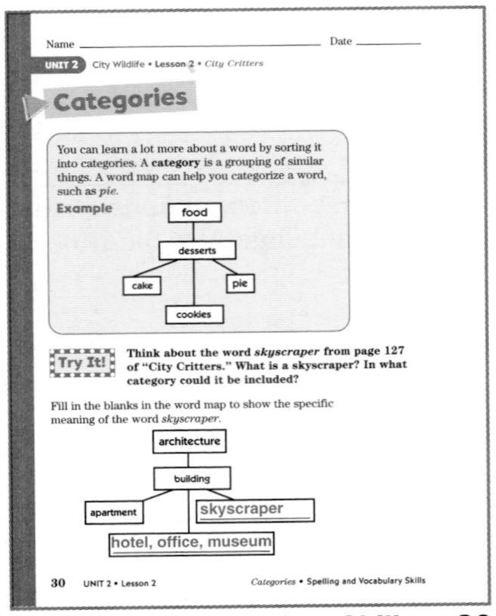
Name ________________ Date ________

UNIT 2 City Wildlife • Lesson 2 • *City Critters*

Categories

You can learn a lot more about a word by sorting it into categories. A **category** is a grouping of similar things. A word map can help you categorize a word, such as *pie*.

Example

Try It! **Think about the word *skyscraper* from page 127 of "City Critters." What is a skyscraper? In what category could it be included?**

Fill in the blanks in the word map to show the specific meaning of the word *skyscraper*.

30 UNIT 2 • Lesson 2 *Categories* • Spelling and Vocabulary Skills

***Spelling and Vocabulary Skills* p. 30**

Writing Process Strategies

Prewriting

Summary Paragraph

Teach

- Review student ideas for summary paragraphs from Day 1.
- Read ***Writer's Workbook,*** page 10, on prewriting summary paragraphs.
- Discuss ***Language Arts Transparency 13,*** Expository Structure. Let students know that they may not need to fill in all of the blanks for a summary paragraph.

Independent Practice

Prewriting

- Have students fill out their audience and purpose on page 10 of the ***Writer's Workbook.***
- Have students complete the graphic organizer on page 11 of the ***Writer's Workbook.***

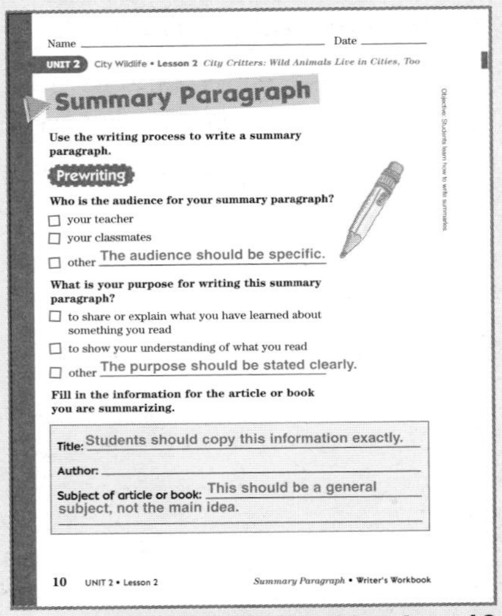
Name ________________ Date ________

UNIT 2 City Wildlife • Lesson 2 *City Critters: Wild Animals Live in Cities, Too*

Summary Paragraph

Use the writing process to write a summary paragraph.

Prewriting

Who is the audience for your summary paragraph?

- ☐ your teacher
- ☐ your classmates
- ☐ other The audience should be specific.

What is your purpose for writing this summary paragraph?

- ☐ to share or explain what you have learned about something you read
- ☐ to show your understanding of what you read
- ☐ other The purpose should be stated clearly.

Fill in the information for the article or book you are summarizing.

Title: Students should copy this information exactly.
Author: ____________
Subject of article or book: This should be a general subject, not the main idea.

Objective: Students learn how to write summaries.

10 UNIT 2 • Lesson 2 *Summary Paragraph* • Writer's Workbook

***Writer's Workbook* p. 10**

Professional Development

Teacher Resource Library CD-ROMs or ***Online Professional Development*** provides courses that help you better understand the Writing instruction in ***Open Court Reading.*** For more information about this program, visit SRAonline.com.

English Language Conventions

Grammar, Usage, and Mechanics

Mechanics: Commas in a Series

Teach

- Refer students to ***Language Arts Handbook,*** page 271, on commas in a series.
- Ask students to name three or more types of animals that live in the city. Then ask them to come up with sentences using the series of animals. Write the sentences on the board and point out the correct placement of the commas.

Guided Practice in Reading

Pages 124, 126, and 128 of "City Critters: Wild Animals Live in Cities, Too" contain series. Ask students to identify these series within a time limit that you set. Let them know that although the literature selection may use the commas differently, they should still be able to identify the series. Write the sentences on the board after they have identified them, and ask the students where the missing commas should go. *(There are three series on page 126, and two on page 128.)*

DAY 3

Word Analysis

Spelling

The /er/ and /or/ Sounds

Teach

- Introduce words found in the story with the /er/ and /or/ sounds.
- Ask students for words with the /or/ sound that rhyme with *fort. (sort, sport, torte)*

Guided Practice

Have students complete page 32 from ***Spelling and Vocabulary Skills*** to begin to learn strategies for spelling words with /er/ and /or/ sounds.

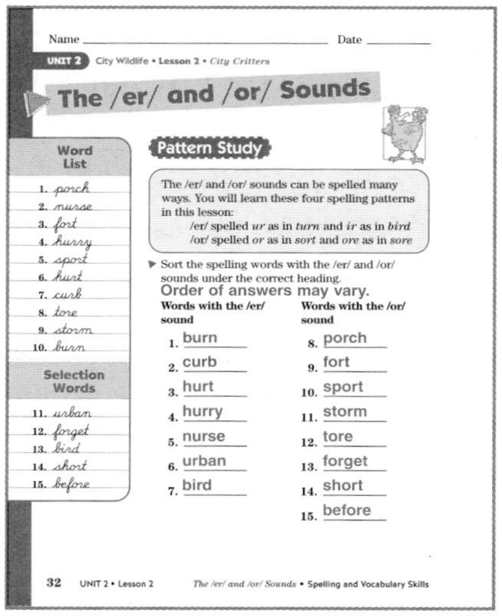
Name ______ Date ______

UNIT 2 City Wildlife • Lesson 2 • *City Critters*

The /er/ and /or/ Sounds

Word List: 1. porch 2. nurse 3. fort 4. hurry 5. sport 6. hurt 7. curb 8. tore 9. storm 10. burn

Selection Words: 11. urban 12. forget 13. bird 14. short 15. before

Pattern Study

The /er/ and /or/ sounds can be spelled many ways. You will learn these four spelling patterns in this lesson:
/er/ spelled *ur* as in *turn* and *ir* as in *bird*
/or/ spelled *or* as in *sort* and *ore* as in *sore*

▶ Sort the spelling words with the /er/ and /or/ sounds under the correct heading.
Order of answers may vary.

Words with the /er/ sound	Words with the /or/ sound
1. burn	8. porch
2. curb	9. fort
3. hurt	10. sport
4. hurry	11. storm
5. nurse	12. tore
6. urban	13. forget
7. bird	14. short
	15. before

32 UNIT 2 • Lesson 2 *The /er/ and /or/ Sounds* • Spelling and Vocabulary Skills

***Spelling and Vocabulary Skills* p. 32**

Vocabulary (continued)

Specific Categories

- Write *scientist* and *biologist* from page 127 of "City Critters" on the board.
- Explain how the structure of these two words is related. *(The* -ist *endings both mean "someone who studies something.")* Circle the *-ist* endings.
- Ask a student to look up *biology* in the dictionary. *(the study of living things)*
- Explain that a *biologist* is a scientist who studies living things.
- Ask students to name other types of scientists. *(paleontologist, botanist)*

Writing Process Strategies

Drafting

Summary Paragraph

Teach

Read ***Writer's Workbook,*** page 11, on drafting a summary paragraph.

Writer's Craft

Organization of Expository Writing

- Explain that expository writing explains or informs readers. This form of writing can be organized in different ways depending on the subject that the writer is explaining.
  - Using examples gives readers a clear picture of your main idea.
  - Explaining reasons or causes helps readers understand your main idea by answering *why.*
  - Stating specific facts that support the main idea helps readers believe what you write.
- Read ***Language Arts Handbook,*** pages 78–79, on expository writing.
- Read ***Comprehension and Language Arts Skills,*** pages 34–35, on organization of expository writing.

Guided Practice

Drafting

Direct students to turn the information on their graphic organizer into a first draft.

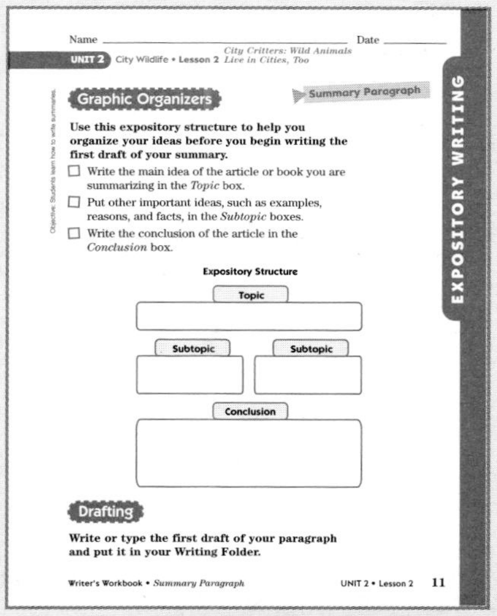
Name ______ Date ______

UNIT 2 City Wildlife • Lesson 2 *City Critters: Wild Animals Live in Cities, Too*

EXPOSITORY WRITING

Graphic Organizers — Summary Paragraph

Objective: Students learn how to write summaries.

Use this expository structure to help you organize your ideas before you begin writing the first draft of your summary.

- ☐ Write the main idea of the article or book you are summarizing in the *Topic* box.
- ☐ Put other important ideas, such as examples, reasons, and facts, in the *Subtopic* boxes.
- ☐ Write the conclusion of the article in the *Conclusion* box.

Expository Structure

Topic

Subtopic | Subtopic

Conclusion

Drafting

Write or type the first draft of your paragraph and put it in your Writing Folder.

Writer's Workbook • *Summary Paragraph* UNIT 2 • Lesson 2 11

***Writer's Workbook* p. 11**

English Language Conventions

Grammar, Usage, and Mechanics

Mechanics: Commas in a Series

Teach

- **Review** commas in a series. Refer again to ***Language Arts Handbook,*** page 271.
- Write the following sentences on the board and point out the use of commas in the series.
  - *I use a blackboard, chalk, and eraser to teach.*
  - *When it gets cold it can snow, the snow can turn to ice, and the ground can get slippery.*
  - *If I study hard I will get good grades, my parents will be proud of me, I'll get a raise in my allowance, and I'll be able to buy the bike I want.*

Guided Practice in Writing

Ask students to write a paragraph on two places they would like to travel. Ask them to include series of what they expect to find in each place.

Informal Assessment

Check students' writing to make sure they are using commas in a series correctly.

Leveled Classroom Library*

Encourage students to read at least 30 minutes daily outside of class. Have them read books in the ***Leveled Classroom Library*** to support the unit theme and help students develop their vocabulary by reading independently.

Birds, Nests and Eggs

BY MEL BORING. NORTHWORD, 1998.

Fourteen birds are introduced to young readers through color illustrations, simple descriptions of their songs and nesting habits, and simple facts. **(Average)**

Come Back Salmon: How a Group of Dedicated Kids Adopted Pigeon Creek and Brought It Back to Life

BY MOLLY CONE. SIERRA JUVENILE CLUB, 1994.

Students from Jackson Elementary School in Everett, Washington, adopt a polluted creek, bring it back to life, and preserve it as a place for salmon to spawn. (Outstanding Science Trade Book) **(Advanced)**

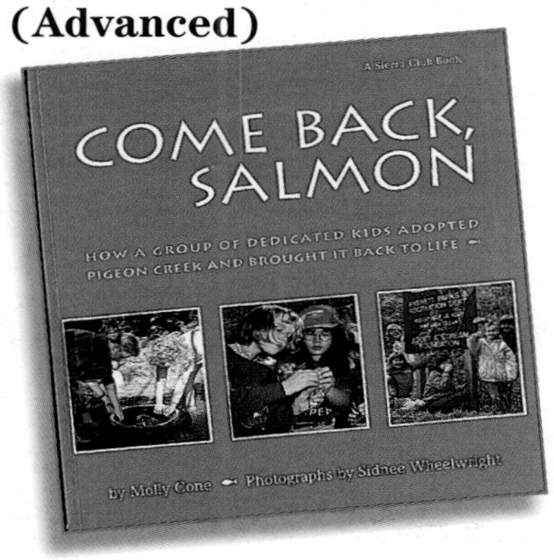

Coyotes in the Crosswalk: True Tales of Animal Life in the Wilds of the City

BY DIANE SWANSON. VOYAGEUR, 1995.

Covering 10 North American animals, this exploration covers the adaptations these animals have developed to ensure survival in the city. (Orbis Pictus Award for outstanding children's nonfiction) **(Challenge)**

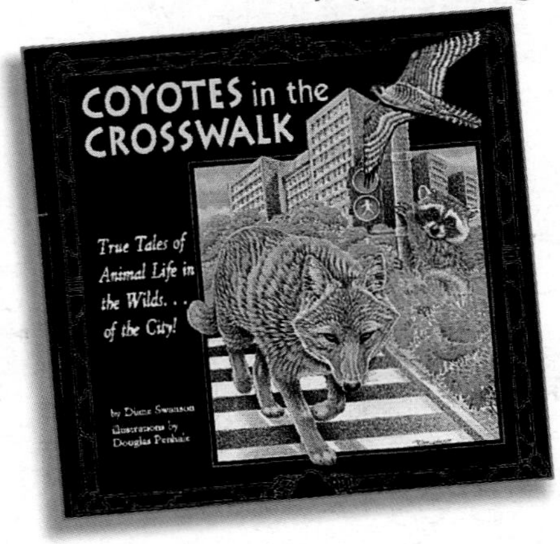

* These books, which all support the unit theme City Wildlife, are part of a 36-book ***Leveled Classroom Librar***y available for purchase from SRA/McGraw-Hill. Note: Teachers should preview any trade books for appropriateness in their classrooms before recommending them to students.

SRA TECHNOLOGY

Web Connections

- City Wildlife Web Site
- Online Professional Development
- Online Phonics
- Online Assessment

CD-ROMs

- Research Assistant
- Decodable Book Activities
- Teacher Resource Library

Audiocassettes/CDs

- Listening Library: City Wildlife
- Sound/Spelling Card Stories

Computer Skills

TechKnowledge

Materials are available through SRA/McGraw-Hill.

Make Way for Ducklings

LESSON PLANNER

Suggested Pacing: 3–5 days	DAY I	DAY 2
	DAY I	DAY 2
1 Preparing to Read **Materials** ■ Student Anthology, Book 1, pp. 136–147 ■ Decodable Book Activities CD-ROM ■ Decodable Book 19 ■ Routine Cards 1, 3, Routines 1–2, 8–9	**Word Knowledge,** p. 136K ■ word families ■ synonyms ■ /əl/ spelled *-le* **About the Words and Sentences,** p. 136K	**Word Knowledge** **Developing Oral Language,** p. 136L
2 Reading & Responding **Materials** ■ Student Anthology, Book 1, pp. 136–147 ■ Program Assessment ■ Reading Transparencies 12, 46, 50 ■ Inquiry Journal, p. 30 ■ Home Connection, p. 21 ■ Science/Social Studies Connection Center ■ Unit 2 Assessment Guide, pp. 10–13 ■ Writer's Notebook ■ Comprehension and Language Arts Skills, pp. 36–37 ■ Routine Cards 1–2, Routines 3–6	**Build Background,** p. 136O **Preview and Prepare,** pp. 136O–136P **Selection Vocabulary,** p. 136P **Reading Recommendations,** pp. 136Q–136R **Student Anthology,** pp. 136–143 First Read ✓ **Comprehension Strategies** ■ Asking Questions, pp. 136, 138 ■ Predicting, pp. 140, 142 **Discussing Strategy Use,** p. 142 **Discussing the Selection,** p. 143A	**Student Anthology,** pp. 136–143 Second Read **Comprehension Skills** ■ Fantasy and Reality, pp. 137, 139, 141, 143 **Checking Comprehension,** p. 143 **Supporting the Reading,** pp. 143C–143D ■ Fantasy and Reality
Inquiry **Materials** ■ Student Anthology, Book 1, pp. 136–147 ■ Inquiry Journal, pp. 40–43 ■ Research Assistant CD-ROM	**Investigation** ■ Investigating Concepts Beyond the Text, p. 145A	**Investigation** ■ Concept/Question Board, p. 145B
3 Language Arts **Materials** ■ Student Anthology, Book 1, pp. 136–147 ■ Comprehension and Language Arts Skills, pp. 36–41 ■ Language Arts Handbook ■ Language Arts Transparency 27 ■ Spelling and Vocabulary Skills, pp. 34–37 ■ The Ultimate Writing and Creativity Center ■ Writer's Workbook, pp. 14–17	**Word Analysis** ✓■ Spelling: The Final /əl/ Sound Pretest, p. 145F **Writing Process Strategies** ■ Expository Writing: Book Review, p. 145F **English Language Conventions** ■ Mechanics: Commas in Dialogue, p. 145F	**Word Analysis** ■ Spelling: Word Sorting, p. 145G ■ Vocabulary: Synonyms, p. 145G **Writing Process Strategies** ■ Expository Writing: Book Review, p. 145G **English Language Conventions** ■ Mechanics: Commas in Dialogue, p. 145G

P Phonics ✓ Informal Assessment Available ✓ Formal Assessment Available

DAY 2 continued	DAY 3	
DAY 3	**DAY 4**	**DAY 5**
Ⓟ **Phonics & Fluency,** p. 136M ■ open syllables with vowel digraphs **About the Words and Sentences,** p. 136M	Ⓟ **Phonics & Fluency** **Developing Oral Language,** p. 136M **Dictation,** p. 136N	**General Review**
Student Anthology ✓■ Concept Connections, p. 144 ■ Meet the Author/Illustrator, p. 145 **Review Selection Vocabulary,** p. 143B **View Fine Art,** p. 143B	**Literary Elements,** p. 143E ■ Fiction vs. Nonfiction **Science Connection** ■ Birds in the City, p. 143F	✓**Selection Assessment** ■ "Make Way for Ducklings," pp. 10–13 **Home Connection,** p. 143B
✓**Investigation** ■ Needs and Plans Phase, p. 145C	**Supporting the Investigation** ■ Tables and Charts, p. 145D	**Investigation** ■ Unit Investigation Continued ■ Update Concept/Question Board
Word Analysis ■ Spelling: The Final /əl/ Sound, p. 145H ■ Vocabulary: Synonyms, p. 145H **Writing Process Strategies** ■ Expository Writing: Book Review, p. 145H **Writer's Craft** ■ Paragraph Form, p. 145H **English Language Conventions** ✓■ Mechanics: Commas in Dialogue, p. 145H	**Word Analysis** ■ Spelling: The Final /əl/ Sound, p. 145I ■ Vocabulary: Synonyms, p. 145I **Writing Process Strategies** ■ Expository Writing: Book Review, p. 145I **English Language Conventions** ✓■ Listening, Speaking, Viewing Language: Language Reflects Cultures, p. 145I	**Word Analysis** ✓■ Spelling: The Final /əl/ Sound Final Test ✓■ Vocabulary: Synonyms, p. 145J **Writing Process Strategies** ✓■ Expository Writing: Book Review, p. 145J **English Language Conventions** ✓■ Penmanship: Cursive Letters *y, z,* and *v*, p. 145J

Below are suggestions for differentiating instruction. These are the same skills shown in the Lesson Planner; however, these pages provide extra practice opportunities or enriching activities to meet the varied needs of students.

WORKSHOP

Differentiating Instruction

Teacher Directed: Individual and Small-Group Instruction

Spend time each day with individuals and small groups to individualize instruction. Each day:

- preteach students who need help with the next lesson.
- reteach students who need to solidify their understanding of content previously taught.
- listen to students read to check their fluency.
- hold writing and inquiry conferences.

Use the following program components to support instruction:

- ***Reteach*** with students who need a bit more practice
- ***Intervention*** for students who exhibit a lack of understanding of the lesson concepts
- ***English Learner Support*** with students who need language help

Student: Independent Activities

Students can work alone, with a partner, or in small groups on such activities as:

- Review sound/spellings
- Practice dictation words
- Partner reading
- Practice fluency
- Independent reading
- Reading Roundtable
- Concept vocabulary
- Selection vocabulary
- Writing in progress
- Conference
- Language Arts
- Challenge activities
- Inquiry and Investigation activities
- Listening Library
- Online Phonics

For Workshop Management Tips, see Appendix pages 41–42.

	DAY I
Decoding/ Word Knowledge	**Teacher Directed** ■ Blending: Final *-le*, ***Intervention Guide,*** p. 80
Fluency	**Independent Activities** ■ Self-test fluency rate ■ Partner reading
Comprehension	**Teacher Directed** ■ Preteach "Make Way for Ducklings," ***Intervention Guide,*** pp. 82–83 ■ Preteach Intervention Selection One, ***Intervention Guide,*** pp. 83–84 ■ ***English Learner Support Guide*** • Vocabulary, pp. 122–123 • Comprehension Strategy: Asking Questions, pp. 123–124 **Independent Activities** ■ Browse ***Leveled Classroom Library*** ■ Add vocabulary in Writer's Notebook ■ Record response to selection in Writer's Notebook ■ ***Listening Library Audiocassette/CD***
Inquiry	**Independent Activities** ■ Concept/Question Board ■ Explore OCR Web site for theme connections ■ Wildlife Dangers Chart, ***Inquiry Journal,*** p. 40
Language Arts	**Teacher Directed** ■ Grammar, Usage, and Mechanics, ***Intervention Guide,*** p. 86 **Independent Activities** ■ Commas in Dialogue, ***Comprehension and Language Arts Skills,*** pp. 38–39

DAY 2	DAY 3	DAY 4	DAY 5
Teacher Directed ▪ Developing Oral Language, ***Intervention Guide,*** p. 80	**Teacher Directed** ▪ Dictation and Spelling: Final *-le*, ***Intervention Guide,*** pp. 80–81	**Teacher Directed** ▪ Blending: Vowel Pairs, ***Intervention Guide,*** p. 81 **Independent Activities** ▪ Read ***Decodable Book 19***	**Teacher Directed** ▪ Developing Oral Language, ***Intervention Guide,*** p. 81 ▪ Dictation and Spelling, ***Intervention Guide,*** pp. 81–82
Independent Activities ▪ Oral reading of selection for fluency ▪ Partner reading	**Independent Activities** ▪ Partner reading of selection	**Independent Activities** ▪ Reread "Make Way for Ducklings" ▪ Partner read ***Decodable Book 19***	**Teacher Directed** ▪ Repeated Readings/Fluency Check, ***Intervention Guide,*** p. 85
Teacher Directed ▪ Preteach "Make Way for Ducklings," ***Intervention Guide,*** pp. 82–83 ▪ Comprehension Strategies, ***Intervention Guide,*** p. 84 ▪ Reread Intervention Selection One, ***Intervention Guide,*** pp. 83–84 ▪ ***English Learner Support Guide*** • Vocabulary, p. 125 • Comprehension Strategy: Asking Questions, pp. 125–127 ▪ Fantasy and Reality, ***Reteach,*** pp. 39–40 **Independent Activities** ▪ Independent reading ▪ Complete Link to Writing in Supporting the Reading, p. 143D ▪ Fantasy and Reality • ***Comprehension and Language Arts Skills,*** pp. 36–37 • ***Challenge,*** p. 35	**Teacher Directed** ▪ Reread "Make Way for Ducklings," ***Intervention Guide,*** pp. 82–83 ▪ Preteach Intervention Selection Two, ***Intervention Guide,*** pp. 84–85 ▪ ***English Learner Support Guide*** • Vocabulary, pp. 127–128 • Comprehension Strategy: Asking Questions, pp. 128–129 ▪ Discuss Concept Connections, p. 144 **Independent Activities** ▪ Read ***Leveled Classroom Library*** book ▪ Add words to Word Bank	**Teacher Directed** ▪ Reread "Make Way for Ducklings," ***Intervention Guide,*** pp. 82–83 ▪ Comprehension Strategies, ***Intervention Guide,*** p. 85 ▪ Reread Intervention Selection Two, ***Intervention Guide,*** pp. 84–85 ▪ ***English Learner Support Guide*** • Vocabulary, pp. 129–130 • Comprehension Strategy: Asking Questions, pp. 130–131 **Independent Activities** ▪ Reread ***Leveled Classroom Library*** book ▪ Complete Independent Practice in Literary Elements, p. 143E ▪ ***English Learner Support Activities,*** p. 17 ▪ Science Connection, p. 143F	**Teacher Directed** ▪ Informal Assessment for Intervention ▪ ***English Learner Support Guide*** • Review Vocabulary, p. 132 • Comprehension Strategy: Asking Questions, pp. 132–133 **Independent Activities** ▪ Read ***Leveled Classroom Library*** book as independent reading ▪ Reading Roundtable ▪ ***English Learner Support Activities,*** p. 18
Independent Activities ▪ Concept/Question Board ▪ Explore OCR Web site for theme connections ▪ Use ***Research Assistant CD-ROM*** to continue investigation	**Teacher Directed** ▪ Discuss needs and plans **Independent Activities** ▪ Concept/Question Board ▪ Research Cycle: Needs and Plans Phase 1, ***Inquiry Journal,*** pp. 41–42	**Independent Activities** ▪ Concept/Question Board ▪ Use ***Research Assistant CD-ROM*** to continue investigation ▪ Tables and Charts, ***Inquiry Journal,*** p. 43	**Independent Activities** ▪ Concept/Question Board ▪ Continue research
Teacher Directed ▪ Grammar, Usage, and Mechanics, ***Intervention Guide,*** p. 86 ▪ Spelling: Word Sort, p. 145G ▪ Commas in Dialogue, ***Reteach,*** p. 43 **Independent Activities** ▪ Seminar: Plan a Fiction Book Review, p. 145G ▪ Vocabulary: Synonyms, ***Spelling and Vocabulary Skills,*** pp. 34–35 ▪ Commas in Dialogue, ***Challenge,*** p. 38	**Teacher Directed** ▪ Writing Activity, ***Intervention Guide,*** p. 87 ▪ Vocabulary: Synonyms, ***Reteach,*** p. 42 **Independent Activities** ▪ Spelling: The Final /əl/ Sound, ***Spelling and Vocabulary Skills,*** p. 36 ▪ Writer's Craft: Paragraph Form, ***Comprehension and Language Arts Skills,*** pp. 40–41 ▪ Vocabulary: Synonyms, ***Challenge,*** p. 37	**Teacher Directed** ▪ Writer's Craft: Paragraph Form, ***Reteach,*** p. 44 ▪ Writing Activity, ***Intervention Guide,*** p. 87 ▪ Spelling: The Final /əl/ Sound, ***Reteach,*** p. 41 **Independent Activities** ▪ Seminar: Revise a Fiction Book Review, p. 145I ▪ Spelling: The Final /əl/ Sound • ***Spelling and Vocabulary Skills,*** p. 37 • ***Challenge,*** p. 36	**Independent Activities** ▪ Seminar: Edit/Proofread and Publish a Fiction Book Review, p. 145J ▪ Penmanship: Practice Cursive Letters *y, z,* and *v,* p. 145J ▪ Writer's Craft: Paragraph Form, ***Challenge,*** p. 39

ASSESSMENT

Formal Assessment Options

Use these summative assessments along with your informal observations to assess student progress.

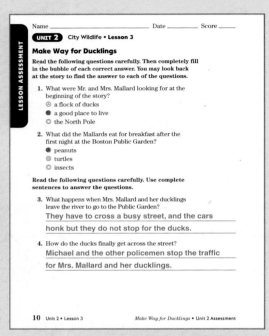

Name ______________ Date ________ Score ______

UNIT 2 City Wildlife • Lesson 3

LESSON ASSESSMENT

Make Way for Ducklings

Read the following questions carefully. Then completely fill in the bubble of each correct answer. You may look back at the story to find the answer to each of the questions.

1. What were Mr. and Mrs. Mallard looking for at the beginning of the story?
   - Ⓐ a flock of ducks
   - ● a good place to live
   - Ⓒ the North Pole
2. What did the Mallards eat for breakfast after the first night at the Boston Public Garden?
   - ● peanuts
   - Ⓑ turtles
   - Ⓒ insects

Read the following questions carefully. Use complete sentences to answer the questions.

3. What happens when Mrs. Mallard and her ducklings leave the river to go to the Public Garden?
   They have to cross a busy street, and the cars honk but they do not stop for the ducks.
4. How do the ducks finally get across the street?
   Michael and the other policemen stop the traffic for Mrs. Mallard and her ducklings.

10 Unit 2 • Lesson 3 *Make Way for Ducklings* • Unit 2 Assessment

Unit 2 Assessment p. 10

Make Way for Ducklings *(continued)*

5. Why does Mrs. Mallard think that the Public Garden is not a good place to raise a family?
   She thinks the Public Garden is not a good place because a boy on a bicycle almost runs her over.
6. Why couldn't Mrs. Mallard visit Michael for a while?
   She laid eight eggs, and she needed to keep them warm.
7. Where does Mr. Mallard go after the baby ducks are born?
   Mr. Mallard decides to take a trip to see what the rest of the river looks like.
8. What does Mrs. Mallard do with the ducklings while Mr. Mallard is away?
   Mrs. Mallard teaches her ducklings how to walk in line, to come when they are called, and to keep away from things with wheels.

Read the following questions carefully. Then completely fill in the bubble of each correct answer.

9. Which of these could happen in real life?
   - ● ducks building a nest on an island in a river
   - Ⓑ ducks telling people how they feel
   - Ⓒ ducks building a bridge over a highway
10. Who did the Mallards visit every day in the park?
    - Ⓐ a swan
    - Ⓑ a boy
    - ● a policeman

Unit 2 Assessment • *Make Way for Ducklings* Unit 2 • Lesson 3 11

Unit 2 Assessment p. 11

Make Way for Ducklings *(continued)*

Read the questions below. Use complete sentences in your answers.

Linking to the Concepts Why is the island a good city home for the Mallards?
Answers will vary. Accept all reasonable answers.

Personal Response Is there a place near where you live that would make a good home for mallards to live in? Why would it be a good place for ducks?
Answers will vary. Accept all reasonable answers.

12 Unit 2 • Lesson 3 *Make Way for Ducklings* • Unit 2 Assessment

Unit 2 Assessment p. 12

Make Way for Ducklings *(continued)*

Vocabulary

Read the following questions carefully. Then completely fill in the bubble of each correct answer.

1. The Mallards think the swan on the boat is an enormous bird. **Enormous** means
   - Ⓐ pretty
   - Ⓑ smart
   - ● huge
2. Mr. Mallard is delighted when Mrs. Mallard says she likes the pond. Another word for **delighted** is
   - ● happy
   - Ⓑ confused
   - Ⓒ bored
3. The Mallards choose a cozy spot to build their nest. In this sentence, **cozy** means
   - Ⓐ bright
   - ● protected
   - Ⓒ rocky
4. Mr. and Mrs. Mallard were bursting with pride over their new ducklings. To be **bursting** with pride means to be
   - Ⓐ afraid of
   - Ⓑ tired about
   - ● filled with
5. It was a big responsibility taking care of so many ducklings. Another word for **responsibility** is
   - ● job
   - Ⓑ idea
   - Ⓒ party

Unit 2 Assessment • *Make Way for Ducklings* Unit 2 • Lesson 3 13

Unit 2 Assessment p. 13

Name ______________ Date ________ Score ______

UNIT 2 City Wildlife

END OF UNIT ASSESSMENT Multiple Choice

Spelling Assessment

Read each sentence carefully. Look for the underlined word that is misspelled. Then completely fill in the bubble of the line where the word is misspelled. If no word is misspelled, fill in the bubble of the line marked "Correct as is."

1. Ⓐ A <u>bubble</u> is filled with air.
   Ⓑ A beard is <u>hair</u> around the chin.
   ● Good behavior is a <u>choyce</u>.
   Ⓓ Correct as is.
2. ● An abacus helps you <u>cownt</u>.
   Ⓖ A seagull is a type of <u>bird</u>.
   Ⓗ Mice have <u>little</u> feet.
   Ⓙ Correct as is.
3. Ⓐ Vegetables are planted in <u>soil</u>.
   Ⓑ Some <u>rare</u> books are expensive.
   Ⓒ An evening <u>gown</u> is fancy.
   ● Correct as is.
4. Ⓕ An igloo is a <u>house</u> built of snow.
   ● Hockey is a rough <u>sporot</u>.
   Ⓗ Snakes can <u>coil</u> into circles.
   Ⓙ Correct as is.
5. ● A <u>candal</u> can be scented.
   Ⓑ Purple is a <u>royal</u> color.
   Ⓒ Water collects in a <u>puddle</u>.
   Ⓓ Correct as is.
6. Ⓕ The <u>fare</u> is the cost of a ticket.
   Ⓖ The sun can <u>burn</u> your skin.
   ● Skiers often <u>ware</u> warm coats.
   Ⓙ Correct as is.

42 *Spelling Assessment* • Unit 2 Assessment

Unit 2 Assessment p. 42

Name ______________ Date ________ Score ______

UNIT 2 City Wildlife

END OF UNIT ASSESSMENT Multiple Choice

Vocabulary Assessment

Read each sentence. Then choose the answer in which the underlined word is used in the same way as it is in the sentence.

SAMPLE

The restaurant <u>bill</u> was very expensive.
Which answer shows the word <u>bill</u> used in the same way?
- ● The plumber sent us a <u>bill</u> for his work.
- Ⓑ That duck had a very large <u>bill</u>.
- Ⓒ The <u>bill</u> was passed in Congress.
- Ⓓ The doctor agreed to <u>bill</u> us later.

1. The duck landed on the <u>bank</u> of the pond.
   Which answer shows the word <u>bank</u> used in the same way?
   - Ⓐ Do not <u>bank</u> on him giving you the answers.
   - Ⓑ My money is in an account at the <u>bank</u>.
   - ● The muddy <u>bank</u> made a good home for the turtle.
   - Ⓓ The <u>bank</u> gave us a loan on our house.
2. A <u>dear</u> friend sent Anna a birthday gift.
   Which answer shows the word <u>dear</u> used in the same way?
   - Ⓕ A buck is a male <u>deer</u>.
   - Ⓖ Most <u>deer</u> are gentle animals.
   - Ⓗ Oh <u>dear</u>! I forgot my keys.
   - ● He gave his <u>dear</u> teddy bear a hug.
3. The <u>new</u> shoes were red with white laces.
   Which answer shows the word <u>new</u> used in the same way?
   - Ⓐ I <u>knew</u> the answer.
   - ● The <u>new</u> penny was shiny.
   - Ⓒ The dog <u>knew</u> his name.
   - Ⓓ The band <u>knew</u> how to play the song.

Unit 2 Assessment • *Vocabulary Assessment* 43

Unit 2 Assessment p. 43

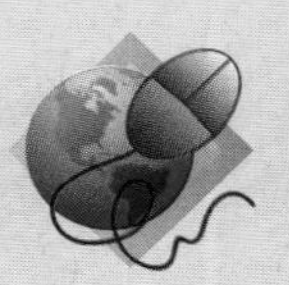

Online Assessment for ***Open Court Reading*** helps teachers differentiate classroom instruction based on students' scores from the weekly and end-of-unit assessments. It provides exercises best suited to meet the needs of each student. For more information, visit SRAonline.com.

Informal Comprehension Strategies Rubrics

Asking Questions

- The student asks questions about ideas or facts presented in the text and attempts to answer these questions by reading the text.

Predicting

- The student makes predictions about the text.
- The student updates predictions during reading, based on information in the text.

Research Rubrics

During Workshop, assess students using the rubrics below. The rubrics range from 1–4 in most categories, with 1 being the lowest score. Record each student's score on the inside back cover of the ***Inquiry Journal***.

Recognizing Information Needs

1 Identifies topics about which more needs to be learned. ("I need to learn more about the brain.")

2 Identifies information needs that are relevant though not essential to the research question. ("To understand how Leeuwenhoek invented the microscope, I need to know what size germs are.")

3 Identifies questions that are deeper than the one originally asked. (Original question: "How does the heart work?" Deeper question: "Why does blood need to circulate?")

Finding Needed Information

1 Collects information loosely related to topic.

2 Collects information clearly related to topic.

3 Collects information helpful in advancing on a research problem.

4 Collects problem-relevant information from varied sources and notices inconsistencies and missing pieces.

5 Collects useful information, paying attention to the reliability of sources and reviewing information critically.

Objectives

- Students practice recognizing word families.
- Students practice recognizing adjective synonyms.
- Students practice recognizing verb synonyms.
- Students practice recognizing /əl/ spelled *-le.*
- Students practice recognizing open syllables with vowel digraphs.

Materials

- Student Anthology, Book 1, pp. 136–147
- Decodable Book Activities CD-ROM
- Decodable Book 19
- Routine Cards 1, 3, Routines 1–2, 8–9

Teacher Tip SYLLABICATION To help students blend words and build fluency, use the syllabication below of the words in the word lines.

sat • is • fy	sat • is • fied
sat • is • fac • tion	sat • is • fac • tor • y
de • cide	de • cid • ed
un • de • cid • ed	de • cis • ion
e • nor • mous	gi • gan • tic
tre • men • dous	im • mense
beck • oned	sig • naled
mo • tioned	ges • tured
peo • ple	tur • tles
lit • tle	wad • dle
whis • tle	

Routine Card
Refer to ***Routine 1*** for whole-word blending and ***Routine 2*** for sentence blending.

Teacher Tip Encourage students to just read the words. Stop and blend only those words that give them problems.

WORD KNOWLEDGE

Word Knowledge

Reading the Words and Sentences

Use the established procedure as you have students read each line of words and the sentences in this and in subsequent lessons. The words in **boldface** are from the selection.

Line 1:	satisfy	**satisfied**	satisfaction	**satisfactory**	
Line 2:	decide	**decided**	undecided	decision	
Line 3:	**enormous**	gigantic	tremendous	immense	
Line 4:	**beckoned**	signaled	motioned	gestured	
Line 5:	**people**	**turtles**	**little**	**waddle**	**whistle**
Sentence 1:	Just as the ducks were getting ready to start on their way, a strange enormous bird came by.				
Sentence 2:	The ducks climbed out on the bank and waddled along.				
Sentence 3:	The policeman raised one hand to stop the traffic, and then beckoned with the other for Mrs. Mallard to cross over.				
Sentence 4:	Some people can whistle many tunes.				

About the Words and Sentences

- **Lines 1–2:** All of the words in Line 1 have the same base word *(satisfy)* and all of the words in Line 2 have the same base word *(decide).* After the words in each line have been read, ask students to identify the base word and discuss how the base word changed part of speech when the prefix or suffix was added.
- **Lines 3–4:** The words in each line are synonyms. Have the students define what synonyms are *(words that have similar meanings).* After reading the words in Line 3, have students use each word in a sentence. Ask students what part of speech the words in Line 3 are *(adjectives).* Have students use the words in Line 4 in a sentence and ask students to identify the part of speech *(verbs).*
- **Line 5:** The words in the last line are found in "Make Way for Ducklings" and introduce the final /əl/ sound spelled *-le.*
- **Sentences 1–3:** These sentences are from the story students are about to read. Ask students to identify the words that have suffixes or prefixes. *(getting, climbed, waddled, raised, beckoned)*
- **Sentence 4:** Have students identify the words in the last sentence that contain the /əl/ sound spelled *-le. (people, whistle)*

Developing Oral Language

Use direct teaching to review the words. Use one or both of the following activities to help students practice reading the words.

- To review synonyms, write the following words on the board: *large, tiny, hard, create.* Have volunteers give synonyms for each of the words on the board.
- Have a student choose a word from Lines 1 or 2, use it in a sentence, and call on another student to use another form of the word in a different sentence.

WORD KNOWLEDGE

Teacher Tip FLUENCY Gaining a better understanding of the spellings of sounds and structure of words will help students as they encounter unfamiliar words in their reading. By this time in Grade 3 students should be reading approximately 107 words per minute with fluency and expression. As students read, you may notice that some need work in building fluency. During Workshop, have these students select a section of the text (a minimum of 160 words) to read several times in order to build fluency.

Spelling
See pages 145E–145J for the corresponding spelling lesson for the /əl/ sound.

Differentiating Instruction

If...	Then...
Students need extra help with word families or synonyms	Use ***Online Phonics***
Students need extra help with the final /əl/ sound spelled *-le*	Use ***Intervention Guide*** pages 80–81

amazing!" and the man who swept the streets said: "Well, now, ain't that nice!" and when Mrs. Mallard heard them she was so proud she tipped her nose in the air and walked along with an extra swing in her waddle.

When they came to the corner of Beacon Street there was the police car with four policemen that Clancy had sent from headquarters. The policemen held back the traffic so Mrs. Mallard and the ducklings could march across the street, right on into the Public Garden.

Inside the gate they all turned round to say thank you to the policemen. The policemen smiled and waved good-by.

When they reached the pond and swam across to the little island, there was Mr. Mallard waiting for them, just as he had promised.

The ducklings liked the new island so much that they decided to live there. All day long they follow the swan boats and eat peanuts.

And when night falls they swim to their little island and go to sleep.

143

Comprehension Skills

Second Read

Fantasy and Reality

Ask students to identify characteristics that make this story a fantasy.

- *The ducklings and Mrs. Mallard say thank you to Michael.*
- *Mr. Mallard was waiting as he had promised.*

Checking Comprehension

- Why is city wildlife so important in this story? *(It's a story about a family of ducks who settle in the pond near the Public Garden in Boston.)*
- What do the events in the story have to do with the title? *(The policeman helps Mrs. Mallard and her ducklings cross the busy streets so they can get to the Public Garden. He stops the traffic so the cars "make way" for the ducklings.)*
- Why do you think that this story is a fantasy? *(It's a fantasy because the animals talk and act the way that people do.)*

Teacher Tip FLUENCY By this time in third grade, good readers should be reading approximately 107 words per minute with fluency and expression. The only way to gain this fluency is through practice. Have students reread the selection to you and to each other during Workshop to help build fluency. As students read, you may notice that some need work in building fluency. During Workshop, have these students select a section of the text (a minimum of 160 words) to read several times in order to build fluency.

COMPREHENSION

Differentiating Instruction

If...	Then...
English Learners need extra help reviewing "Make Way for Ducklings"	Use ***English Learner Support Guide*** pages 132–133

Formal Assessment

See pages 10–13 in the ***Unit 2 Assessment*** to test the students' comprehension of "Make Way for Ducklings."

Routine Card
Refer to ***Routine 6*** for the *handing-off process.*

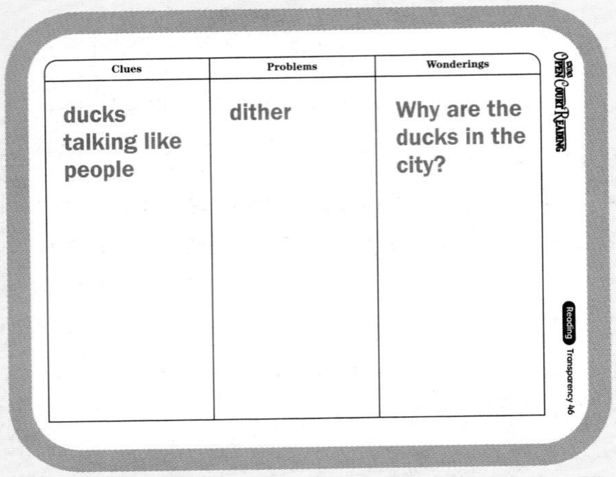

Clues	Problems	Wonderings
ducks talking like people	dither	Why are the ducks in the city?

Reading Transparency 46

www.sra4kids.com
Web Connection
Some students may choose to conduct a computer search for additional books or information about city wildlife. Invite them to make a list of these books and sources of information to share with classmates and the school librarian. Check the Reading link of the SRA Web page for additional links to theme-related Web sites.

Teacher Tip For information regarding humane and environmental issues, contact the National Association for Humane and Environmental Education, the Youth Education Division of The Humane Society of the United States. This association offers resources for classroom teachers and educators to teach the value of, and respect for, animals and our natural environment.

Discussing the Selection

After the first read, the whole group discusses the selection and any personal thoughts, reactions, problems, or questions that it raises. To stimulate discussion, students can ask one another the kinds of questions that good readers ask themselves about a text: *How does it connect to city wildlife? What have I learned that is new? What did I find interesting? What is important here? What was difficult to understand? Why would someone want to read this?* Throughout the discussion, ensure that students are using specific information from the text to defend their interpretations.

Handing-Off Process Seeing you as a contributing member of the group sets a strong example for students. However, to help students learn to keep the discussion student-centered, have each student choose the next speaker instead of handing the discussion back to you. Using the *handing-off process* will help students to take responsibility for the discussion.

Engage students in a discussion to determine whether they have grasped the following ideas:

- what Mr. and Mrs. Mallard were looking for and why
- why they made the choice they made
- how people posed a threat to their safety
- how people helped them
- what advantages and disadvantages city life posed for the Mallard family

During this time, have students return to the clues, problems, and wonderings they noted during browsing to determine whether the clues were borne out by the selection, whether and how their problems were solved, and whether their wonderings were answered or deserve further discussion and investigation. Let the students decide which items deserve further discussion.

Also have students return to the Focus Questions on the first page of the selection. Select a student to read the questions aloud, and have volunteers answer the questions. If students do not know the answers to the questions, have them return to the text to find the answers.

You may wish to review the elements of fantasy with the students at this time. Discuss with them how they can tell that "Make Way for Ducklings" is a fantasy.

Have students break into small groups to discuss what this story tells them about wildlife in urban areas or the relationship between people and wildlife in urban areas. Groups can discuss their ideas with the rest of the class.

Writer's Notebook

Students may wish to record their personal responses to the selection. If students have ever seen ducks or other birds in a city, or participated in efforts to help city wildlife, encourage them to record these events.

Review Selection Vocabulary

Have students review the definitions of the selection vocabulary words that they wrote in the vocabulary section of their Writer's Notebooks. Remind them that they discussed the meanings of these words before reading the selection. Have students write sentences for each of the vocabulary words after the definitions in the same section of their Writer's Notebooks. They can use the definitions and the sentences to study for the vocabulary portion of their Lesson Assessments. Have them add any other interesting words that they clarified while reading to the Personal Dictionary section of their Writer's Notebooks. Encourage students to refer to the selection vocabulary words throughout the unit. The words from the selection are:

enormous	**delighted**	**cozy**
bursting	**responsibility**	**beckoned**

Have students include this lesson's words in the Word Bank for this unit. Encourage students to find words from other resources, their investigations, and family discussions to add to the Word Bank.

View Fine Art

Have students reflect on the painting ***Lunch in the Gardens*** on page 146 of the ***Student Anthology*** and share their thoughts and reactions with the class. Explain that the painting by Beryl Cook provides a humorous look at life in New York. The artist often portrays her subjects with both humor and affection. Here, she shows businessmen in suits eating french fries, as imploring pigeons surround them. The pigeons here are just as much a part of the city life as the businessmen.

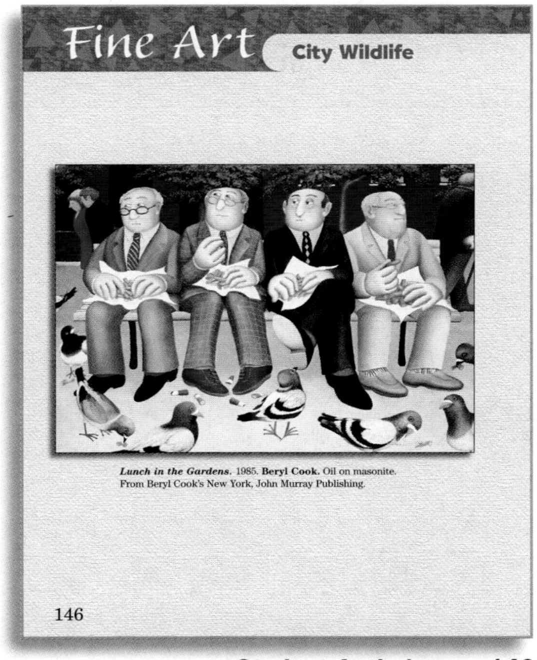
Fine Art City Wildlife

Lunch in the Gardens. 1985. **Beryl Cook.** Oil on masonite. From Beryl Cook's New York, John Murray Publishing.

146

Student Anthology p. 146

Home Connection

Send home the ***Home Connection*** letter for "Make Way for Ducklings" on page 21. Parents and students can learn how to make a snack mix containing the ducklings' favorite food—peanuts. A Spanish version of this letter appears on page 22.

DIFFERENTIATING INSTRUCTION

English Learner Tip

PICTURE STORY Ask each English Learner to pick three nouns from the story, and to copy each word carefully onto an individual sheet of paper. On the reverse side of each sheet, the word may be illustrated. Then have each student take a turn improvising a fantasy story that contains the three words. When a student uses one of the chosen words, he or she can hold it up and display it to the class.

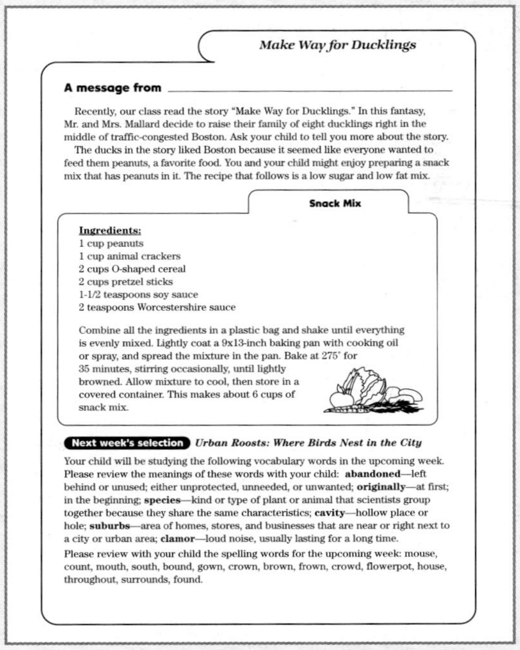
Make Way for Ducklings

A message from ______________________

Recently, our class read the story "Make Way for Ducklings." In this fantasy, Mr. and Mrs. Mallard decide to raise their family of eight ducklings right in the middle of traffic-congested Boston. Ask your child to tell you more about the story.

The ducks in the story liked Boston because it seemed like everyone wanted to feed them peanuts, a favorite food. You and your child might enjoy preparing a snack mix that has peanuts in it. The recipe that follows is a low sugar and low fat mix.

Snack Mix

Ingredients:
1 cup peanuts
1 cup animal crackers
2 cups O-shaped cereal
2 cups pretzel sticks
1-1/2 teaspoons soy sauce
2 teaspoons Worcestershire sauce

Combine all the ingredients in a plastic bag and shake until everything is evenly mixed. Lightly coat a 9x13-inch baking pan with cooking oil or spray, and spread the mixture in the pan. Bake at 275° for 35 minutes, stirring occasionally, until lightly browned. Allow mixture to cool, then store in a covered container. This makes about 6 cups of snack mix.

Next week's selection ***Urban Roosts: Where Birds Nest in the City***

Your child will be studying the following vocabulary words in the upcoming week. Please review the meanings of these words with your child: **abandoned**—left behind or unused; either unprotected, unneeded, or unwanted; **originally**—at first; in the beginning; **species**—kind or type of plant or animal that scientists group together because they share the same characteristics; **cavity**—hollow place or hole; **suburbs**—area of homes, stores, and businesses that are near or right next to a city or urban area; **clamor**—loud noise, usually lasting for a long time.

Please review with your child the spelling words for the upcoming week: mouse, count, mouth, south, bound, gown, crown, brown, frown, crowd, flowerpot, house, throughout, surrounds, found.

Home Connection p. 21

Reading Transparency 50

Teacher Tip LITERARY TERMINOLOGY Incorporate into the discussion literary terms that students have discussed so far this year. Students should be able to discuss plot, characterization, realistic fiction, fantasy, and nonfiction.

Differentiating Instruction

If...	Then...
Students have demonstrated an understanding of fantasy	Have them read other fantasy stories and compare and contrast the elements of this genre in the stories they read

Supporting the Reading

Comprehension Skills: Fantasy and Reality

Teach Tell students that learning to identify different types of writing helps them to anticipate or predict the content of texts they read, increases their comprehension of those texts, and allows them to choose what type of reading they want to do. Gaining experience with many different types of texts also allows students to develop their own personal preferences in reading material.

Guided Practice Use a two-column chart on ***Reading Transparency 50*** to show information about Fantasy and Reality. Label the chart columns *Fantasy* and *Reality*. Have students reread pages 136–143 and record events from the story under the appropriate column. In the other column, ask students to note how the event would have been treated in realistic fiction or nonfiction. You can use the following as an example to get started.

Fantasy	Reality
Mr. and Mrs. Mallard looked for a good place to live.	The two ducks flew around the city. They built a nest by the pond.

Independent Practice Read through the Focus and Identify sections of ***Comprehension and Language Arts Skills,*** page 36, with students. Guide students through the Identify portion, and help them come up with examples found in the story. Then have students complete the Practice and Apply portions of ***Comprehension and Language Arts Skills,*** page 37.

Link to Writing Tell students that fantasy writing places no limits on their imagination. Have them use the topic they chose for the Apply section of the ***Comprehension and Language Arts Skills*** activity they just completed to create their own fantasy story. They are free to choose another topic if they like, or to use the titles on the worksheet as a starting point for ideas. Encourage students to use words that they learned while reading the selection in their writing.

Name ______________________ Date __________

UNIT 2 City Wildlife • Lesson 3 *Make Way for Ducklings*

Fantasy and Reality

Focus An author may write a story that is based on reality or on fantasy.

- **Fantasy** stories are stories that could not happen in real life. Fantasy stories may have make-believe characters.
- A **realistic** story tells of something that could happen in real life.

Identify

Look through "Make Way for Ducklings." Find examples that show that this is a fantasy story. Write two examples and explain why you chose them. Answers will vary. Possible answers given.

Page: 137

What makes it a fantasy story? Mr. and Mrs. Mallard talk as humans do.

Explanation: Real animals do not talk just like people.

Page: ______

What makes it a fantasy story? ______________________

Explanation: ______________________

36 UNIT 2 • Lesson 3 Comprehension and Language Arts Skills

Name ______________________ Date __________

UNIT 2 City Wildlife • Lesson 3 *Make Way for Ducklings*

Fantasy and Reality

COMPREHENSION

Practice

Read the list of story topics. Write an **F** beside each topic that is a fantasy story.

1. Ali, Juan, and Sue go to school. ______
2. A cat speaks in poems. F
3. A giant eats the trees in your backyard. F
4. A girl's family moves to a new town. ______
5. A boy breaks a window with a football. ______
6. Three girls fly out of their bedroom windows at night. F
7. Cali's pig can fly around their farm. F
8. Kevin gets a toy truck for his birthday. ______

Apply

Choose one of the story topics that you did not mark with an **F**. Write the topic below. Then write how to turn it into a fantasy story. Answers will vary.

Topic chosen: ______________________

How to turn it into a fantasy story: ______________________

Comprehension and Language Arts Skills UNIT 2 • Lesson 3 37

Comprehension and Language Arts Skills pp. 36–37

Differentiating Instruction

If...	Then...
Students need extra practice with fantasy and reality	Use ***Reteach*** pages 39–40
Students have an understanding of fantasy and reality and would enjoy a challenge	Use ***Challenge*** page 35

Skills Trace

Fantasy and Reality

Introduced in Grade 1.

Scaffolded throughout Grade 3.

REINTRODUCED: Unit 2, Lesson 3
Unit 3, Lesson 2

TESTED: Unit 2 Assessment

Teacher Tip Using the elements of a fantasy and what students know about improving their writing, have the class develop a revision checklist. Encourage them to use this checklist to revise their writing.

Teacher Tip The Guided Practice portion of this lesson could also be a Workshop activity. Display the books around the classroom. Number each book so students can independently classify the genres of the books in their Writer's Notebooks.

DIFFERENTIATING INSTRUCTION

If...	Then...
Students are having difficulty distinguishing fiction from nonfiction	Have them read or browse several examples of each genre with you during Workshop. Help students identify the differences between fiction and nonfiction.

Literary Elements

Fiction vs. Nonfiction

Teach Ask students what they remember about the difference between fiction and nonfiction. Prompt students to identify "Make Way for Ducklings" as fiction and also as fantasy. Remind students that fantasy is a story that could not happen in the real world.

Guided Practice On the board, write the headings *Fiction* and *Nonfiction.* Under *Fiction,* list the elements of fiction. Under *Nonfiction* list the corresponding elements.

Arrange to have ten or twelve children's books at hand in the classroom, including fiction, nonfiction, fantasy, and realistic fiction. Display one book at a time and have the students identify which type of story each book represents. Encourage students to identify and distinguish fiction from nonfiction, and fantasy from reality as they do independent reading throughout the school year.

Independent Practice Ask students to look in their ***Writing Folders*** or through any of their previous writings, and identify the fiction and nonfiction selections. Alternatively, if students have compiled some resources for their investigations, ask them to identify which ones are nonfiction and which are fiction. (These will likely be mostly nonfiction.)

If you would like to assign a writing project, you might have students write a short fiction story and a short nonfiction story about an animal or bird.

Science Connection

Birds in the City

In "Make Way for Ducklings," students read about a family of ducks that settled in the middle of Boston, in part because people fed them peanuts. For this activity, encourage students to observe a bird over the course of several days. Make a journal of what it eats. If first-hand observation is not possible, students may conduct research to learn about the bird's diet. Define the terms *producers* (produces food for other species), *consumers* (consumes food produced by other species), *carnivores* (meat-eating animals), *herbivores* (plant-eating animals), and *omnivores* (plant- and meat-eating animals) for students and ask them to use the terms that apply to the bird they are studying when they present information to the class. Based on this information, ask students to explain what impact the species might have on its environment. Ask them to provide references to support their conjectures. Student groups may incorporate these findings into their unit investigations if they are related to their research problem or question.

Teacher Tip MATERIALS
- ✔ notebook
- ✔ birds in urban setting
- ✔ poster boards
- ✔ colored pencils or markers

Teacher Tip PURPOSE To learn about the diet of one type of city-dwelling bird and how that species' activities impact its environment.

DAY 5

Word Analysis

Spelling

Assessment: Final Test

The Final /əl/ Sound

Teach

Repeat the Pretest or use the Final Test on page 31 of ***Unit 2 Assessment*** as summative assessment for student understanding of the final /əl/ sound spelling pattern.

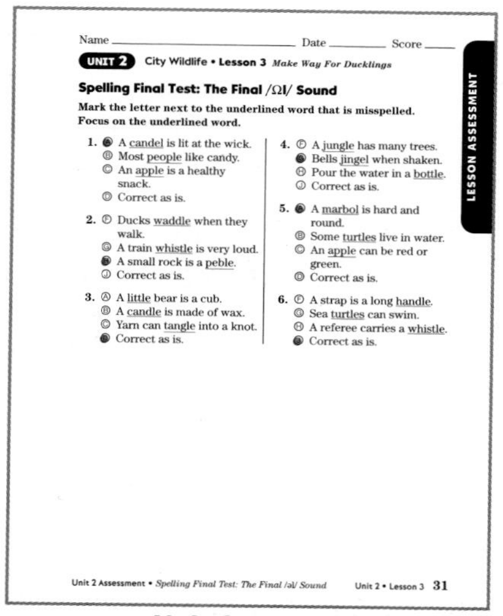
Name ______ Date ______ Score ______

UNIT 2 City Wildlife • Lesson 3 *Make Way For Ducklings*

Spelling Final Test: The Final /Ωl/ Sound

Mark the letter next to the underlined word that is misspelled. Focus on the underlined word.

1. Ⓐ A candel is lit at the wick.
   Ⓑ Most people like candy.
   Ⓒ An apple is a healthy snack.
   Ⓓ Correct as is.
2. Ⓕ Ducks waddle when they walk.
   Ⓖ A train whistle is very loud.
   Ⓗ A small rock is a peble.
   Ⓙ Correct as is.
3. Ⓐ A little bear is a cub.
   Ⓑ A candle is made of wax.
   Ⓒ Yarn can tangle into a knot.
   Ⓓ Correct as is.
4. Ⓕ A jungle has many trees.
   Ⓖ Bells jingel when shaken.
   Ⓗ Pour the water in a bottle.
   Ⓙ Correct as is.
5. Ⓐ A marbol is hard and round.
   Ⓑ Some turtles live in water.
   Ⓒ An apple can be red or green.
   Ⓓ Correct as is.
6. Ⓕ A strap is a long handle.
   Ⓖ Sea turtles can swim.
   Ⓗ A referee carries a whistle.
   Ⓙ Correct as is.

LESSON ASSESSMENT

Unit 2 Assessment • *Spelling Final Test: The Final /əl/ Sound* Unit 2 • Lesson 3 31

Unit 2 Assessment p. 31

Guided Practice

Have students categorize any mistakes they made on the Final Test. Are they careless errors? Are they lesson-pattern problems? Check student writing samples for /əl/ spellings.

Vocabulary

Informal Assessment

Ask students to think of synonyms and antonyms for *little*. Draw a word map with *little* in a center box. Label the left side *Antonyms* and label the right side *Synonyms*. See if students can name antonyms and synonyms to complete a word map for *little*. (antonyms: *big, large, huge*; synonyms: *small, petite, tiny*) Have students add new words to their word list in their Writer's Notebooks.

Writing Process Strategies

Editing/Proofreading and Publishing

Book Review, Fiction

Teach

Read ***Writer's Workbook,*** page 17, on editing/proofreading and publishing.

Guided Practice

Editing/Proofreading and Publishing

- Have students edit their fiction book reviews.
- Direct students to use the checklist in the ***Writer's Workbook,*** page 17, to help them edit their writing.
- Have students make a neat final copy in their best cursive handwriting or print it on the computer.

Formal Assessment

Total Point Value: 10

1. There is a topic sentence for each paragraph. (2 points)
2. The main idea or plot is clearly stated in the first paragraph. (2 points)
3. Opinions are supported with examples, reasons, facts, or details. (2 points)
4. The final copy is neat, clean, and easy to read. (2 points)
5. Mechanics: capitalization, punctuation, and spelling are correct. (2 points)

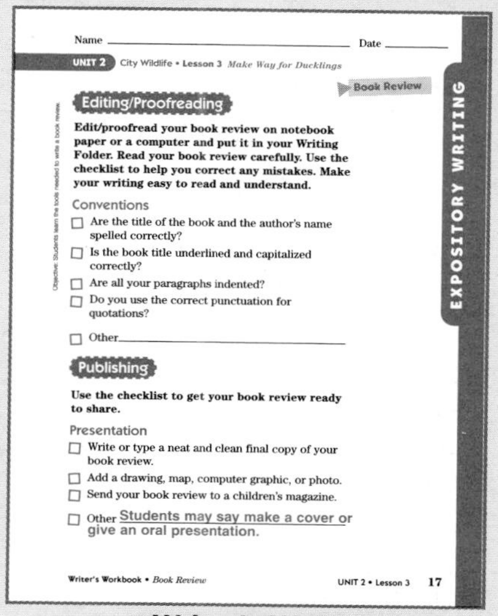
Name ______ Date ______

UNIT 2 City Wildlife • Lesson 3 *Make Way for Ducklings*

Book Review

Editing/Proofreading

Edit/proofread your book review on notebook paper or a computer and put it in your Writing Folder. Read your book review carefully. Use the checklist to help you correct any mistakes. Make your writing easy to read and understand.

Conventions

- ☐ Are the title of the book and the author's name spelled correctly?
- ☐ Is the book title underlined and capitalized correctly?
- ☐ Are all your paragraphs indented?
- ☐ Do you use the correct punctuation for quotations?
- ☐ Other ______

Publishing

Use the checklist to get your book review ready to share.

Presentation

- ☐ Write or type a neat and clean final copy of your book review.
- ☐ Add a drawing, map, computer graphic, or photo.
- ☐ Send your book review to a children's magazine.
- ☐ Other Students may say make a cover or give an oral presentation.

EXPOSITORY WRITING

Objective: Students learn the tools needed to write a book review.

Writer's Workbook • *Book Review* UNIT 2 • Lesson 3 17

Writer's Workbook p. 17

English Language Conventions

Penmanship

Cursive Letters *y, z,* and *v*

Teach

- **Teacher Model:** On the board, introduce the formation of lowercase cursive *y*, *z*, and *v* as overcurve letters.

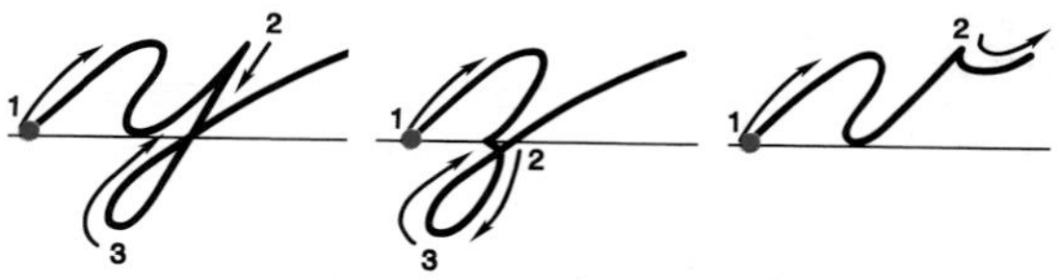

y Starting point, overcurve
Slant down
Undercurve, slant down
Loop back into overcurve: small *y*

z Starting point, overcurve
Slant down, overcurve, down
Loop into overcurve: small *z*

v Starting point, overcurve
Slant down
Undercurve
Small curve to right: small *v*

- **Teacher Model:** Write the words *zipper*, *fly*, and *vase* to model proper letter formation.
- Draw slanted lines through the letters to demonstrate proper slant. Tell them all their letters must slant to the right.

Guided Practice

- Invite students to come to the board and trace the letters *y*, *z*, and *v*.
- Have students practice writing rows of *y*s, *z*s, and *v*s in their Writer's Notebooks.
- From "Make Way for Ducklings," have students write the words *everyone*, *lady*, and *amazing*, and draw slanted lines through the letters to check for proper slant.

Informal Assessment

Check students' handwriting for proper slant to the right.

LESSON WRAP-UP

Reading and Language Arts Skills Traces

Language Arts

WORD ANALYSIS

Skills Trace

Spelling: The Final /əl/ Sound

Introduced in Grade 3.
Scaffolded throughout Grades 3–5.

INTRODUCED: Unit 2, **Lesson 3**, p. 145E
PRACTICED: Unit 2, **Lesson 3**, pp. 145F–145J
Spelling and Vocabulary Skills, pp. 36–37
TESTED: Unit 2, **Lesson 3**, p. 145F (Pretest)
Unit 2, **Lesson 3**, p. 31 (Final Test)
Unit 2 Assessment

Skills Trace

Vocabulary: Synonyms

Introduced in Grade 1.
Scaffolded throughout Grades 2–5.

REINTRODUCED: Unit 2, **Lesson 3**, p. 145E
PRACTICED: Unit 2, **Lesson 3**, pp. 145G–145J
Spelling and Vocabulary Skills, pp. 34–35
TESTED: Unit 2 Assessment

WRITING PROCESS STRATEGIES

Skills Trace

Expository Writing: Book Review—Fiction

Introduced in Grade 1.
Scaffolded throughout Grades 3–6.

REINTRODUCED: Unit 2, **Lesson 3**, p. 145F
PRACTICED: Unit 2, **Lesson 3**, pp. 145G–145J
Writer's Workbook, pp. 14–17
TESTED: Unit 2, **Lesson 2**,
Formal Assessment, p. 145J
Unit 2 Assessment

Skills Trace

Writer's Craft: Paragraph Form

Introduced in Grade 1.
Scaffolded throughout Grades 2–6.

REINTRODUCED: Unit 2, **Lesson 3**, p. 145H
PRACTICED: Unit 2, **Lesson 3**, p. 145H
Comprehension and Language Arts Skills, pp. 40–41
TESTED: Unit 2 Assessment

ENGLISH LANGUAGE CONVENTIONS

Skills Trace

Mechanics: Commas in Dialogue

Introduced in Grade 2.
Scaffolded throughout Grades 3–6.

REINTRODUCED: Unit 2, **Lesson 3**, p. 145F
PRACTICED: Unit 2, **Lesson 3**, p. 145G
Unit 2, **Lesson 3**, p. 145H
Comprehension and Language Arts Skills, pp. 38–39
TESTED: Unit 2, **Lesson 3**,
Informal Assessment, p. 145H
Unit 2 Assessment

Skills Trace

Listening, Speaking, Viewing Language: Language Reflects Culture

Introduced in Grade 3.
Scaffolded throughout Grade 4.

INTRODUCED: Unit 2, **Lesson 3**, p. 145I
TESTED: Unit 2, **Lesson 3**,
Informal Assessment, p. 145I

Skills Trace

Penmanship: Cursive Letters *y, z,* and *v*

Introduced in Grade 3 (*y*), and Grade 2 (*z, v*).
Scaffolded throughout Grades 4–6 and Grades 3–6.

INTRODUCED: Unit 2, **Lesson 3**, p. 145J
TESTED: Unit 2, **Lesson 3**,
Informal Assessment, p. 145J

Reading

COMPREHENSION

Skills Trace

Fantasy and Reality

Introduced in Grade 1.
Scaffolded throughout Grade 3.

REINTRODUCED: Unit 2, Lesson 3
REINFORCED: Unit 3, Lesson 2
TESTED: Unit 2 Assessment

Professional Development: Writing

Getting Started: A Writing Tool Kit

A Writing Area, writing folders, and some simple rules not only eliminate management problems but also foster independence, encourage risk taking, and cultivate sharing. Work on these as a class at the beginning of the year, and make changes as needed.

Writing Area

A Writing Area promotes independence and provides teachers with more time to hold conferences with students. Have students participate in setting up this Writing Area so they know what materials are in the Writing Area and how to use them.

Materials The Writing Area contains a variety of writing materials for students to use, from the initial writing of their papers to the making of their final drafts. Materials in the Writing Area should include the following:

- Pencils, pens, crayons, markers, and paints
- Computer paper that has alternating green and white lines for drafting
- Different sizes of unlined paper to be used for drafting as well as for final copies
- Books for authors to browse through for ideas
- Magazines for photos
- Dictionaries and other reference materials
- Cardboard, tag board, and construction paper
- Wallpaper samples for covers
- Stencils for titles
- String, yarn, dental floss, staplers, and three-hole punches for binding

Writing Folders

Writing folders help keep writing organized. Every student should have a writing folder in which to keep drafts, revisions, and pieces that need a rest. Students also may want to keep a list of ideas for writing as well as checklists for revising and editing. Folders can be used by teachers for evaluation and for showing parents how their children are growing and exploring different types of writing. Many young authors like to personalize their folders. This can serve as an introductory writing activity.

One concern teachers have is that folders get messy, and they wonder if a notebook might work better. Notebooks, unfortunately, do not serve the same purpose that folders do, because they discourage students from looking back and comparing drafts. Students find it easier to have their earlier drafts right there next to the page they are revising.

Following are a few simple hints to help students manage their writing folders:

- Have students put their name and date on each piece, and have them note if the piece is a first draft, a revision, or an edited piece. If it is a revision, have them use a paper clip to hold the draft and revision together.
- Students may want to list the titles of their works somewhere on their writing folder.
- Periodically, students may want to go through their folders and remove drafts of published works or pieces that no longer interest them; however, they should not throw everything away. Encourage students during small-group conferences to talk about why they are keeping some items and throwing away others.

Professional Development

Teacher Resource Library CD-ROMs or ***Online Professional Development*** provides courses that help you better understand the Writing instruction in ***Open Court Reading.***

For more information about this program, visit SRAonline.com.

Additional information about writing as well as resource references can be found in the ***Professional Development Guide: Writing.***

Viewing the Theme Through Fine Art

Students can use the artworks on these pages to investigate the unit theme of City Wildlife in images rather than in words. Encourage students to talk about their impressions of the artworks and about how each piece of art might relate to the unit theme City Wildlife.

Below is some background information about each of the artworks. Share with students whatever you feel is appropriate. You may also wish to encourage students to find out more about artists and artistic styles that interest them.

Lunch In the Gardens

BERYL COOK (1926–) was born in Egham, Surrey, England, and has also lived in Zimbabwe. She became interested in painting after she taught her son how to paint with his toy watercolor set. It was not until 1975, when a friend persuaded her to exhibit some of her paintings in an antique shop, that Cook began selling her work. Since then, she has regularly exhibited her paintings and also illustrated *Seven Years and a Day* by Colette O'Hare.

Lunch in the Gardens is a humorous look at life in New York. The four men in their business suits are, perhaps, people-watching as they eat a lunch of french fries and feed the imploring pigeons. The birds, like the men, are an important part of city life and add to the wit of this painting. By focusing on the four men, Cook invites the viewer to take part in a humorous glimpse of her observations of ordinary people and their attitudes and actions. Her subjects are often portrayed with both humor and affection.

Fine Art

City Wildlife

Lunch in the Gardens. 1985. **Beryl Cook.** Oil on masonite. From Beryl Cook's New York, John Murray Publishing.

146

Cable Car Festival. 1988. **Dong Kingman.** Watercolor on paper. 30" × 22". Conacher Gallery, San Francisco.

147

Cable Car Festival

Dong Kingman (1911–2000) was born in Oakland, California, and moved at the age of five to Hong Kong with his parents. Encouraged by his mother, he began painting in the traditional Chinese medium of watercolor as a child. In 1929 he returned to the United States and experimented with oil paints, but eventually went back to watercolors. Unlike the traditional Chinese watercolors, where only black and white were used, Kingman introduces vibrant colors. He began his paintings by first drawing his subject matter and then layering washes of color to create a sense of liveliness.

Cable Car Festival is one of the later watercolor paintings created by Kingman. It pictures the city of San Francisco during a cable car celebration. By stacking and overlapping the buildings and crowding the figures together, Kingman is able to ellicit the feeling of a crowded, somewhat cramped space. His use of bright colors and festive decorations gives the scene energy and excitement. The smooth areas of gray wash recede into the background as the splashes of color carry the viewers' eyes from the right side of the painting to the cable car. Notice how even the city wildlife on the sidewalk enjoy the celebration and become an integral part of life in the city.

Focus Questions Many different species of birds survive in busy cities. How do you think this is possible? Do you think that people or wildlife adapt more easily to their environments? Why?

Urban Roosts

Where Birds Nest in the City

from the book by
Barbara Bash

Early in the morning you can hear something rustling up on the ledge of an old stone building. Even before the city awakens, the birds are stirring in their urban roosts.

All across the country, as their natural habitats have been destroyed, birds have moved to town. The ones that have been able to adapt are thriving in the heart of the city.

One familiar urban dweller is the pigeon. Long ago it was called a rock dove, because it lived in the rocky cliffs along the coast of Europe. Today it flourishes all over the United States in the nooks and crannies of our cities.

148

SELECTION INTRODUCTION

Selection Summary

Genre: Expository Text

In this selection, Barbara Bash tells about the types of birds that make their homes in cities. How do birds live in the city with all its buildings, streets, and concrete? What do they eat? Where do they nest? Students will learn how city birds have adapted to their urban habitats. Detailed descriptions help the students locate and identify both familiar and rare birds that flourish in the city. Students are encouraged to observe their environment to learn about wildlife living around them. Bold, colorful artwork infuses the expository text with a sense of drama.

Major elements of expository text include:

- Expository text gives information. It tells people something.
- It contains facts about real events or people.
- It presents information in a straightforward way.
- It give events in the order in which they happen.
- It may be organized by topics.
- It might contain diagrams, photographs, and other illustrations.
- It contains information that can be checked by looking at other sources.

About the Author/Illustrator

Working as a professional calligrapher in Berkeley, California, **BARBARA BASH** became interested in botanical illustration. This fascination led her to a study of ecosystems, an interest she continued to pursue after moving to Boulder, Colorado. Bash illustrated several natural-science books including *Tiger Lilies and Other Beastly Plants.* The first book she wrote and illustrated for young readers was *Desert Giant: The World of the Saguaro Cactus.* Her curiosity led her to visit Africa. The result was *Tree of Life: The World of the African Baobab.* The following year, *Urban Roosts: Where Birds Nest in the City,* was published and was awarded the Outstanding Science Trade Book Award and was named an IRA Teachers' Choice title. Currently, Bash lives in urban Brooklyn, New York.

Students can read more about Barbara Bash on page 163 of the ***Student Anthology.***

Inquiry Connections

Wild creatures have the ability to adapt to new environments. Many birds live successfully in urban habitats. They roost, build nests, have young, and find food while surrounded by tall buildings and miles of concrete. Birds are so much a part of the urban scene that few human city dwellers notice them.

This selection encourages students to notice wildlife around them by pointing out where to look.

- Urban birds find unusual places to roost, adapting to urban habitats by building nests in both hidden and public places.
- Some birds migrate seasonally to cities.

Before reading the selection:

- Point out that students may post a question, concept, word, illustration, or object on the Concept/Question Board at any time during the course of their unit investigation. Be sure that students include their name or initials on the items they post so that others will know whom to go to if they have an answer or if they wish to collaborate on a related activity.
- Students should feel free to write an answer or a note on someone else's question or to consult the Board for ideas for their own investigations throughout the unit.
- Encourage students to read about city wildlife at home and to bring in articles or pictures that are good examples to post on the Board.

Concept/Question Board

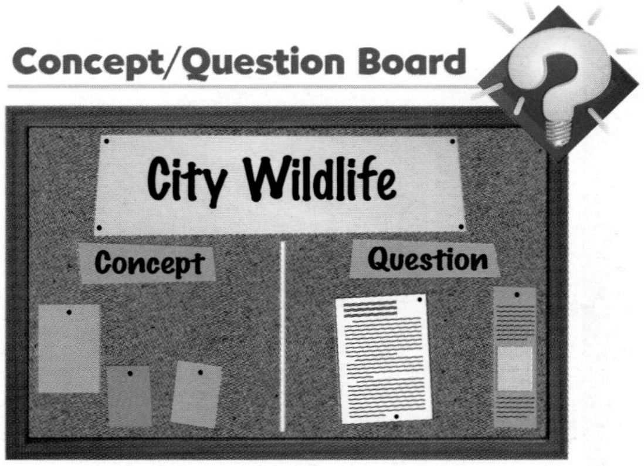

PROGRAM RESOURCES

Leveled Practice

Reteach
Pages 45–48

Challenge
Pages 40–43

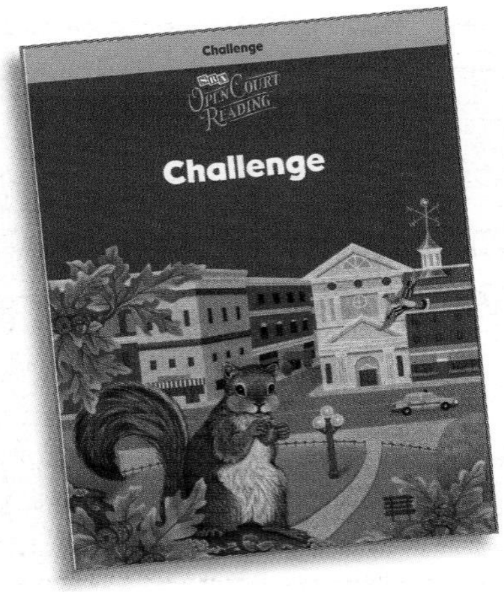

English Learner Support Activities

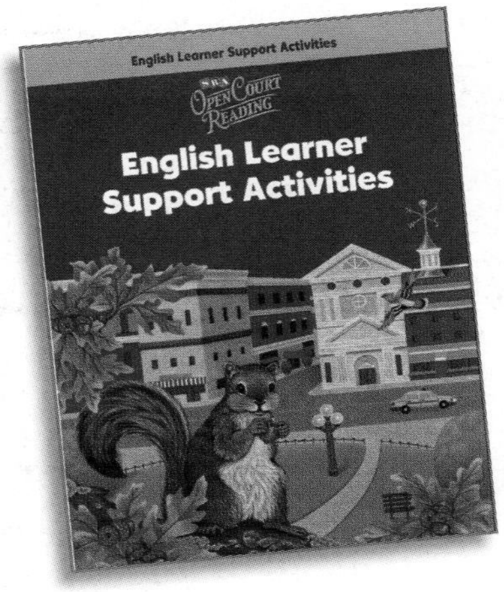

Intervention Workbook

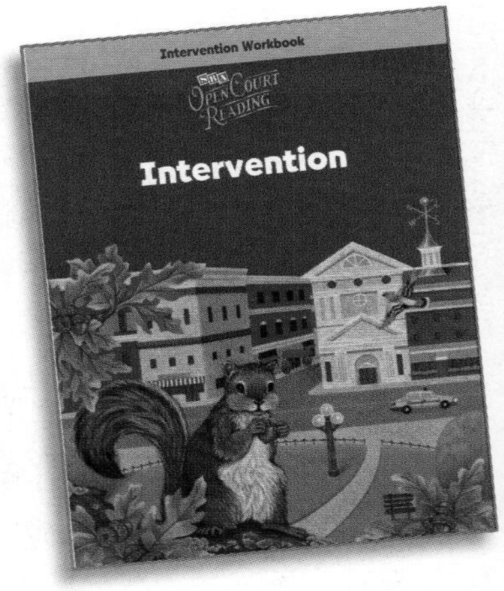

Decodable Book 20

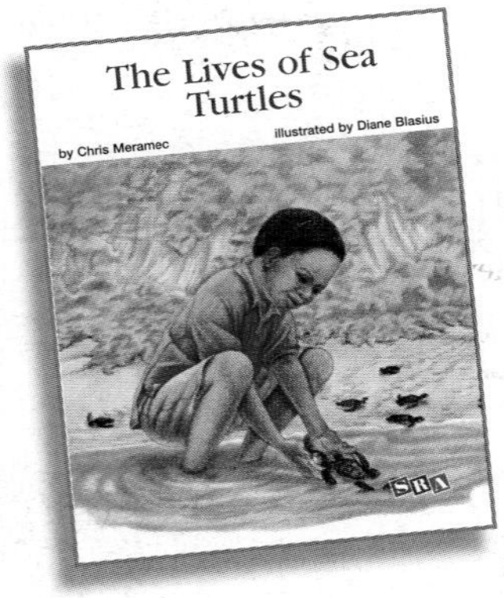

Leveled Classroom Library*

Encourage students to read at least 30 minutes daily outside of class. Have them read books in the ***Leveled Classroom Library*** to support the unit theme and help students develop their vocabulary by reading independently.

Farewell to Shady Glade

BY BILL PEET. HOUGHTON, 1981.

A humorous and unique look at what happens to the wildlife in a place when the bulldozers and city life move in. (Southern California Council on Literature for Children and Young People Award) **(Easy)**

Birds, Nests and Eggs

BY MEL BORING. NORTHWORD, 1998.

Fourteen birds are introduced to young readers through color illustrations, simple descriptions of their songs and nesting habits, and simple facts. **(Average)**

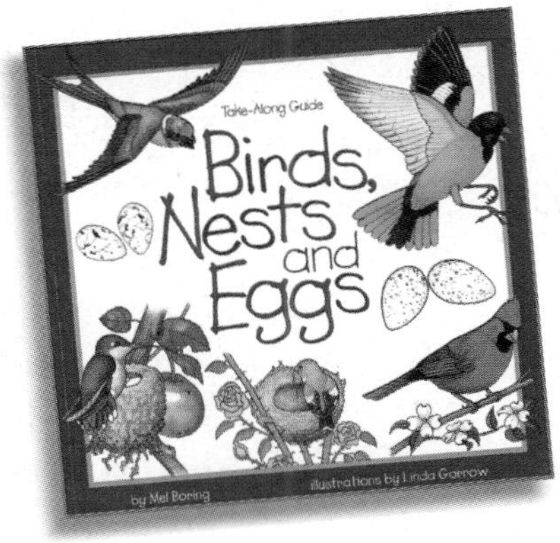

Come Back Salmon: How a Group of Dedicated Kids Adopted Pigeon Creek and Brought It Back to Life

BY MOLLY CONE. SIERRA JUVENILE CLUB, 1994.

Students from Jackson Elementary School in Everett, Washington, adopt a polluted creek, bring it back to life, and preserve it as a place for salmon to spawn. (Outstanding Science Trade Book) **(Advanced)**

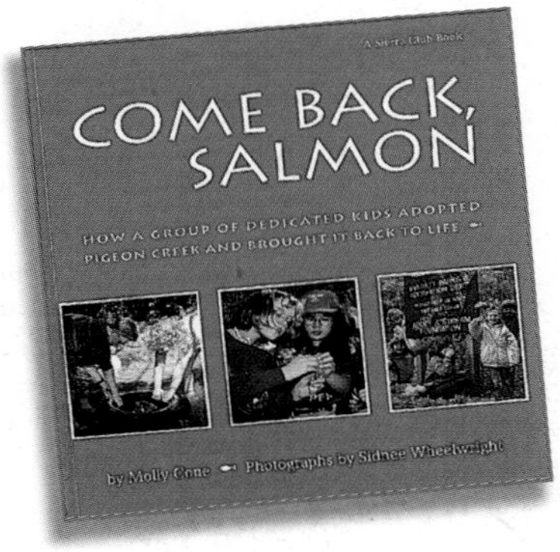

* These books, which all support the unit theme City Wildlife, are part of a 36-book ***Leveled Classroom Library*** available for purchase from SRA/McGraw-Hill. Note: Teachers should preview any trade books for appropriateness in their classrooms before recommending them to students.

SRA TECHNOLOGY

Web Connections

- City Wildlife Web Site
- Online Professional Development
- Online Phonics
- Online Assessment

CD-ROMs

- Research Assistant
- Decodable Book Activities
- Teacher Resource Library

Audiocassettes/CDs

- Listening Library: City Wildlife
- Sound/Spelling Card Stories

Computer Skills

TechKnowledge

Materials are available through SRA/McGraw-Hill.

Set Purposes

Encourage students to set their own purposes for reading. As students read, have them notice what the selection teaches them about city wildlife and how it might answer questions they might have.

Selection Vocabulary

As students study vocabulary, they will use a variety of skills to determine the meaning of a word. These include context clues, word structure, and apposition. Students will apply these same skills while reading to clarify additional unfamiliar words.

Display ***Reading Transparency 13*** before reading the selection to introduce and discuss the following words and their meanings.

abandoned: left behind or unused; either unprotected, unneeded, or unwanted (page 150)

originally: at first, in the beginning (page 151)

species: kind or type of plant or animal that scientists group together because the plants or animals share many of the same characteristics (page 151)

cavity: hollow place or hole (page 151)

suburbs: areas of homes, stores, and businesses that are near or right next to a city or urban area (page 154)

clamor: loud noise, usually for a long time (page 158)

Have students read the words in the word box, stopping to blend any words that they have trouble reading. Demonstrate how to decode multisyllabic words by breaking the words into syllables and blending the syllables. If students still have trouble, refer them to the ***Sound/Spelling Cards.*** If the word is not decodable, give the students the pronunciation. Other words that may be unfamiliar to students should be clarified during reading, with each definition tied to the way that the word is used in the story *(examples: camouflaged, intersection)*. Students can write their definitions in their Writer's Notebooks.

Have students read the sentences on the transparency to determine the meaning of the underlined words. Each word has two sentences that students will read and from which they should be able to derive the meaning of the underlined word. Remind them to use one or more of the skills they have learned—context clues, word structure, or apposition—to figure out the meaning before using a dictionary. Be sure students explain which skills they are using and how they figured out the meanings of the words. Have students reread the sentence, substituting the definition to see if the sentence makes sense. Have a volunteer create a new sentence using the underlined word.

DIFFERENTIATING INSTRUCTION

If...	Then...
Students need extra help with selection vocabulary	Use *Intervention Guide* pages 91–92

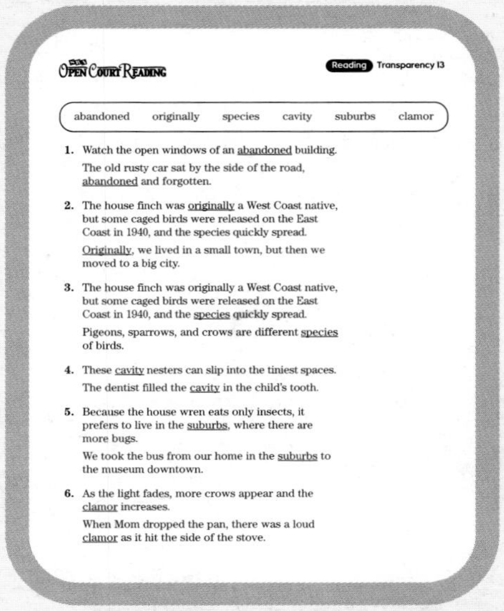

OPEN COURT READING — Reading Transparency 13

abandoned originally species cavity suburbs clamor

1. Watch the open windows of an abandoned building.
   The old rusty car sat by the side of the road, abandoned and forgotten.
2. The house finch was originally a West Coast native, but some caged birds were released on the East Coast in 1940, and the species quickly spread.
   Originally, we lived in a small town, but then we moved to a big city.
3. The house finch was originally a West Coast native, but some caged birds were released on the East Coast in 1940, and the species quickly spread.
   Pigeons, sparrows, and crows are different species of birds.
4. These cavity nesters can slip into the tiniest spaces.
   The dentist filled the cavity in the child's tooth.
5. Because the house wren eats only insects, it prefers to live in the suburbs, where there are more bugs.
   We took the bus from our home in the suburbs to the museum downtown.
6. As the light fades, more crows appear and the clamor increases.
   When Mom dropped the pan, there was a loud clamor as it hit the side of the stove.

Reading Transparency 13

Teacher Tip **SELECTION VOCABULARY** To help students decode words, divide them into syllables when you are saying them, as shown below. The information following each word tells how students can figure out the meaning of each word. When writing words on the board, do not divide them into syllables.

a • ban • doned	context clues
o • rig • i • nal • ly	context clues
spe • cies	context clues
cav • i • ty	context clues
sub • urbs	context clues
clam • or	context clues

Routine Card
Refer to *Routine 3* for the vocabulary procedure.

Differentiating Instruction

Intervention Tip

PREREADING THE SELECTION During Workshop, sit with students who need extra support reading "Urban Roosts" and help them read the story before the whole-class reading.

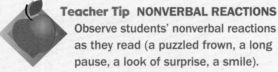

If...	Then...
Students need extra help with clarifying	Use ***Intervention Guide*** pages 92–93
Students need extra help with summarizing	Use ***Intervention Guide*** pages 93–94

Routine Card
Refer to ***Routine 5*** for the procedure on reading the selection.

Teacher Tip **NONVERBAL REACTIONS** Observe students' nonverbal reactions as they read (a puzzled frown, a long pause, a look of surprise, a smile). When you see such reactions, ask students to share their questions and/or comments.

Teacher Tip **COMPREHENSION STRATEGIES** Remind students as they read on the second day to summarize what they learned from the first day.

Reading Recommendations

Oral Reading

Oral reading is suggested, since the selection contains extensive natural science information and vocabulary that may be challenging to the students. Students may also find it helpful to periodically sum up the information in the selection. Use the think-aloud prompts to help students generate their own think-alouds during reading. Students should read aloud fluently with appropriate expression and intonation. Make sure that students attend to punctuation and read in phrases.

Help students make use of the comprehension strategies listed below to help them understand the selection. Have them stop reading periodically or wait until they have completed the selection to discuss the reading strategies. After the students have finished reading the selection, use the Discussing the Selection questions on page 161A to see if they understand what they have read.

Using Comprehension Strategies First Read

Comprehension strategy instruction allows students to become aware of how good readers read. Good readers constantly check their understanding as they are reading and ask themselves questions. In addition, skilled readers recognize when they are having problems and stop to use various comprehension strategies to help them make sense of what they are reading.

During the reading of "Urban Roosts," you will model and prompt the use of the following reading strategies:

- **Monitoring and Clarifying** takes different forms, including clarifying the meaning of words and clarifying difficult ideas or passages. In order to clarify meanings, students can use Context, use Structural Analysis, use Apposition, reread the text, use charts or graphic organizers, or use resources outside of the text.
- **Summarizing** prompts readers to keep track of what they are reading and to focus their minds on important information.
- **Asking Questions** helps readers focus attention on what they are reading and engages them in deeper understanding of themes, concepts, and ideas.

As students read, they should be using a variety of strategies to help them understand the selection. Encourage students to use the strategies listed above as the class reads the story aloud. Do this by stopping at the points indicated by the numbers in the magenta circles on the reduced student page and modeling for the students the use of a particular strategy. Students can also stop reading periodically to discuss what they have learned and what problems they may be having.

Building Comprehension Skills Second Read

Revisiting or rereading a selection allows readers to apply skills that give them a more complete understanding of the text. Some follow-up comprehension skills help students organize information. Others lead to deeper understanding—to "reading between the lines," as mature readers do. In this selection, students will review the following comprehension skill:

Cause and Effect: Readers identify what causes events to happen or what caused characters to behave in certain ways, which helps readers put together logical explanations in the text.

Reading with a Purpose

Have students look for ways birds find homes in cities.

Research in Action

Remember to discuss with the students difficulties that occur during reading. While problems that arise during reading should be addressed as they occur, it is important to reflect on the problems and how they were solved. After reading, have students identify the difficulties. Probe with questions that foster metacognition, or thinking about thinking, such as *What did you find difficult here? How did you try to figure it out? Did that work? What else might work?*
(Michael Pressley)

Teacher Tip Dismiss any preconceived ideas you might have about a selection. Expect the unexpected.

During Workshop, and after the selection has been read at least once, have students listen to the recording of this lesson's selection on the ***Listening Library Audiocassette/CD.*** After students have listened, have them discuss their personal preferences of the selections read. Ask them what other things they have listened to and like to listen to on the radio, on audiocassettes, or on CDs.

Professional Development

Teacher Resource Library CD-ROMs or ***Online Professional Development*** provides courses that help you better understand the Comprehension/Knowledge Building instruction in ***Open Court Reading.*** For more information about this program, visit SRAonline.com.

COMPREHENSION

This selection is broken into two parts. On the first day, read pages 148–154. On the second day, read pages 155–161.

Comprehension Strategies

First Read

Begin prompting students for responses. Praise answers that are appropriate even if they do not match the student sample. This will encourage students to use strategies as they read.

Prompting

1 Monitoring and Clarifying *I'm confused about the meaning of urban roosts. I'll look for clues in the selection and in the illustrations to help me figure out the meaning. I can see that the birds are resting on an arch in the city. I bet I'll find out more clues as I continue to read. What do you think* urban roosts *means? Make sure you clarify any confusing sections while you read.*

Student Samples

2 Monitoring and Clarifying
The word urban *was a vocabulary word for the story "City Critters," so I already know that* urban *means* city. *When I read page 149, I found out that a roost is a place where birds go for shelter. Now I know that urban roosts are the birds' homes in the city.*

Word Knowledge

SCAFFOLDING: The skills students are reviewing in Word Knowledge should help them in reading the story. This lesson focuses on compound words, related words, synonyms, and vivid verbs.

vivid verbs: **rustling**, **stirring**, **flourishes**

First Reading Recommendation

ORAL • CHORAL

Focus Questions Many different species of birds survive in busy cities. How do you think this is possible? Do you think that people or wildlife adapt more easily to their environments? Why?

Urban Roosts
Where Birds Nest in the City

from the book by
Barbara Bash

Early in the morning you can hear something rustling up on the ledge of an old stone building. Even before the city awakens, the birds are stirring in their urban roosts. 1

All across the country, as their natural habitats have been destroyed, birds have moved to town. The ones that have been able to adapt are thriving in the heart of the city.

One familiar urban dweller is the pigeon. Long ago it was called a rock dove, because it lived in the rocky cliffs along the coast of Europe. Today it flourishes all over the United States in the nooks and crannies of our cities.

148

Informal Assessment

Observe individual students as they read and use the Teacher Observation Log, found in the ***Program Assessment Teacher's Edition,*** to record anecdotal information about each student's strengths and weaknesses.

Teacher Tip COMPREHENSION STRATEGIES Let students know that good readers are using Clarifying all the time. Students should use this strategy whenever they read.

To the pigeon, the city may look like a wilderness full of high cliffs and deep canyons. The cliffs are buildings made of stone and brick and glass, and the canyons are windy avenues full of cars and people. Flying together in flocks, pigeons explore the city canyons looking for food and spots to roost.

A roost is a place where birds go for protection when they sleep and for shelter **2** from the rain and cold. Pigeons roost under highway overpasses, on window ledges, under building archways, on top of roofs, and under eaves. Sometimes their roosts are so well hidden you have to watch carefully to find them.

149

Differentiating Instruction

If...	Then...
English Learners need extra help with vocabulary	Use ***English Learner Support Guide*** pages 136–137
English Learners need extra help with cause and effect	Use ***English Learner Support Guide*** pages 137–138

Comprehension Skills

Second Read

Cause and Effect

Review with the students what they know about cause and effect. Remind students that "what happened" in a story is called the effect. Explain that "what prompted it to happen" is called the cause. Tell the students that as they read they must think about what happened in a story and why it happened. Remind students that sometimes we know the effect before we learn the cause. You may want to use an overhead transparency to chart the cause and effect relationships throughout the selection.

- Point out that pigeons fly in flocks, exploring the city as mentioned on page 149. This is "what happened"—the effect.
- Ask the students to find information on page 149 that explains why the pigeons explore the city in flocks *(looking for food and spots to roost)*. This is "why it happened"—the cause.

Word Knowledge

compound words: **highway** **overpasses** **archways**

Skills Trace

Cause and Effect

Introduced in Grade 1.
Scaffolded throughout Grades 2 and 3.

REINTRODUCED: Unit 1, Lesson 2
REINFORCED: Unit 1, Lesson 4
Unit 2, Lesson 4
TESTED: Unit 2, Assessment

Second Reading Recommendation

ORAL • **SILENT**

COMPREHENSION

COMPREHENSION

Comprehension Strategies

First Read

Prompting

3 Monitoring and Clarifying

Does anyone want to clarify something in the selection so far that confuses them? Clarifying helps us to figure out unknown words and phrases. There are a lot of words in this story that may be unfamiliar. Who would like to begin to clarify a confusing word or phrase?

Student Sample

Monitoring and Clarifying *I don't know what* clutch *means. I know you are supposed to look at how the word is used. The story says "...the female sits quietly on her clutch." Then it says that "...after eighteen days, fuzzy chicks begin to appear." The story also talks about pigeons laying eggs and hatching their young. When I put all these clues together, I figured out that* clutch *means "the eggs that the bird sits on and hatches."*

Word Knowledge

vivid verbs: **roosting**
flying

Teacher Tip When a passage is confusing, prompt students to think about whether the meanings of some words are unknown or whether necessary information seems to be missing.

Teacher Tip **MONITORING AND ADJUSTING READING SPEED** Remind students to pay attention to their reading speed, especially with this selection, as it contains challenging natural-science vocabulary.

Look up under the train trestle. Pigeons may be roosting along the dark beams. Watch the open windows of an abandoned building. Hundreds of pigeons could be living inside, flying in and out all day long.

A nest is a place where birds lay their eggs and raise their chicks. Often it's in the same spot as the roost. Pigeons build a flimsy platform of sticks and twigs and debris up on a ledge, or on a windowsill, or in a flowerpot out on a fire escape, or in the curve of a storefront letter.

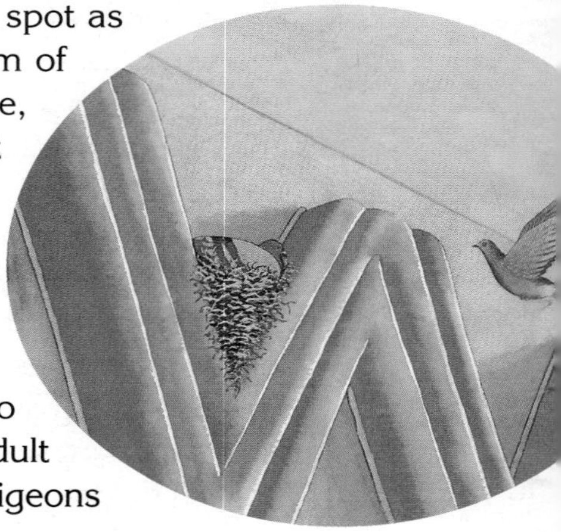

Throughout the year, pigeons lay eggs and hatch their young. The female sits quietly on her clutch, and after
3 eighteen days, fuzzy chicks begin to appear. Five weeks later, after their adult feathers are fully developed, the young pigeons fly away to find homes of their own.

150

Science/Social Studies Connection Center

Refer to the ***Science/Social Studies Connection Center*** Card 12 for a science activity that students can investigate.

Sparrows and finches are successful city dwellers, too. Introduced from England in 1870 to control insects, the house sparrow has chosen to live close to people all across the United States. The house finch was originally a West Coast native, but some caged birds were released on the East Coast in 1940, and the species quickly spread. Sparrows and finches don't migrate, so you can watch them at backyard feeders throughout the year, chirping and chattering as they pick up seeds.

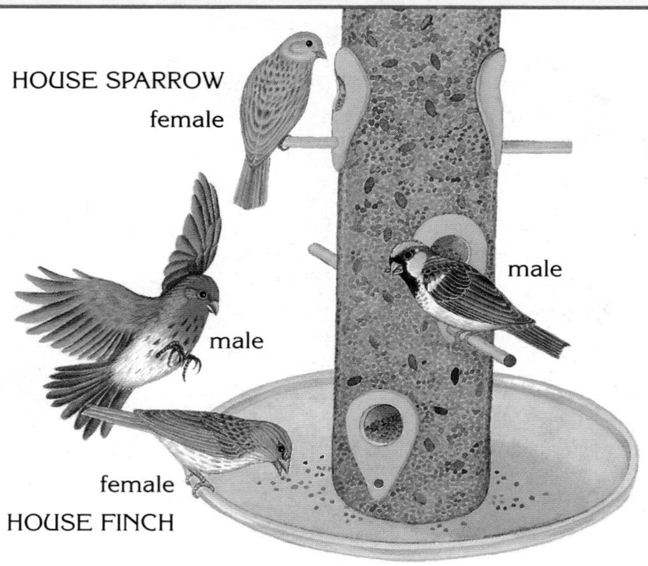

The little hollows in and around building ornaments and Gothic sculptures are favorite nesting spots for sparrows and finches. These cavity nesters can slip into the tiniest spaces. Some of their nests are visible and others are completely hidden from view.

In the spring, you may see a small bird flying overhead with a twig in its beak. If you follow its flight, it will lead you to its nest.

151

COMPREHENSION

Comprehension Skills

Second Read

Cause and Effect

Have students continue to read carefully in order to find out what happened and why it happened. Write the headings *Cause: Why It Happened* and *Effect: What Happened* on the board.

Ask the students to identify information on pages 148–151 that explains cause-and-effect relationships.

Examples include:

Cause	Effect
abandoned building windows left open	*pigeons fly inside to roost*

Cause	Effect
sparrows and finches introduced to America to control insects	*species spread from coast to coast*

Word Knowledge

vivid verbs: **chirping**
chattering

Teacher Tip As students read aloud, listen for appropriate pacing, intonation, and expression.

Differentiating Instruction

If...	Then...
English Learners need extra help with vocabulary	Use ***English Learner Support Guide*** pages 139–140
English Learners need extra help with cause and effect	Use ***English Learner Support Guide*** pages 140–141

Literary Elements

Details

Teach Explain to students that writers make their texts vivid and interesting by carefully choosing the details they add. Details help readers imagine settings and actions, helping them to visualize and understand what they read. Details may take the form of vivid adjectives or verbs or very precise step-by-step instructions. Nonfiction and fiction authors both carefully choose details to help readers connect with the text. Attention to detail can make the difference between a satisfactory piece of writing and a lively, engaging piece of writing.

Guided Practice Invite students to reread "Urban Roosts," paying attention to all the descriptive language, not just the vivid verbs. Ask students to identify details that bring the text to life, and write on the board the words or phrases they suggest. Point out the difference between the vivid language of details, and the ordinary language of stating facts. For example, if students notice "sleekly built with powerful wings," point out that without attention to detail, this phrase might have been, "The thin bird has strong wings," or "soar" might have been "went."

Independent Practice Ask students to look in their ***Writing Folders*** for a piece of writing they would like to revise by adding vivid, descriptive details. Students may wish to share their revised pieces with the class. Encourage students to make note of examples of vivid language in their Writer's Notebooks in the section Identifying the Writer's Craft.

Teacher Tip This study of the literary element Details will help students with their comprehension skills and strategies.

Teacher Tip Ask students to identify other techniques of language a writer might use to engage an audience. *(rhymes, onomatopoeia, choice of vocabulary)*

Teacher Tip MATERIALS
- ✔ poster boards
- ✔ colored pencils or markers

Teacher Tip PURPOSE To learn about how wildlife adapts to change.

Science Connection

Adapting to Change

In "Urban Roosts," students read about different types of birds that live and roost in urban environments. Have students choose one type of urban creature or plant they have observed in the local environment to study. Students should conduct research to explain how the wildlife has changed to survive in its new environment. Point out that insects, for example, adapt rapidly to chemical sprays that are used to destroy them. The same process happens in plants. Some birds' feathers even change color to match the color of smog pollution. What happens to wildlife that does not adapt to change? What happens to wildlife that adapts more quickly than other species?

To present their findings, students should use the given materials to create an artistic representation. This could include making a collage, a mobile, a picture, or a storybook. Encourage the students to attempt a mode of presentation they have not tried before.

Social Studies Connection

Native American Homes

Different birds build different homes and communities in which to live. Just as the kildeer lays its eggs out in the open, without a nest, the peregrine falcon makes a nest up high on the ledge of skyscrapers. People organize themselves in the same way, adapting to their environment. Explain that now this is harder to see in our country due to technology. But this idea is best evidenced with the indigenous Native American tribes throughout the country. Their homes, clothing, and cultural traditions differed greatly, depending on the resources available, climate, and lay of the land.

Assign groups of students different regions of the Unites States, including the local region, and have the students research the homes in which the Native Americans lived. Have them find the reasons for the style of home; for example, the teepee was used as a temporary lodging for more nomadic tribes. The students should draw pictures or make models of their researched area's homes. The researched information should be presented to the class, but could also be displayed on a board for students to investigate at a later time.

Teacher Tip MATERIALS

- ✔ paper
- ✔ colored pencils

Teacher Tip PURPOSE To show that both people and animals adapt to their environment, including explaining how the environment dictates human lives and activities.

Concept Connections

Linking the Selection

- Birds that roost in high cliffs away from the city choose high buildings and bridges. Ground-nesting birds choose flat rooftops.
- They provide the birds with shelter.

Exploring Concept Vocabulary

The concept word for this lesson is ***shelter.*** Write it on the board. Work with students to develop a definition that clearly links to the unit theme. Have students copy the word and definition into the Vocabulary section of their Writer's Notebooks.

Shelter: a place that covers and protects someone or something from danger. For example, some birds find shelter in crevices under train trestles.

- City wildlife needs to be protected from things that might harm it.
- The birds found shelter under highway overpasses, in traffic lights, and behind roof tiles.

Each student should create a sentence using the word ***shelter*** and one of the selection vocabulary words. The sentence should demonstrate the student's understanding of the words.

Expanding the Concept

You may want to do a whole-group discussion to help students continue to develop their ability to engage in meaningful dialogue. However, students may conduct these dialogues in small groups. If students work in small groups, bring the groups together and have them share their ideas with the whole class.

As students complete their discussions, have them record their ideas and impressions about the selection on page 30 of their ***Inquiry Journals.***

Urban Roosts

Where Birds Nest in the City

Concept Connections

Linking the Selection

Writer's Notebook

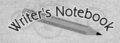

Think about the following questions, and then record your responses in the Response Journal section of your Writer's Notebook.

- How are the birds' homes in the city like the homes they would have away from the city?
- Why are these similarities important?

Exploring Concept Vocabulary

The concept word for this lesson is ***shelter.*** If you do not know what this word means, look it up in a dictionary. Answer these questions:

- Why is it important for city wildlife to have ***shelter?***
- What kinds of ***shelter*** did the birds find in the city?

In the Vocabulary section of your Writer's Notebook, write a sentence that includes the word ***shelter*** and one of the selection vocabulary words.

Expanding the Concept

Think about the city wildlife in the selection "City Critters." How are the birds in "Urban Roosts" similar to other city wildlife?

Try to use the word ***shelter*** in your discussion about the similarities.

Add new ideas about city wildlife to the Concept/Question Board.

162

Informal Assessment

This may be a good time to observe students working in small groups and to mark your observations in the Teacher Observation Log found in the *Program Assessment Teacher's Edition.*

Teacher Tip CONCEPT VOCABULARY Developing a repertoire of concept-related vocabulary will help students deepen their understanding of theme concepts, help facilitate class discussions, and help students formulate ideas, problems, and questions for inquiry.

Meet the Author and Illustrator

Barbara Bash began her love of art through her love of letters. *"My first connection to art and creativity was through the alphabet. I loved to draw the twenty-six letters. All through elementary school I experimented with their forms constantly."* Her love for art and letters led her to study calligraphy, the art of making fancy letters. From there, she went on to study nature and began learning how to draw it. Her love of nature gave her the desire to create books for children.

Before she writes a book, she learns everything she can about the subject through books, photographs, and films. Then she travels to the area where she can watch the subject. She has gone to Arizona to learn about the cactus and to East Africa to learn about the baobab tree. For this book, Barbara Bash walked through New York City to find where birds make their nests in the city.

163

Meet the Author/Illustrator

After students have read about Barbara Bash, discuss the following questions with them:

- When Barbara Bash set out to illustrate a story about birds in a city environment, she traveled to New York to get ideas for her illustrations. Looking at the pictures in "Urban Roosts," point out examples of how this practice of researching a topic before drawing it enabled Bash to better illustrate the story. *(Answers will vary, but students might focus on the skyscrapers, architectural details, and city skyline that seems to reflect a firsthand view of New York City.)*
- Barbara Bash first learned to draw letters, then worked at creating fancy lettering, called calligraphy, and finally decided to try writing and illustrating books for children. How do you think spending so much time learning to carefully letter the alphabet may have helped Bash be a better illustrator? *(Answers may vary, but students might comment that carefully lettering the alphabet may have taught Bash to pay close attention to detail.)*

Differentiating Instruction

If...	Then...
Students enjoyed reading "Urban Roosts: Where Birds Nest in the City"	Encourage them to browse or read Barbara Bash's other nature books such as *Desert Giant: The World of the Saguaro Cactus* and *Tree of Life: The World of the African Baobab*

Objectives

- Students learn about the different types of wildlife that live in cities.
- Students will gain a deeper understanding of issues related to city wildlife.
- Student groups revise plans as necessary and continue investigating.
- Students learn about the different parts of a book.

Materials

- Student Anthology, Book 1, pp. 148–165
- Inquiry Journal, pp. 44–47
- Research Assistant CD-ROM

Teacher Tip To complete the supplementary activity, students might need to combine first-hand observation with investigating. Take this opportunity to review the terms *primary* and *secondary* sources.

INVESTIGATION

Investigating Concepts Beyond the Text

Student groups should be entering "Needs and Plans Phase 2." During this phase, meet with investigation groups to discuss difficulties they are having and to help them revise their investigation problems, conjectures, needs, or plans, if necessary. Make sure students are identifying investigation needs related to their conjectures. Some groups may have discovered by this time that their problem is not very promising. Remind groups that they can still change their investigation problems and questions. Some groups may choose to keep the same general problem but reformulate it more precisely. Additionally, some students might wish to change groups because they have become more interested in the problem of another group. Remember that these revision discussions have no specific agenda, but are open to anything that needs changing. There must, however, be a reason for changing. New facts, new insights, or new inferences may be the basis for various revisions.

After reading "Urban Roosts," discuss with students what different animals look for in their urban habitat. It would be helpful to have students pinpoint locations on a map designating different biomes in which animals live. Then have students explain how the urban habitat has similar features to the biomes. Ask students to find passages in the selection that discuss specifically what interests different types of birds. For example, the author mentions that pigeons choose buildings that might remind them of cliffs and canyons, and the snowy owl chooses airport landing fields perhaps because they are similar to the tundra landscape. Student groups might wish to compare the natural habitat with the urban habitat some wildlife has chosen. Students can use the chart on page 44 of the ***Inquiry Journal*** to help them organize information. Tell students that they may want to return to this chart as they proceed with their investigations.

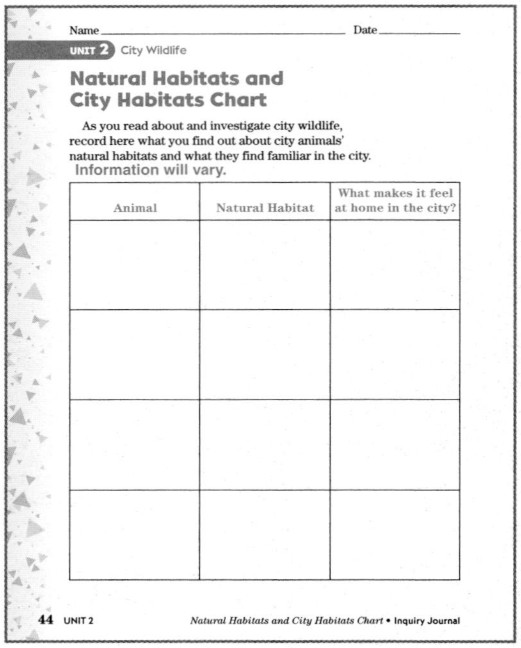

Name ______________ Date ______

UNIT 2 City Wildlife

Natural Habitats and City Habitats Chart

As you read about and investigate city wildlife, record here what you find out about city animals' natural habitats and what they find familiar in the city.

Information will vary.

Animal	Natural Habitat	What makes it feel at home in the city?

44 UNIT 2 *Natural Habitats and City Habitats Chart* • Inquiry Journal

Inquiry Journal p. 44

Concept/Question Board

After reading each selection, students should use the Concept/Question Board to:

- Post any questions they asked about a selection before reading that have not been answered yet.
- Refer to as they formulate statements about concepts that apply to their investigations.
- Post general statements formulated by each collaborative group.
- Continue to post news articles or other items that they find during the unit investigation.
- Read and think about posted questions, articles, or concepts that interest them and provide answers to the questions.

Unit 2 Investigation Management

Lesson 1	Introduce investigation possibilities. Groups form and brainstorm initial plans. Plans are presented to the whole class and discussed. Groups can take a neighborhood tour to identify city wildlife.
Lesson 2	Groups refine problems and form conjectures. Students can invite an expert to class.
Lesson 3	Groups create investigation plans, assign tasks, and begin investigation. Groups can hold a discussion about the benefits and dangers of city living.
Lesson 4	**Collaborative Investigation** **Groups revise plans and continue investigation.** **Supplementary Activity** **Groups can compare urban and natural animal habitat.**
Lesson 5	Groups present informal presentations, make necessary revisions, and continue investigation. Groups can investigate and lead a panel discussion on the issue of disappearing natural habitat and how wildlife is affected.
Lesson 6	Groups make final preparations and presentation of findings. Groups can create a proposal for protecting wildlife in urban areas.

INVESTIGATION

Research Assistant

The *Research Assistant CD-ROM* can assist students in their investigations.

Teacher Tip For information regarding humane and environmental issues, contact the National Association for Humane and Environmental Education, the Youth Education Division of The Humane Society of the United States. This association offers resources for classroom teachers and educators to teach the value of, and respect for, animals and our natural environment.

Teacher Tip Remind students of the recursive nature of the investigation process. Students will be continually finding and discussing new information and revising questions and conjectures. Their readings, activities, and research will assist them as they continue through the investigation cycle.

Formal Assessment

Use the Research Rubrics on page 148J to assess students' ability to recognize information needs.

INVESTIGATION

Needs and Plans Phase 2

During this phase, conduct whole-class discussion to help you determine which groups are having trouble identifying knowledge needs related to their conjectures. You might need to direct them to resources that best answer their questions and help them use these books effectively. (See page 163D, Parts of a Book.) You might also need to assist groups that have decided to reformulate their problem.

During Workshop, groups can meet to make revisions to their research problem, identification of knowledge needs, and individual job assignments. As you observe the groups making final job assignments, have students take on tasks that are related to their strengths and preferences. For example, a student who loves to draw might particularly enjoy planning and making the visual portion of the investigation or examining photographs, illustrations, and diagrams for useful information. Groups can use ***Inquiry Journal,*** page 45, to help them keep track of their revisions.

Name ______________________ Date ________

City Wildlife UNIT 2

Research Cycle: Needs and Plans Phase 2

Our problem: Answers will vary.

____

____

Knowledge Needs—Information we need to find or figure out in order to help investigate the problem:

A. Answers will vary.

B. ______________________

C. ______________________

D. ______________________

E. ______________________

F. ______________________

Group Members	Main Jobs

Hint: To save rewriting Knowledge Needs in the Main Jobs section, write the capital letter marking the Knowledge Need line on the Main Job line.

Inquiry Journal • *Research Cycle: Needs and Plans Phase 2* UNIT 2 45

Inquiry Journal p. 45

Parts of a Book (Index)

Teach Ask students to tell what they know about using an index. Review the following points:

- An index is an alphabetical list of key words and topics.
- A topic may have a subtopic.
- An index may refer readers to other topics.
- Each key word may reference one or more pages.

Guided Practice Have students refer to the index on page 46 of their ***Inquiry Journal.*** Ask students the following questions:

- Is there a listing in the index for pigeons? *(yes)*
- What are the subtopics under *pigeon? (babies, calls, descriptions, in the city, mating, nests)*
- On what pages would you find information about pigeon babies? *(pages 49–50)*
- What topics does the index refer you to under the topic *Pigeons? (dove, passenger pigeon, racing pigeon)*

For additional practice with indexes, have students complete ***Inquiry Journal,*** pages 46–47.

Independent Practice Instruct students to use indexes for any research they are doing involving books. Using the index will help them quickly find the specific information they need. In addition, checking the index of a book can help them decide whether it will be useful in their investigations.

Name________________ Date________

UNIT 2 City Wildlife

Using an Index

This is a page from the index of a book called *Finding Out About Our Feathered Friends.* Use it to answer the questions on the next page.

Using an Index *(continued)*

1. How many topics are there that start with the letter *O*? 3
   What are they? Oriole, Osprey, Owl
2. On which pages can you find information about *Parrots*? 18, 19, 20
3. What subtopics are listed under *Parakeet*? and learning, caring for
4. What specific types of Owls does the index refer you to under the topic *Owls*? Barn owl, Great horned owl
5. Is there a listing in the index for *Ravens*? yes
6. On which pages can you find information about *Materials for Nests*? 32–35, 38, 50
7. On which page can you find a description of a *Pelican*? 115
8. On which pages can you find information about the *National Audubon Society*? 3, 14, 79, 85

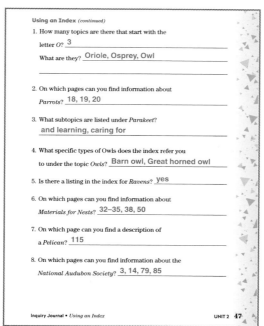

Inquiry Journal pp. 46–47

SUPPORTING THE INVESTIGATION

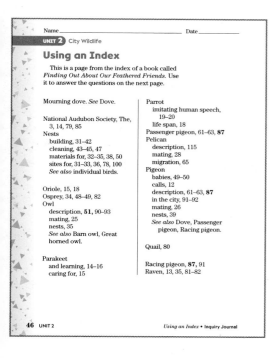

Teacher Tip Encourage the students to comment on one another's ideas.

DIFFERENTIATING INSTRUCTION

If...	Then...
Students are having difficulty understanding and using an index	• Help them with ***Inquiry Journal*** pages 46–47 during Workshop • Provide additional examples of indexes for them to explore

Presentation

Phrasing

Poetry is a special kind of writing that is often best experienced aloud. Poets play with sounds, rhythm, and phrasing to create a mood or communicate a message. Reading poetry aloud gives students the opportunity to experiment with phrasing. Phrasing can affect which parts of the poem stand out and which ones flow into the next.

Read the poem aloud for students. This time, draw their attention to how one phrase flows to the next and where the short and long pauses occur. Read smoothly through the lines, pausing at commas and stopping at periods. Demonstrate how different the poem sounds when a long pause is inserted at the end of each line.

Allow students to practice phrasing. Volunteers may wish to try reading one of these two poems aloud for the class. Encourage students to read other poems to the class as well. They can read one of their own, or they can choose from books in the classroom or school library. Students might wish to practice phrasing during Workshop, working with a partner.

DIFFERENTIATING INSTRUCTION

If...	Then...
Students need help building fluency	Have them preview the poems to find punctuation that identifies places they should slow down, show emotion, or stop

Focus Questions How do you think deer find their way into the city? What can be done to protect the deer in the city?

Two Days in May

Harriet Peck Taylor
illustrated by Leyla Torres

Early one Saturday morning in May, I went to our fire escape window and rubbed the sleep from my eyes. I looked down at the small garden I had planted behind our apartment building. Five animals were grazing on the new lettuce in my garden!

"Mama! Mama!" I called. "Come see what's in our yard!"

Mama hurried over to the window and gasped. "Sonia, those animals are deer, but how did they get here?" she asked. "I'll run and tell Mr. Donovan."

166

SELECTION INTRODUCTION

Selection Summary

Genre: Realistic Fiction

"Two Days in May," is the story of an urban community that comes together out of a common desire to protect wildlife. All the neighbors were touched by this unexpected encounter with wildlife, threatened by rapidly disappearing habitats and forced into the city to look for food. Although this story is based on a real event (Chicago, 1996), the author depicts a fictional account here. The characters, point of view, and dialogue, though based on fact, come from the writer's imagination.

Some elements of realistic fiction include:

- The characters behave as people do in real life.
- The setting of the story is a real place or could be a real place.
- The events in the story could happen in real life.

About the Author

HARRIET PECK TAYLOR incorporates different Native American legends into many of her stories. She has used Anasazi rock art; Siksika, Wasco, Tewa, and Seneca legends; and regionalism to inform her readers of the different ways of life across the country. Often using animals as the central characters, Taylor shows the struggle between nature and environment in her stories, such as "Two Days in May."

Students can read more about the author on page 181 of their ***Student Anthologies.***

About the Illustrator

LEYLA TORRES was raised in Bogota, Colombia. While her parents ran a local elementary school, Torres entertained herself by painting, reading, and creating rag dolls. As she studied fine arts at the university, Torres was surprised to learn that drawing anything well took a lot of practice and patience. Now she lives in New York City with her husband. She has won the 1999 Parents Choice Recommendation for her illustrations in *Subway Sparrow*. Other works include: *Saturday Sancocho* and *Liliana's Grandmothers*.

Students can read more about the illustrator on page 181 of their ***Student Anthologies.***

Inquiry Connections

This story illustrates how people can help wildlife in urban surroundings. The story characters also serve as examples of how to react to wildlife when we encounter it—with gentleness, respect, and protectiveness. The story shows the relationships and interactions between wildlife and people in ever-expanding urban settings. It also demonstrates how wildlife is affected by the rapidly expanding development of wild areas.

- Sometimes wildlife needs the help of people to survive.
- Rapidly expanding urban areas threaten wildlife habitat.
- Efforts to protect wildlife help not only the wildlife, but also the community of people involved in the effort.
- Sometimes, simple acts are all that is necessary to make a big difference in protecting wildlife.

Before reading the selection:

- Point out that students may post a question, concept, word, illustration, or object on the Concept/Question Board at any time during the course of their unit investigation. Be sure that students include their name or initials on the items they post so that others will know whom to go to if they have an answer or if they wish to collaborate on a related activity.
- Students should feel free to write an answer or a note on someone else's question or to consult the Board for ideas for their own investigations throughout the unit.
- Encourage students to read about city wildlife at home and to bring in articles or pictures that are good examples to post on the Board.

Concept/Question Board

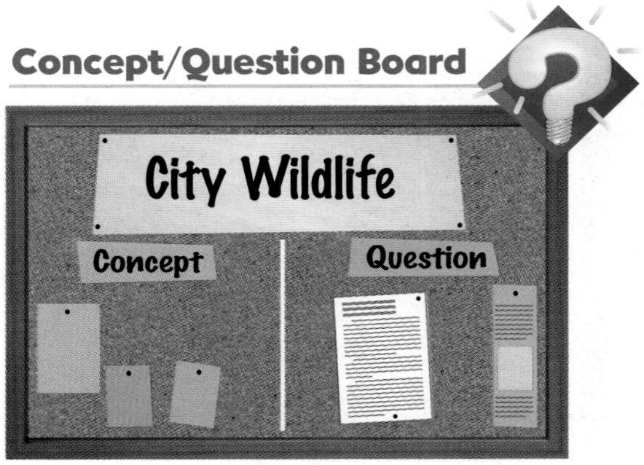

Leveled Practice

Reteach
Pages 49–54

Challenge
Pages 44–48

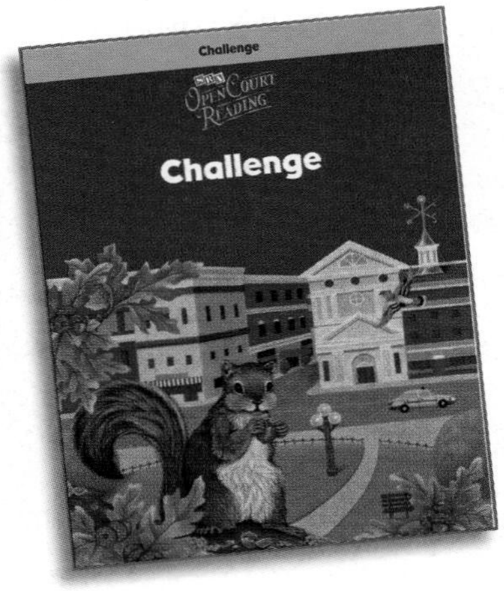

English Learner Support Activities

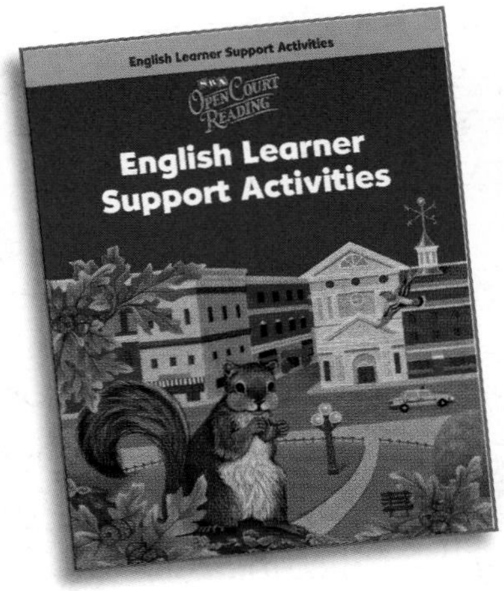

Intervention Workbook

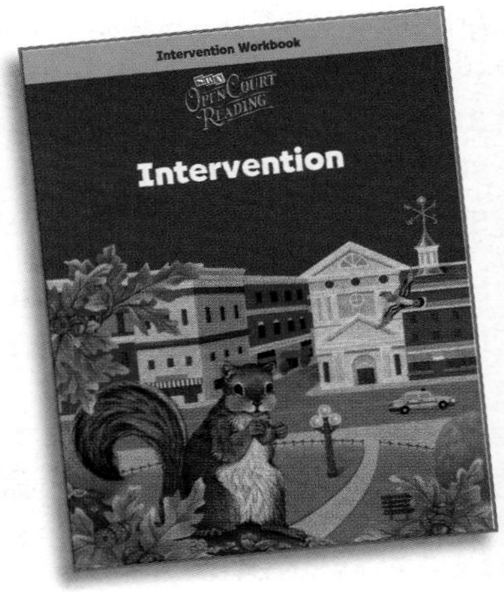

Decodable Book 21

Leveled Classroom Library*

Encourage students to read at least 30 minutes daily outside of class. Have them read books in the ***Leveled Classroom Library*** to support the unit theme and help students develop their vocabulary by reading independently.

Wild in the City

BY JAN THORNHILL. FIREFLY, 1999.

The wild animals in Jenny's backyard must work diligently to find food and raise their young while Jenny sleeps soundly. **(Easy)**

City Park

BY WENDY DAVIS. CHILDREN'S PRESS, 1997.

Amidst the skyscrapers, cars, buses, machinery, and bustling people of a city lives a very different environment. The city park is alive with trees, birds, animals, and human visitors. This colorful and informative book gives students a close-up look at the habitat of a city park. **(Average)**

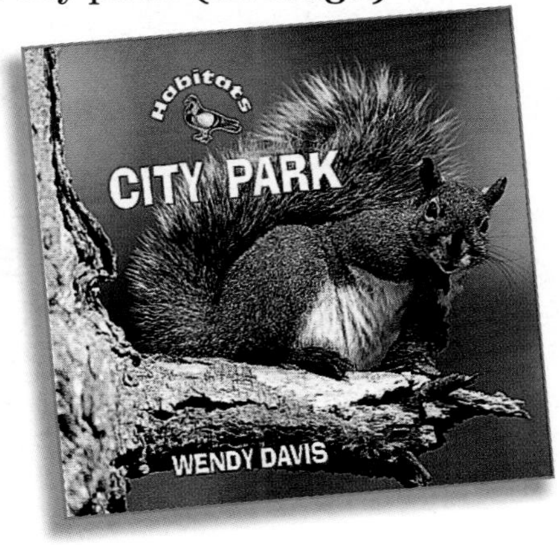

Coyotes in the Crosswalk: True Tales of Animal Life in the Wilds of the City

BY DIANE SWANSON. VOYAGEUR, 1995.

Covering 10 North American animals, this exploration covers the adaptation these animals have developed to ensure survival in the city. (Orbis Pictus Award for outstanding children's nonfiction) **(Challenge)**

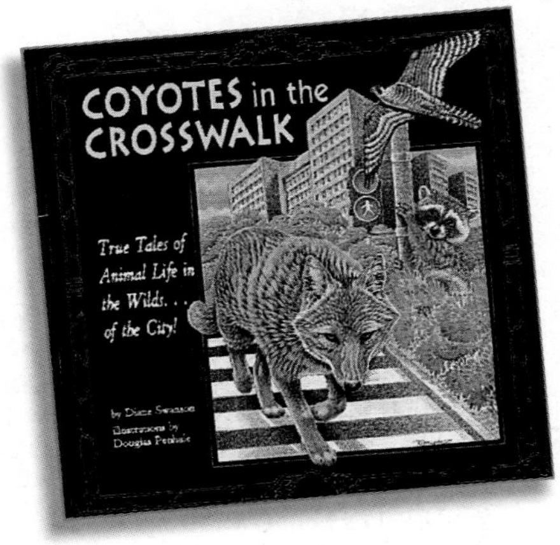

* These books, which all support the unit theme City Wildlife, are part of a 36-book ***Leveled Classroom Library*** available for purchase from SRA/McGraw-Hill. Note: Teachers should preview any trade books for appropriateness in their classrooms before recommending them to students.

SRA TECHNOLOGY

Web Connections

- City Wildlife Web Site
- Online Professional Development
- Online Phonics
- Online Assessment

CD-ROMs

- Research Assistant
- Decodable Book Activities
- Teacher Resource Library

Audiocassettes/CDs

- Listening Library: City Wildlife
- Sound/Spelling Card Stories

Computer Skills

TechKnowledge

Materials are available through SRA/McGraw-Hill.

Suggested Pacing: 3–5 days

LESSON PLANNER	DAY 1	DAY 2
	DAY 1	DAY 2
1 Preparing to Read **Materials** ■ Student Anthology, Book 1, pp. 166–181 ■ Decodable Book Activities CD-ROM ■ Sound/Spelling Cards ■ Decodable Book 21 ■ Routine Cards 1, 3, Routines 1–2, 8–9	**Word Knowledge, p. 166K** ■ contractions ■ suffix *-ing* and *-ly* ■ prefix *un-* ■ /oi/ spelled *_oy* and *oi* **About the Words and Sentences, p. 166K**	**Developing Oral Language, p. 166L**
2 Reading & Responding **Materials** ■ Student Anthology, Book 1, pp. 166–181 ■ Program Assessment ■ Reading Transparencies 14, 46, 50 ■ Inquiry Journal, p. 31 ■ Home Connection, p. 25 ■ Writer's Notebook ■ Unit 2 Assessment Guide, pp. 18–21 ■ Comprehension and Language Arts Skills, pp. 46–47 ■ Routine Cards 1–2, Routines 3–6 ■ Science/Social Studies Connections Center Cards 14, 15	**Build Background, p. 166O** **Preview and Prepare, pp. 166O–166P** **Selection Vocabulary, p. 166P** **Reading Recommendations, pp. 166Q–166R** **Student Anthology, pp. 166–172** First Read ✓**Comprehension Strategies** ■ Asking Questions pp. 166, 170 ■ Making Connections, p. 168 ■ Summarizing, p. 172	**Student Anthology, pp. 173–179** First Read **Comprehension Strategies** ■ Making Connections, p. 174 ■ Asking Questions, p. 176 ■ Summarizing, p. 178 **Discussing Strategy Use, p. 178** **Discussing the Selection, p. 179A** ■ Review Selection ■ Complete Discussion ✓**Concept Connections, p. 180** **Meet the Author/Illustrator, p. 181**
Inquiry **Materials** ■ Student Anthology, Book 1, pp. 166–181 ■ Inquiry Journal, pp. 48–50 ■ Research Assistant CD-ROM	✓**Investigation** ■ Investigating Concepts Beyond the Text: Reevaluating Problems and Questions, p. 181A	**Investigation** ■ Concept/Question Board, p. 181B
3 Language Arts **Materials** ■ Student Anthology, Book 1, pp. 166–181 ■ Comprehension and Language Arts Skills, pp. 46–51 ■ Language Arts Handbook ■ Language Arts Transparencies 10, 17 ■ Sound/Spelling Card 43 ■ Spelling and Vocabulary Skills, pp. 42–45 ■ The Ultimate Writing and Creativity Center ■ Writer's Workbook, pp. 22–25	**Word Analysis** ✓■ Spelling: The /oi/ Sound Pretest, p. 181F **Writing Process Strategies** ■ Expository Writing: Explaining a Process, p. 181F **English Language Conventions** ■ Mechanics: Question Marks and Exclamation Points, p. 181F	**Word Analysis** ■ Spelling: The /oi/ Sound, p. 181G ■ Vocabulary: Homophones, p. 181G **Writing Process Strategies** ■ Expository Writing: Explaining a Process, p. 181G **Writer's Craft** ■ Purpose and Audience, p. 181G **English Language Conventions** ■ Mechanics: Question Marks and Exclamation Points, p. 181G

Ⓟ Phonics ✓Informal Assessment Available ✓Formal Assessment Available

DAY 2 continued	DAY 3	
DAY 3	**DAY 4**	**DAY 5**
Ⓟ **Phonics & Fluency,** p. 166M ■ /le/ spelled *le* with long and short vowels **About the Words and Sentences,** p. 166M	**Developing Oral Language,** p. 166N **Dictation,** p. 166N	**Review Word Knowledge and Phonics**
Student Anthology, pp. 166–172 Second Read **Comprehension Skills** ■ Cause and Effect, pp. 167, 169, 171 **Supporting the Reading,** pp. 179C–179D ■ Cause and Effect	**Student Anthology,** pp. 173–179 Second Read **Comprehension Skills** ■ Cause and Effect, pp. 173, 175, 177, 179 **Checking Comprehension,** p. 179 **Review Selection Vocabulary,** p. 179B **Literary Elements,** p. 179E ■ Setting	✓ **Selection Assessment** ■ "Two Days in May," pp. 18–21 **Home Connection,** p. 179B **Social Studies Connection** ■ Making Laws, p. 179F
Investigation ✓■ Revise Conjectures, p. 181C	**Supporting the Investigation** ■ Note Taking, p. 181D	**Investigation** ■ Unit Investigation Continued ■ Update Concept/Question Board
Word Analysis ■ Spelling:The /oi/ Sound, p. 181H ■ Vocabulary: Homophones, p. 181H **Writing Process Strategies** ■ Expository Writing: Explaining a Process, p. 181H **English Language Conventions** ✓■ Mechanics: Question Marks and Exclamation Points, p. 181H	**Word Analysis** ■ Spelling:The /oi/ Sound, p. 181I ■ Vocabulary: Homophones, p. 181I **Writing Process Strategies** ■ Expository Writing: Explaining a Process, p. 181I **English Language Conventions** ✓■ Listening, Speaking, Viewing Interacting: Asking Questions, p. 181I	**Word Analysis** ✓■ Spelling: The /oi/ Sound Final Test ✓■ Vocabulary: Homophones, p. 181J **Writing Process Strategies** ✓■ Expository Writing: Explaining a Process, p. 181J **English Language Conventions** ✓■ Penmanship: Cursive Letters *h* and *k*, p. 181J

Below are suggestions for differentiating instruction. These are the same skills shown in the Lesson Planner; however, these pages provide extra practice opportunities or enriching activities to meet the varied needs of students.

WORKSHOP

Differentiating Instruction

Teacher Directed: Individual and Small-Group Instruction

Spend time each day with individuals and small groups to individualize instruction. Each day:

- preteach students who need help with the next lesson.
- reteach students who need to solidify their understanding of content previously taught.
- listen to students read to check their fluency.
- hold writing and inquiry conferences.

Use the following program components to support instruction:

- ***Reteach*** with students who need a bit more practice
- ***Intervention*** for students who exhibit a lack of understanding of the lesson concepts
- ***English Learner Support*** with students who need language help

Student: Independent Activities

Students can work alone, with a partner, or in small groups on such activities as:

- Review sound/spellings
- Practice dictation words
- Partner reading
- Practice fluency
- Independent reading
- Reading Roundtable
- Concept vocabulary
- Selection vocabulary
- Writing in progress
- Conference
- Language Arts
- Challenge activities
- Inquiry and Investigation activities
- Listening Library
- Online Phonics

For Workshop Management Tips, see Appendix pages 41–42.

	DAY I
Decoding/ Word Knowledge	**Teacher Directed** ▪ Blending: Contractions, ***Intervention Guide,*** p. 98
Fluency	**Independent Activities** ▪ Self-test fluency rate ▪ Oral reading of selection for fluency
Comprehension	**Teacher Directed** ▪ Preteach "Two Days in May," ***Intervention Guide,*** pp. 100–101 ▪ Preteach Intervention Selection One, ***Intervention Guide,*** pp. 101–102 ▪ ***English Learner Support Guide*** • Vocabulary, pp. 150–151 • Comprehension Skill: Cause and Effect, pp. 151–153 **Independent Activities** ▪ Browse ***Leveled Classroom Library*** ▪ Add vocabulary in Writer's Notebook
Inquiry	**Teacher Directed** ▪ Reevaluating Problems and Questions, p. 181A **Independent Activities** ▪ Concept/Question Board ▪ Explore OCR Web site for theme connections ▪ Disappearing Habitat Chart, ***Inquiry Journal,*** p. 48
Language Arts	**Teacher Directed** ▪ Grammar, Usage, and Mechanics, ***Intervention Guide,*** p. 104 **Independent Activities** ▪ Question Marks and Exclamation Points, ***Comprehension and Language Arts Skills,*** pp. 48–49

DAY 2	DAY 3	DAY 4	DAY 5
Teacher Directed ▪ Developing Oral Language, ***Intervention Guide,*** p. 98	**Teacher Directed** ▪ Dictation and Spelling: Contractions, ***Intervention Guide,*** pp. 98–99 **Independent Activities** ▪ ***Online Phonics***	**Teacher Directed** ▪ Blending: Final *-le*, ***Intervention Guide,*** p. 99 **Independent Activities** ▪ Read ***Decodable Book 21,*** *Nesting and Burrowing Birds*	**Teacher Directed** ▪ Developing Oral Language, ***Intervention Guide,*** p. 99 ▪ Dictation and Spelling: Final *-le*, ***Intervention Guide,*** pp. 99–100
Independent Activities ▪ Oral reading of "Two Days in May" for fluency ▪ Partner reading	**Independent Activities** ▪ Partner reading of selection	**Independent Activities** ▪ Reread "Two Days in May" ▪ Partner read ***Decodable Book 21,*** *Nesting and Burrowing Birds*	**Teacher Directed** ▪ Repeated Readings/Fluency Check, ***Intervention Guide,*** p. 103 **Independent Activities** ▪ Reread ***Decodable Book 21***
Teacher Directed ▪ Preteach "Two Days in May," ***Intervention Guide,*** pp. 100–101 ▪ Comprehension Strategies, ***Intervention Guide,*** p. 102 ▪ Reread Intervention Selection One, ***Intervention Guide,*** pp. 101–102 ▪ ***English Learner Support Guide*** • Vocabulary, pp. 153–155 • Comprehension Skill: Cause and Effect, pp. 154–156 ▪ Discuss Concept Connections, p. 180 **Independent Activities** ▪ Independent reading ▪ Record response to selection in Writer's Notebook ▪ ***Listening Library Audiocassette/CD***	**Teacher Directed** ▪ Reread "Two Days in May," ***Intervention Guide,*** pp. 100–101 ▪ Preteach Intervention Selection Two, ***Intervention Guide,*** pp. 102–103 ▪ ***English Learner Support Guide*** • Vocabulary, pp. 156–158 • Comprehension Skill: Cause and Effect, pp. 157–159 ▪ Cause and Effect, ***Reteach,*** pp. 49–50 **Independent Activities** ▪ Read ***Leveled Classroom Library*** book ▪ Complete Link to Writing in Supporting the Reading, p. 179D ▪ Cause and Effect • ***Comprehension and Language Arts Skills,*** pp. 46–47 • ***Challenge,*** p. 44	**Teacher Directed** ▪ Reread "Two Days in May," ***Intervention Guide,*** pp. 100–101 ▪ Comprehension Strategies, ***Intervention Guide,*** p. 103 ▪ Reread Intervention Selection Two, ***Intervention Guide,*** pp. 102–103 ▪ ***English Learner Support Guide*** • Vocabulary, pp. 159–160 • Comprehension Skill: Cause and Effect, pp. 160–161 **Independent Activities** ▪ Independent reading ▪ Add words to Word Bank ▪ Complete Independent Practice in Literary Elements, p. 179E ▪ ***English Learner Support Activities,*** p. 21	**Teacher Directed** ▪ ***English Learner Support Guide*** • Review Vocabulary, p. 162 • Comprehension Skill: Cause and Effect, pp. 162–163 **Independent Activities** ▪ Read ***Leveled Classroom Library*** book as independent reading ▪ Reading Roundtable ▪ Social Studies Connection, p. 179F ▪ ***English Learner Support Activities,*** p. 22
Independent Activities ▪ Concept/Question Board ▪ Use ***Research Assistant CD-ROM*** to continue investigation	**Independent Activities** ▪ Concept/Question Board ▪ Explore OCR Web site for theme connections ▪ Revising Conjectures, p. 181C	**Independent Activities** ▪ Concept/Question Board ▪ Complete Independent Practice in Supporting the Investigation, p. 181D ▪ Note-Taking Guidelines, ***Inquiry Journal,*** pp. 49–50	**Independent Activities** ▪ Concept/Question Board ▪ Use ***Research Assistant CD-ROM*** to continue investigation
Teacher Directed ▪ Grammar, Usage, and Mechanics, ***Intervention Guide,*** p. 104 ▪ Question Marks and Exclamation Points, ***Reteach,*** p. 53 **Independent Activities** ▪ Vocabulary: Homophones, ***Spelling and Vocabulary Skills,*** pp. 42–43 ▪ Writer's Craft: Audience and Purpose, ***Comprehension and Language Arts Skills,*** pp. 50–51 ▪ Question Marks and Exclamation Points, ***Challenge,*** p. 47	**Teacher Directed** ▪ Writing Activity, ***Intervention Guide,*** pp. 105–106 ▪ Vocabulary: Homophones, ***Reteach,*** p. 52 **Independent Activities** ▪ Seminar: Draft an Explanation of a Process, p. 181H ▪ Spelling: The /oi/ Sound, ***Spelling and Vocabulary Skills,*** p. 44 ▪ Vocabulary: Homophones, ***Challenge,*** p. 46	**Teacher Directed** ▪ Writer's Craft: Audience and Purpose, ***Reteach,*** p. 54 ▪ Writing Activity, ***Intervention Guide,*** p. 106 ▪ Spelling: The /oi/ Sound, ***Reteach,*** p. 51 **Independent Activities** ▪ Spelling: The /oi/ Sound • ***Spelling and Vocabulary Skills,*** p. 45 • ***Challenge,*** p. 45	**Independent Activities** ▪ Seminar: Edit/Proofread and Publish an Explanation of a Process, p. 181J ▪ Penmanship: Practice Cursive Letters *h* and *k*, p. 181J ▪ Writer's Craft: Audience and Purpose, ***Challenge,*** p. 48

ASSESSMENT

Formal Assessment Options

Use these summative assessments along with your informal observations to assess student progress.

Name ____________ Date ________ Score ______

UNIT 2 City Wildlife • Lesson 5

LESSON ASSESSMENT

Two Days in May

Read the following questions carefully. Then completely fill in the bubble of each correct answer. You may look back at the story to find the answer to each of the questions.

1. Why couldn't the deer stay in the city?
   - Ⓐ There was not enough food.
   - ● It was not a safe place.
   - Ⓒ People wanted them for pets.
2. Who decides to call the wildlife rescuer?
   - Ⓐ Mr. Donovan
   - Ⓑ Papa
   - ● Mr. Benny

Read the following questions carefully. Use complete sentences to answer the questions.

3. How do the neighbors protect the deer from the animal control officer?
   They stand around the deer and do not leave until the wildlife rescuer arrives.
4. What words tell about the city's sounds in this story?
   The words that tell about the city's sounds are rumbling, honking, beeping, humming, and buzzing.
5. How do the deer seem to feel about all the crowd?
   They are not comfortable. They are alert and careful.

18 Unit 2 • Lesson 5 *Two Days in May* • Unit 2 Assessment

Unit 2 Assessment p. 18

Two Days in May *(continued)*

LESSON ASSESSMENT

6. How do the neighbors pass the time while they wait?
   They get to know each other better and share what they know about deer.
7. What do Mr. Smiley and the Pigeon Lady think about each other at the end of the story?
   They are no longer angry with each other and become friends.
8. Where does Carl Jackson take the deer?
   He takes them to the woods outside of the city.

Read the following questions carefully. Then completely fill in the bubble of each correct answer.

9. Why do deer sometimes wander into cities?
   - Ⓐ the new roads make it easy
   - Ⓑ the cities seem interesting
   - ● the forests are disappearing
10. At the end of the story, how many deer did the people really save?
    - Ⓐ five
    - ● seven
    - Ⓒ nine

Unit 2 Assessment • *Two Days in May* Unit 2 • Lesson 5 19

Unit 2 Assessment p. 19

Two Days in May *(continued)*

LESSON ASSESSMENT

Read the questions below. Use complete sentences in your answers.

Linking to the Concepts What lessons can be learned about working together from this story?
Answers will vary. Accept all reasonable answers.

Personal Response After reading this story, what would you do if you found a wild animal that needed rescuing?
Answers will vary. Accept all reasonable answers.

20 Unit 2 • Lesson 5 *Two Days in May* • Unit 2 Assessment

Unit 2 Assessment p. 20

Two Days in May *(continued)*

LESSON ASSESSMENT

Vocabulary

Read the following questions carefully. Then completely fill in the bubble of each correct answer.

1. At the end of the story, one of the does gives birth to two fawns. **Does** are
   - Ⓐ baby deer
   - ● female deer
   - Ⓒ male deer
2. In this story, **bucks** are
   - Ⓐ dollars
   - Ⓑ female deer
   - ● male deer
3. The neighbors decide to call a wildlife rescue organization. An **organization** is most like
   - ● a group working together
   - Ⓑ an apartment
   - Ⓒ a group of tourists
4. There aren't enough woods left, so deer sometimes wander far away looking for territory to call their own. **Territory** is another word for
   - ● land
   - Ⓑ streets
   - Ⓒ towns
5. The rescue organization relocates animals that have been stranded. To **relocate** something means to
   - Ⓐ chase it
   - Ⓑ repair it
   - ● move it

Unit 2 Assessment • *Two Days in May* Unit 2 • Lesson 5 21

Unit 2 Assessment p. 21

Name ____________ Date ________ Score ______

UNIT 2 City Wildlife • Lesson 5 *Two Days in May*

LESSON ASSESSMENT

Spelling Pretest: The /oi/ Sound

Fold this page back on the dotted line. Take the Pretest. Then correct any word you misspelled by crossing out the word and rewriting it next to the incorrect spelling.

1. ________	1. boy
2. ________	2. enjoy
3. ________	3. broil
4. ________	4. loyal
5. ________	5. oil
6. ________	6. boil
7. ________	7. soil
8. ________	8. coil
9. ________	9. coin
10. ________	10. join
11. ________	11. destroy
12. ________	12. poison
13. ________	13. royal
14. ________	14. point
15. ________	15. voices

34 Unit 2 • Lesson 5 *Spelling Pretest: The /oi/ Sound* • Unit 2 Assessment

Unit 2 Assessment p. 34

Name ____________ Date ________ Score ______

UNIT 2 City Wildlife • Lesson 5 *Two Days in May*

LESSON ASSESSMENT

Spelling Final Test: The /oi/ Sound

Mark the letter next to the underlined word that is misspelled. Focus on the underlined word.

1. Ⓐ Dogs enjoy playing fetch.
   ● A rare coyn is valuable.
   Ⓒ Fans are loyal to something.
   Ⓓ Correct as is.
2. Ⓕ Machines drill to find oil.
   Ⓖ Tornadoes can destroy cities.
   Ⓗ Cows join to form a herd.
   ● Correct as is.
3. ● A young boi is a child.
   Ⓑ Vines coil as they grow.
   Ⓒ Some plants can poison pets.
   Ⓓ Correct as is.
4. Ⓕ Liquids boil over fire.
   Ⓖ Purple is a royal color.
   ● Gardeners coyl a water hose.
   Ⓙ Correct as is.
5. ● The poynt of a needle is sharp.
   Ⓑ A dime is a small coin.
   Ⓒ Cakes are made with oil.
   Ⓓ Correct as is.
6. Ⓕ A poison is dangerous.
   ● Plant flowers in rich soyl.
   Ⓗ People enjoy vacations.
   Ⓙ Correct as is.

Unit 2 Assessment • *Spelling Final Test: The /oi/ Sound* Unit 2 • Lesson 5 35

Unit 2 Assessment p. 35

Online Assessment for *Open Court Reading* helps teachers differentiate classroom instruction based on students' scores from the weekly and end-of-unit assessments. It provides exercises best suited to meet the needs of each student. For more information, visit SRAonline.com.

Informal Comprehension Strategies Rubrics

Asking Questions

- The student asks questions about ideas or facts presented in the text and attempts to answer these questions by reading the text.

Making Connections

- The student activates prior knowledge and related knowledge.
- The student uses prior knowledge to explain something encountered in the text.
- The student connects ideas presented later in the text to ideas presented earlier in the text.
- The student notes ideas in the text that are new or conflict with what he or she thought previously.

Summarizing

- The student paraphrases the text, reporting main ideas and a summary of what is in the text.
- The student decides which parts of the text are important in his or her summary.
- The student draws conclusions from the text.
- The student makes global interpretations of the text, such as recognizing the genre.

Research Rubrics

During Workshop, assess students using the rubrics below. The rubrics range from 1–4 in most categories, with 1 being the lowest score. Record each student's score on the inside back cover of the ***Inquiry Journal***.

Finding Needed Information

1 Collects information loosely related to topic.
2 Collects information clearly related to topic.
3 Collects information helpful in advancing on a research problem.
4 Collects problem-relevant information from varied sources and notices inconsistencies and missing pieces.
5 Collects useful information, paying attention to the reliability of sources and reviewing information critically.

Revising Problems and Conjectures

1 No revision.
2 Produces new problems or conjectures with little relation to earlier ones.
3 Tends to lift problems and conjectures directly from reference material.
4 Progresses to deeper, more refined problems and conjectures.

1 Preparing to Read

Two Days in May

Objectives

- Students practice recognizing contractions.
- Students practice recognizing base words and affixes, including the suffixes *-ly* and *-ing* and the prefix *un-*.
- Students practice spelling words with the /oi/ sounds spelled *oi* and *_oy*.
- Students practice recognizing words ending in *-le* with long and short vowels.

Materials

- Student Anthology, Book 1, pp. 166–181
- Decodable Book Activities CD-ROM
- Decodable Book 21
- Routine Cards 1, 3, Routines 1–2, 8–9
- Sound/Spelling Cards

Teacher Tip SYLLABICATION To help students blend words and build fluency, use the syllabication below of the words in the word lines.

build • ing	camp • ing	sleep • ing	gent • ly
prob • a • bly	friend • ly	bright • ly	
com • fort • a • ble		un • com • fort • a • ble	
stead • y	un • stead • y	voic • es	point
roy • al	pois • on	de • stroy	

Routine Card
Refer to ***Routine 1*** for whole-word blending and ***Routine 2*** for sentence blending.

Spelling
See pages 181E–181J for the corresponding spelling lesson for the /oi/ sound.

WORD KNOWLEDGE

Word Knowledge

Reading the Words and Sentences

Use the established procedure as you have students blend each line of words and the sentences in this and in subsequent lessons. The words in **boldface** are from the selection.

Line 1:	can't	aren't	it's	that's	
Line 2:	they'll	they're	we'll	I'll	
Line 3:	building	camping	sleeping		
Line 4:	gently	probably	friendly	brightly	
Line 5:	comfortable	uncomfortable	steady	unsteady	
Line 6:	voices	point	royal	poison	destroy

Sentence 1: "They probably smelled your garden," he explained.
Sentence 2: The Pigeon Lady came up to Peach and me and said, "Oh, girls, aren't they wonderful!"
Sentence 3: I could see that the people made them uncomfortable and it helped me appreciate that these really were wild animals.
Sentence 4: Screaming and shouting can destroy people's voices.

About the Words and Sentences

- **Lines 1–2:** The words in Lines 1 and 2 are contractions. Have students tell you the two words that make up each contraction.
- **Line 3:** The words in Line 3 have the suffix *-ing* added to them. Have the class identify the base words. Ask students to tell you how the suffix changes the meaning of the words.
- **Line 4:** The words in Line 4 have the suffix *-ly* added to them. Have the class identify the base words. Ask students to tell you how the suffix changes the meaning of the words.
- **Line 5:** These words in Line 5 have the prefix *un-* added to them. Ask students to tell you how the prefix changes the meaning of the words. Because *un-* means *not*, this is a good time to review antonyms with students as well. Point out that adding the prefix creates an antonym of the base word.
- **Line 6:** The spelling words in the last line are found in "Two Days in May" and review the /oi/ sound spelled *_oy* and *oi*.
- **Sentences 1–3:** These sentences are from the story students are about to read. Ask students to identify the contraction *(aren't)*. Have students identify the word with the suffix *-ly (probably)*. Have students identify the word with the prefix *un- (uncomfortable)*.
- **Sentence 4:** Have students identify the spelling words in the last sentence that contain the /oi/ sound spelled *_oy* and *oi*. *(destroy, voices)*

Developing Oral Language

Use direct teaching to review the words. Use one or both of the following activities to help students practice the words aloud.

- Have a student choose a word and call out only the line and the position of the word in the line, for example, "Line 1, Word 3." Have the student select a classmate to read the words. Then ask the student to use the word in a sentence.
- Point to a word on the board and select a student to read the word and use it in a sentence. Then that student can point to a word on the board and choose another student to read it and use it in a sentence. Erase the words as they are selected and continue until all the words have been erased.

WORD KNOWLEDGE

Teacher Tip PROOFREADING Remind students whether they are writing on the board or on paper, they should proofread their work.

Teacher Tip FLUENCY Gaining a better understanding of the spellings of sounds and structure of words will help students as they encounter unfamiliar words in their reading. By this time in Grade 3 students should be reading approximately 107 words per minute with fluency and expression. As students read, you may notice that some need work in building fluency. During Workshop, have these students select a section of the text (a minimum of 160 words) to read several times in order to build fluency.

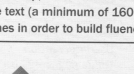

Research in Action
Segmentation

The ability to decode single words accurately and fluently is dependent upon the ability to segment words and syllables into phonemes.
(G. Reid Lyon)

Differentiating Instruction

If...	Then...
Students need extra help with contractions	Use ***Intervention Guide*** pages 98–99

We stayed all afternoon, waiting anxiously, hoping to hear from the rescue organization. We got to know one another better, and we learned more about the deer.

Peach's eyes were wide and bright. "Look how they rotate their big soft ears to the left and right," she exclaimed.

Clarence said, "We studied deer in science. Their hearing is very sharp. It helps them detect enemies approaching from far away."

Mr. Benny nodded as he walked over to us. "I sometimes see this kind of deer at night, in the headlights, when I drive way past the city limits. When they're startled by the taxi's lights, their tails go up like flags. The tails are white underneath, which means the animals are white-tailed deer."

The deer grazed and slept cautiously, always alert to danger. They watched us with curious, intelligent eyes. I could see that the people made them uncomfortable, and it helped me appreciate that these really were wild animals. We tried to keep our distance and not make any sudden movements.

173

Comprehension Skills

Second Read

Cause and Effect

Have students continue to look for the cause-and-effect relationships in the story. Remind them that certain clue words can be used to show these relationships. Even if the writer does not use these words in the story, students can use the words to explain cause and effect. Have them practice using clue words in sentences to explain causes and effects.

- *The neighbors were not leaving the deer* so that *the deer would remain unharmed.*
- *The deer slept cautiously* because *the people made them feel uncomfortable.*
- Since *they are wildlife and not used to being around people, the deer were uncomfortable.*

Word Knowledge

***-ly* endings:** **anxiously**
cautiously

Teacher Tip Ask students one or more of the following questions to make sure they are understanding what they are reading: Is anyone confused? Do you need clarification? Can you summarize what you have read so far? Does what you are reading make sense to you?

COMPREHENSION

Science/Social Studies Connection Center

Refer to the ***Science/Social Studies Connection Center*** Card 14 for a social studies activity that students can investigate.

COMPREHENSION

Comprehension Strategies

First Read

Prompting

5 Making Connections *This scene reminds me of a real experience I had once. Does anyone else have a connection here? What is it?*

Student Sample

Making Connections *I have a connection here. This reminds me of the time I went camping with my family this fall. Mom brought lots of quilts and blankets for us because it's chilly outside at night. We all slept snuggled under the blankets outside. The blankets were warm, but I remember the wind felt cold on my nose and forehead.*

Word Knowledge

***-ly* endings:** **sadly**

Teacher Tip Be sure to encourage all the students to use strategies. Call on various students to share which strategies they are using and to tell how they are using them to figure out the meaning of the text.

When evening came, the crowd grew. We talked quietly and told jokes as we kept watch over our silent friends. We ordered pizza from Giuseppe's.

Ana Sánchez spoke to the animal control officer. "Would you like a slice of pizza?" she asked.

"Thanks so much," he said. "My name is Steve Scully, and I understand how hard this must be for all of you. This is the part of my job I dislike.

"The problem is population growth. We've built towns and highways where there were once forests and streams. Now there is very little habitat left for the deer. There is no easy solution." He shook his head sadly.

174

I begged Papa to let me sleep outside all night, since almost everyone was staying. Mama came out with my baby brother, Danny. She brought blankets, a quilt, a jacket, and even my stuffed dog, Hershey.

Mama sat close and draped her arm across my shoulders. "Are you sure you'll be warm enough, Sonia?" she asked.

"I'm sure," I said.

We sat silently together, admiring the deer.

Finally she said, "I have to go put Danny to bed." She kissed me on the top of my head. "Sweet dreams, pumpkin."

I slept like a bear cub, curled in a ball against Papa's broad back. 5

175

Comprehension Skills

Second Read

Cause and Effect

Have students continue to identify the cause-and-effect relationships in the story. Remind them to use clue words in their own sentences.

- *Since we've built towns and highways where there were forests and streams, there is no habitat left for the deer.*
- *Sonia's mother had to leave so she could put Danny to bed.*

Word Knowledge

contractions: **you'll**
I'm

Teacher Tip Remind students that when authors don't use words to clue the cause-and-effect relationship, readers have to make inferences.

COMPREHENSION

Differentiating Instruction

If...	Then...
English Learners need extra help with vocabulary	Use ***English Learner Support Guide*** pages 156–158
English Learners need extra help with cause and effect	Use ***English Learner Support Guide*** pages 157–159

COMPREHENSION

Comprehension Strategies

First Read

Prompting

6 **Asking Questions** *I have questions now. Who else has questions now?*

Student Sample

Asking Questions *I have questions too. Is someone from the organization going to get there in the morning? How will they move the deer? Where will they move them?*

Prompting

7 **Answering Questions** *Now that I've read more, a lot of my questions have been answered. Have your questions been answered?*

Student Sample

Answering Questions *I see now that the organization got there in the morning. They had to tranquilize the deer and then put them in crates. I still wonder where they will take them. I'll read on to see if I can find out.*

Word Knowledge

***-ing* endings:** **buzzing**, **camping**, **sleeping**, **laughing**

Teacher Tip Help students to understand that each person's response to a text is a very individual matter and that no two people will respond in exactly the same way. Encourage students to respect each other's contributions.

Teacher Tip When listening to students answer questions, instruct them on responding with appropriate elaboration.

Next morning, I awoke with the sun in my eyes and city sounds buzzing in my ears. Papa hugged me and asked how I liked camping out.

"I dreamed I was sleeping with the deer in cool forests under tall trees."

"You were, Sonia!" he said, laughing. "But not in the forest."

I looked at the deer. "Has the wildlife rescuer called back?" I asked.

"Yes, Sonia. The organization called late last night and hopes to get someone out here this morning." 6

The group was quiet as we all continued to wait.

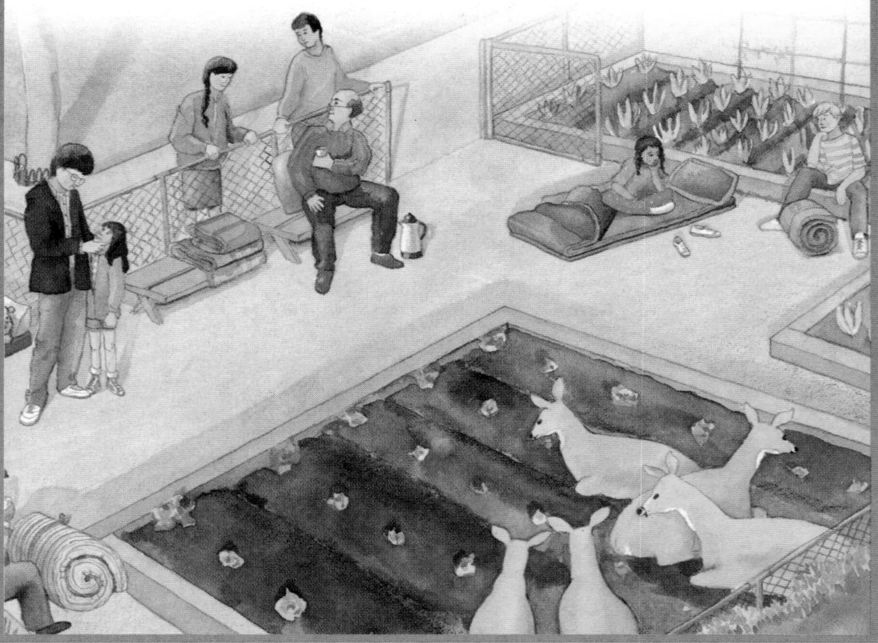

176

Later that morning, a rusty orange truck pulled up. The man who got out had a friendly, open face. All eyes were on him.

"Hi, folks. My name is Carl Jackson, and I'm with the wildlife rescue organization," he said. "I need to put the deer in crates in order to take them to our center. Don't be alarmed—I'm going to shoot them with a small amount of tranquilizer to make them sleep for a little while." Then, as they wobbled on unsteady legs, he grabbed them gently and guided them toward the wooden crates. 7

177

Comprehension Skills

Second Read

Cause and Effect

Have students continue to read carefully to identify causes and effects. Encourage them to continue using clue words as they explain cause-and-effect relationships.

- *Sonia woke up with the city noises buzzing in her ears because she slept outside all night in the city.*
- *Carl Jackson shot the deer with tranquilizers so he could put them in the crates.*

Word Knowledge

prefix *un-*: **unsteady**

COMPREHENSION

Differentiating Instruction

If...	Then...
English Learners need extra help with vocabulary	Use ***English Learner Support Guide*** pages 159–160
English Learners need extra help with cause and effect	Use ***English Learner Support Guide*** pages 160–161

COMPREHENSION

Comprehension Strategies

First Read

Prompting

8 **Summarizing** *I want to stop here and make sure I understand everything that's happened. Who would like to summarize the story here?*

Student Sample

Summarizing *I'd like to summarize. Sonia saw deer in her garden. Then her dad called animal control, and animal control wanted to shoot the deer. The neighbors wanted to save the deer and called an organization to come and rescue them. The neighbors stayed outside all night with the deer to make sure they were OK. Then the rescue organization got there and took the deer out of the city. The organization found a home in the woods for the deer.*

Discussing Strategy Use

Encourage students to share any problems encountered and to tell what strategies they used.

- What connections did they make between the reading and what they already know?
- What questions did they ask as they read?
- Where did they pause in the reading to summarize?

These are questions good readers ask after they read a text. After reading, the students should always be asking, "What did I find interesting? What is important here?" Later, remind the students again that whenever they conclude a reading, they should ask themselves questions about what was in the text.

Word Knowledge

contractions: **I'm**
I'll
they'll

Carl turned to the crowd and smiled. "I'm an animal lover, too, and all of you should feel proud for helping save these deer. I'll find a home for them in the woods, where they'll be safe and happy and have plenty to eat."

Steve Scully came forward and extended his hand to Carl. "Glad you came, man."

A cheer went up from the crowd. People slapped each other on the back. Isidro high-fived everyone, including Mr. Donovan and the Pigeon Lady. Peach and I hugged each other, and Papa shook hands with Carl and Steve. I said goodbye to Teresa and Sandy Yasamura and to Mr. Benny.

I even saw Mr. Smiley shake the Pigeon Lady's hand. "Maybe you can feed the pigeons *behind* my Laundromat," he said. "I have a little space back there."

The Pigeon Lady smiled.

178

Informal Assessment

Use the Informal Comprehension Strategies Rubrics on page 166J to determine whether a student is using the strategies being taught.

Teacher Tip BUILDING FLUENCY As students read, you may notice that some need work in building fluency. During Workshop, have these students select a section of the text (a minimum of 160 words) to read several times in order to build fluency.

A few days later, Papa got a call from Carl. One of the does had given birth to two fawns! And Carl had found a home for all seven deer in a wooded area northwest of the city. 8

Sometimes, when I'm sitting on the fire escape, watching the flickering city lights, I think of the deer. In my mind, they're gliding silently across tall grass meadows all aglow in silver moonlight.

Comprehension Skills

Second Read

Cause and Effect

Remind students that identifying the cause-and-effect relationships in a story can help them better understand what they read. Encourage students to think about and discuss these causes and effects after reading this story.

- *A cheer went up from the crowd because they were rescued.*
- *Mr. Smiley and the Pigeon Lady talked to each other because they had shared an important experience together.*

Checking Comprehension

Ask students the following questions to check their comprehension of the story.

- Why did the deer end up in the city? *(They were looking for food in the city probably because their habitat had been destroyed.)*
- What was so remarkable about what the neighbors did? *(They took the time to protect wildlife. They made a difference by participating in a peaceful protest.)*
- How did the experience help the neighbors? *(The neighbors got to spend time together and some that had not been getting along even had a chance to talk and make up.)*

Teacher Tip FLUENCY By this time in third grade, good readers should be reading approximately 107 words per minute with fluency and expression. The only way to gain this fluency is through practice. Have students reread the selection to you and to each other during Workshop to help build fluency.

Differentiating Instruction

If...	Then...
English Learners need extra help reviewing "Two Days in May"	Use ***English Learner Support Guide*** pages 162–163

Formal Assessment

See pages 18–21 in ***Unit 2 Assessment*** to test students' comprehension of "Two Days in May."

Teacher Tip LITERARY TERMINOLOGY Take advantage of discussion time to introduce into the conversation literary terms students have studied, such as theme, plot, conflict, and characterization, in the context of conversation.

Routine Card
Refer to ***Routine* 6** for the *handing-off process.*

Clues	Problems	Wonderings
deer grazing in city garden	courtyard	How did the deer get there?

Open Court Reading
Reading Transparency 46

***Reading Transparency* 46**

www.sra4kids.com
Web Connection
Some students may choose to conduct a computer search for additional books or information about city wildlife. Invite them to make a list of these books and sources of information to share with classmates and the school librarian. Check the Reading link of the SRA Web page for additional links to the theme-related Web site.

Discussing the Selection

After the first read, the whole group discusses the selection and any personal thoughts, reactions, problems, or questions that it raises. To stimulate discussion, students can ask one another the kinds of questions that good readers ask themselves about a text: *What did I find interesting about this story? What is important here? What was difficult to understand? Why would someone want to read this?* Throughout the discussion, make sure students use specific information from the text to defend their interpretations.

Handing-Off Process Seeing you as a contributing member of the group sets a strong example for students. To emphasize that you are part of the group, actively participate in the *handing-off process:* Raise your hand to be called on by the last speaker when you have a contribution to make. Point out unusual and interesting insights verbalized by students so that these insights are recognized and discussed. As the year progresses, students will take more and more responsibility for the discussions of the selections.

Engage students in a discussion to determine whether they have grasped the following ideas:

- why the deer were looking for food in the city
- how the neighbors saved the deer
- how working together to save the deer helped the neighbors

During this time, have students return to the clues, problems, and wonderings they noted during browsing to determine whether the clues were borne out by the selection, whether and how their problems were solved, and whether their wonderings were answered or deserve further discussion and investigation. Let the students decide which items deserve further discussion.

Also have students return to the Focus Questions on the first page of the selection. Select a student to read the questions aloud, and have volunteers answer the questions. If students do not know the answers to the questions, have them return to the text to find the answers.

You may wish to review the elements of realistic fiction with the students at this time. Discuss with them how they can tell that "Two Days in May" is realistic fiction.

Have students break into small groups to discuss what this story tells them about city wildlife. Groups can discuss their ideas with the rest of the class.

Writer's Notebook

If students have ever had first-hand experience observing deer or helping to rescue wildlife, encourage them to record these events.

Review Selection Vocabulary

Have students review the definitions of the selection vocabulary words that they wrote in the vocabulary section of their Writer's Notebooks. Remind them that they discussed the meanings of these words before reading the selection. Have students write sentences for each of the vocabulary words after the definitions in the same section of their Writer's Notebooks. They can use the definitions and the sentences to study for the vocabulary portion of their Lesson Assessments. Have them add any other interesting words that they clarified while reading to the Personal Dictionary section of their Writer's Notebooks. Encourage students to refer to the selection vocabulary words throughout the unit. The words from the selection are:

does	**territory**	**relocates**
bucks	**organization**	**population**

If you created a Word Bank of key words related to the theme city wildlife, remind students to find words from other resources, from their activities, and from family discussions and add them to the Word Bank. Students may also place synonyms and antonyms in the Word Bank, organizing the words by lesson.

Home Connection

Distribute ***Home Connection,*** page 25. Encourage students to discuss "Two Days in May" with their families. Students will have the opportunity to discuss wildlife conservation issues and read library books about the issue with their families. A Spanish version of this page appears on page 26.

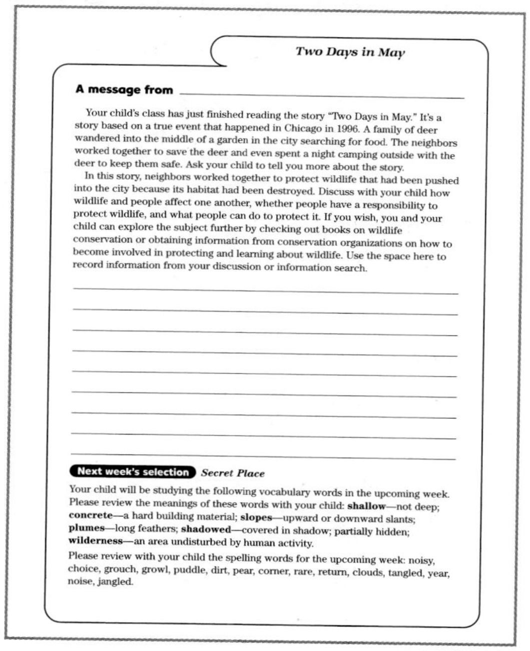

Two Days in May

A message from ______________________

Your child's class has just finished reading the story "Two Days in May." It's a story based on a true event that happened in Chicago in 1996. A family of deer wandered into the middle of a garden in the city searching for food. The neighbors worked together to save the deer and even spent a night camping outside with the deer to keep them safe. Ask your child to tell you more about the story.

In this story, neighbors worked together to protect wildlife that had been pushed into the city because its habitat had been destroyed. Discuss with your child how wildlife and people affect one another, whether people have a responsibility to protect wildlife, and what people can do to protect it. If you wish, you and your child can explore the subject further by checking out books on wildlife conservation or obtaining information from conservation organizations on how to become involved in protecting and learning about wildlife. Use the space here to record information from your discussion or information search.

Next week's selection ***Secret Place***

Your child will be studying the following vocabulary words in the upcoming week. Please review the meanings of these words with your child: **shallow**—not deep; **concrete**—a hard building material; **slopes**—upward or downward slants; **plumes**—long feathers; **shadowed**—covered in shadow; partially hidden; **wilderness**—an area undisturbed by human activity.

Please review with your child the spelling words for the upcoming week: noisy, choice, grouch, growl, puddle, dirt, pear, corner, rare, return, clouds, tangled, year, noise, jangled.

Home Connection p. 25

DAY 3

Word Analysis

Spelling

The /oi/ Sound

Teach

- Introduce *voices* with the /oi/ sound found in "Two Days in May."
- Ask students to think of things with the /oi/ sound found in a kitchen. *(foil, oil, oysters)*

Guided Practice

Have students complete page 44 from ***Spelling and Vocabulary Skills*** to learn strategies for spelling words with the /oi/ sound.

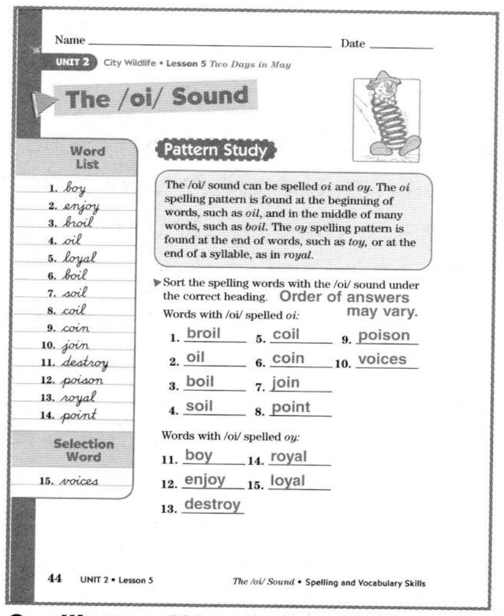
Name ____ Date ____

UNIT 2 City Wildlife • Lesson 5 *Two Days in May*

The /oi/ Sound

Word List: 1. boy 2. enjoy 3. broil 4. oil 5. loyal 6. boil 7. soil 8. coil 9. coin 10. join 11. destroy 12. poison 13. royal 14. point

Selection Word: 15. voices

Pattern Study

The /oi/ sound can be spelled *oi* and *oy*. The *oi* spelling pattern is found at the beginning of words, such as *oil*, and in the middle of many words, such as *boil*. The *oy* spelling pattern is found at the end of words, such as *toy*, or at the end of a syllable, as in *royal*.

▶ Sort the spelling words with the /oi/ sound under the correct heading. Order of answers may vary.

Words with /oi/ spelled *oi*:

1. broil 2. oil 3. boil 4. soil 5. coil 6. coin 7. join 8. point 9. poison 10. voices

Words with /oi/ spelled *oy*:

11. boy 12. enjoy 13. destroy 14. royal 15. loyal

44 UNIT 2 • Lesson 5 *The /oi/ Sound* • Spelling and Vocabulary Skills

***Spelling and Vocabulary Skills* p. 44**

Vocabulary (continued)

Homophones

- Write *tails* on the board. Read the sentence on page 167 of "Two Days in May" that contains *tails*. Ask students what *tails* means.
- Write *tales* on the board. Say *tales* aloud. Ask a student to find the definition for *tales* in a dictionary. *(stories, old fables)*
- Ask if the words are homophones. *(Yes, because the two words have the same sound, but different spellings and meanings.)* Discuss ways to memorize the spellings. *(A t<u>ai</u>l has h<u>ai</u>r on it; a tale does not have the* ai *spelling pattern.)*

Writing Process Strategies

Drafting

Explanation of a Process

Teach

- Review purpose and audience with students.
- Read ***Writer's Workbook*** page 23 on drafting an explanation of a process.

Guided Practice

Drafting

- Have students write the drafts of their explanations of a process.
- If you have computers in the classroom, you may want to give students the option of using word processing software to make their drafts.

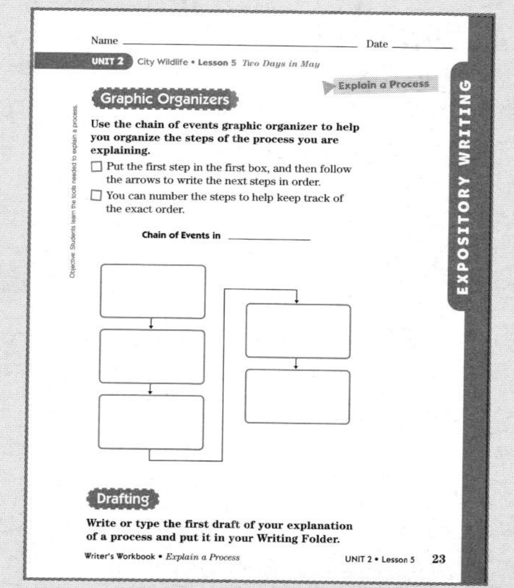
Name ____ Date ____

UNIT 2 City Wildlife • Lesson 5 *Two Days in May*

Explain a Process

EXPOSITORY WRITING

Graphic Organizers

Use the chain of events graphic organizer to help you organize the steps of the process you are explaining.

- ☐ Put the first step in the first box, and then follow the arrows to write the next steps in order.
- ☐ You can number the steps to help keep track of the exact order.

Chain of Events in ____

Objective: Students learn the tools needed to explain a process.

Drafting

Write or type the first draft of your explanation of a process and put it in your Writing Folder.

Writer's Workbook • *Explain a Process* UNIT 2 • Lesson 5 23

***Writer's Workbook* p. 23**

Professional Development

Teacher Resource Library CD-ROMs or ***Online Professional Development*** provides courses that help you better understand the Writing instruction in ***Open Court Reading.*** For more information about this program, visit SRAonline.com.

English Language Conventions

Grammar, Usage, and Mechanics

Mechanics: Question Marks and Exclamation Points

Teach

- **Review** the uses of question marks and exclamation points using ***Language Arts Handbook,*** page 270.
- **Review** that all end punctuation goes inside quotation marks.

Guided Practice in Writing

Have students write sentences with question marks and exclamation points. Ask some of them to write their sentences on the board.

Informal Assessment

Check students' writing for the correct use of question marks and exclamation points.

DAY 4

Word Analysis

Spelling

The /oi/ Sound

Teach

Explain that the exercises in ***Spelling and Vocabulary Skills*** are designed to help students learn to recognize similar spellings in words that sound alike.

Guided Practice

Have students complete page 45 of ***Spelling and Vocabulary Skills*** to reinforce the spelling patterns for the /oi/ sound.

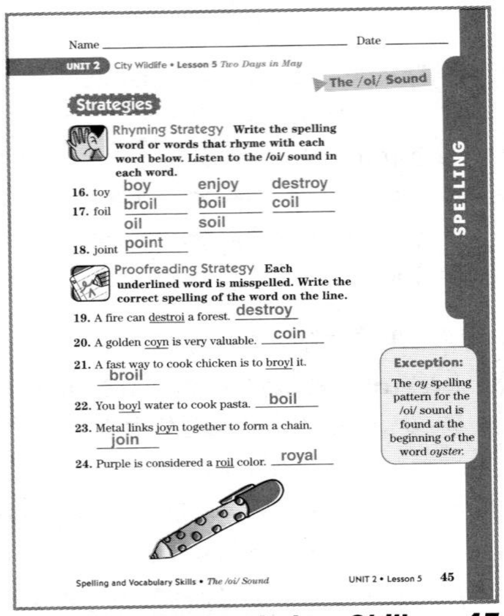

Name ____________ Date ______

UNIT 2 City Wildlife • Lesson 5 *Two Days in May*

The /oi/ Sound

Strategies

Rhyming Strategy **Write the spelling word or words that rhyme with each word below. Listen to the /oi/ sound in each word.**

16. toy boy enjoy destroy
17. foil broil boil coil oil soil
18. joint point

Proofreading Strategy **Each underlined word is misspelled. Write the correct spelling of the word on the line.**

19. A fire can destroi a forest. destroy
20. A golden coyn is very valuable. coin
21. A fast way to cook chicken is to broyl it. broil
22. You boyl water to cook pasta. boil
23. Metal links joyn together to form a chain. join
24. Purple is considered a roil color. royal

Exception: The *oy* spelling pattern for the /oi/ sound is found at the beginning of the word *oyster*.

SPELLING

Spelling and Vocabulary Skills • *The /oi/ Sound* UNIT 2 • Lesson 5 45

***Spelling and Vocabulary Skills* p. 45**

Vocabulary (continued)

Homophones

- Write *way* from "Two Days in May" (page 167) in a box. Write *weigh* in a box next to the *way* box. You will make parallel word maps to visualize the differences between homophone pairs.
- Draw a box under *way*, and write *ay* in it. Draw a box under *weigh* with *eigh* in it. Explain that *ay* and *eigh* are two different spellings for the /ā/ sound.
- Draw one box under the *ay* box and one under the *eigh* box. As a class, find the definitions for the words and write them in the boxes. (way: *a direction;* weigh: *heaviness, test of weight*)

Writing Process Strategies

Revising

Explaining a Process

Teach

- Read ***Writer's Workbook,*** page 24, on revising an explanation of a process.
- Discuss ***Language Arts Transparency 17,*** Revising: Adding Copy.

Troubleshooting

- Forgetting a step makes it difficult for readers to follow your explanation.
- The accuracy of information is sometimes not verified.
- Unfamiliar words specific to the process being explained are sometimes left undefined.
- When the other sentences in a paragraph stray away from the main idea in the topic sentence, readers can get lost or lose interest.

Guided Practice

Revising

- Have students revise their explanations of a process. Remind them to keep their purpose and audience in mind when revising.
- Direct students to use the checklist and the proofreading marks in the ***Writer's Workbook,*** page 24, to help them revise their writing.

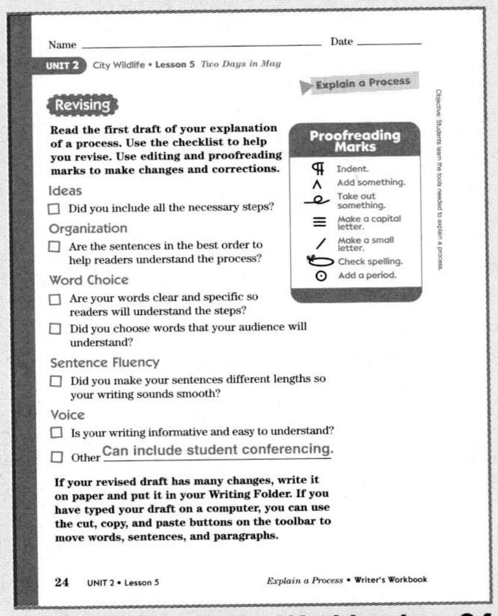

Name ____________ Date ______

UNIT 2 City Wildlife • Lesson 5 *Two Days in May*

Explain a Process

Revising

Read the first draft of your explanation of a process. Use the checklist to help you revise. Use editing and proofreading marks to make changes and corrections.

Ideas
- ☐ Did you include all the necessary steps?

Organization
- ☐ Are the sentences in the best order to help readers understand the process?

Word Choice
- ☐ Are your words clear and specific so readers will understand the steps?
- ☐ Did you choose words that your audience will understand?

Sentence Fluency
- ☐ Did you make your sentences different lengths so your writing sounds smooth?

Voice
- ☐ Is your writing informative and easy to understand?
- ☐ Other Can include student conferencing.

If your revised draft has many changes, write it on paper and put it in your Writing Folder. If you have typed your draft on a computer, you can use the cut, copy, and paste buttons on the toolbar to move words, sentences, and paragraphs.

Proofreading Marks
- ¶ Indent.
- ^ Add something.
- Take out something.
- ≡ Make a capital letter.
- / Make a small letter.
- Check spelling.
- ⊙ Add a period.

Objective: Students learn the tools needed to explain a process.

24 UNIT 2 • Lesson 5 *Explain a Process* • Writer's Workbook

***Writer's Workbook* p. 24**

English Language Conventions

Listening, Speaking, Viewing

Interacting: Asking Questions

Teach

- Explain that we interact with others in order to share, to have fun, and to learn. In order to do all these things, we should be able to ask each other questions and respond to questions with appropriate answers.
- Remind the class that asking and answering questions takes a lot of thought. Before we speak, we should carefully think about what we want to say, and how we are going to say it. This will help us clarify ideas and explain information.

Guided Practice

- In pairs, have students take turns asking one another questions about "Two Days in May" or about a subject of wildlife. *(Why did the deer leave the woods? Food supply is low; space is shrinking. What are the terms for a female deer, male deer, and baby deer?* Doe, buck, fawn.) Remind them to ask questions carefully, and to listen and answer questions thoughtfully. Each student should ask two questions.
- As a class, invite the students to share what they learned from one another. Students should be able to paraphrase each other's words and comments.

Informal Assessment

Observe whether students are able to ask and respond to questions.

DAY 5

Word Analysis

Spelling

Assessment: Final Test

The /oi/ Sound

Teach

Repeat the Pretest or use the Final Test on page 35 of ***Unit 2 Assessment*** as summative assessment for student understanding of the /oi/ sound spelling patterns.

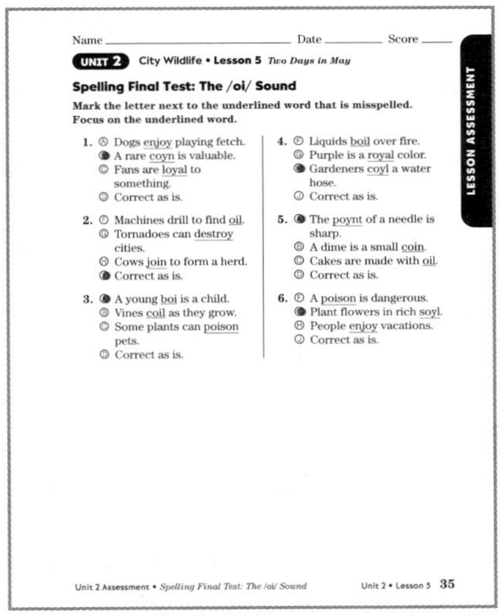

Name ______ Date ______ Score ______

UNIT 2 City Wildlife • Lesson 5 *Two Days in May*

Spelling Final Test: The /oi/ Sound

Mark the letter next to the underlined word that is misspelled. Focus on the underlined word.

1. Ⓐ Dogs enjoy playing fetch.
   Ⓑ A rare coyn is valuable.
   Ⓒ Fans are loyal to something.
   Ⓓ Correct as is.
2. Ⓕ Machines drill to find oil.
   Ⓖ Tornadoes can destroy cities.
   Ⓗ Cows join to form a herd.
   Ⓙ Correct as is.
3. Ⓐ A young boi is a child.
   Ⓑ Vines coil as they grow.
   Ⓒ Some plants can poison pets.
   Ⓓ Correct as is.
4. Ⓕ Liquids boil over fire.
   Ⓖ Purple is a royal color.
   Ⓗ Gardeners coyl a water hose.
   Ⓙ Correct as is.
5. Ⓐ The poynt of a needle is sharp.
   Ⓑ A dime is a small coin.
   Ⓒ Cakes are made with oil.
   Ⓓ Correct as is.
6. Ⓕ A poison is dangerous.
   Ⓖ Plant flowers in rich soyl.
   Ⓗ People enjoy vacations.
   Ⓙ Correct as is.

LESSON ASSESSMENT

Unit 2 Assessment • *Spelling Final Test: The /oi/ Sound* Unit 2 • Lesson 5 35

Unit 2 Assessment p. 35

Guided Practice

Have students categorize any mistakes they made on the Final Test as careless errors or lesson-pattern problems.

Vocabulary

Homophones

Informal Assessment

Ask students what the meaning of *days* is in the title "Two Days in May." *(more than one day, more than 24 hours)* Write *daze* on the board. Discuss the sound, spellings, and meanings that make these words homophones. Ask for a sentence using both words. See if students recognize the differences in homophone spellings and meanings within their writing. Have students add new words to the word list in their Writer's Notebooks.

Writing Process Strategies

Editing/Proofreading and Publishing

Explaining a Process

Teach

- Read ***Writer's Workbook,*** page 25, on editing/proofreading and publishing.
- Remind students to look for the correct use of question marks and exclamation points in their writing.

Guided Practice

Editing/Proofreading and Publishing

- Direct students to use the checklist in the ***Writer's Workbook,*** page 25, to help them edit their writing.
- Have students make a neat final copy in their best cursive handwriting or print it out on the computer.

Formal Assessment

Total Point Value: 10

1. The main idea is clearly stated. (2 points)
2. The steps of the process are easy to understand and follow. (2 points)
3. The word choices and sentence lengths fit the audience. (2 points)
4. The final copy is neat, clean, and easy to read. (2 points)
5. Mechanics: capitalization, punctuation, and spelling are correct. (2 points)

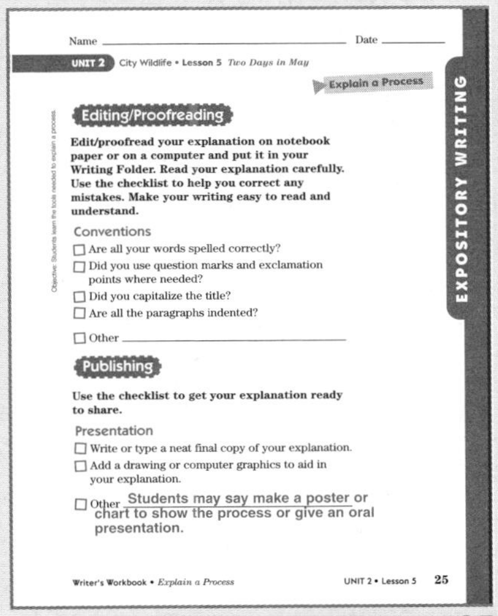

Name ______ Date ______

UNIT 2 City Wildlife • Lesson 5 *Two Days in May*

Explain a Process

Editing/Proofreading

Edit/proofread your explanation on notebook paper or on a computer and put it in your Writing Folder. Read your explanation carefully. Use the checklist to help you correct any mistakes. Make your writing easy to read and understand.

Conventions

- ☐ Are all your words spelled correctly?
- ☐ Did you use question marks and exclamation points where needed?
- ☐ Did you capitalize the title?
- ☐ Are all the paragraphs indented?
- ☐ Other ______

Publishing

Use the checklist to get your explanation ready to share.

Presentation

- ☐ Write or type a neat final copy of your explanation.
- ☐ Add a drawing or computer graphics to aid in your explanation.
- ☐ Other Students may say make a poster or chart to show the process or give an oral presentation.

EXPOSITORY WRITING

Writer's Workbook • *Explain a Process* UNIT 2 • Lesson 5 25

Writer's Workbook p. 25

English Language Conventions

Penmanship

Cursive Letters *h* and *k*

Teach

- **Teacher Model:** On the board, introduce the formation of lowercase cursive *h* and *k* as letters with loops.

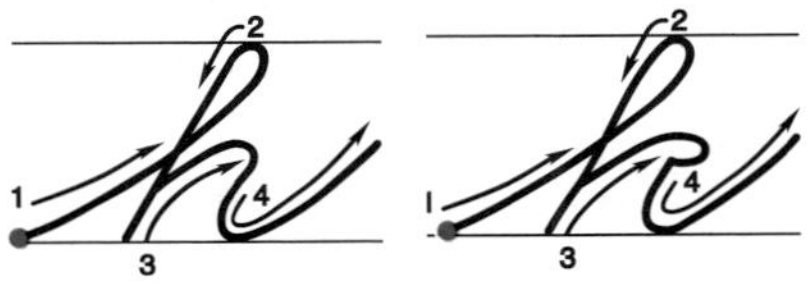

h Starting point, undercurve
Loop back, slant down
Overcurve, slant down into undercurve: small *h*

k Starting point, undercurve
Loop back, slant down
Overcurve
Curve forward, curve under
Slant down into undercurve: small *k*

- Tell the students that the loops in *h* and *k* should both touch the top line. Explain that proper size of letters makes their writing easier to read.
- **Teacher Model:** Write the words *help, kitten,* and *hats* on the board to demonstrate proper letter formation.

Guided Practice

- Invite students to come to the board and trace the letters *h* and *k*.
- Have students practice writing rows of *h*s and *k*s in their Writer's Notebooks.
- From "Two Days in May," have students write the words *block, here,* and *neighborhood* to practice letter formation.

Informal Assessment

Check students' handwriting for properly formed *h* and *k*.

Reading and Language Arts Skills Traces

Language Arts

WORD ANALYSIS

Skills Trace

Spelling: The /oi/ Sound

Introduced in Grade 1.
Scaffolded throughout Grades 2–5.

REINTRODUCED: Unit 2, Lesson 5, p. 181E
PRACTICED: Unit 2, Lesson 5, pp. 181F–181J
Spelling and Vocabulary Skills, pp. 44–45
TESTED: Unit 2, Lesson 5, p. 181F (Pretest)
Unit 2, Lesson 5, p. 35 (Final Test)
Unit 2 Assessment

Skills Trace

Vocabulary: Homophones

Introduced in Grade 1.
Scaffolded throughout Grades 2–5.

REINTRODUCED: Unit 2, Lesson 5, p. 181E
PRACTICED: Unit 2, Lesson 5, pp. 181G–181J
Spelling and Vocabulary Skills, pp. 42–43
TESTED: Unit 2 Assessment

WRITING PROCESS STRATEGIES

Skills Trace

Expository Writing: Explaining a Process

Introduced in Grade 1.
Scaffolded throughout Grades 2–4, 6.

REINTRODUCED: Unit 2, Lesson 5, p. 181F
PRACTICED: Unit 2, Lesson 5, pp. 181G–181J
Writer's Workbook, pp. 22–25
TESTED: Unit 2, Lesson 5, Formal Assessment, p. 181J
Unit 2 Assessment

Skills Trace

Writer's Craft: Audience and Purpose

Introduced in Grade 1.
Scaffolded throughout Grades 2–6.

REINTRODUCED: Unit 2, Lesson 5, p. 181G
PRACTICED: Unit 2, Lesson 5, pp. 181G
Comprehension and Language Arts Skills, pp. 50–51
TESTED: Unit 2 Assessment

ENGLISH LANGUAGE CONVENTIONS

Skills Trace

Mechanics: Exclamation Points and Question Marks

Introduced in Grade K.
Scaffolded throughout Grades 1–6.

REINTRODUCED: Unit 2, Lesson 5, p. 181F
PRACTICED: Unit 2, Lesson 5, p. 181G
Unit 2, Lesson 5, p. 181H
Comprehension and Language Arts Skills, pp. 48–49
TESTED: Unit 2, Lesson 5, Informal Assessment, p. 181H
Unit 2 Assessment

Skills Trace

Listening, Speaking, Viewing Interacting: Asking Questions

Introduced in Grade K.
Scaffolded throughout Grades 1–6.

REINTRODUCED: Unit 2, Lesson 5, p. 181I
TESTED: Unit 2, Lesson 5, Informal Assessment, p. 181I

Skills Trace

Penmanship: Cursive Letters *h* and *k*

Introduced in Grade 2 (*h*) and Grade 3 (*k*).
Scaffolded throughout Grades 3–6 and Grades 4–6.

INTRODUCED: Unit 2, Lesson 5, p. 181J
TESTED: Unit 2, Lesson 5, Informal Assessment, p. 181J

Reading

COMPREHENSION

Skills Trace

Cause and Effect

Introduced in Grade 1.
Scaffolded throughout Grades 2 and 3.

REINTRODUCED: Unit 1, Lesson 2
REINFORCED: Unit 1, Lesson 4
Unit 2, Lesson 4
Unit 2, Lesson 5
Unit 4, Lesson 2
Unit 4, Lesson 7
Unit 6, Lesson 6
TESTED: Unit 2 Assessment

Professional Development: Phonics

Alphabetic Knowledge

Without the ability to name the letters and to identify and discriminate their shapes—*alphabetic knowledge*—phonemic awareness is of limited value. Further, until children can identify the shape of each letter and discriminate one letter from another, it is pointless to introduce them to the *alphabetic principle*. Unless children can recognize letters quickly and with ease, they cannot begin to appreciate that all words are made up of letters and spelling patterns. However, once children are able to identify letters quickly, they have little difficulty learning letter sounds and word spellings (Adams, 1990).

The progression of difficulty in learning how the system of written language works is somewhat the reverse of the system for learning spoken language; that is, it begins with the smallest unit (letters) and advances to the largest unit (text). As they attempt to reproduce the letters they see in print, children gain awareness of how lines work together to make letters. Next, they notice how these letters can be combined to form words, and finally how words can work together to make text (Maxim, 1993). Unless children can recognize the shapes of letters automatically, without having to stop and think about what letter is made by what combination of lines, they cannot recognize words quickly.

What Does Research Tell Us About Alphabetic Knowledge?

Along with phonemic awareness, alphabetic knowledge measured at the beginning of kindergarten is one of the best predictors of reading success at the end of kindergarten and first grade (Chall, 1996; Share, Jorm, Maclean, & Matthews, 1984). Alphabetic knowledge is correlated strongly with children's ability to remember the forms of written words and with their ability to understand that words are sequences of letters (Ehri, 1987; Ehri & Wilce, 1985). Children with little or limited alphabetic knowledge at school entry are likely to have difficulty later on in learning letter sounds and in recognizing words (Mason, 1980; Sulzby, 1983).

It appears that children develop alphabetic knowledge by first learning to name the letters, then to discriminate their shapes, and finally to identify and map their sounds (Mason, 1980). Many children enter school with a great deal of alphabetic knowledge. They have gained this knowledge through listening to storybooks; singing songs; reciting nursery rhymes; playing with alphabet books, blocks, and shapes; watching and listening to children's television shows; and playing computer and CD alphabet games.

Learning to print letters is an excellent way to develop alphabetic knowledge and to promote children's interest in using written language to communicate. Indeed, for many children who read well before starting school, writing comes before reading (Durkin, 1966). Interestingly, analyses of early writing efforts show that as young children decide how to use letters to make words, they rely heavily on letter names, not letter sounds: *YL* (while), *PPL* (people) (Chomsky, 1979).

Professional Development

Teacher Resource Library CD-ROMs or ***Online Professional Development*** provides courses that help you better understand the Phonics and Fluency instruction in ***Open Court Reading.*** For more information about this program, visit SRAonline.com.

Additional information about phonics as well as resource references can be found in the ***Professional Development Guide: Phonics.***

SELECTION INTRODUCTION

Focus Questions What would it be like to discover a secret place in the city that animals call home? Why is it so important to protect such a secret place? What can you do to help protect the wildlife near you?

Secret Place

Eve Bunting
illustrated by Ted Rand

In the heart of the city where I live
there is a secret place.
Close by is a freeway
where cars and trucks boom,
and a railroad track
with freight trains that shunt and grunt.

There are warehouses
with windows blinded by dust
and names paint-scrawled on their brick walls.

The lines on the telephone and electric poles
web the sky.
Smokestacks blow clouds to dim the sun.

But in the heart of the city where I live,
low down, hidden,
a river runs.
The water is dark and shallow
in its concrete bed.
Bushes and tangled weeds
cling to the slopes of the concrete walls.

Hardly anyone knows the river is here.
Hardly anyone cares.

182

Selection Summary

Genre: Realistic Fiction

"Secret Place" tells about a small, hidden spot in the middle of the city where wildlife thrives. Only a handful of people know about it and come to keep an eye on it. Where could the secret place be? Could it be near where you live?

Some major elements of realistic fiction include:

- The characters behave as people do in real life.
- The setting of the story is a real place or could be a real place.
- The events in the story could happen in real life.

About the Author

Eve Bunting is known as one of the world's most prolific writers of juvenile literature. At the age of nine, she went to a boarding school in Belfast, Ireland. It was there, in the telling of tales after "lights out," that she got her first taste of storytelling and developed her lifelong love of books and reading. Nine years after Bunting married, she and her family moved to the United States. Bunting's first book, *The Two Giants*, was a tremendous success. The recipient of numerous awards, Bunting received the Classroom Choice Award from Scholastic Paperbacks for *Skateboard. One More Flight* was selected as one of the Child Association of America's Children's Books of the Year, and *Winter's Coming* was named one of the New York Times Top Ten Books. Bunting has also written on many controversial themes, such as divorce and rioting. She won the Caldecott Medal for a book about the latter, detailed through the eyes of a child in *Smoky Night.*

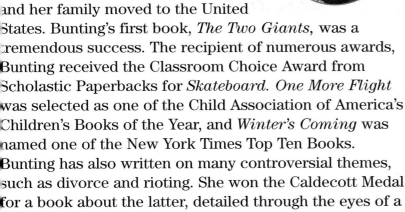

Students can read more about writer Eve Bunting on page 195 of the ***Student Anthology.***

About the Illustrator

Ted Rand no longer accepts portrait commissions so that he can spend his time illustrating children's books. *"The technical freedom, the opportunity to work in a great variety of styles, the people I work with, the common goal of getting children to read, all these combine to put this at the top of my list."* Rand attended the Cornish School in Seattle. *The Ghost Eye* was named a 1986 Children's Choice Book.

Students can read more about the illustrator on page 195 of their ***Student Anthologies.***

Inquiry Connections

This story shows how wildlife can thrive even in the midst of concrete, abandoned factories, noise, and pollution. It also illustrates the fact that wildlife surrounds us, even in cities, although most people don't even notice it. How can the wildlife be cared for? How does the wildlife enhance the lives of people? Key concepts explored are:

- By looking closely, people can find wildlife almost everywhere, even in the middle of large cities.
- People have a deep need to be near and have a connection with wildlife.
- Wildlife must be protected.
- Sometimes, simple acts are all that is necessary to make a big difference in protecting wildlife.

Before reading the selection:

- Point out that students may post a question, concept, word, illustration, or object on the Concept/Question Board at any time during the course of their unit investigation. Be sure that students include their name or initials on the items they post so that others will know whom to go to if they have an answer or if they wish to collaborate on a related activity.
- Students should feel free to write an answer or a note on someone else's question or to consult the Board for ideas for their own investigations throughout the unit.
- Encourage students to read about city wildlife at home and to bring in articles or pictures that are good examples to post on the Board.

Concept/Question Board

- As students prepare to read the selection, have them browse the Focus Questions on the first page of the selection. Tell them to keep these questions in mind as the selection is read.

Set Purposes

Encourage students to set their own purposes for reading this selection. As they read, have students think about the questions they have about city wildlife that this selection might answer or help answer.

Selection Vocabulary

As students study vocabulary, they will use a variety of skills to determine the meaning of a word. These include context clues, word structure, and apposition. Students will apply these same skills while reading to clarify additional unfamiliar words.

Display ***Reading Transparency 15*** before reading the selection to introduce and discuss the following words and their meanings.

shallow:	not deep (page 182)
concrete:	a hard building material (page 182)
slopes:	upward or downward slant (page 182)
plumes:	feathers (page 184)
shadowed:	covered in shadow; partially hidden (page 189)
wilderness:	area undisturbed by human activity (page 190)

Have students read the words in the Word Box, stopping to blend any words that they have trouble reading. Help students decode multisyllabic words by breaking the words into syllables and blending the syllables. If students still have trouble, refer them to the ***Sound/Spelling Cards.*** If the word is not decodable, give the students the pronunciation. Students can write their definitions in their Writer's Notebooks.

Have students read the sentences on the transparency to determine the meaning of the underlined words. Each word has two sentences that students will read and from which they should be able to derive the meaning of the underlined word. Remind them to use one or more of the skills they have learned—context clues, word structure, or apposition—to figure out the meaning before using a dictionary. Be sure students explain which skills they are using and how they figured out the meanings of the words. Have students reread the sentence, substituting the definition to see if the sentence makes sense. Have a volunteer create a new sentence using the underlined word.

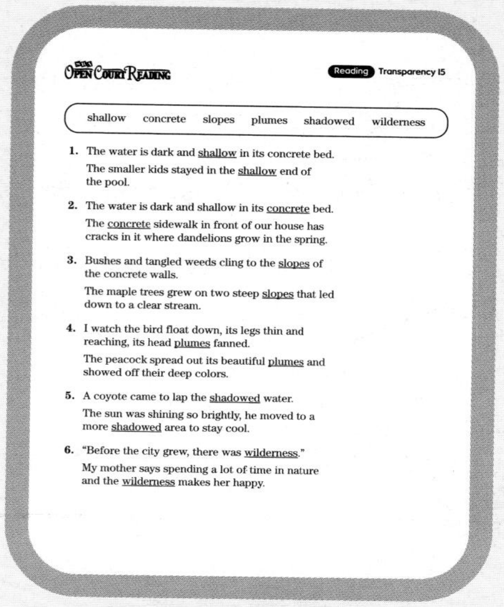

OPEN COURT READING — Reading Transparency 15

shallow concrete slopes plumes shadowed wilderness

1. The water is dark and shallow in its concrete bed.
   The smaller kids stayed in the shallow end of the pool.
2. The water is dark and shallow in its concrete bed.
   The concrete sidewalk in front of our house has cracks in it where dandelions grow in the spring.
3. Bushes and tangled weeds cling to the slopes of the concrete walls.
   The maple trees grew on two steep slopes that led down to a clear stream.
4. I watch the bird float down, its legs thin and reaching, its head plumes fanned.
   The peacock spread out its beautiful plumes and showed off their deep colors.
5. A coyote came to lap the shadowed water.
   The sun was shining so brightly, he moved to a more shadowed area to stay cool.
6. "Before the city grew, there was wilderness."
   My mother says spending a lot of time in nature and the wilderness makes her happy.

Reading Transparency 15

Teacher Tip SETTING PURPOSES Remind students as they set purposes to check the Concept/Question Board for questions and problems that this story might address.

Teacher Tip SELECTION VOCABULARY To help students decode words, divide them into syllables when you are saying them, as shown below. The information following each word tells how students can figure out the meaning of each word. When writing words on the board, do not divide them into syllables.

shal • low	context clues
con • crete	context clues
slopes	context clues
plumes	context clues
shad • owed	word structure
wil • der • ness	word structure

Routine Card
Refer to ***Routine 3*** for the vocabulary procedure.

Teacher Tip COMPREHENSION STRATEGIES Let the students know that they are to use comprehension strategies like good readers use them—that is, they are not supposed to wait for the teacher to remind them to use strategies, but rather are to use them on their own to understand a text.

Routine Card
Refer to ***Routine 5*** for the procedure on reading the selection.

Differentiating Instruction

If...	Then...
Students need extra help with visualizing	Use ***Intervention Guide*** pages 111–112

Teacher Tip COMPREHENSION STRATEGIES Remind students on the second day as they read the story to summarize what they learned from the first day.

Teacher Tip For extra practice in oral fluency, have individual students read aloud to you a selection they have previously read, either from a ***Decodable Book*** or a passage from the ***Student Anthology.*** Time each student for one minute. If the student reads more than 107 words correctly, have the student retell the selection he or she has just read. Use one prompt if the student seems to be stuck, and allow a maximum of one minute for the student to retell the story. If the student does not read more than 107 words correctly, have the student try reading from an earlier ***Decodable Book*** to help you determine where the problem lies.

Reading Recommendations

Oral Reading

This selection should not pose many difficulties for students who wish to read this selection silently. However, reading this story aloud will give students an opportunity to enjoy its poetic language, give you the opportunity to continue modeling comprehension strategies for students, and give students practice using the strategies aloud. For this reason, oral reading is recommended.

Have students make use of the comprehension strategies listed below to help them understand the selection. Have them stop reading periodically or wait until they have completed the selection to discuss the reading strategies. After the students have finished reading the selection, use the Discussing the Selection questions on page 193A to see if they understand what they have read.

Using Comprehension Strategies First Read

Comprehension strategy instruction allows students to become aware of how good readers read. Good readers constantly check their understanding as they are reading and ask themselves questions. In addition, skilled readers recognize when they are having problems and stop to use various comprehension strategies to help them make sense of what they are reading.

During the reading of "Secret Place," teacher model and prompt the use of the following comprehension strategies.

- **Monitoring and Adjusting Reading Speed** can be used when it is necessary for readers to slow down and reread in order to obtain all of the information.
- **Summarizing** prompts readers to keep track of what they are reading and to focus their minds on important information.
- **Visualizing** requires readers to mentally picture the events or characters in the story, resulting in a more vivid and imaginative understanding of the story.

As students read, they should be using a variety of strategies to help them understand the selection. Encourage students to use the strategies listed above as the class reads the story aloud. Do this by stopping at the points indicated by the numbers in the magenta circles on the reduced student page and using a particular strategy. Students can also stop reading periodically to discuss what they have learned and what problems they may be having.

Building Comprehension Skills Second Read

Revisiting or rereading a selection allows students to apply skills that give them a more complete understanding of the text. Some follow-up comprehension skills help students organize information. Others lead to deeper understanding—to "reading between the lines," as mature readers do.

An extended lesson on the comprehension skill, Author's Purpose, can be found in the Supporting the Reading section page 193C–193D. This lesson is intended to give students extra practice with Author's Purpose. However, it may be used at this time to introduce the comprehension skill to students.

- **Author's Purpose (Introduction):** Readers determine the purpose the author had for writing the text. Readers can then sort out what is important in a text from what is less important. Knowing the author's purpose also gives readers an idea of what they can expect to find in the text.

Reading with a Purpose

Have students look for ways city wildlife adapts. Also have them find ways people help wildlife.

Research in Action

The children are reading all day every day. Encourage them to bring to class examples of intriguing characters, interesting ways authors have presented characters, and effective passages of dialogue from things they read outside of class. *(Marsha Roit)*

During Workshop, and after the selection has been read at least once, have students listen to the recording of this lesson's selection on the ***Listening Library Audiocassette/CD.*** After students have listened, have them discuss their personal preferences of the selections read. Ask them what other things they have listened to and like to listen to on the radio, on audiocassettes, or on CDs.

COMPREHENSION

This selection is broken into two parts. On the first day, read pages 182–187. On the second day, read pages 188–193.

Comprehension Strategies

First Read

Read the story aloud, taking turns with the students. Start by modeling the use of strategies for the students.

Teacher Modeling

1 Monitoring and Adjusting Reading Speed *After reading this passage, I think I misunderstood something. The speaker says there is a river. I know he's in a city. Is he saying that no one knows the river is there in the city? Maybe I read the passage too quickly. I'd better slow down to make sure I understand what is going on. Let's read on a bit slower this time.*

Word Knowledge

SCAFFOLDING The skills students are reviewing in Word Knowledge should help them in reading the story. This lesson focuses on compound words, the inflectional ending *-ed,* antonyms, and vivid verbs and nouns.

vivid verbs: **boom**
shunt
grunt

Teacher Tip Although Monitoring and Adjusting Reading Speed is the strategy being modeled, encourage students to use any strategy they have learned as they read the story.

Writer's Craft

Effective Beginnings
Point out how effective the beginning of the story is. A sense of mystery is created by the knowledge that hardly anyone knows about the secret place. This makes the reader want to read the story to learn about the secret place. See Writer's Craft, page 195H.

First Reading Recommendation

ORAL • CHORAL

Focus Questions What would it be like to discover a secret place in the city that animals call home? Why is it so important to protect such a secret place? What can you do to help protect the wildlife near you?

Secret Place

Eve Bunting
illustrated by Ted Rand

In the heart of the city where I live
there is a secret place.
Close by is a freeway
where cars and trucks boom,
and a railroad track
with freight trains that shunt and grunt.

There are warehouses
with windows blinded by dust
and names paint-scrawled on their brick walls.

The lines on the telephone and electric poles
web the sky.
Smokestacks blow clouds to dim the sun.

But in the heart of the city where I live,
low down, hidden,
a river runs.
The water is dark and shallow
in its concrete bed.
Bushes and tangled weeds
cling to the slopes of the concrete walls.

Hardly anyone knows the river is here. **1**
Hardly anyone cares.

182

Informal Assessment

Observe individual students as they read, and use the Teacher Observation Log, found in the ***Program Assessment Teacher's Edition,*** to record anecdotal information about each student's strengths and weaknesses.

Mrs. Arren knows,
and Mr. Ramirez,
and Peter and Janet who are married.

I know, and my father knows, too.
He works a forklift
in one of the brick warehouses,
and I showed him the secret place
the day I found it.

183

Skills Trace

Author's Purpose

Introduced in Grade 2.
Scaffolded throughout Grade 3.

REINTRODUCED:	Unit 2, Lesson 6
REINFORCED:	Unit 3, Lesson 1
	Unit 4, Lesson 4
TESTED:	Unit 2 Assessment

COMPREHENSION

Comprehension Skills

Second Read

Author's Purpose

During a second reading of the story tell students to look for clues to the author's purpose for this text. Understanding the author's purpose helps readers focus in on important details in a text and also helps them make sense of these details. Ask students what information they see here and what that information tells them about the author's purpose. Record, in note form, the details students notice and what they think those details reveal about the author's purpose.

- On the first page are details about the city—the sounds and sights. I think the writer is describing setting so she can tell a story about something that happens there.
- The last line of the first page says, "Hardly anyone cares." In addition to telling an entertaining story, I think the author might also have a message to share.

Word Knowledge

***-ed* endings:** **married**, **showed**, **amazed**

Teacher Tip AUTHOR'S PURPOSE Tell students that they should try to figure out the author's purpose whenever they are reading.

Second Reading Recommendation

ORAL • **SILENT**

COMPREHENSION

Comprehension Strategies

First Read

Begin prompting students for responses. Praise answers that are appropriate, even if they do not match the student sample. This will encourage students to use strategies as they read.

Prompting

2 Monitoring and Adjusting Reading Speed *After slowing down and reading further, I think I know what the boy meant when he said no one knows. Who would like to share what they learned when they slowed down their reading?*

Student Sample

Monitoring and Adjusting Reading Speed *I see now that he was talking about a part of the river where there is still a lot of wildlife. That's unusual in the middle of a big city. I bet he meant no one knows about just that special part of the river where all the wildlife live.*

Word Knowledge

***-ed* endings:** **fanned**

Teacher Tip FLUENCY Remind students to notice spelling changes to base words when suffixes are added.

Teacher Tip Tell students that good readers keep thinking about the questions that come up about the topic, and they keep coming back to those questions. As they read, tell them to keep the questions on the Concept/Question Board in mind. Have them make notes to themselves in the Response Journal section of their Writer's Notebooks about which questions seem really most important. Tell them that good readers always think about what is important in selections, and they try to remember this important information.

The white egret found it, too.
I watch the bird float down,
its legs thin and reaching,
its head plumes fanned.

184

Differentiating Instruction

If...	Then...
English Learners need extra help with vocabulary	Use ***English Learner Support Guide*** pages 166–167
English Learners need extra help with summarizing	Use ***English Learner Support Guide*** pages 167–168

The green-winged teal knows.
The buffleheads that come to water-skim know.
And the circling mallards know.
I've seen them here before.
Peter says last year
there was a mallard nest
lined with feathers from the mother's breast.
Later there were ducklings.
"They'll nest here again," Peter says. **2**
I jump up and down. "Ducklings! Perfect!"

185

Comprehension Skills

Second Read

Author's Purpose

Remind students to look for specific details, then ask themselves: *Why did the author include this information? What is she trying to say? Is she trying to entertain? Inform? Persuade?*

- I see here that the author is including lots of details about how the wildlife looks. I bet she adds these details to help readers picture the scene.
- I noticed earlier that I thought the author might also have a message to share. With all these details about wildlife, I bet the message is related to appreciating or respecting wildlife.

Word Knowledge

antonyms:
before (after)
with (without)
later (earlier)
up (down)

Teacher Tip As students read aloud, listen for appropriate pacing, intonation, and expression.

COMPREHENSION

COMPREHENSION

Comprehension Strategies

First Read

Prompting

❸ **Monitoring and Adjusting Reading Speed** *I see some other things here that require me to slow down my reading speed. What about anyone else? Would anyone here like to clarify something they overlooked before they checked their reading speed?*

Student Sample

Monitoring and Adjusting Reading Speed *By looking at the illustration, I see that Peter is naming the birds in the secret place. Since some of the names are in the illustration, I started reading slower without thinking about it. Now I know that Peter was telling the boy about all the different birds and that leads me to understand that this secret place is bigger than I originally thought.*

Teacher Tip Remind students to use all the reading strategies they have learned so far in order to better understand and appreciate the story.

Teacher Tip COMPREHENSION Good readers are active readers. They interact with the text as they read by emoting, reacting, responding, and problem solving in their efforts to construct and maintain meaning.

Differentiating Instruction

If...	Then...
English Learners need extra help with vocabulary	Use ***English Learner Support Guide*** page 169
English Learners need extra help with summarizing	Use ***English Learner Support Guide*** pages 169–171

Mrs. Arren and Mr. Ramirez and Janet and Peter
bring binoculars.
They let me look through them.
The sparrows lined up on the barbed wire fence
seem big as mud hens.

Peter tells me the names of the birds.
He is like a bird himself,
with hair the color of a cinnamon teal. **3**

187

Comprehension Skills

Second Read

Author's Purpose

Have students continue to identify the author's purpose as they read. They can consider the author's purpose for including specific details and also think about the author's overall purpose for the entire text.

- Here the author describes how the characters can get a closer look at wildlife. The author's purpose here might be to show that the characters are true nature lovers. This detail might develop characterization.
- I also think the author has a message to send with this story. Maybe the purpose of this detail is also to give people an example of how to observe nature.

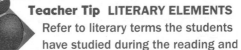

Word Knowledge

***-ed* endings:** **lined**
barbed

Teacher Tip LITERARY ELEMENTS
Refer to literary terms the students have studied during the reading and after the reading during discussion. This will help students understand the terminology and be able to use it in discussions about literature.

COMPREHENSION

INVESTIGATION

Concept/Question Board

Tell students this is a good time to post on the Concept/Question Board any new questions they have about city wildlife that "Secret Place" might have raised. Remind them of your earlier discussion about the Concept/Question Board and ask them to tell what they remember about that discussion.

After reading each selection, students should use the Concept/Question Board to:

- Post any questions they asked about a selection before reading that have not been answered yet.
- Refer to as they formulate statements about concepts that apply to their investigations.
- Post general statements formulated by each collaborative group.
- Continue to post news articles or other items that they find during their unit investigations.
- Read and think about posted questions, articles, or concepts that interest them and provide answers to their questions.

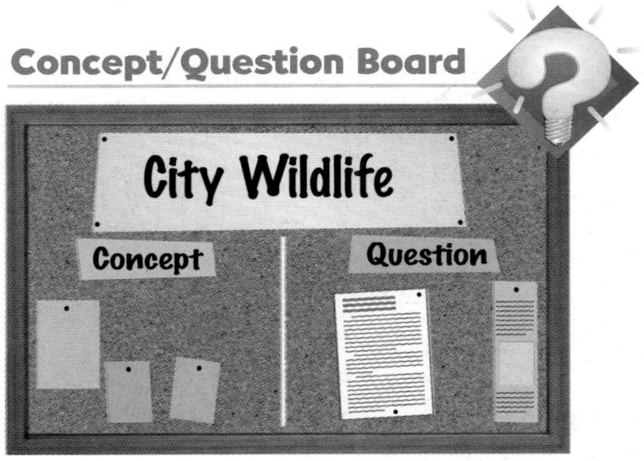

Unit 2 Investigation Management

Lesson 1	Introduce investigation possibilities. Groups form and brainstorm initial plans. Plans are presented to the whole class and discussed. Groups can take a neighborhood tour to identify city wildlife.
Lesson 2	Groups refine problems and form conjectures. Students can invite an expert to class.
Lesson 3	Groups create investigation plans, assign tasks, and begin investigation. Groups can hold a discussion about the benefits and dangers of city living.
Lesson 4	Groups revise plans and continue investigation. Groups can compare urban and natural animal habitats.
Lesson 5	Groups present formal presentations, make necessary revisions, and continue investigation. Groups can investigate and lead a panel discussion on the issue of disappearing natural habitats and how wildlife is affected.
Lesson 6	Collaborative Investigation **Groups make final preparations and presentations of findings.** Supplementary Activity **Groups can create a proposal for protecting wildlife in urban areas.**

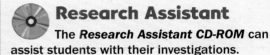

Teacher Tip If students' investigations have been going well, they will be eager for a chance to share their findings and not so eager to hear how others are doing. If you have students who are anxious to share information, let them report briefly to remove that pressure. Then return to the larger group and refocus discussion.

Research Assistant

The ***Research Assistant CD-ROM*** can assist students with their investigations.

Teacher Tip Remind students that their investigation topics are on-going. The unit investigations are not performed to find final conclusions or come to final decisions regarding any one topic. Instead, they are designed to stimulate further thinking and investigation of the topic, lasting past the end of a unit or the end of the school year.

Informal Assessment

Observe and assess students during their oral presentations. Record your observations in the Teacher Observation Log found in the ***Program Assessment Teacher's Edition.***

Formal Assessment

Use the Research Rubrics on page 182J to make an overall assessment of students' research.

INVESTIGATION

Presentations

Now that students have been investigating city wildlife and related issues for several weeks, students may have new insights they would like to discuss with others or record for themselves. Looking over the entries they've made in their ***Inquiry Journals*** will show them how far they have come in their investigations.

As students are concluding their investigations and preparing formal presentations, remind them to think about the questions and ideas they had at the beginning of the unit. Have those ideas changed? If so, in what ways have they changed? What do they know now that they didn't know before?

Have students propose new questions and form new conjectures based on their readings, activities, and investigations of this unit's theme. Encourage students to pursue these questions on their own if they desire. Remind them of the never-ending nature of research and investigation and of the discoveries that will be made along the way.

iagrams

each Ask students what they know about diagrams. If necessary, give them ıe following information: diagrams are pictures that show something and bel its parts. Diagrams are often used as a way to illustrate how to put ›mething together when the written directions of how to do so seem ›mplicated or confusing. Some people can follow pictures better than they ın written or oral directions. Ask students to share occasions on which they ay have seen or used diagrams.

uided Practice Write the following directions for assembling an ice ream cone on the board: 1) Get a cone. 2) Put ice cream in it. Ask students to ad the directions and comment on the clarity. (Hopefully, students will ›tice that there is no mention of how one should get the ice cream from the ırton into the cone.) Now draw simple pictures to go with each step. For the cond step, make sure you show the carton of ice cream and a scoop or ›oon digging into the ice cream and putting the scoop of ice cream on top of ıe cone. Discuss with students how the pictures make the directions clearer.

ndependent Practice Ask students to think of the steps required to ake a peanut butter and banana sandwich. Have them write each step in the rections and then make a diagram to clarify the steps.

or additional practice with diagrams, have students complete pages 51–52 of ***quiry Journal.***

Name________________ Date________

City Wildlife UNIT 2

Diagrams

A diagram is a plan, drawing, or outline that shows how something works, that labels or explains parts of something, or that shows the relationship between parts of something.

Look at the diagram of THE TONGUE. Use the diagram to answer the questions.

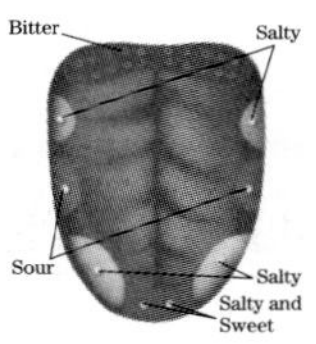

1. What taste bud is at the back of the tongue? bitter
2. What taste buds are on the tip of the tongue? salty and sweet
3. What taste buds are on the side of the tongue? sour and salty

Inquiry Journal • *Diagrams* UNIT 2 51

Diagrams *(continued)*

Look at the diagram of THE EAR. Use the diagram to answer the questions.

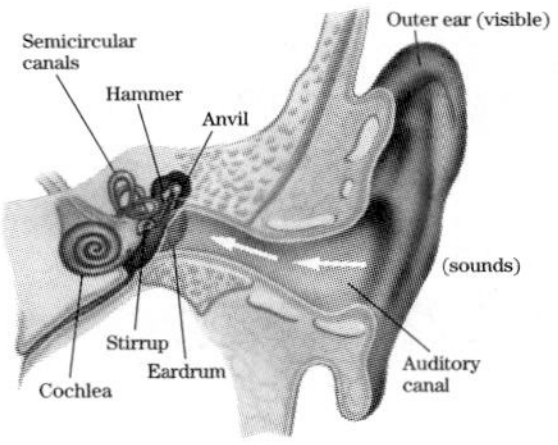

1. Name the part of the ear that you can see. outer ear
2. Through what part of the ear do noises enter? auditory canal
3. What part of the ear is farthest from the outer ear? cochlea

52 UNIT 2 *Diagrams* • Inquiry Journal

Inquiry Journal pp. 51–52

SUPPORTING THE INVESTIGATION

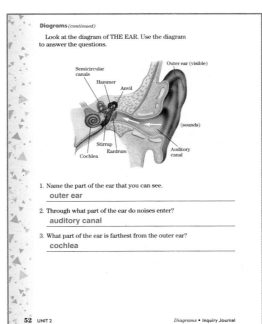

Encourage students to use ***TechKnowledge*** to learn more about how to use a computer for various tasks.

Differentiating Instruction

If...	Then...
Students are having difficulty writing the steps for making a peanut butter and banana sandwich	Act out each step for students and have them record it
Students are having difficulty with diagrams	• Help them create a diagram showing the steps for making a peanut butter and banana sandwich • Help them complete pages 51–52 in their ***Inquiry Journals*** during Workshop

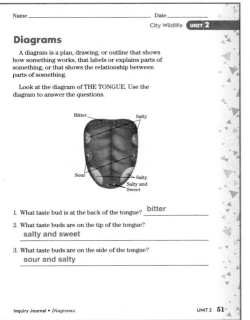

Objectives

Word Analysis

Spelling

- **Review Sound Spelling Patterns from Unit 2.** Review understanding of the /âr/, /ar/, /or/, /er/, /əl/, /oi/, and /ow/ sound spelling patterns from Unit 2 as introduced in Phonics and Fluency.

Vocabulary

- **Review Vocabulary Strategies.** Using words from "Secret Place," review the strategies for learning about homophones, word concept, categories, antonyms, and synonyms from Unit 2.

Writing Process Strategies

- **Expository Writing: Research Report.** Learn the form and process of writing a research report.

English Language Conventions

Grammar, Usage, and Mechanics

- **Review.** This lesson reviews the skills learned in Lessons 1–5.

Listening, Speaking, Viewing

- **Presenting: Chronological Order.** Use chronological order to practice the organization of ideas.

Penmanship

- **Cursive Letters *f* and *b*.** Develop handwriting skills by practicing formation of cursive *f* and *b*.

Materials

- Language Arts Handbook
- Comprehension and Language Arts Skills, pp. 52–57
- Writer's Workbook, pp. 26–29
- Language Arts Transparencies 20, 31
- Spelling and Vocabulary Skills, pp. 46–49
- Student Anthology
- Sound/Spelling Cards 27, 29, 39, 43
- Spelling Software
- Routine Card 2, Routine 7

Differentiating Instruction

Reteach, Challenge, and ***Intervention*** lessons are available to support the language arts instruction in this lesson.

Research in Action

Writing is, for most, laborious and slow. The mind travels faster than the pen; consequently, writing becomes a question of learning to make occasional wing shots, bringing down the bird of thought as it flashes by.
(William Strunk, Jr. and E. B. White, The Elements of Style)

Language Arts Overview

Word Analysis

Spelling The Spelling activities on the following pages review the /âr/ sound spellings, /or/ sound spellings, /er/ sound spellings, /əl/ sound spelled *le*, /oi/ sound spelled *oi* or *_oy*, and the /ow/ sound spelled *ou_* or *ow*.

Selection Spelling Words

These words from "Secret Place" review the sound spelling patterns from Unit 2.

clouds **tangled** **year** **noise** **jangled**

Vocabulary The Vocabulary activities review homophones, synonyms, antonyms, levels of specificity, and word concept.

Vocabulary Skill Words

there **plumes*** **binoculars** **mallards** **together**

**Also Selection Vocabulary*

Additional Materials: dictionary, thesaurus

Writing Process Strategies

The Writing Process Strategies lesson involves instruction in researching and writing a research report. Students will show what they know or have learned by objectively presenting verifiable facts, ideas, or events.

SRA TECH KNOWLEDGE: To learn basic computer skills for writing, have students practice keying the Symbol keys and help them review letters, punctuation, special keys, numbers, and symbols previously learned. ***TechKnowledge,*** Level 3, Lessons 29–30, teach these keyboarding skills.

English Language Conventions

Grammar, Usage, and Mechanics **Review.** Display knowledge and understanding of all of the skills learned in Lessons 1–5.

Listening, Speaking, Viewing **Presenting: Chronological Order.** In this Presenting lesson, students will use chronological order to practice the organization of ideas.

Penmanship **Cursive Letters *f* and *b*.** This lesson develops cursive handwriting skills by having students learn correct formation of *f* and *b*. Students then practice writing words from the literature selection that contain those letters.

DAY 1

Word Analysis

Spelling

Assessment: Pretest
Unit 2 Review

Teach
Give students the Pretest on page 36 of ***Unit 2 Assessment.*** Have them proofread and correct any misspelled words.

Pretest Sentences

1. **noisy** Concert fans are **noisy**.
2. **choice** Restaurants offer a **choice** of foods.
3. **grouch** A **grouch** is in a bad mood.
4. **growl** Dogs **growl** at strangers.
5. **puddle** Water can form a **puddle.**
6. **dirt** Some **dirt** can stain clothing.
7. **pear** A **pear** is a sweet fruit.
8. **corner** A **corner** is an angle.
9. **rare** A **rare** antique is very expensive.
10. **return** Birds often **return** to the same nest.
11. **clouds** Some **clouds** look fluffy.
12. **tangled** Insects get **tangled** in a spider's web.
13. **cradle** A baby sleeps in a **cradle**.
14. **noise** A kazoo makes a funny **noise**.
15. **jangled** Long ago, dinner bells **jangled** for supper.

Diagnose any misspellings by determining whether students misspelled sound spelling patterns from Unit 2 or some other part of the word. Then use the Pretest as a take-home list to review the spellings of words with sound spelling patterns from Unit 2.

Writing Process Strategies

Getting Ideas
Research Report

Teach
Introduce Research Reports

- Read ***Language Arts Handbook,*** pages 108–113, to introduce research reports.
- Share the Formal Assessment Rubrics with the students (see Day 5 of this lesson).

Inspiration

Teacher Model: *"Even though the story 'Secret Place' is fiction, the author describes real wild animals doing the things real wild animals do. I want to know more about these creatures. Once I do, I could write a research report to share what I have learned with others."*

Brainstorming

Encourage students to suggest topics for a research report. Make a list of students' suggestions on the board.

Guided Practice
Getting Ideas

Direct students to write ideas for a research report and possible sources of information in their Writer's Notebooks.

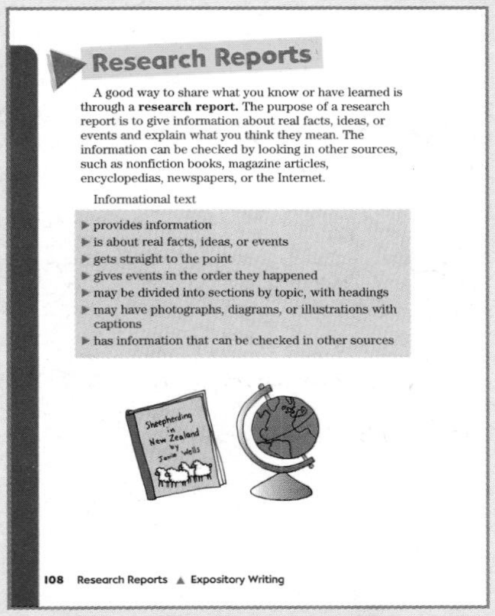
Research Reports

A good way to share what you know or have learned is through a **research report.** The purpose of a research report is to give information about real facts, ideas, or events and explain what you think they mean. The information can be checked by looking in other sources, such as nonfiction books, magazine articles, encyclopedias, newspapers, or the Internet.

Informational text

- provides information
- is about real facts, ideas, or events
- gets straight to the point
- gives events in the order they happened
- may be divided into sections by topic, with headings
- may have photographs, diagrams, or illustrations with captions
- has information that can be checked in other sources

108 Research Reports ▲ Expository Writing

Language Arts Handbook p. 108

English Language Conventions

Grammar, Usage, and Mechanics
Review

Teach
- Review the skills from Lessons 1–5.
  - Lesson 1, Quotation marks: Make sure students know that quotation marks are used to set off dialogue and the titles of short stories, poems, songs, and chapters of books.
  - Lesson 2, Commas in a series: Make sure students understand that commas are used to separate three or more words or phrases in a series.
  - Lesson 3, Commas in dialogue: Make sure students know how to properly place commas in dialogue.
  - Lesson 4, Capitalization of places: Make sure students understand that the names of specific cities, states, countries, parks, and buildings are capitalized.
  - Lesson 5, Question marks and exclamation points: Make sure students know how to use question marks and exclamation points correctly.

Independent Practice
Have students complete ***Comprehension and Language Arts Skills,*** pages 54–55, which review all the skills in the unit.

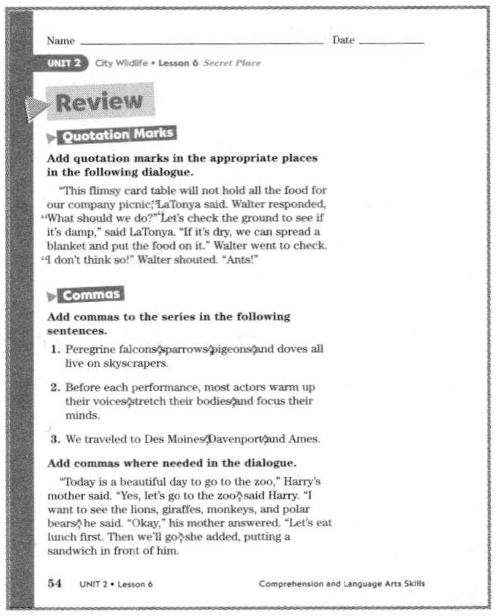
Name ________ Date ________

UNIT 2 City Wildlife • Lesson 6 *Secret Place*

Review

Quotation Marks

Add quotation marks in the appropriate places in the following dialogue.

"This flimsy card table will not hold all the food for our company picnic," LaTonya said. Walter responded, "What should we do?" "Let's check the ground to see if it's damp," said LaTonya. "If it's dry, we can spread a blanket and put the food on it." Walter went to check. "I don't think so!" Walter shouted. "Ants!"

Commas

Add commas to the series in the following sentences.

1. Peregrine falcons, sparrows, pigeons, and doves all live on skyscrapers.
2. Before each performance, most actors warm up their voices, stretch their bodies, and focus their minds.
3. We traveled to Des Moines, Davenport, and Ames.

Add commas where needed in the dialogue.

"Today is a beautiful day to go to the zoo," Harry's mother said. "Yes, let's go to the zoo," said Harry. "I want to see the lions, giraffes, monkeys, and polar bears," he said. "Okay," his mother answered. "Let's eat lunch first. Then we'll go," she added, putting a sandwich in front of him.

54 UNIT 2 • Lesson 6 Comprehension and Language Arts Skills

Comprehension and Language Arts Skills p. 54

DAY 2

Word Analysis

Spelling

Word Sorting

- Review ***Sound/Spelling Cards 27, 29, 39,*** and ***43.***
- Have students complete the Spelling Bee activity for Unit 2 on the ***Spelling Software.***

Vocabulary

Review of Homophones

Teach

- Write *there* (page 182 of "Secret Place") on the board. Ask a student to read the sentence with *there* and explain its meaning in the sentence. *(located, where the warehouses are)*
- Write *their* on the board next to *there.* Ask what the definition of *their* is. *(ownership, personal, belonging to them)*
- Remind students that *there* and *their* are homophones.
- Underline the different spelling patterns found in *there* and *their.* As a class, think of ways to memorize the spellings.

Guided Practice

Use ***Spelling and Vocabulary Skills,*** page 46, to review word concepts. Ask students to complete page 47 as independent practice.

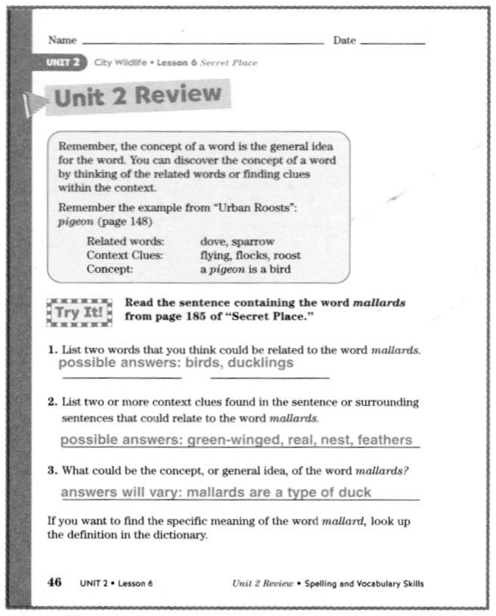
Name ______ Date ______

UNIT 2 City Wildlife • Lesson 6 *Secret Place*

Unit 2 Review

Remember, the concept of a word is the general idea for the word. You can discover the concept of a word by thinking of the related words or finding clues within the context.

Remember the example from "Urban Roosts": *pigeon* (page 148)

Related words:	dove, sparrow
Context Clues:	flying, flocks, roost
Concept:	a *pigeon* is a bird

Try It! **Read the sentence containing the word *mallards* from page 185 of "Secret Place."**

1. List two words that you think could be related to the word *mallards.*
possible answers: birds, ducklings
2. List two or more context clues found in the sentence or surrounding sentences that could relate to the word *mallards.*
possible answers: green-winged, real, nest, feathers
3. What could be the concept, or general idea, of the word *mallards?*
answers will vary: mallards are a type of duck

If you want to find the specific meaning of the word *mallard,* look up the definition in the dictionary.

46 UNIT 2 • Lesson 6 *Unit 2 Review* • Spelling and Vocabulary Skills

***Spelling and Vocabulary Skills* p. 46**

Writing Process Strategies

Prewriting

Research Report

Teach

- Review student suggestions for research report topics and information sources from Day 1.
- Read ***Writer's Workbook,*** page 26, on prewriting for a research report.
- Remind students to use their own words when writing down information for their research reports.

Independent Practice

Prewriting

- Have students fill out their audience and purpose for a research report on page 26 of the ***Writer's Workbook.***
- Have students complete the graphic organizer on page 27 of the ***Writer's Workbook.***

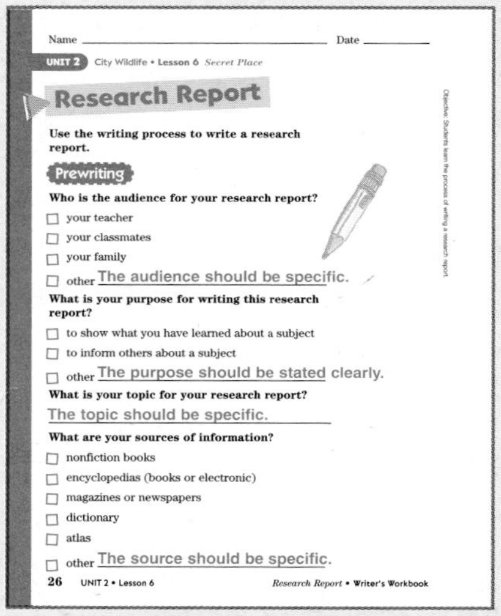
Name ______ Date ______

UNIT 2 City Wildlife • Lesson 6 *Secret Place*

Research Report

Use the writing process to write a research report.

Prewriting

Who is the audience for your research report?

- ☐ your teacher
- ☐ your classmates
- ☐ your family
- ☐ other The audience should be specific.

What is your purpose for writing this research report?

- ☐ to show what you have learned about a subject
- ☐ to inform others about a subject
- ☐ other The purpose should be stated clearly.

What is your topic for your research report?

The topic should be specific.

What are your sources of information?

- ☐ nonfiction books
- ☐ encyclopedias (books or electronic)
- ☐ magazines or newspapers
- ☐ dictionary
- ☐ atlas
- ☐ other The source should be specific.

Objective: Students learn the process of writing a research report.

26 UNIT 2 • Lesson 6 *Research Report* • Writer's Workbook

***Writer's Workbook* p. 26**

English Language Conventions

Grammar, Usage, and Mechanics

Review

Teach

- Review quotation marks by asking students when they would use them. Write their answers on the board. *(Quotation marks are used in dialogue and to set off the titles of short stories, poems, songs, and chapters of books.)*
- Review commas in a series by reminding students that commas should be used between three or more words or phrases in a series. Write these sentences on the board and ask students to come to the board and insert commas where necessary.
  - We have water*(,)* snacks*(,)* and a first-aid kit for our hike.
  - Yesterday I had to clean my room*(,)* do my homework*(,)* and help with dinner.
- Review commas in dialogue by explaining that commas are used in dialogue to set off the words of the speaker from the rest of the sentence.
- Review capitalization of places by explaining that proper nouns naming specific cities, states, countries, parks, and buildings should always be capitalized.
- Review question marks and exclamation points by reminding students that question marks are used in interrogative sentences and exclamation points are used in exclamatory sentences and interjections.

Guided Practice in Reading

Have students look for examples of the grammar, usage, and mechanics skills from this unit in "Secret Place." *(It will not be possible to find examples of all of these in the selection.)*

DAY 3

Word Analysis

Spelling

Unit 2 Review

Teach

- Introduce the spelling words found in "Secret Place."
- Ask students to think of words with the /oi/ or /ow/ sounds that are seen on the playground. *(soil, flowers, clouds)*

Guided Practice

Have students complete page 48 of ***Spelling and Vocabulary Skills*** to review strategies for spelling words with sound spelling patterns from Unit 2.

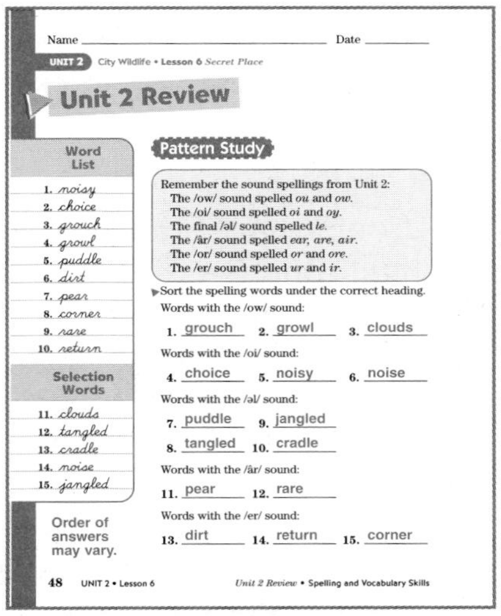

Name ______________ Date ________

UNIT 2 City Wildlife • Lesson 6 *Secret Place*

Unit 2 Review

Word List
1. noisy
2. choice
3. grouch
4. growl
5. puddle
6. dirt
7. pear
8. corner
9. rare
10. return

Selection Words
11. clouds
12. tangled
13. cradle
14. noise
15. jangled

Pattern Study

Remember the sound spellings from Unit 2:
The /ow/ sound spelled *ou* and *ow*.
The /oi/ sound spelled *oi* and *oy*.
The final /əl/ sound spelled *le*.
The /âr/ sound spelled *ear*, *are*, *air*.
The /or/ sound spelled *or* and *ore*.
The /er/ sound spelled *ur* and *ir*.

Sort the spelling words under the correct heading.

Words with the /ow/ sound:
1. grouch 2. growl 3. clouds

Words with the /oi/ sound:
4. choice 5. noisy 6. noise

Words with the /əl/ sound:
7. puddle 9. jangled
8. tangled 10. cradle

Words with the /âr/ sound:
11. pear 12. rare

Words with the /er/ sound:
13. dirt 14. return 15. corner

Order of answers may vary.

48 UNIT 2 • Lesson 6 *Unit 2 Review* • Spelling and Vocabulary Skills

***Spelling and Vocabulary Skills* p. 48**

Vocabulary (continued)

Review of Antonyms

- Write *together* on the board.
- Ask a student to read the sentence on page 188 of "Secret Place" with *together.* Ask students to think of the meaning of *together.* *(joined, with someone, not alone)*
- Write *apart* on the board. Explain that *together* and *apart* are antonyms, words with opposite meanings.
- Ask the class to think of definitions for *apart*, knowing that it is an antonym for *together.* *(not together, without anyone, alone)*

Writing Process Strategies

Drafting

Research Report

Teach

Read ***Writer's Workbook,*** page 27, on drafting a research report.

Writer's Craft

Effective Beginnings

- Explain that an effective beginning is one that grabs the reader's attention and makes them want to read more.
- List these five ways to write effective beginnings on the board:
  - Ask a question.
  - Tell something that happened to a person.
  - Use an interesting or surprising fact.
  - Give a quote.
  - State a problem.
- Read ***Language Arts Handbook,*** pages 202–205, on effective beginnings and endings.
- Read ***Comprehension and Language Arts Skills,*** pages 56–57, on effective beginnings.

Guided Practice

Drafting

Have students write the drafts of their research reports.

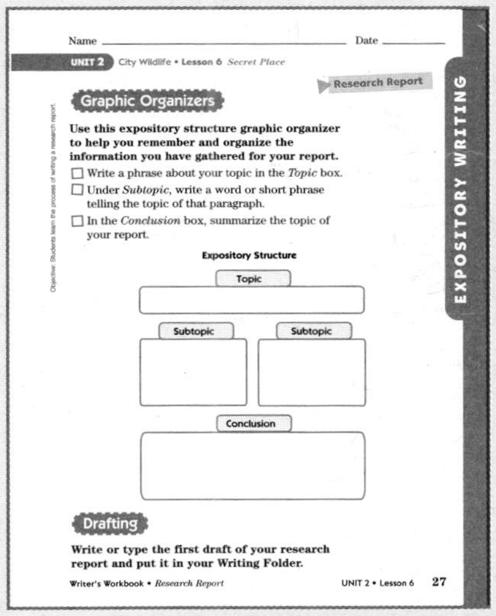

Name ______________ Date ________

UNIT 2 City Wildlife • Lesson 6 *Secret Place*

Research Report

Graphic Organizers

Use this expository structure graphic organizer to help you remember and organize the information you have gathered for your report.

☐ Write a phrase about your topic in the *Topic* box.
☐ Under *Subtopic,* write a word or short phrase telling the topic of that paragraph.
☐ In the *Conclusion* box, summarize the topic of your report.

Expository Structure

Topic

Subtopic | Subtopic

Conclusion

Drafting

Write or type the first draft of your research report and put it in your Writing Folder.

EXPOSITORY WRITING

Writer's Workbook • *Research Report* UNIT 2 • Lesson 6 27

***Writer's Workbook* p. 27**

English Language Conventions

Grammar, Usage, and Mechanics

Review

Teach

- Write the following sentences on the board. Point out the rules you are illustrating.
  - "There are three eggs in the nest," said Emilio. *(quotation marks in dialogue, commas in dialogue)*
  - Maria's favorite song is "You Are My Sunshine." *(quotation marks to set off title of song)*
  - Chris and his grandfather saw bucking broncos, cowboys, Brahma bulls, and clowns at the livestock show at Madison Square Garden. *(commas in a series, capitalization of specific building)*
  - Don't do that! Do you want to break it? *(exclamation points and question marks)*

Guided Practice in Writing

Ask students to write a short dialogue between the egret and the possum in "Secret Place" about what they think of their home in the city. Encourage students to use as many of the grammar, usage, and mechanics skills covered in Unit 2 as they can.

Informal Assessment

Check students' writing to make sure they are using the skills from this unit properly.

DAY 4

Word Analysis

Spelling

Unit 2 Review

Teach

Explain that the strategies for the exercises in ***Spelling and Vocabulary Skills*** are designed to help them learn to become better spellers of words with the sound spelling patterns introduced in Unit 2.

Guided Practice

Have students complete page 49 of ***Spelling and Vocabulary Skills*** to review the sound spelling patterns from Unit 2.

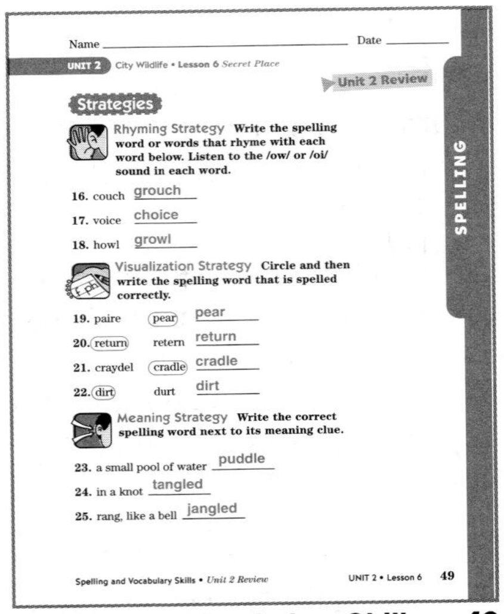

Name ______ Date ______

UNIT 2 City Wildlife • Lesson 6 *Secret Place*

Unit 2 Review

SPELLING

Strategies

Rhyming Strategy **Write the spelling word or words that rhyme with each word below. Listen to the /ow/ or /oi/ sound in each word.**

16. couch grouch
17. voice choice
18. howl growl

Visualization Strategy **Circle and then write the spelling word that is spelled correctly.**

19. paire (pear) pear
20. (return) retern return
21. craydel (cradle) cradle
22. (dirt) durt dirt

Meaning Strategy **Write the correct spelling word next to its meaning clue.**

23. a small pool of water puddle
24. in a knot tangled
25. rang, like a bell jangled

Spelling and Vocabulary Skills • *Unit 2 Review* UNIT 2 • Lesson 6 49

***Spelling and Vocabulary Skills* p. 49**

Vocabulary (continued)

Review Synonyms

- Write *plumes* from page 184 of "Secret Place" on the board.
- Ask students to find clues from the sentences that can help them understand the meaning of *plumes*. *(bird, head, fanned)*
- Ask students to think of a synonym for *plumes* or look in a thesaurus. *(feathers)*

Writing Process Strategies

Revising

Research Report

Teach

- Read ***Writer's Workbook,*** page 28, on revising a research report.
- Go over ***Language Arts Transparency 20,*** Revising: Rearranging.
- **Troubleshooting**
  - Do not copy text source exactly unless you are using just a small part for a quotation.
  - Double check any details you are unsure of.
  - Include a short definition of unusual or uncommon words.

Routine Card
Refer to *Routine 7* for Writing Conferences.

Guided Practice

Revising

- Have students revise their drafts on paper or a computer, using the Effective Beginnings skills they learned on Day 3.
- Direct students to use the checklist and the proofreading marks in the ***Writer's Workbook,*** page 28, to help them revise their writing.

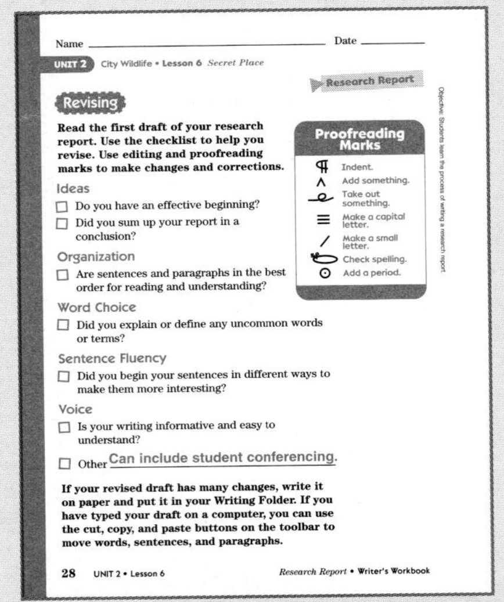

Name ______ Date ______

UNIT 2 City Wildlife • Lesson 6 *Secret Place*

Research Report

Revising

Read the first draft of your research report. Use the checklist to help you revise. Use editing and proofreading marks to make changes and corrections.

Ideas
- ☐ Do you have an effective beginning?
- ☐ Did you sum up your report in a conclusion?

Organization
- ☐ Are sentences and paragraphs in the best order for reading and understanding?

Word Choice
- ☐ Did you explain or define any uncommon words or terms?

Sentence Fluency
- ☐ Did you begin your sentences in different ways to make them more interesting?

Voice
- ☐ Is your writing informative and easy to understand?
- ☐ Other Can include student conferencing.

Proofreading Marks
- ¶ Indent.
- ^ Add something.
- Take out something.
- ≡ Make a capital letter.
- / Make a small letter.
- Check spelling.
- ⊙ Add a period.

Objective: Students learn the process of writing a research report.

If your revised draft has many changes, write it on paper and put it in your Writing Folder. If you have typed your draft on a computer, you can use the cut, copy, and paste buttons on the toolbar to move words, sentences, and paragraphs.

28 UNIT 2 • Lesson 6 *Research Report* • Writer's Workbook

***Writer's Workbook* p. 28**

English Language Conventions

Listening, Speaking, Viewing

Presenting: Chronological Order

Teach

- Explain that when something is in chronological order, it means events are listed in the order in which they happened. *Chronological* refers to when the events happened in time. *Beginning, middle,* and *end* are words that show chronological order.
- Explain that the chronological order of events is one way to present information in an oral presentation. We can pick out the major points or events we wish to discuss, and list them in the order that they happened. This gives our presentation a certain order that makes it easier to understand.

Guided Practice

- In small groups, have students pick out a few points from "Secret Place" that are important to the story. Have students organize the points into chronological order (beginning, middle, and end) as if they were preparing a presentation. *(Beginning—crowded city, busy streets, concrete buildings; Middle—peaceful river, wildlife, trees in the middle of the city; End—nighttime, the place remains a secret.)*
- Invite the students to share the points they found important. Do the students agree on the chronological order?

Informal Assessment

Observe whether students are able to organize ideas into chronological order.

DAY 5

Word Analysis

Spelling

Assessment: Final Test

Unit 2 Review

Teach

Repeat the Pretest or use the Final Test on page 37 of ***Unit 2 Assessment*** as summative assessment of student understanding of the sound spelling patterns from Unit 2.

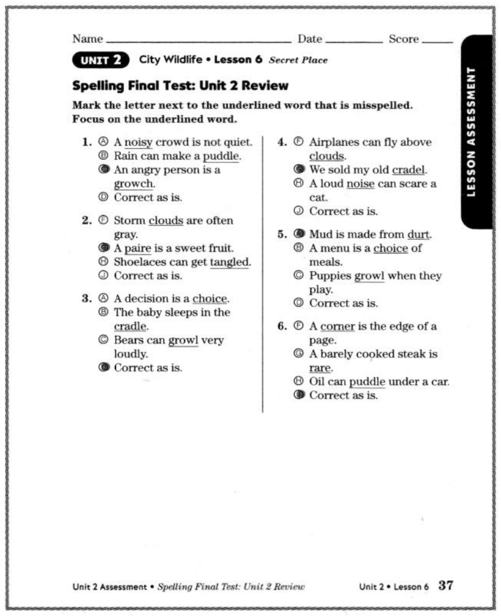
Name ______ Date ______ Score ______

UNIT 2 City Wildlife • Lesson 6 *Secret Place*

Spelling Final Test: Unit 2 Review

Mark the letter next to the underlined word that is misspelled. Focus on the underlined word.

1. Ⓐ A noisy crowd is not quiet.
   Ⓑ Rain can make a puddle.
   ● An angry person is a growch.
   Ⓓ Correct as is.
2. Ⓕ Storm clouds are often gray.
   ● A paire is a sweet fruit.
   Ⓗ Shoelaces can get tangled.
   Ⓙ Correct as is.
3. Ⓐ A decision is a choice.
   Ⓑ The baby sleeps in the cradle.
   Ⓒ Bears can growl very loudly.
   ● Correct as is.
4. Ⓕ Airplanes can fly above clouds.
   ● We sold my old cradel.
   Ⓗ A loud noise can scare a cat.
   Ⓙ Correct as is.
5. ● Mud is made from durt.
   Ⓑ A menu is a choice of meals.
   Ⓒ Puppies growl when they play.
   Ⓓ Correct as is.
6. Ⓕ A corner is the edge of a page.
   Ⓖ A barely cooked steak is rare.
   Ⓗ Oil can puddle under a car.
   ● Correct as is.

LESSON ASSESSMENT

Unit 2 Assessment • *Spelling Final Test: Unit 2 Review* Unit 2 • Lesson 6 37

***Unit 2 Assessment* p. 37**

Guided Practice

Have students categorize any mistakes they made on the Final Test as careless errors or lesson-pattern problems.

Vocabulary

Informal Assessment

Assess student knowledge of the reviewed strategies by asking students to choose one unfamiliar word from their word list in the Writer's Notebook. Ask them to apply one of the reviewed strategies to discover the meaning of the word (homophones, word concept, categories, antonyms, or synonyms). Have students add any new words to the running word list in the Writer's Notebook.

Writing Process Strategies

Editing/Proofreading and Publishing

Research Report

Teach

- Read ***Writer's Workbook,*** page 29, on editing/proofreading and publishing.
- Discuss ***Language Arts Transparency 31,*** Proofreader's Marks.

Independent Practice

Editing/Proofreading and Publishing

- Direct students to use the checklist in the ***Writer's Workbook,*** page 29.
- Have students make a neat final copy.

Formal Assessment

Total Point Value: 10

1. **The main idea is clearly stated. (2 points)**
2. **There is at least one supporting detail or example for each topic sentence. (2 points)**
3. **All information is written in the student's own words, except for quotations. (2 points)**
4. **The final copy is neat, clean, and easy to read. (2 points)**
5. **Mechanics: capitalization, punctuation, and spelling are correct. (2 points)**

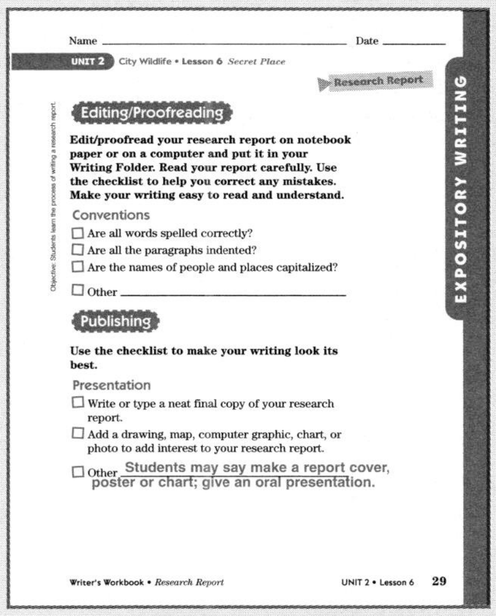
Name ______ Date ______

UNIT 2 City Wildlife • Lesson 6 *Secret Place*

Research Report

Objective: Students learn the process of writing a research report.

Editing/Proofreading

Edit/proofread your research report on notebook paper or on a computer and put it in your Writing Folder. Read your report carefully. Use the checklist to help you correct any mistakes. Make your writing easy to read and understand.

Conventions

- ☐ Are all words spelled correctly?
- ☐ Are all the paragraphs indented?
- ☐ Are the names of people and places capitalized?
- ☐ Other ______

Publishing

Use the checklist to make your writing look its best.

Presentation

- ☐ Write or type a neat final copy of your research report.
- ☐ Add a drawing, map, computer graphic, chart, or photo to add interest to your research report.
- ☐ Other Students may say make a report cover, poster or chart; give an oral presentation.

EXPOSITORY WRITING

Writer's Workbook • *Research Report* UNIT 2 • Lesson 6 29

***Writer's Workbook* p. 29**

English Language Conventions

Penmanship

Cursive Letters *f* and *b*

Teach

- **Teacher Model:** On the board, introduce the formation of lowercase cursive letters *f* and *b* as letters with loops.

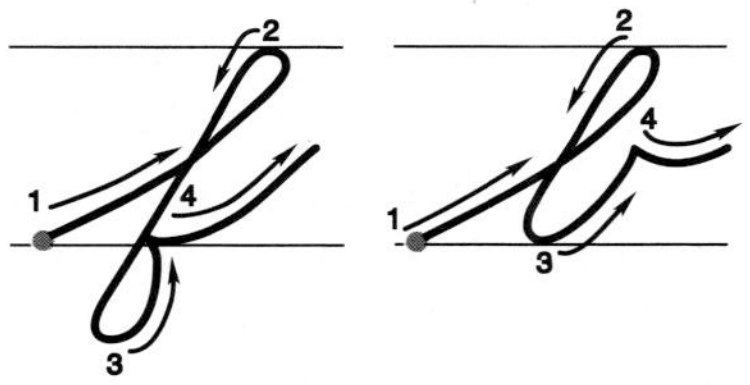

f Starting point, undercurve
Loop back, slant down
Loop forward, undercurve: small *f*

b Starting point, undercurve
Loop back, slant down
Undercurve, small curve to right: small *b*

- **Teacher Model:** Write the words *found, baby,* and *bird* on the board to model proper letter formation.
- Tell students not to make loops for letters that do not need loops.

Guided Practice

- Invite students to come to the board and trace the letters *f* and *b*.
- Have students practice writing rows of *f* and *b* in their Writer's Notebooks.
- From "Secret Place," have students write the words *by, freeway, boom,* and *freight* to practice letter formation.

Informal Assessment

Check students' handwriting for loops in letters that should not be looped.

LESSON WRAP-UP

Reading and Language Arts Skills Traces

Language Arts

WORD ANALYSIS

Skills Trace

Spelling: Unit 2 Review

Introduced in Grade 1.
Scaffolded throughout Grades 2–5.

REINTRODUCED: Unit 2, Lessons 1–5
PRACTICED: Unit 2, Lessons 1–5
Spelling and Vocabulary Skills, pp. 48–49
TESTED: Unit 2, Lesson 6, p. 195F (Pretest)
Unit 2, Lesson 6, p. 37 (Final Test)
Unit 2 Assessment

Skills Trace

Vocabulary: Unit 2 Review

Introduced in Grade 1.
Scaffolded throughout Grades 2–5.

REINTRODUCED: Unit 2, Lessons 1–5
PRACTICED: Unit 2, Lessons 1–5
Spelling and Vocabulary Skills, pp. 46–47
TESTED: Unit 2 Assessment

WRITING PROCESS STRATEGIES

Skills Trace

Expository Writing: Research Report

Introduced in Grade 3.
Scaffolded throughout Grades 4–6.

INTRODUCED: Unit 2, Lesson 6, p. 195F
PRACTICED: Unit 2, Lesson 6, pp. 195G–195J
Writer's Workbook, pp. 26–29
TESTED: Unit 2, Lesson 6, Formal Assessment, p. 195J
Unit 2 Assessment

Skills Trace

Writer's Craft: Effective Beginnings

Introduced in Grade 2.
Scaffolded throughout Grades 3–6.

REINTRODUCED: Unit 2, Lesson 6, p. 195H
PRACTICED: Unit 2, Lesson 6, p. 195H
Comprehension and Language Arts Skills, pp. 56–57
TESTED: Unit 2 Assessment

ENGLISH LANGUAGE CONVENTIONS

Skills Trace

Listening, Speaking, Viewing Presenting: Chronological Order

Introduced in Grade 2.
Scaffolded throughout Grade 3.

REINTRODUCED: Unit 2, Lesson 6, p. 195I
TESTED: Unit 2, Lesson 6, Informal Assessment, p. 195I

Skills Trace

Penmanship: Cursive Letters *f* and *b*

Introduced in Grade 2 (*f*) and Grade 3 (*b*).
Scaffolded throughout Grades 3–6 and Grades 4–6.

INTRODUCED: Unit 2, Lesson 6, p. 195J
TESTED: Unit 2, Lesson 6, Informal Assessment, p. 195J

Reading

COMPREHENSION

Skills Trace

Author's Purpose

Introduced in Grade 2.
Scaffolded throughout Grade 3.

REINTRODUCED: Unit 2, Lesson 6
REINFORCED: Unit 3, Lesson 1
Unit 4, Lesson 4
Unit 5, Lesson 2
Unit 5, Lesson 3
Unit 6, Lesson 4
TESTED: Unit 2 Assessment

Professional Development: Comprehension

Reading Comprehension Strategies

The primary aim of reading is comprehension. Without comprehension, neither intellectual nor emotional responses to reading are possible—other than the response of frustration. Good readers are problem solvers. They bring their critical faculties to bear on everything they read. Experienced readers generally understand most of what they read, but just as important, they recognize when they do not understand, and they have at their command an assortment of strategies for monitoring and furthering their understanding.

The goal of comprehension strategy instruction is to turn responsibility for using strategies over to the students as soon as possible. Research has shown that students' comprehension and learning problems are not a matter of mental capacity but rather their inability to use strategies to help them learn. Good readers use a variety of strategies to help them make sense of the text and get the most out of what they read. Trained to use a variety of comprehension strategies, children dramatically improve their learning performance. In order to do this, the teacher models strategy use and gradually incorporates different kinds of prompts and possible student think-alouds as examples of the types of thinking students might do as they read to comprehend what they are reading.

Comprehension Strategies

The following are descriptions of some of the types of strategies good readers use to comprehend text.

Predicting Good readers predict what will happen next. When reading fiction, they make predictions about what they are reading and then confirm or revise those predictions as they go.

Visualizing Good readers visualize what is happening in the text. They form mental images as they read. They picture the setting, the characters, and the action in a story. Visualizing helps readers understand descriptions of complex activities or processes. Visualizing can also be helpful when reading expository text. When a complex process or an event is described, the reader can follow the process or the event better by visualizing each step or episode. Sometimes an author helps the reader by providing illustrations, diagrams, or maps.

Summarizing Good readers sum up to check their understanding as they read. Sometimes they reread to fill in gaps in their understanding. Good readers use the strategy of summarizing to keep track of what they are reading and to focus their minds on important information. The process of putting the information in one's own words not only helps good readers remember what they have read but also prompts them to evaluate how well they understand the information. Sometimes the summary reveals that one's understanding is incomplete, in which case it might be appropriate to reread the previous section to fill in the gaps. Good readers usually find that the strategy of summarizing is particularly helpful when they are reading long or complicated text.

Professional Development

Teacher Resource Library CD-ROMs or ***Online Professional Development*** provides courses that help you better understand the Comprehension/Knowledge Building instruction in ***Open Court Reading.*** For more information about this program, visit SRAonline.com.

Additional information about comprehension as well as resource references can be found in the ***Professional Development Guide: Comprehension.***

Pronunciation Key: **a**t; l**ā**te; c**â**re; f**ä**ther; s**e**t; m**ē**; **i**t; k**ī**te; **o**x; r**ō**se; **ô** in b**ou**ght; c**oi**n; b**o͝o**k; t**o͞o**; f**o**rm; **ou**t; **u**p; **ū**se; t**û**rn; ə sound in **a**bout, chick**e**n, penc**i**l, cann**o**n, circ**u**s; **ch**air; **hw** in **wh**ich; ri**ng**; **sh**op; **th**in; **th**ere; **zh** in trea**s**ure.

manners (ma´ nərz) *n.* Habits of behavior.

margin (mär´ jin) *n.* The blank edge of a paper.

marvelous (märv´ ə ləs) *adj.* Outstanding.

mayor (mā´ ər) *n.* The chief elected official of a city.

metallic (mə tal´ ik) *adj.* As if made of metal.

microscope (mī´ krə skōp´) *n.* An instrument that makes small things look larger.

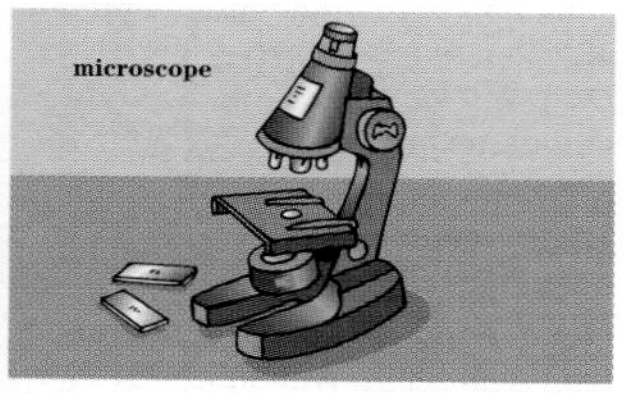

migrate (mī´ grāt) *v.* To move from colder to warmer lands and back again.

miniature (min´ ē ə chər) *adj.* Tiny; very small.

molt (mōlt) *v.* To lose or shed hair, feathers, or a shell.

monument (mon´ yə mənt) *n.* Anything built to honor a person or event.

mood (mo͞od) *n.* A general state of mind.

mottled (mot´ ld) *adj.* Spotted or blotched with different colors.

mound (mound) *n.* A pile or heap of something.

mustache (mus´ tash) *n.* Hair grown on the upper lip.

N

nervous (nər´ vəs) *adj.* Moving in an excited or jumpy way.

nest (nest) *v.* To build a home. —*n.* A shelter made by animals; a home.

nestling (nest´ ling) *n.* A bird too young to leave the nest.

nibble (ni´ bəl) *v.* To take small bites.

nimbly (nim´ blē) *adv.* Quickly and easily.

nook (no͝ok) *n.* A small, hidden place.

O

observation (ob´ zûr vā´ shən) *n.* The act of studying or noticing.

observe (əb zûrv´) *v.* To see; to look at.

occasion (ə kā´ zhən) *n.* An event.

ocotillo (ō´ kə tēl´ yō) *n.* A desert bush with sharp spines.

opportunity (op´ ər to͞o´ ni tē) *n.* A good chance.

ordinary (ôr´ dən er´ ē) *adj.* The usual kind.

organization (or´ gə nə zā´ shən) *n.* A group of people who join together for one purpose; a club.

originality (ə rij´ ə nal´ i tē) *n.* Newness; freshness.

originally (ə rij´ ə nl ē) *adv.* At first; in the beginning.

outfit (out´ fit´) *n.* A group of people with a common purpose or belief.

overpass (ō´ vər pas´) *n.* A road that crosses above another road.

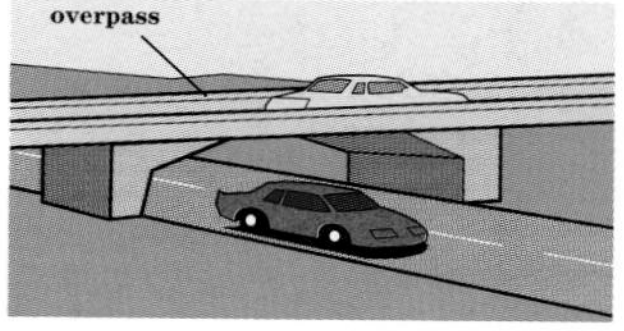

P

parachute (par´ ə sho͞ot´) *n.* An umbrella-shaped object that helps other objects float down slowly from heights.

parade (pə rād´) *v.* To march in an orderly fashion.

parasite (par´ ə sīt´) *n.* An animal that lives and feeds on another animal.

patch (pach) *n.* A small area.

particular (pər tik´ yə lər) *adj.* Only; special.

patient (pā´ shənt) *adj.* Calmly putting up with something difficult.

passageway (pas´ ij wā´) *n.* A narrow place to walk between two buildings.

pattern (pat´ ərn) *n.* The way in which things are placed.

peer (pēr) *v.* To look.

peregrine (per´i grin) *n.* A type of falcon that catches other birds in flight.

period (pēr´ ē əd) *n.* An amount of time.

permission (pər mi´ shən) *n.* Consent that allows one to do something.

petition (pə tish´ ən) *n.* A written request to someone in charge, signed by those who agree.

Pronunciation Key: **a**t; l**ā**te; c**â**re; f**ä**ther; s**e**t; m**ē**; **i**t; k**ī**te; **o**x; r**ō**se; **ô** in b**ou**ght; c**oi**n; b**o͝o**k; t**o͞o**; f**or**m; **ou**t; **u**p; **ū**se; t**û**rn; **ə** sound in **a**bout, chick**e**n, penc**i**l, cann**o**n, circ**u**s; **ch**air; **hw** in **wh**ich; ri**ng**; **sh**op; **th**in; **th**ere; **zh** in trea**s**ure.

petroleum jelly (pe´ trō´ lē əm jel´ ē) *n.* A greasy, sticky substance used to coat things.

plantain (plan´ tin) *n.* A weed that has large leaves and long spikes with small flowers.

plaster (plas´ tər) *n.* A substance like cement that is used to make walls and ceilings.

plume (plo͞om) *n.* A long feather.

poet (pō´ ət) *n.* A person who writes or composes poems.

pollution (pə lo͞o´ shən) *n.* Harmful or dirty material added to the air, water, or soil.

population (pä´ pyə lā´ shən) *n.* A count of how many in a group.

porcupine (por´ kyə pīne) *n.* An animal with stiff pointy hairs.

portion (por´ shən) *n.* A part.

possess (pə zes´) *v.* To have; to own.

post (pōst) *n.* A position that one is appointed to.

pottery (pot´ ə rē) *n.* Bowls, pots, plates, and other objects shaped from moist clay and hardened by heat.

practical (prak´ ti kəl) *adj.* Useful.

prejudice (prej´ ə dis) *n.* Unfairness; an opinion formed without knowing the facts.

prickly (prik´ lē) *adj.* Full of sharp points that stick or sting.

privet (priv´ it) *n.* A shrub related to the lilac bush and the olive tree. It has small white flowers and smooth, dark fruit; all parts are poisonous.

probably (prä´ bə blē) *adv.* Most likely to happen.

procession (prə se´ shən) *n.* A group of people that moves along in a formal manner.

proclaim (prō klām) *v.* To declare; to announce officially.

proper (pro´ pər) *adj.* Acceptable.

protest (prō´ test´) *n.* A statement against something.

proud (proud) *adj.* Feeling very pleased with something.

provoke (prə vōk´) *v.* To cause.

Q

Queen Anne's lace (kwēn´ anz´ lās´) *n.* A wild form of the carrot plant with lacy white flowers.

quill (kwil) *n.* The stiff pointy hairs on a porcupine.

R

racial (rā´ shəl) *adj.* Having to do with a race of people.

rebel (ri bəl´) *v.* To resist a ruler's power.

rectangle (rek´ tan´ gəl) *n.* A four-sided shape with four right angles.

regardless (ri gärd´ lis) *adv.* Without concern for.

relocate (rē lō´ kāt´) *v.* To move to a different place.

rescue (res´ kū´) *v.* To save from harm or danger.

resist (ri zist´) *v.* To fight against.

respond (ri spond´) *v.* To answer.

responsibility (ri spon´ sə bil´ i tē) *n.* A duty; a job.

rotate (rō´ tāt´) *v.* To move as though going around in a circle.

routine (ro͞o tēn´) *n.* The same actions done over and over.

royal (roi´ əl) *adj.* Owned by a king or a queen.

S

scenery (sē´ nə rē) *n.* The painted pictures and objects used on stage in a play.

scholar (sko´ lər) *n.* A person who has learned a great deal about a subject.

scrawl (skrôl) *v.* To write in a fast, messy way. —*n.* A scribble.

sculpt (skulpt) *v.* To make a figure, statue, or design by carving wood or stone or by forming clay.

sculpture (skulp´ chər) *n.* A figure, statue, or design carved out of something solid.

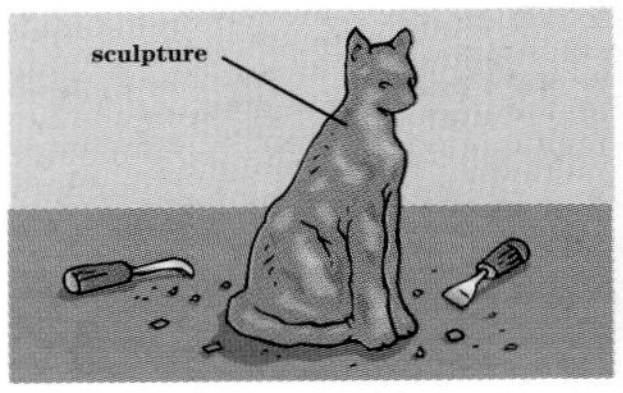

segregation (seg´ ri gā´ shən) *n.* Keeping different races of people apart from each other.

seldom (sel´ dəm) *adv.* Rarely; not often.

sensitive (sen´ si tiv) *adj.* Able to feel things well.

seriously (sir´ ē əs lē) *adv.* Thoughtfully, sincerely.

sesame (ses´ə mē) *n.* The seed of an Asian plant which is used to add flavor to food.

severe (sə vir´) *adj.* Harsh or extreme.

sewer (so͞o´ ər) *n.* An underground pipe that carries dirty water away from buildings.

Pronunciation Key: **at**; **lāte**; **câre**; **fäther**; **set**; **mē**; **it**; **kīte**; **ox**; **rōse**; **ô** in **bought**; **coin**; **bŏŏk**; **tōō**; **form**; **out**; **up**; **ūse**; **tûrn**; **ə** sound in **about**, **chicken**, **pencil**, **cannon**, **circus**; **chair**; **hw** in **which**; **ring**; **shop**; **thin**; **there**; **zh** in **treasure**.

shades (shādz) *n.* Sunglasses.

shadowed (sha´ dōd) *adj.* Covered in shadow; partially hidden.

shallow (shal´ ō) *adj.* Being close to the bottom; not deep.

sharp (shärp) *n.* A musical note that sounds one-half tone higher than it usually does. —*adj.* 1. Clear. 2. Keen.

shock (shok) *v.* To surprise and upset at the same time.

shutter (shut´ ər) *n.* A doorlike cover that opens and closes over a window.

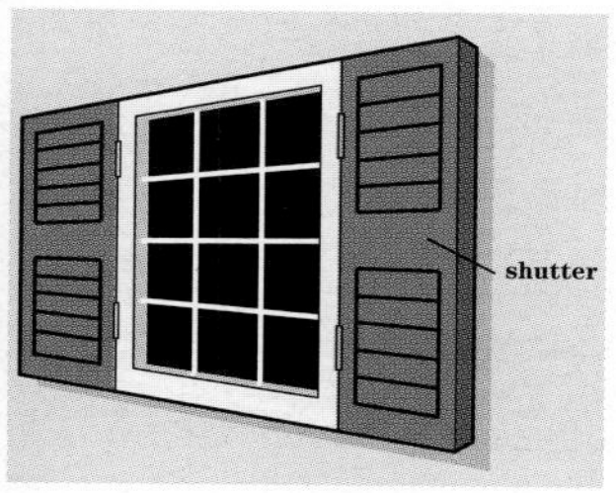

skyscraper (skī´ skrā´ pər) *n.* A very tall building found in a city.

slope (slōp) *n.* An upward or downward slant.

smokestack (smōk´ stak´) *n.* A large, tall chimney from which smoke is released.

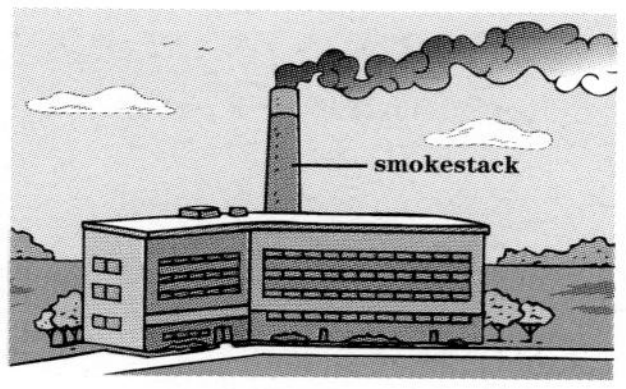

soar (sor) *v.* To fly at a great height.

solemnly (so´ ləm lē) *adv.* In a serious way.

solution (sə lōō´ shən) *n.* A way to solve a problem.

sought (sôt) *v.* Past tense of **seek:** To look for.

species (spē´ shēz) *n.* An animal family; a kind of animal.

splinter (splin´ tər) *n.* A small sharp piece of wood broken off from a larger piece.

squeegee (skwē´ jē) *v.* To make a squeaking sound by rubbing as if using a squeegee, which is a rubber-edged tool for removing excess water from windows.

squiggle (skwig´ əl) *n.* A line that is curved or wavy.

stalk (stôk) *n.* The stem of a plant.

starve (stärv) *v.* To die from hunger.

statue (stach´ ōō) *n.* A carved figure of a person or an animal.

sternly (stûrn´ lē) *adv.* In a strict or harsh way.

stiff (stif) *adj.* Something not easily bent; not flexible.

stitch (stich) *v.* To join two pieces of cloth together with tight loops of thread.

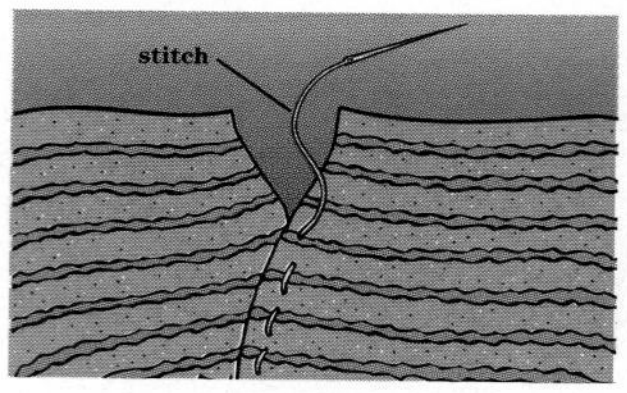

stout (stout) *adj.* Sturdy; strong.

stucco (stuk´ ō) *n.* Plaster that covers outside walls.

sturdy (stər´ dē) *adj.* Solidly built.

style (stīl) *n.* The way something is done.

subject (səb´ jikt) *n.* A person who is ruled over.

suburb (sub´ ûrb) *n.* A town on the outer edge of a larger city.

suitable (sōō´ tə bəl) *adj.* Fitting; right.

sycamore (sik´ ə mor´) *n.* A shade tree; a buttonwood tree.

T

taunt (tônt) *n.* Spoken words that make fun of someone in a mean way.

tease (tēz) *v.* To annoy continuously.

temperature (tem´ pər ə chər) *n.* The hotness or coldness of a thing.

territory (ter´ ə tor´ ē) *n.* An area of land.

toil (toi´ əl) *v.* To work hard.

trace (trās) *v.* To form carefully; to sketch.

trainer (trā´ nər) *n.* Teacher, coach.

traitor (trā´ tər) *n.* Someone who betrays another's trust.

triangle (trī´ an´ gəl) *n.* A three-sided shape with three angles.

trestle (tres´ əl) *n.* A framework that holds up train tracks above a river or above the ground.

trill (tril) *v.* To make a vibrating sound, like the sound some birds make.

Pronunciation Key: **at**; **lāte**; **câre**; **fäther**; **set**; **mē**; **it**; **kīte**; **ox**; **rōse**; **ô** in **bought**; **coin**; **bŏŏk**; **tōō**; **form**; **out**; **up**; **ūse**; **tûrn**; **ə** sound in **about**, **chicken**, **pencil**, **cannon**, **circus**; **chair**; **hw** in **which**; **ring**; **shop**; **thin**; **there**; **zh** in **treasure**.

tundra (tun´ drə) *n.* In the arctic regions, a flat plain with no trees.

twitter (twi´ tər) *v.* To chatter noisily; to sound like chirping birds.

tyrant (tī´ rənt) *n.* A harsh, unjust ruler.

U

urban (ûr´ bən) *adj.* In a city.

V

vacant (vā´ kənt) *adj.* Empty.

vigilante (vij´ ə lan´ tē) *n.* A person who acts as if he or she is the law.

violently (vī´ ə lənt lē) *adv.* With destructive force.

visible (viz´ ə bəl) *adj.* Able to be seen.

W

wardrobe (wor´ drōb´) *n.* A collection of clothes.

warehouse (war´ hous´) *n.* A building where products and materials are stored.

whine (hwīn) *v.* To talk in a complaining, annoying voice.

wilderness (wil´ dər nəs) *n.* A wild, natural area that has not been developed or occupied by people.

windswept (wind´ swept´) *adj.* Blown by wind constantly.

Program Appendix

Program Appendix

The Program Appendix includes a step-by-step explanation of procedures for research-based, effective practices in reading instruction that are repeatedly used throughout ***SRA/Open Court Reading.*** These practices may also be used in other instructional materials.

Table of Contents

Reading Materials and Techniques

PROGRAM APPENDIX

Different reading materials and techniques are appropriate at different stages of reading development. The purpose of this section is to discuss different types of reading materials and how they may be used most effectively.

Reading Big Books

Purpose

Many students come from homes where they are read to often, but a significant number of other students have not had this valuable experience. Big Books (Levels K and 1) offer all students crucial opportunities to confirm and expand their knowledge about print and reading. They are especially useful for shared reading experiences in the early grades.

The benefits of reading Big Books include engaging even nonreaders in:

- unlocking the books' messages.
- developing print awareness.
- participating in good reading behaviors.
- observing what a good reader does: remarking on the illustrations and the title, asking questions about the content and what might happen, making predictions, and clarifying words and ideas.
- promoting the insight that a given word is spelled the same way every time it occurs as high-frequency words are pointed out.
- reinforcing the correspondence between spoken and written words and spelling patterns.
- enjoying the illustrations and connecting them to the text to help students learn to explore books for enjoyment and information.
- interpreting and responding to literature and expository text before they can read themselves.

Procedure for Reading Big Books

During the first reading of the Big Books, you will model reading behaviors and comprehension strategies similar to those that will later be taught formally. During the second reading, you will address print awareness and teach comprehension skills such as classifying and categorizing or sequencing, which help the reader organize information. In addition, you will teach skills such as making inferences and drawing conclusions, which help the reader focus on the deeper meaning of the text. At first, teachers should expect to do all of the reading but should not prevent students from trying to read on their own or from reading words they already know.

- **Activate Prior Knowledge.** Read the title of the selection and the author's and illustrator's names. At the beginning of each Big Book, read the title of the book and discuss what the whole book is about before going on to reading the first selection.
- **Discuss Prior Knowledge.** Initiate a brief discussion of any prior knowledge the students have that might help them understand the selection.
- **Browse the Selection.** Ask students to tell what they think the story might be about just from looking at the illustrations. This conversation should be brief so that the students can move on to a prereading discussion of print awareness.

Big Books offer all students crucial opportunities to confirm and expand their knowledge about print and reading.

- **Develop Print Awareness.** The focus of browsing the Big Books is to develop awareness of print. Urge students to tell what words or letters they recognize rather than what they expect the selection to be about.

  To develop print awareness, have students look through the selection page by page and comment on whatever they notice in the text. Some students may know some of the words, while others may only recognize specific letters or sounds. The key is to get the students to look at the print separately from the illustrations even before they have heard the actual text content. This process isolates print awareness so that it is not influenced by content. It also gives you a clearer idea of what your students do or do not know about print.
- **Read Aloud.** Read the selection aloud expressively. The reading enables the students simply to hear and enjoy the text as it is read through once. With this reading, you will model behaviors and comprehension strategies that all students will need to develop to become successful readers—for example, asking questions; clarifying unfamiliar words, first by using the pictures and later by using context; or predicting what might happen next.
- **Reread.** Read the selection expressively again. During the second reading of the stories, you will focus on teaching comprehension skills. Also, to develop print awareness, point to each word as it is read, thus demonstrating that text proceeds from left to right and from top to bottom and helping advance the idea that words are individual spoken and written units. Invite the students to identify the rhyming words in a poem or chime in on repetitive parts of text as you point to the words. Or students can read with you on this second reading, depending on the text.
- **Discuss Print.** Return to print awareness by encouraging discussion of anything the students noticed about the words. Young students should begin to realize that you are reading separate words that are separated by spaces. Later, students will begin to see that each word is made up of a group of letters. The students should be encouraged to discuss anything related to the print. For example, you might ask students to point to a word or count the number of words on a line. Or you might connect the words to the illustrations by pointing to a word and saying it and then asking the students to find a picture of that word.
- **Responding.** Responding to a selection is a way of insuring comprehension. Invite students to tell about the story by asking them what they like about the poem or story or calling on a student to explain in his or her own words what the poem or story tells about. Call on others to add to the telling as needed. For nonfiction selections, this discussion might include asking students what they learned about the topic and what they thought was most interesting.

Tips for Using Big Books

- Make sure the entire group is able to see the book clearly while you are reading.
- If some students are able to read or predict words, encourage them to do so during the rereading.
- Encourage students to present and use their knowledge of print.
- Allow students to look at the Big Books whenever they wish.
- Provide small versions of the Big Books for students to browse through and try to read at their leisure.
- The reader of the Big Book should try to be part of the collaborative group of learners rather than the leader.

Using the Pre-Decodable Books

Purpose

Pre-Decodable Books play an important role in students' early literacy development by providing them with meaningful "reading" experiences before they are actually reading on their own and by expanding their awareness of the forms and uses of print. By following along as you read aloud a **Pre-Decodable Book,** students learn about the left-to-right and top-to-bottom progression of print on a page, the clues that indicate the beginnings and endings of sentences, the connections between pictures and words, and important book conventions, such as front and back covers, authors' and illustrators' names, title pages, and page numbers.

The **Pre-Decodable Books** provide students with opportunities to apply their growing knowledge of letter names, shapes, and sounds, and to become familiar with individual words.

Through retelling the story in a **Pre-Decodable Book,** predicting or wondering about what will happen, and asking and responding to questions about the book, students not only learn about the relationship between spoken and written language, they learn to think about what they have read.

About the Pre-Decodable Books

Each **Pre-Decodable Book** contains a story that engages students' interest as it provides them with opportunities to practice what they are learning in their lessons. These "Pre-Decodable" stories each contain several high-frequency words that most students already have in their spoken vocabularies and that are a basic part of all meaningful stories. Learning to identify high-frequency words quickly, accurately, and effortlessly is a critical part of students' development as fluent, independent readers. The inside back cover of each **Pre-Decodable Book** contains a list of high-frequency words.

How to Read the Pre-Decodable Books

- Before reading a **Pre-Decodable Book,** take time to familiarize students with any new **high-frequency words** in the book and to review previously introduced words. To reinforce the idea that it is important to know these words because they are used so often in print, always point out the words in context. For example, focus students' attention on the words in Big Book selections or on signs and posters around the classroom.
- Give each student a copy of the book. Tell students that you will read the book together. Hold up your book. Read the title. If the title has a rebus picture, point to it and tell the students what it is. Then point to the word beneath it and explain that the picture represents that word. Point to and read the names of the author and illustrator, reminding students that an author writes a book and an illustrator draws the pictures. Page through the book, pointing to and naming the rebus pictures. Have the students say the name of each rebus. To avoid confusion, always *tell* them the *exact* word that a rebus represents. *Don't encourage them to guess at its meaning.*
- Allow students time to browse through the book on their own, commenting on what they see in the illustrations and making predictions about what they think the book will be about. Encourage them to comment on anything special they notice about the story, the illustrations, or the words in the book.
- Help the students to find page 3. Read the book aloud without stopping. As you read, move your hand beneath the words to show the progression of print. Pause at each rebus as you say the word it represents, pointing first to the rebus, then to the word beneath it.
- Reread the book. This time, ask the students to point to and read the high-frequency words.
- Tell the students to follow along in their books as you read the story again. Read the title aloud, and then have the students read it with you. Reread page 3. Point to each rebus picture and ask a volunteer to "read" it. Point to the word beneath the picture and remind students that the picture shows what the word is. Continue through each page of the book, calling on volunteers to "read" and stopping as necessary to clarify and help students with words.
- After reading, answer any questions the students might have about the book. Encourage them to discuss the illustrations and to explain what is happening in each one.

Reading Decodables and Building Fluency

Purpose

The most urgent task of early reading instruction is to make written thoughts intelligible to students. This requires a balanced approach that includes systematic instruction in phonics as well as experiences with authentic literature. Thus, from the very beginning, ***Open Court Reading*** includes the reading of literature. At the beginning of first grade, when students are learning phonics and blending as a tool to access words, the teacher reads aloud. During this time students are working on using comprehension strategies and skills and discussing stories. As students learn the code and blend words, recognize critical sight words, and develop some level of fluency, they take more responsibility for the actual reading of the text.

This program has a systematic instruction in phonics that allows the students to begin reading independently. This instruction is supported by ***Open Court Reading*** **Decodable Books.**

Practice

The ***Open Court Reading*** **Decodable Books** are designed to help the students apply, review, and reinforce their expanding knowledge of sound/spelling correspondences. Each story supports instruction in new phonic elements and incorporates elements and words that have been learned earlier. There are eight page and sixteen page **Decodable Books.** Grade K has eight-page **Decodable Books.** In Grade 1 the eight-page books focus on the new element introduced in the lesson, while the sixteen-page books review and reinforce the elements that have been taught since the last sixteen-page book. They review sounds from several lessons and provide additional reading practice. Grades 2–3 have eight-page **Decodable Books** in Getting Started, and sixteen-page books in the first 4–5 units of the grade level. The primary purpose is to provide practice reading the words. It is important that the students also attach meaning to what they are reading. Questions are often included in the ***Teacher's Edition*** to check both understanding and attention to words.

Fluency

Fluency is the effortless ability to read or access words with seemingly little attention to decoding. It also involves grouping words into meaningful units and using expression appropriately. Fluency is critical but not sufficient for comprehension.

To become proficient readers who fully understand what they read, the whole process of decoding must become as automatic as possible. The students need to be so familiar with the sound/spellings and with the most common nondecodable sight words that they automatically process the letters or spellings and expend most of their energy on comprehending the meaning of the text.

While fluency begins in first grade, many students will continue to need practice in building fluency in second and third grades. Initially, students can use the ***Open Court Reading*** **Decodable Books** in grades 2 and 3, but fluency practice should include using materials from actual literature the students are reading.

Procedure

Preparing to Read

- Introduce and write on the board any nondecodable high-frequency or story words introduced or reviewed in the story. Tell the students how to pronounce any newly introduced high-frequency words. Then point to each new word and have the students say it. Have them read any previously introduced sight word in the Word Bank list. All of the ***Open Court Reading*** **Decodable Books** contain high-frequency words that may not be decodable. For example, the word *said* is a very common high-frequency word that is not decodable. Including words like *said* makes the language of the story flow smoothly and naturally. The students need to be able to recognize these words quickly and smoothly.
- Read the title. At the beginning of the year, you may need to read the title of the book to the students, but as the year goes on, you should have a student read it whenever possible. The sixteen-page ***Open Court Reading*** **Decodable Books** contain two related chapters, each using the same sounds and spellings. In such cases, read the title of the **Decodable** book, and then point out the two individual chapter titles. Have volunteers read the title of the chapter you are about to read.
- Browse the story. Have the students look through the story, commenting on whatever they notice in the text or illustrations and telling what they think the story will tell them.

Reading the Story

After this browsing, the students will read the story a page at a time. Again, these books are designed to support the learning of sounds and spellings. The focus should not be on comprehension. Students should understand what they are reading, and they should feel free to discuss anything in the story that interests them. Any areas of confusion are discussed and clarified as they arise, as described below.

- Have the students read a page to themselves. Then call on one student to read the page aloud, or have the whole group read it aloud.
- If a student has difficulty with a word that can be blended, help her or him blend the word. Remind the student to check the **Sound/Spelling Cards** for help. If a word cannot be blended using the sound/spellings learned so far, pronounce the word for the student.
- If a student has trouble with a word or sentence, have the reader call on a classmate for help, and then continue reading after the word or sentence has been clarified. After something on a page has been clarified or discussed, have that page reread by a different student before moving on to the next page.
- Repeat this procedure for each page.
- Reread the story twice more, calling on different students to read or reading it in unison. These readings should go more quickly, with fewer stops for clarification.

Responding to the Story

Once the story has been read aloud a few times, have the students respond as follows:

- Ask the students what hard words they found in the story and how they figured them out. They may mention high-frequency words they didn't recognize, words they had to blend, and words whose meanings they did not know.
- Invite the students to tell about the story, retelling it in their own words, describing what they liked about it, or citing what they found interesting or surprising. Specific suggestions to use are listed in the ***Teacher's Edition.***
- Questions are provided in the ***Teacher's Edition.*** They are designed to focus the students' attention on the words and not just the pictures. The questions require answers that cannot be guessed by looking at the pictures alone, such as a name, a bit of dialogue, or an action or object that is not pictured. Have the students point to the words, phrases, or sentences that answer the questions.

Building Fluency

Building fluency is essential to gaining strong comprehension. The more fluent the students become, the more they can attend to the critical business of understanding the text. Opportunities for students to build fluency may include:

- Have students "partner read" the most recent ***Open Court Reading*** **Decodable Book** twice, taking turns reading a page at a time. The partners should switch the second time through so they are reading different pages from the ones they read the first time. If there is time left, the partners should choose any of the previously read stories to read together. Use this time for diagnosis, having one student at a time read with you.
- Making sure that the ***Open Court Reading*** **Decodable Books** are readily available in the classroom.
- Reading **Decodable Books** with as many students as possible one at a time.
- Reminding the students that they may read with partners during Workshop.

The only way the students can become fluent readers is to read as much and as often as possible.

Reading the Student Anthologies

Purpose

Reading is a complex process that requires students not only to decode what they read but also to understand and respond to it. The purpose of this section is to help you identify various reading behaviors used by good readers and to encourage those behaviors in your students.

Reading Behaviors and Comprehension Strategies

There are four basic behaviors that good readers engage in during reading. These behaviors include the application of certain comprehension strategies, which are modeled while reading the Student Anthology (Levels 1–6).

Setting Reading Goals and Expectations

Good readers set reading goals and expectations before they begin reading. This behavior involves a variety of strategies that will help students prepare to read the text.

- **Activate prior knowledge.** When good readers approach a new text, they consider what they already know about the subject or what their experiences have been in reading similar material.
- **Browse the text.** To get an idea of what to expect from a text, good readers look at the title and the illustrations. They may look for potential problems, such as difficult words. When browsing a unit, have students glance quickly at each selection, looking briefly at the illustrations and the print. Have them tell what they think they might be learning about as they read the unit.
- **Decide what they expect from the text.** When reading for pleasure, good readers anticipate enjoying the story or the language. When reading to learn something, they ask themselves what they expect to find out.

Responding to Text

Good readers are active readers. They interact with text by using the following strategies:

- **Making connections.** Good readers make connections between what they read and what they already know. They pay attention to elements in the text that remind them of their own experiences.
- **Visualizing, or picturing.** Good readers visualize what is happening in the text. They form mental images as they read. They picture the setting, the characters, and the action in a story. When reading expository text, good readers picture the objects, processes, or events described. Visualizing helps readers understand descriptions of complex activities or processes.
- **Asking questions.** Good readers ask questions that may prepare them for what they will learn. If their questions are not answered in the text, they may try to find answers elsewhere and thus add even more to their store of knowledge.
- **Predicting.** Good readers predict what will happen next. When reading fiction, they make predictions about what they are reading and then confirm or revise those predictions as they go.
- **Thinking about how the text makes you feel.** Well-written fiction touches readers' emotions; it sparks ideas.

Checking Understanding

One of the most important behaviors good readers exhibit is the refusal to continue reading when something fails to make sense. Good readers continually assess their understanding of the text with strategies such as:

- **Interpreting.** As they read, good readers make inferences that help them understand and appreciate what they are reading.
- **Summing up.** Good readers sum up to check their understanding as they read. Sometimes they reread to fill in gaps in their understanding.
- **Monitoring and adjusting reading speed.** Good readers monitor their understanding of what they read. They slow down as they come to difficult words and passages. They speed up as they read easier passages.

Monitoring and Clarifying Unfamiliar Words and Passages

- **Apply decoding skills** to sound out unknown words.
- **Determine what is unclear** to find the source of the confusion.
- **Apply context clues** in text and illustrations to figure out the meanings of words or passages.
- **Reread the passage** to make sure the passage makes sense.
- **Check a dictionary or the glossary** to understand the meanings of words not clarified by clues or rereading.

Procedures

Modeling and Thinking Aloud

Modeling and encouraging students to think aloud as they attempt to understand text can demonstrate for everyone how reading behaviors are put into practice. The most effective models will be those that come from your own reading. Using questions such as the following, as well as your students' questions and comments, will make both the text and the strategic reading process more meaningful to students.

- What kinds of things did you wonder about?
- What kinds of things surprised you?
- What new information did you learn?
- What was confusing until you reread or read further?

Model comprehension strategies in a natural way, and choose questions and comments that fit the text you are reading. Present a variety of ways to respond to text.

- Pose questions that you really do wonder about.
- Identify with characters by comparing them with yourself.
- React emotionally by showing joy, sadness, amusement, or surprise.
- Show empathy with or sympathy for characters.
- Relate the text to something that has happened to you or to something you already know.
- Show interest in the text ideas.
- Question the meaning or clarity of the author's words and ideas.

Encouraging Students' Responses and Use of Strategies

Most students will typically remain silent as they try to figure out an unfamiliar word or a confusing passage. Encourage students to identify specifically what they are having difficulty with. Once the problem has been identified, ask the students to suggest a strategy for dealing with the problem. Remind students to:

- Treat problems encountered in text as interesting learning opportunities.
- Think out loud about text challenges.
- Help each other build meaning. Rather than tell what a word is, students should tell how they figured out the meanings of challenging words and passages.
- Consider reading a selection again with a partner after reading it once alone. Partner reading provides valuable practice in reading for fluency.
- Make as many connections as they can between what they are reading and what they already know.
- Visualize to clarify meanings or enjoy descriptions.
- Ask questions about what they are reading.
- Notice how the text makes them feel.

Whole-Word Blending

Once students are comfortable with sound-by-sound blending, they are ready for whole-word blending.

- Write the whole word to be blended on the board or an overhead transparency.
- Ask the students to blend the sounds as you point to them.
- Then have the students say the whole word.
- Ask the students to use the word in a sentence and then to extend the sentence.
- When all of the words have been blended, point to words randomly and ask individuals to read them.

Blending Syllables

In reading the ***Student Anthologies,*** students will often encounter multisyllabic words. Some students are intimidated by long words, yet many multisyllabic words are easily read by reading and blending the syllables rather than the individual sounds. Following a set of rules for syllables is difficult since so many of the rules have exceptions. Students need to remember that each syllable in a word contains one vowel sound.

- Have students identify the vowel sounds in the word.
- Have students blend the first syllable sound by sound if necessary or read the first syllable.
- Handle the remaining syllables the same way.
- Have students blend the syllables together to read the word.

Blending Sentences

Blending sentences is the logical extension of blending words. Blending sentences helps students develop fluency, which is critical to comprehension. Encourage students to reread sentences with phrasing and natural intonation.

- Write the sentence on the board or on a transparency, underlining any high-frequency sight words—words that the students cannot decode either because they are irregular or because they contain sounds or spellings that the students have not yet learned or reviewed. If the students have not read these words before, write the words on the board or an overhead transparency and introduce them before writing the sentence. These words should not be blended but read as whole words.

Building for Success

A primary cause of students' blending failure is their failure to understand how to use the **Sound/Spelling Cards**. Students need to practice sounds and spellings when the **Sound/Spelling Cards** are introduced and during initial blending. They also need to understand that if they are not sure of how to pronounce a spelling, they can check the cards.

Early blending may be frustrating. You must lead the group almost constantly. Soon, however, leaders in the group will take over. Watch to see whether any students are having trouble during the blending. Include them in small-group instruction sessions. At that time you may want to use the vowel-first procedure described below to reteach blending lines.

Extra Help

In working with small groups during **Workshop**, you may want to use some of the following suggestions to support students who need help with blending.

Vowel-First Blending

Vowel-first blending is an alternative to sound-by-sound and whole-word blending for students who need special help. Used in small-group sessions, this technique helps students who have difficulty with the other two types of blending to focus on the most important part of each word, the vowels, and to do only one thing at a time. These students are not expected to say a sound and blend it with another at virtually the same time. The steps to use in vowel-first blending follow:

Blending is the heart of phonics instruction and the key strategy students must learn to open the world of written language.

1. Across the board or on an overhead transparency, write the vowel spelling in each of the words in the line. For a short vowel, the line may look like this:
   a a a
   For a long vowel, the line may look like this:
   ee ea ea
2. Point to the spelling as the students say the sound for the spelling.
3. Begin blending around the vowels. In front of the first vowel spelling, add the spelling for the beginning sound of the word. Make the blending motion, and have the students blend through the vowel, adding a blank to indicate that the word is still incomplete. Repeat this procedure for each partial word in the line until the line looks like this:
   ma__ sa__ pa__
   see__ mea__ tea__
4. Have the students blend the partial word again as you make the blending motion and then add the spelling for the ending sound.
5. Make the blending motion, and have the students blend the completed word—for example, *mat* or *seed.*
6. Ask a student to repeat the word and use it in a sentence. Then have another student extend the sentence.
7. Repeat steps 4, 5, and 6 for each word in the line, which might look like this:
   mat sad pan
   or
   seed meat team

Tips

- In the early lessons, do blending with as much direction and dialogue as is necessary for success. Reduce your directions to a minimum as soon as possible. You have made good progress when you no longer have to say, "Sound—Sound—Blend," because the students automatically sound and blend as you write.
- Unless the line is used to introduce or to reinforce a spelling pattern, always ask a student to use a word in a sentence and then to extend the sentence immediately after you've developed the word. If the line is used to introduce or to reinforce a spelling pattern, however, ask the students to give sentences at the end of the line. Students will naturally extend sentences by adding phrases to the ends of the sentences. Encourage them to add phrases at the beginning or in the middle of the sentence.
- Use the vowel-first procedure in small group preteaching or reteaching sessions with students who are having a lot of trouble with blending. Remember that you must adapt the blending lines in the lessons to the vowel-first method.
- The sight words in the sentences cannot be blended. The students must approach them as sight words to be memorized. If students are having problems reading sight words, tell them the words.
- Cue marks written over the vowels may help students.
  - ✓ Straight line cue for long vowels
    EXAMPLES: *āpe, mē, fīne, sō, ūse*
  - ✓ Curved line cue for short vowels
    EXAMPLES: *că t, pĕt, wĭn, hŏt, tŭg*
  - ✓ Tent cue for variations of a and o
    EXAMPLES: *âll, ôff*
  - ✓ Dot cue for schwa sound with multiple-syllable words
    EXAMPLES: *salȧd, planėt, pencil, wagȯn*

Dictation and Spelling

Purpose

The purpose of dictation is to teach the students to spell words based on the sounds and spellings. In addition, learning dictation gives students a new strategy for reflecting on the sounds they hear in words to help them with their own writing.

As the students learn that sounds and spellings are connected to form words and that words form sentences, they begin to learn the standard spellings that will enable others to read their writing. As students learn to encode correctly, they develop their visual memory for words (spelling ability) and hence increase their writing fluency. Reinforcing the association between sounds and spellings and words through dictation gives students a spelling strategy that provides support and reassurance for writing independently. Reflecting on the sounds they hear in words will help students develop writing fluency as they apply the strategy to writing unfamiliar words.

A dictation activity is a learning experience; it is not a test. The students should be encouraged to ask for as much help as they need. The proofreading techniques are an integral part of dictation. Students' errors lead to self-correction and, if need be, to reteaching. The dictation activities must not become a frustrating ordeal. The students should receive reinforcement and feedback.

There are two kinds of dictation: Sounds-in-Sequence Dictation and Whole-Word Dictation. The two types differ mainly in the amount of help they give the students in spelling the words. The instructions vary for each type.

Procedure

Sounds-in-Sequence Dictation

Sounds-in-Sequence Dictation gives the students the opportunity to spell words sound by sound, left to right, checking the spelling of each sound as they write. (Many students write words as they think they hear and say the words, not as the words are actually pronounced or written.)

- Pronounce the first word to be spelled. Use the word in a sentence and say the word again (word/sentence/word). Have students say the word.
- Tell students to think about the sounds they hear in the word. Ask, "What's the first sound in the word?"
- Have students say the sound.
- Point to the **Sound/Spelling Card**, and direct the students to check the card. Ask what the spelling is. The students should say the spelling and then write it.
- Proceed in this manner until the word is complete.
- Proofread. You can write the word on the board as a model, or have a student do it. Check the work by referring to the **Sound/Spelling Cards**. If a word is misspelled, have the students circle the word and write it correctly, either above the word or next to it.

Whole-Word Dictation

Whole-Word Dictation gives the students the opportunity to practice this spelling strategy with less help from the teacher.

- Pronounce the word, use the word in a sentence, and then repeat the word (word/sentence/word). Have the students repeat the word. Tell the students to think about the word. Remind the students to check the **Sound/Spelling Cards** for spellings and to write the word.
- Proofread. Write or have a volunteer write the word on the board as a model. Check the word by referring to the **Sound/Spelling Cards**.

Sentence Dictation

Writing dictated sentences. Help students apply this spelling strategy to writing sentences. Dictation supports the development of fluent and independent writing. Dictation of a sentence will also help the students apply conventions of written language, such as capitalization and punctuation.

- Say the complete sentence aloud.
- Dictate one word at a time following the procedure for Sounds-in-Sequence Dictation.

Continue this procedure for the rest of the words in the sentence. Remind the students to put a period at the end. Then proofread the sentence, sound by sound, or word by word. When sentences contain sight words, the sight words should be dictated as whole words, not sound by sound. As the students learn to write more independently, the whole sentence can be dictated word by word.

Proofreading

Whenever the students write, whether at the board or on paper, they should proofread their work. Proofreading is an important technique because it allows the students to learn by self-correction and it gives them an immediate second chance for success. It is the same skill students will use as they proofread their writing. Students should proofread by circling—not by erasing—each error. After they circle an error, they should write the correction beside the circle. This type of correction allows you and the students to see the error as well as the correct form. Students also can see what needs to be changed and how they have made their own work better.

You may want to have students use a colored pencil to circle and write in the correction. This will make it easier for them to see the changes.

Procedure for Proofreading

- Have a student write the word or sentence on the board or on an overhead transparency.
- Have students tell what is good.
- Have students identify anything that can be made better.
- If there is a mistake, have the student circle it and write it correctly.
- Have the rest of the class proofread their own work.

The Word Building Game

The major reason for developing writing alongside reading is that reading and writing are complementary communicative processes. Decoding requires that students blend the phonemes together into familiar cohesive words. Spelling requires that students segment familiar cohesive words into separate phonemes. Both help students develop an understanding of how the alphabetic principle works.

The Word Building game gives the students a chance to exercise their segmentation abilities and to practice using the sounds and spellings they are learning. The game is a fast-paced activity in which the students spell related sets of words with the teacher's guidance. (Each successive word in the list differs from the previous one by one sound.)

For the Word Building game, the students use their ***Individual Letter Cards*** (Levels K and 1) to build the words. (As an alternative they can use pencil and paper.) You will be writing at the board.

Give the students the appropriate ***Letter Cards***. For example, if the list for the Word Building game is *am*, *at*, *mat*, they will need their *a*, *m*, and *t* ***Letter Cards***.

- Say the first word, such as *am*. (Use it in a sentence if you wish.) Have the students repeat the word. Say the word slowly, sound by sound. Tell the students to look at the ***Sound/Spelling Cards*** to find the letters that spell the sounds. Touch the first sound's card, in this case the Lamb card, and have students say the sound. Continue the process with the second sound. Write the word on the board while the students use their ***Letter Cards*** to spell it. Have students compare their words with your word, make changes as needed, and then blend and read the word with you.
- The students will then change the first word to make a different word. Say the next word in the list, (*at*). Segment the sounds of the word, and have students find the ***Sound/Spelling Cards*** that correspond. Write the new word (*at*) under the first word (*am*) on the board and have the students change their cards to spell the new word. Have them compare their words to yours and make changes as needed. Blend and read the word with the students. Continue in a like manner through the word list.

Spelling Strategies

Spelling

Many people find English difficult, because English sound/spelling patterns seem to have a million exceptions. The key to becoming a good speller, however, is not just memorization. The key is recognizing and internalizing English spelling patterns. Some people do this naturally as they read and develop large vocabularies. They intuitively recognize spelling patterns and apply them appropriately. Others need explicit and direct teaching of vocabulary and spelling strategies and spelling patterns before they develop spelling consciousness.

Purpose

Spelling is a fundamental skill in written communication. Although a writer may have wonderful ideas, he or she may find it difficult to communicate those ideas without spelling skills. Learning to spell requires much exposure to text and writing. For many it requires a methodical presentation of English spelling patterns.

English Spelling Patterns

A basic understanding of English spelling patterns will help provide efficient and effective spelling instruction. Just as the goal of phonics instruction is to enable students to read fluently, the goal of spelling instruction is to enable students to write fluently so they can concentrate on ideas rather than spelling.

- **Sound Patterns** Many words are spelled the way they sound. Most consonants and short vowels are very regular. Once a student learns the sound/spelling relationships, he or she has the key to spelling many words.
- **Structural Patterns** Structural patterns are employed when adding endings to words. Examples of structural patterns include doubling the final consonant, adding *–s* or *–es* to form plurals, and dropping the final *e* before adding *–ing*, *-ed*, *-er*, or *–est.* Often these structural patterns are very regular in their application. Many students have little trouble learning these patterns.
- **Meaning Patterns** Many spelling patterns in English are *morphological;* in other words, the meaning relationship is maintained regardless of how a sound may change. Prefixes, suffixes, and root words that retain their spellings regardless of how they are pronounced are further examples of meaning patterns.
- **Foreign Language Patterns** Many English words are derived from foreign words and retain those language patterns. For example, *kindergarten* (German), *boulevard* (French), and *ballet* (French from Italian) are foreign language patterns at work in English.

Developmental Stages of Spelling

The most important finding in spelling research in the past thirty years is that students learn to spell in a predictable developmental sequence, much as they learn to read. It appears to take the average student three to six years to progress through the developmental stages and emerge as a fairly competent, mature speller.

Prephonemic The first stage is the *prephonemic* stage, characterized by random letters arranged either in continuous lines or in word-like clusters. Only the writer can "read" it, and it may be "read" differently on different days.

Semiphonemic As emergent readers learn that letters stand for sounds, they use particular letters specifically to represent the initial consonant sound and sometimes a few other very salient sounds. This marks the discovery of *phonemic awareness* that letters represent speech sounds in writing.

Phonemic When students can represent most of the sounds they hear in words, they have entered the *phonemic* stage of spelling. They spell what they hear, using everything they know about letter sounds, letter names, and familiar words. Many remedial spellers never develop beyond this stage and spell a word the way it sounds whenever they encounter a word they can't spell.

Transitional or Within Word Pattern As they are exposed to more difficult words, students discover that not all words are spelled as they sound. They learn that they must include silent letters, spell past tenses with *–ed*, include a vowel even in unstressed syllables, and remember how words look. The *transitional* stage represents the transition from primarily phonemic strategies to rule-bound spelling.

Derivational The *derivational* stage occurs as transitional spellers accumulate a large spelling vocabulary and gain control over affixes, contractions, homophones and other meaning patterns. They discover that related or derived forms of words share spelling features even if they do not sound the same. As spellers gain control over these subtle word features and spell most words correctly, they become conventional spellers.

Procedures

The spelling lessons are organized around different spelling patterns, beginning with phonetic spelling patterns and progressing to other types of spelling patterns in a logical sequence. Word lists including words from the literature selection focus on the particular patterns in each lesson. In general, the sound patterns occur in the first units at each grade, followed by structural patterns, meaning patterns, and foreign language patterns in the upper grade levels.

- As you begin each new spelling lesson, have students identify the spelling pattern and how it is like and different from other patterns.
- Give the pretest to help students focus on the lesson pattern.
- Have students proofread their own pretests immediately after the test, crossing out any misspellings and writing the correct spelling.
- Have them diagnose whether the errors they made were in the lesson pattern or in another part of the word. Help students determine where they made errors and what type of pattern they should work on to correct them.
- As students work through the spelling pages from the ***Spelling and Vocabulary Skills*** book, encourage them to practice the different spelling strategies in the exercises.

Sound Pattern Strategies

✓ **Pronunciation Strategy** As students encounter an unknown word, have them say the word carefully to hear each sound. Encourage them to check the **Sound/Spelling Cards.** Then have them spell each sound. (/s/ + /i/ + /t/: *sit)*

✓ **Consonant Substitution** Have students switch consonants. The vowel spelling usually remains the same. *(bat, hat, rat, flat, splat)*

✓ **Vowel Substitution** Have students switch vowels. The consonant spellings usually remain the same. (CVC: *hit, hat, hut, hot;* CVCV: *mane, mine;* CVVC: *boat, beat, bait, beet)*

✓ **Rhyming Word Strategy** Have students think of rhyming words and the rimes that spell a particular sound. Often the sound will be spelled the same way in another word. *(cub, tub, rub)*

Structural Pattern Strategies

✓ **Conventions Strategy** Have students learn the rule and exceptions for adding endings to words (dropping *y*, dropping *e*, doubling the final consonant, and so on).

✓ **Proofreading Strategy** Many spelling errors occur because of simple mistakes. Have students check their writing carefully and specifically for spelling.

✓ **Visualization Strategy** Have students think about how a word looks. Sometimes words "look" wrong because a wrong spelling pattern has been written. Have them double-check the spelling of any word that looks wrong.

Meaning Pattern Strategies

✓ **Family Strategy** When students are not sure of a spelling, have them think of how words from the same base word family are spelled. *(critic, criticize, critical; sign, signal, signature)*

Spelling and Vocabulary Strategies (continued)

✓ **Meaning Strategy** Have students determine a homophone's meaning to make sure they are using the right word. Knowing prefixes, suffixes, and base words will also help.

✓ **Compound Word Strategy** Tell students to break a compound apart and spell each word. Compounds may not follow conventions rules for adding endings. *(homework, nonetheless)*

✓ **Foreign Language Strategy** Have students think of foreign language spellings that are different from English spelling patterns. *(ballet, boulevard, sauerkraut)*

✓ **Dictionary Strategy** Ask students to look up the word in a dictionary to make sure their spelling is correct. If they do not know how to spell a word, have them try a few different spellings and look them up to see which one is correct. *(fotograph, photograph)* This develops a spelling consciousness.

Use the Final Test to determine understanding of the lesson spelling pattern and to identify any other spelling pattern problems. Encourage student understanding of spelling patterns and use of spelling strategies in all their writing to help transfer spelling skills to writing.

Vocabulary Strategies

Purpose

Strong vocabulary skills are correlated to achievement throughout school. The purpose of vocabulary strategy instruction is to teach students a range of strategies for learning, remembering, and incorporating unknown vocabulary words into their existing reading, writing, speaking, and listening vocabularies.

Procedures

The selection vocabulary instruction in the first and second part of the lesson focuses on teaching specific vocabulary necessary for understanding the literature selection more completely. The weekly vocabulary instruction in the Language Arts part of each lesson is geared toward teaching vocabulary skills and strategies to build and secure vocabulary through word relationships or develop vocabulary strategies for unknown words.

General Strategies

There is no question that having students read and reading to students are effective vocabulary instructional strategies. Most word learning occurs through exposure to words in listening and reading. Multiple exposures to words, particularly when students hear, see, say, and write words, is also effective. Word play, including meaning and dictionary games, helps to develop a word consciousness as well.

Vocabulary Skills and Strategies

Word Relationships People effectively learn new words by relating them to words they already know. An understanding of different word relationships enables students to quickly and efficiently secure new vocabulary. The weekly vocabulary lessons are organized around these types of word groups. Word relationships include:

- **Antonyms** Words with opposite or nearly opposite meanings. *(hot/cold)*
- **Synonyms** Words with similar meanings. *(cup, mug, glass)*
- **Multiple Meanings** Words that have more than one meaning. *(run, dressing, bowl)*
- **Shades of Meaning** Words that express degrees of a concept or quality. *(like, love, worship)*
- **Levels of Specificity** Words that describe at different levels of precision. *(living thing, plant, flower, daffodil)*
- **Analogies** Pairs of words that have the same relationship. *(ball is to baseball as puck is to hockey)*
- **Compound Words** Words comprised of two or more words. *(daylight)*
- **Homographs** Words that are spelled the same but have different meanings and come from different root words. *(bear, count)*
- **Homophones** Words that sound the same but have different spellings and meanings. *(mane/main, to/two/too)*
- **Base Word Families** Words that have the same base word. *(care, careless, careful, uncaring, carefree)*
- **Prefixes** An affix attached before a base word that changes the meaning of the word. *(misspell)*
- **Suffixes** An affix attached to the end of a base word that changes the meaning of the word. *(careless)*
- **Concept Vocabulary** Words that help develop understanding of a concept. *(space, sun, Earth, satellite, planet, asteroid)*
- **Classification and Categorization** Sorting words by related meanings. *(colors, shapes, animals, foods)*

Contextual Word Lists Teaching vocabulary in context is another way to secure understanding of unknown words. Grouping words by subject area such as science, social studies, math, descriptive words, new words, and so on enables students to connect word meanings and build vocabulary understanding.

- **Figurative Language** Idioms, metaphors, similes, personification, puns, and novel meanings need to be specifically taught, especially for English language learners.
- **Derivational Word Lists** Presenting groups of words derived from particular languages or with specific roots or affixes is an effective way to reinforce meanings and spellings of foreign words and word parts.

Vocabulary Strategies for Unknown Words

Different strategies have been shown to be particularly effective for learning completely new words. These strategies are included in the ***Spelling and Vocabulary Skills*** activities.

Key Word This strategy involves providing or having students create a mnemonic clue for unknown vocabulary. For example, the word *mole* is defined in chemistry as a "gram molecule." By relating *mole* to *molecule*, students have a key to the meaning of the word.

Definitions Copying a definition from a dictionary is somewhat effective in learning new vocabulary. Combining this with using the word in writing and speaking adds to the effectiveness of this strategy. Requiring students to explain a word or use it in a novel sentence helps to ensure that the meaning is understood.

Context Clues Many words are learned from context, particularly with repeated exposure to words in reading and listening. Without specific instruction in consciously using context clues, however, unknown words are often ignored.

- **Syntax** How a word is used in a sentence provides some clue to its meaning.
- **External Context Clues** Hints about a word's meaning may appear in the setting, words, phrases, or sentences surrounding a word in text. Other known words in the text may be descriptive, may provide a definition (apposition), may be compared or contrasted, or may be used synonymously in context. Modeling and teaching students to use context to infer a word's meaning can help in learning unknown words.

Word Structure Examining the affixes and roots of a word may provide some clue to its meaning. Knowing the meaning of at least part of the word can provide a clue to its meaning. (For example, *unenforceable* can be broken down into meaningful word parts.)

Semantic Mapping Having students create a semantic map of an unknown word after learning its definition helps them to learn it. Have students write the new word and then list in a map or web all words they can think of that are related to it.

Semantic Feature Analysis A semantic feature analysis helps students compare and contrast similar types of words within a category to help secure unknown words. Have students chart, for example, the similarities and differences between different types of sports, including new vocabulary such as *lacrosse* and *cricket*.

Developing Vocabulary

Purpose

Vocabulary is closely connected to comprehension. Considerable vocabulary growth occurs incidentally during reading. A clear connection exists between vocabulary development and the amount of reading a person does, and there are strong indications that vocabulary instruction is important and that understanding the meaning of key words helps with comprehension.

In ***Open Court Reading,*** vocabulary is addressed before, during, and after reading. Before reading, the teacher presents vocabulary words from the selection. Students use skills such as context clues, apposition, and structural analysis to figure out the meaning of the words. These selection vocabulary words are not only important to understanding the text but are also high-utility words that can be used in discussing and writing about the unit theme.

During reading, students monitor their understanding of words and text. When they do not understand something, they stop and clarify what they have read. Students will use these same skills—context clues, apposition, structural elements, and the like—to clarify the meanings of additional words encountered while reading. Figuring out the meanings of words while reading prepares students for the demands of independent reading both in and out of school.

After reading, students review the vocabulary words that they learned before reading the selection. They also review any interesting words that they identified and discussed during reading. Students record in their Writer's Notebook both the selection vocabulary words and the interesting words they identified during their reading and are encouraged to use both sets of words in discussion and in writing.

Procedure

Before students read a selection, the teacher uses an overhead transparency to introduce the selection vocabulary to the class. The transparency contains two sentences for each selection vocabulary word. Students must use context clues, apposition, or word structure in the sentences to figure out the meaning of the underlined vocabulary words. If students cannot figure out the meaning of the word using one of these skills, they can consult the glossary or dictionary.

Below are suggestions for modeling the use of context clues, apposition, or word structure to figure out the meaning of a word.

Modeling Using Context Clues

Have students read the sentences on the transparency. Explain to students that they will use *context clues,* or other words in the sentence, to figure out the meaning of the underlined word. For example, if the word is "treacherous," the sentences might include:

1. Mrs. Frisby must undertake a <u>treacherous</u> journey to bring her son some medicine.
2. We took a <u>treacherous</u> walk near a swamp filled with crocodiles.

Have students look for clues in the sentences that might help them understand the meaning of the underlined word. Point out that a good clue in the second sentence is "near a swamp filled with crocodiles." This clue should help them understand that *treacherous* probably has something to do with danger. Guide students until they can give a reasonable definition of *treacherous.* To consolidate understanding of the word, ask another student to use the definition in a sentence.

Modeling Using Apposition

Have students read the sentences on the transparency. Explain to students that they will use *apposition* to figure out the meaning of the word. In apposition, the word is followed by the definition, which is set off by commas. For example, if the word is "abolitionist," the sentences might include the following:

1. The conductor thought he was an <u>abolitionist</u>, a person who wanted to end slavery.
2. John Brown was a famous <u>abolitionist</u>, a person who wanted to end slavery.

It should be pretty clear to students using apposition that the definition of the word *abolitionist* is "a person who wanted to end slavery."

Modeling Using Word Structure

Have students read the sentences on the transparency. Explain to students that they will use *word structure,* or parts of the selection vocabulary word, to figure out the meaning. For example, if the word is "uncharted," the sentences might include:

1. The strong wind blew Ivan's ship away into <u>uncharted</u> seas.
2. The explorers Lewis and Clark went into <u>uncharted</u> territory.

Have students look at the word *uncharted* and break it into parts: the prefix *un-, chart,* and the suffix *–ed.* Students should know that the suffix *un-* means "not," and that the suffix *–ed* usually indicates the past tense of a verb. However, you may need to remind students about the meanings of these affixes. Ask students for the meaning of the word *chart.* Students should know that a chart could be a "map" or a "table." Guide them as they put together the definitions of the word parts, *un-* (not), *charted* (mapped or tabled). They should be able to come up with the definition "not mapped" or "unmapped" or even "unknown." Have them substitute their definition in the sentences to see if the definition makes sense. So, for instance, the first sentence would read "The strong wind blew Ivan's ship away into unmapped (or unknown) seas." Confirm with students that the new sentence makes sense, and then repeat the same process for the second sentence.

Reading Comprehension

Everything the students learn about phonemic awareness, phonics, and decoding has one primary goal—to help them understand what they are reading. Without comprehension, there is no reading.

Reading Comprehension Strategies

Purpose

The primary aim of reading is comprehension. Without comprehension, neither intellectual nor emotional responses to reading are possible—other than the response of frustration. Good readers are problem solvers. They bring their critical faculties to bear on everything they read. Experienced readers generally understand most of what they read, but just as importantly, they recognize when they do not understand, and they have at their command an assortment of strategies for monitoring and furthering their understanding.

The goal of comprehension strategy instruction is to turn responsibility for using strategies over to the students as soon as possible. Research has shown that students' comprehension and learning problems are not a matter of mental capacity but rather their inability to use strategies to help them learn. Good readers use a variety of strategies to help them make sense of the text and get the most out of what they read. Trained to use a variety of comprehension strategies, students dramatically improve their learning performance. In order to do this, the teacher models strategy use and gradually incorporates different kinds of prompts and possible student think-alouds as examples of the types of thinking students might do as they read to comprehend what they are reading.

Setting Reading Goals

Even before they begin reading and using comprehension strategies, good readers set reading goals and expectations. Readers who have set their own goals and have definite expectations about the text they are about to read are more engaged in their reading and notice more in what they read. Having determined a purpose for reading, they are better able to evaluate a text and determine whether it meets their needs. Even when the reading is assigned, the reader's engagement is enhanced when he or she has determined ahead of time what information might be gathered from the selection or how the selection might interest him or her.

Comprehension Strategies

Descriptions of strategies good readers use to comprehend the text follow.

Summarizing

Good readers sum up to check their understanding as they read. Sometimes they reread to fill in gaps in their understanding. Good readers use the strategy of summarizing to keep track of what they are reading and to focus their minds on important information. The process of putting the information in one's own words not only helps good readers remember what they have read, but also prompts them to evaluate how well they understand the information. Sometimes the summary reveals that one's understanding is incomplete, in which case it might be appropriate to reread the previous section to fill in the gaps. Good readers usually find that the strategy of summarizing is particularly helpful when they are reading long or complicated text.

Monitoring and Clarifying

Good readers constantly monitor themselves as they read in order to make sure they understand what they are reading. They note the characteristics of the text, such as whether it is difficult to read or whether some sections are more challenging or more important than others are. In addition, when good readers become aware that they do not understand, they take appropriate action, such as rereading, in order to understand the text better. As they read, good readers stay alert for problem signs such as loss of concentration, unfamiliar vocabulary, or lack of sufficient background knowledge to comprehend the text. This ability to self-monitor and identify aspects of the text that hinder comprehension is crucial to becoming a proficient reader.

Asking Questions

Good readers ask questions that may prepare them for what they will learn. If their questions are not answered in the text, they may try to find answers elsewhere and thus add even more to their store of knowledge. Certain kinds of questions occur naturally to a reader, such as clearing up confusion or wondering why something in the text is as it is. Intentional readers take this somewhat informal questioning one step further by formulating questions with the specific intent of checking their understanding. They literally test themselves by thinking of questions a teacher might ask and then by determining answers to those questions.

Predicting

Good readers predict what will happen next. When reading fiction, they make predictions about what they are reading and then confirm or revise those predictions as they go.

Making Connections

Good readers make connections between what they are reading and what they already know from past experience or previous reading.

Visualizing

Good readers visualize what is happening in the text. They form mental images as they read. They picture the setting, the characters, and the action in a story. Visualizing can also be helpful when reading expository text. Visualizing helps readers understand descriptions of complex activities or processes. When a complex process or an event is being described, the reader can follow the process or the event better by visualizing each step or episode. Sometimes an author or an editor helps the reader by providing illustrations, diagrams, or maps. If no visual aids have been provided, it may help the reader to create one.

Monitoring and Adjusting Reading Speed

Good readers understand that not all text is equal. Because of this, good readers continuously monitor what they are reading and adjust their reading speed accordingly. They skim parts of the text that are not important or relevant to their reading goals and they purposely slow down when they encounter difficulty in understanding the text.

Procedures

Modeling and Thinking Aloud

One of the most effective ways to help students use and understand the strategies good readers use is to make strategic thinking public. Modeling these behaviors and encouraging students to think aloud as they attempt to understand text can demonstrate for everyone in a class how these behaviors are put into practice. Suggestions for think-alouds are provided throughout the **Teacher's Edition.**

The most effective models you can offer will be those that come from your own reading experiences. What kinds of questions did you ask yourself? What kinds of things surprised you the first time you read a story? What kinds of new information did you learn? What kinds of things were confusing until you reread or read further? Drawing on these questions and on your students' questions and comments as they read will make the strategic reading process more meaningful to the students. Below are suggestions for modeling each of the comprehension strategies.

- **Modeling Setting Reading Goals.** To model setting reading goals, engage students in the following:

- **Activate prior knowledge.** As you approach a new text, consider aloud what you already know about the subject or what your experiences have been in reading similar material.
- **Browse the text.** To get an idea of what to expect from a text, look at the title and the illustrations. Look for potential problems, such as difficult words. Have students glance quickly at the selection, looking briefly at the illustrations and the print. Have them tell what they think they might be learning about as they read the selection.
- **Decide what to expect from the text.** Anticipate enjoying the story, the language of the text, or the new information you expect to gain from the selection.

- **Modeling Summarizing.** Just as the strategy of summarizing the plot and then predicting what will happen next can enhance a student's reading of fiction, so too can the same procedure be used to the student's advantage in reading nonfiction. In expository text, it is particularly logical to stop and summarize at the end of a chapter or section before going on to the next. One way to model the valuable exercise of making predictions and at the same time expand knowledge is to summarize information learned from a piece of expository writing and then predict what the next step or category will be. Appropriate times to stop and summarize include the following:
  - when a narrative text has covered a long period of time or a number of events
  - when many facts have been presented
  - when an especially critical scene has occurred
  - when a complex process has been described
  - any time there is the potential for confusion about what has happened or what has been presented in the text
  - when returning to a selection
- **Modeling Monitoring and Clarifying.** A reader may need clarification at any point in the reading. Model this strategy by stopping at points that confuse you or that may confuse your students. Indicate that you are experiencing some confusion and need to stop and make sure you understand what is being read. Difficulty may arise from a challenging or unknown word or phrase. It may also stem from the manner in which the information is presented. Perhaps the author did not supply needed information. As you model this strategy, vary the reasons for stopping to clarify so that the students understand that good readers do not simply skip over difficult or confusing material—they stop and figure out what they don't understand.
- **Modeling Asking Questions.** Learning to ask productive questions is not an easy task. Students' earliest experiences with this strategy take the form of answering teacher-generated questions. However, students should be able to move fairly quickly to asking questions like those a teacher might ask. Questions that can be answered with a simple yes or no are not typically very useful for helping them remember and understand what they have read. Many students find it helpful to ask questions beginning with *Who? What? When? Where? How?* or *Why?* As students become more accustomed to asking and answering questions, they will naturally become more adept at phrasing their questions. As their question-asking becomes more sophisticated, they progress from simple questions that can be answered with explicit information in the text to questions that require making inferences based on the text.

Good readers use a variety of strategies to help them make sense of the text and get the most out of what they read.

- **Modeling Predicting.** Predicting can be appropriate at the beginning of a selection—on the basis of the titles and the illustrations—or at any point while reading a selection. At first, your modeling will take the form of speculation about what might happen next, but tell students from the start what clues in the text or illustrations helped you predict, in order to make it clear that predicting is not just guessing. When a student makes a prediction—especially a far-fetched one—ask what in the selection or in his or her own experience the prediction is based on. If the student can back up the prediction, let the prediction stand; otherwise, suggest that the student make another prediction on the basis of what he or she already knows. Often it is appropriate to sum up before making a prediction. This will help students consider what has come before as they make their predictions about what will happen next. When reading aloud, stop whenever a student's prediction has been confirmed or contradicted. Have students tell whether the prediction was correct. If students seem comfortable with the idea of making predictions but rarely do so on their own, encourage them to discuss how to find clues in the text that will help them.
- **Modeling Making Connections.** To model making connections, share with students any thoughts or memories that come to mind as you read the selection. Perhaps a character in a story reminds you of a childhood friend, allowing you to better identify with interactions between characters. Perhaps information in an article on Native-American life in the Old West reminds you of an article that you have read on the importance of the bison to Native Americans. Sharing your connections will help students become aware of the dynamic nature of reading and show them another way of being intentional, active learners.
- **Modeling Visualizing.** Model visualizing by describing the mental images that occur to you as you read. A well-described scene is relatively easy to visualize, and if no one does so voluntarily, you may want to prompt students to express their own visualizations. If the author has not provided a description of a scene, but a picture of the scene would make the story more interesting or comprehensible, you might want to model visualizing as follows: "Let's see. The author says that the street was busy, and we know that this story is set during the colonial period. From what I already know about those times, there were no cars, and the roads were different from the roads of today. The street may have been paved with cobblestones. Horses would have been pulling carriages or wagons. I can almost hear the horses' hoofs going clip-clop over the stones." Remind students that different readers may picture the same scene quite differently, which is fine. Every reader responds to a story in her or his own way.
- **Modeling Monitoring and Adjusting Reading Speed.** Just as readers need to monitor for problems, they need to be aware that different texts can be approached in different ways. For example, if reading a story or novel for enjoyment, the reader will typically read at a relaxed speed that is neither so fast as to be missing information nor as slow as they might read a textbook. If on the other hand, the reader is reading a textbook, he or she will probably decrease speed to assure understanding and make sure that all important information is read and understood. When modeling this strategy, be sure you indicate why you, as the reader, have chosen to slow down or speed up. Good readers continually monitor their speed and ability to understand throughout reading.

Reading Comprehension (continued)

Reading Aloud

At the beginning of the year, students should be encouraged to read selections aloud. This practice will help you and them understand some of the challenges posed by the text and how different students approach these challenges.

Reading aloud helps students build fluency, which in turn will aid their comprehension. Students in grades K–3 can use **Decodable Books** to build fluency, while students in grades 4–6 can use the literature from the **Student Anthologies.** Fluent second graders read between 82 and 124 words per minute with accuracy and understanding, depending on the time of the year (fall/spring). Fluent third graders can be expected to read between 107 and 142 words per minute; fourth (125/143); fifth (126/151); sixth (127/153).

Make sure that you set aside time to hear each student read during the first few days of class—the days devoted to Getting Started are perfect for this—so that you can determine students' abilities and needs. **Workshop** is also a good time to listen to any students who do not get to read aloud while the class is reading the selection together.

If your students have not previously engaged in the sort of strategic thinking aloud that is promoted throughout the ***SRA/Open Court Reading*** program, you will have to do all or most of the modeling at first, but encourage the students to participate as soon as possible.

As the year progresses, students should continue reading aloud often, especially with particularly challenging text. Model your own use of strategies, not only to help students better understand how to use strategies, but also to help them understand that actively using strategies is something that good, mature readers do constantly.

Most students are unaccustomed to thinking out loud. They will typically stand mute as they try to figure out an unfamiliar word or deal with a confusing passage. When this happens, students should be encouraged to identify specifically what they are having difficulty with. A student might identify a particular word, or he or she may note that the individual words are familiar but the meaning of the passage is unclear.

Active Response

Not only are good readers active in their reading when they encounter problems, but they respond constantly to whatever they read. In this way they make the text their own. As students read they should be encouraged to:

- Make as many connections as they can between what they are reading and what they already know.
- Visualize passages to help clarify their meanings or simply to picture appealing descriptions.
- Ask questions about what they are reading. The questions that go through their minds during reading will help them to examine, and thus better understand, the text. Doing so may also interest them in pursuing their own investigations. The questions may also provide a direction for students' research or exploration.
- Summarize and make predictions as a check on how well they understand what they are reading.

Tips

- Remember that the goal of all reading strategies is comprehension. If a story or article does not make sense, the reader needs to choose whatever strategies will help make sense of it. If one strategy does not work, the reader should try another.
- Always treat problems encountered in text as interesting learning opportunities rather than something to be avoided or dreaded.
- Encourage students to think out loud about text challenges.
- Encourage students to help each other build meaning from text. Rather than telling each other what a word is or what a passage means, students should tell each other how they figured out the meanings of challenging words and passages.
- Assure students that these are not the only strategies that can be used while reading. Any strategy that they find helpful in understanding text is a good useful strategy.
- Encourage students to freely share strategies they have devised on their own. You might want to write these on a large sheet of paper and tape them to the board.
- An absence of questions does not necessarily indicate that students understand what they are reading. Be especially alert to students who never seem to ask questions. Be sure to spend tutorial time with these students occasionally, and encourage them to discuss specific selections in the context of difficulties they might have encountered and how they solved them as well as their thoughts about unit concepts.
- Observing students' responses to text will enable you to ascertain not only how well they understand a particular selection but also their facility in choosing and applying appropriate strategies. Take note of the following:
  - ✓ Whether the strategies a student uses are effective in the particular situation.
  - ✓ Whether the student chooses from a variety of appropriate strategies or uses the same few over and over.
  - ✓ Whether the student can explain to classmates which strategies to use in a particular situation and why.
  - ✓ Whether the student can identify alternative resources to pursue when the strategies she or he has tried are not effective.
  - ✓ Whether students' application of a given strategy is becoming more effective over a period of time.

Becoming familiar and comfortable with these self-monitoring techniques gives readers the confidence to tackle material that is progressively more difficult. A good, mature reader knows that he or she will know when understanding what he or she is reading is becoming a problem and can take steps to correct the situation.

Reading Comprehension Skills

Purpose

An important purpose of writing is to communicate thoughts from one person to another. The goal of instruction in reading comprehension skills is to make students aware of the logic behind the structure of a written piece. If the reader can discern the logic of the structure, he or she will be more able to understand the author's logic and gain knowledge both of the facts and the intent of the selection. By keeping the organization of a piece in mind and considering the author's purpose for writing, the reader can go beyond the actual words on the page and make inferences or draw conclusions based on what was read. Strong, mature readers utilize these "between the lines" skills to get a complete picture of not only what the writer is saying, but what the writer is trying to say.

Effective comprehension skills include:

Author's Point of View

Point of view involves identifying who is telling the story. If a character in the story is telling the story, that one character describes the action and tells what the other characters are like. This is first-person point of view. In such a story, one character will do the talking and use the pronouns *I*, *my*, *me*. All other characters' thoughts, feelings, and emotions will be reported through this one character.

If the story is told in third-person point of view, someone outside the story who is aware of all of the characters' thoughts and feelings and actions is relating them to the reader. All of the characters are referred to by their names or the pronouns *he/she*, *him/her*, *it*.

If students stay aware of who is telling a story, they will know whether they are getting the full picture or the picture of events as seen through the eyes of only one character.

Sequence

The reader can't make any decisions about relationships or events if he or she has no idea in which order the events take place. The reader needs to pay attention to how the writer is conveying the sequence. Is it simply stated that first this happened and then that happened? Does the writer present the end of the story first and then go back and let the reader know the sequence of events? Knowing what the sequence is and how it is presented helps the reader follow the writer's line of thought.

Fact and Opinion

Learning to distinguish fact from opinion is essential to critical reading and thinking. Students learn what factors need to be present in order for a statement to be provable. They also learn that an opinion, while not provable itself, should be based on fact. Readers use this knowledge to determine for themselves the validity of the ideas presented in their reading.

Main Idea and Details

An author always has something specific to say to his or her reader. The author may state this main idea in different ways, but the reader should always be able to tell what the writing is about.

To strengthen the main point or main idea of a piece, the author provides details to help the reader understand. For example, the author may use comparison and contrast to make a point, provide examples, provide facts, give opinions, give descriptions, give reasons or causes, or give definitions. The reader needs to know what kinds of details he or she is dealing with before making a judgment about the main idea.

Compare and Contrast

Using comparison and contrast is one of the most common and easiest ways a writer uses to get his or her reader to understand a subject. Comparing and contrasting unfamiliar thoughts, ideas, or things with familiar thoughts, ideas, and things gives the reader something within his or her own experience base to use in understanding.

Cause and Effect

What made this happen? Why did this character act the way he or she did? Knowing the causes of events helps the reader to see the whole story. Using this information to identify the probable outcomes (effects) of events or actions will help the reader anticipate the story or article.

Classify and Categorize

The relationships of actions, events, characters, outcomes, and such in a selection should be clear enough for the reader to see the relationships. Putting like things or ideas together can help the reader understand the relationships set up by the writer.

Author's Purpose

Everything that is written is written for a purpose. That purpose may be to entertain, to persuade, or to inform. Knowing why a piece is written—what purpose the author had for writing the piece—gives the reader an idea of what to expect and perhaps some prior idea of what the author is going to say.

If a writer is writing to entertain, then the reader can generally just relax and let the writer carry him or her away. If, on the other hand, the purpose is to persuade, it will help the reader understand and keep perspective if he or she knows that the purpose is to persuade. The reader can be prepared for whatever argument the writer delivers.

Drawing Conclusions

Often, writers do not directly state everything—they take for granted their audience's ability to "read between the lines." Readers draw conclusions when they take from the text small pieces of information about a character or event and use this information to make a statement about that character or event.

Making Inferences

Readers make inferences about characters and events to understand the total picture in a story. When making inferences, readers use information from the text, along with personal experience or knowledge, to gain a deeper understanding of a story event and its implications.

Procedure

Read the Selection

First, have students read the selection using whatever strategies they need to help them make sense of the selection. Then discuss the selection to assure that students did, indeed, understand what they read. Talk about any confusion they may have, and make any necessary clarifications.

Reread

Revisiting or rereading a selection allows the reader to note specific techniques that authors use to organize and present information in narratives and expository genres. Once students have a basic understanding of the piece, have them reread the selection in whole or in part, concentrating on selected skills. Choose examples of how the writer organized the piece to help the reader understand.

Limit this concentration on specific comprehension/writing skills to one or two that can be clearly identified in the piece. Trying to concentrate on too many things will just confuse students and make it harder for them to identify any of the organizational devices used by the writer. If a piece has many good examples of several different aspects, then go back to the piece several times over a span of days.

Write

Solidify the connection between how an author writes and how readers make sense of a selection by encouraging students to incorporate these organizational devices into their own writing. As they attempt to use these devices, they will get a clearer understanding of how to identify them when they are reading.

Remind students often that the purpose of any skill exercise is to give them tools to use when they are reading and writing. Unless students learn to apply the skills to their own reading—in every area of reading and study—then they are not gaining a full understanding of the purpose of the exercise.

Grammar, Usage, and Mechanics

PROGRAM APPENDIX

Writing is a complicated process. A writer uses handwriting, spelling, vocabulary, grammar, usage, genre structures, and mechanics skills with ideas to create readable text. In addition, a writer must know how to generate content, or ideas, and understand genre structures in order to effectively present ideas in writing. Many students never progress beyond producing a written text that duplicates their everyday speech patterns. Mature writers, however, take composition beyond conversation. They understand the importance of audience and purpose for writing. They organize their thoughts, eliminating those that do not advance their main ideas, and elaborating on those that do so that their readers can follow a logical progression of ideas in an essay or story. Mature writers also know and can use the conventions of grammar, usage, spelling, and mechanics. They proofread and edit for these conventions, so their readers are not distracted by errors.

Purpose

The Study of English Conventions

Over the years the study of grammar, usage, and mechanics has gone in and out of favor. In the past century much research has been done to demonstrate the effectiveness of traditional types of instruction in the conventions of English. Experience and research have shown that learning grammatical terms and completing grammar exercises have little effect on the student's practical application of these skills in the context of speaking or writing. These skills, in and of themselves, do not play a significant role in the way students use language to generate and express their ideas—for example during the prewriting and drafting phases of the writing process. In fact, emphasis on correct conventions has been shown to have a damaging effect when it is the sole focus of writing instruction. If students are evaluated only on the proper use of spelling, grammar, and punctuation, they tend to write fewer and less complex sentences.

Knowledge of English conventions is, however, vitally important in the editing and proofreading phases of the writing process. A paper riddled with mistakes in grammar, usage, or mechanics is quickly discounted. Many immature writers never revise or edit. They finish the last sentence and turn their papers in to the teacher. Mature writers employ their knowledge of English language conventions in the editing phase to refine and polish their ideas.

The study of grammar, usage, and mechanics is important for two reasons.

1. Educated people need to know and understand the structure of their language, which in large part defines their culture.
2. Knowledge of grammar gives teachers and students a common vocabulary for talking about language and makes discussions of writing tasks more efficient and clearer.

Procedure

The key issue in learning grammar, usage, and mechanics is *how* to do it. On the one hand, teaching these skills in isolation from writing has been shown to be ineffective and even detrimental if too much emphasis is placed on them. On the other hand, not teaching these skills and having students write without concern for conventions is equally ineffective. The answer is to teach the skills in a context that allows students to directly apply them to a reading or writing activity. Students should be taught proper use of punctuation or subject/verb agreement at the same time they are taught to proofread for those conventions. As they learn to apply their knowledge of conventions during the final stages of the writing process, they will begin to see that *correcting* errors is an editorial, rather than a composition skill.

History of English

A basic understanding of the history and structure of the English language helps students understand the rich but complex resource they have for writing.

Old English

The English language began about AD 450 when the Angles, Jutes, and Saxons—three tribes that lived in northern Europe—invaded the British Isles. Much of their language included words that had to do with farming (*sheep, dirt, tree, earth*). Many of their words are the most frequently used words in the English language today. Because of Latin influences, English became the first of the European languages to be written down.

Middle English

In 1066 William the Conqueror invaded England and brought Norman French with him. Slowly Old English and Norman French came together, and Middle English began to appear. Today 40% of Modern English comes from French. With the introduction of the printing press English became more widespread.

Modern English

With the Renaissance and its rediscovery of classical Greek and Latin, many new words were created from Greek and Latin word elements. This continued intensively during the Early Modern English period. This rich language was used in the writings of Shakespeare and his contemporaries and profoundly influenced the nature and vocabulary of English. With dictionaries and spelling books, the English language became more standardized, although it continues to be influenced by other languages and new words and trends. These influences continue to make English a living, dynamic language.

Punctuation

Early writing had no punctuation or even spaces between words. English punctuation had its beginning in ancient Greece and Rome. Early punctuation reflected speaking, rather than reading. By the end of the eighteenth century, after the invention of printing, most of the rules for punctuation were established, although they were not the same in all languages.

The Structure of English

Grammar is the sound, structure, and meaning system of language. People who speak the same language are able to communicate because they intuitively know the grammar system of that language, the rules of making meaning. All languages have grammar, and yet each language has its own grammar.

Traditional grammar study usually involves two areas:

- **Parts of speech** (nouns, verbs, adjectives, adverbs, pronouns, prepositions, conjunctions) are typically considered the content of grammar. The parts of speech involve the *form* of English words.
- **Sentence structure** (subjects, predicates, objects, clauses, phrases) is also included in grammar study. Sentence structure involves the *function* of English.

Mechanics involves the conventions of punctuation and capitalization. Punctuation helps readers understand writers' messages. Proper punctuation involves marking off sentences according to grammatical structure. In speech students can produce sentences as easily and unconsciously as they can walk, but in writing they must think about what is and what is not a sentence.

In English there are about 14 punctuation marks (period, comma, quotation marks, question mark, exclamation point, colon, semicolon, apostrophe, hyphen, ellipsis, parentheses, brackets, dash, and underscore). Most immature writers use only three: period, comma, and question mark. The experienced writer or poet with the command of punctuation adds both flexibility and meaning to his or her sentences through his or her use of punctuation.

Usage is the way in which we speak in a given community. Language varies over time, across national and geographical boundaries, by gender, across age groups, and by socioeconomic status. When the variation occurs within a given language, the different versions of the same language are called *dialects.* Every language has a *prestige dialect* associated with education and financial success. In the United States, this *dialect* is known as Standard English and is the language of school and business.

Usage involves the word choices people make when speaking certain dialects. Word choices that are perfectly acceptable in conversation among friends may be unacceptable in writing. Usage is often the most obvious indicator of the difference between conversation and composition. Errors in word usage can make a writer seem ignorant and thus jeopardize his or her credibility, no matter how valid or important his or her overall message might be. Usage depends on a student's cultural and linguistic heritage. If the dialect students have learned is not the formal language of school settings or if it is not English, students must master another dialect or language in order to write Standard English.

The English Language Conventions lessons in ***Open Court Reading*** are structured to focus on grammar and usage or mechanics skills presented in a logical sequence. A skill is introduced on the first day of the lesson with appropriate models and then practiced in reading and writing on subsequent days to ensure that skills are not taught in isolation. Encourage students to use the focused English language convention presented in each lesson as they complete each Writing Process Strategies activity. Also encourage them to reread their writing, checking for proper use of the conventions taught. With practice, students should be able to apply their knowledge of conventions to any writing they do.

Tips

- Some of the errors students make in writing are the result simply of not carefully reading their final drafts. Many errors occur because the writer's train of thought was interrupted and a sentence is not complete or a word is skipped. These may look like huge errors that a simple rereading can remedy. Most often the writer can correct these types of errors on his or her own. A major emphasis of any English composition program should be to teach the editing and proofreading phases of the writing process so students can eliminate these types of errors themselves. This involves a shift in perception—from thinking of grammar as a set of discrete skills that involve mastery of individual rules, to understanding grammar as it applies to the act of communicating in writing.
- As students learn English language conventions, they should be expected to incorporate them into their written work. A cumulative student checklist of the grammar, usage, and mechanics skills covered in a grade level appears in the back of the ***Writer's Workbook.***
- Sometimes, students write sentences that raise grammatically complex problems that require a deep understanding of English grammar. Use the Sentence Lifting strategies outlined in the **Proofreading** part of the Appendix to identify and discuss these more sophisticated types of errors that can include:
  - **Faulty Parallelism.** Parts of a sentence parallel in meaning are not parallel in structure.
  - **Nonsequitors.** A statement does not follow logically from something said previously.
  - **Dangling Modifiers.** A phrase or clause does not logically modify the word next to it.
  - **Awkwardness.** Sentences are not written simply.
  - **Wordiness.** Thoughts are not written in as few words as possible.
  - **Vocabulary.** Precise words are not used.

Listening, Speaking, Viewing

Some people are naturally good listeners, and others have no trouble speaking in front of groups. Many people, however, need explicit instruction on how to tune in for important details and how to organize and make an oral presentation. While some people naturally critique what they read, hear, and see, many others need specific guidance to develop skills for analyzing what they encounter in images and the media. The abilities to listen appropriately and to speak in conversations and in groups, as well as to critically evaluate the information with which they are presented, are fundamental skills that will serve students throughout their lives.

Purpose

In addition to reading and writing, listening, speaking, and viewing complete the language arts picture. Through the development of these language arts skills, students gain flexibility in communicating orally, visually, and in writing. When speaking and listening skills are neglected, many students have difficulty speaking in front of groups, organizing a speech, or distinguishing important information they hear. A top anxiety for many adults is speaking in front of groups. Much of this anxiety would not exist if listening, speaking, and viewing skills were taught from the early years.

The Listening, Speaking, and Viewing instruction focuses on the literature selection or the Writing Process Strategies to provide context, reinforce other elements of the lesson, and integrate the other language arts. Many of the Listening, Speaking, and Viewing skills are very similar to reading or writing skills. For example, listening for details is the same type of skill as reading for details. Preparing an oral report employs many of the same skills as preparing a written report. Learning to use these skills effectively gives students flexibility in how they approach a task.

Procedure

Listening, speaking, and viewing skills are presented with increasing sophistication throughout every grade level of ***Open Court Reading*** in the Language Arts part of each lesson. Every unit includes at least one lesson on each of the following skills so that students encounter the skills again and again throughout a grade level:

- **Listening.** Listening skills include comprehending what one hears and listening for different purposes, such as to identify sequence or details, to summarize or draw conclusions, or to follow directions.
- **Speaking.** Speaking skills include speaking formally and conversationally, using appropriate volume, giving oral presentations, and using effective grammar. Speaking skills also include using descriptive words, using figurative language, and using formal and informal language.
- **Viewing.** Viewing skills include comprehending main ideas and messages in images, mass media, and other multimedia.
- **Interaction.** Interaction instruction focuses on a combination of listening and speaking skills. These include asking and responding to questions, nonverbal cues such as eye contact, facial expression, and posture, and contributing to and interacting in group settings.
- **Presenting Information.** The last Listening, Speaking, and Viewing lesson in every unit usually focuses on presentation skills. These include sharing ideas, relating experiences or stories, organizing information, and preparing for speeches. These lessons often parallel the Writing Process Strategies instruction, so that students can prepare their information in written or oral form.

Tips

- Point out the parallels among the language arts skills: providing written and oral directions, telling or writing a narrative, and so on. Encourage students to see that they have choices for communicating. Discuss the similarities and differences between different forms of communication, and determine whether one is preferable in a given situation.
- Ensure that all students have opportunities to speak in small groups and whole-class situations.
- Provide and teach students to allow appropriate wait time before someone answers a question.

Writing

PROGRAM APPENDIX

The ability to write with clarity and coherence is essential to students' success in school as well as in life. Communicating through writing is becoming more and more important in this age of computers. Yet, writing remains a major problem for students at all levels, as well as adults in the workplace.

Purpose

Writing is a complex process. It requires the ability to use a variety of skills (penmanship, grammar, usage, mechanics, spelling, vocabulary) fluently and appropriately at the same time one's creative and critical thinking processes create and structure an idea. Familiarity with the structures of writing and different genres, audiences, and purposes is necessary to write appropriately as well. The art of writing well also involves writer's craft, the ability to manipulate words and sentences for effect.

As strange as it may seem, the better a writer is, the *harder* he or she works at writing. The best writers are not the best because they are naturally talented. They are the best usually because they work the hardest. Good writers really do take *more* time than others in the planning and revising stages of the writing process. Poorer writers make writing look easy by writing without planning and typically build a composition sentence by sentence. They turn in their papers with little or no correction.

The goals of writing instruction have many facets:

- To model and practice writing in a variety of writing genres so that students can choose and write in an appropriate form.
- To model and practice a writing process to help students develop routines for planning their work and then revising and editing it.
- To practice using spelling, vocabulary, and English language conventions skills in writing so that students can use them fluently.
- To develop writing traits: ideas, organization, voice, word choice, sentence fluency, and presentation so that students become effective writers.

Just as the goal of phonics instruction is to teach students to read, the Writing Process Strategies instruction in ***Open Court Reading*** focuses on skills, structures, and strategies for writing. The goal of this instruction is to learn how to write, rather than to develop a particular idea. From this instruction, students will have a comprehensive bank of tools for writing, which they can then employ in the development of their Research and Inquiry investigations in each unit or in any other writing application.

The best writers are not the best because they are naturally talented. They are the best usually because they work the hardest. Good writers really do take more *time than others in the planning and revising stages of the writing process.*

Procedures

Writing Genres

There are several different genres students are typically asked to write. These usually include many creative stories and a few reports. The only narrative writing most adults do, however, is summaries of meetings. The bulk of adult writing consists of writing reports, letters, analyses, memos, and proposals. College students, as well, typically write research reports or critiques. A literate student needs to be able to choose and write in an appropriate genre.

- Narrative writing is story writing, which has a beginning, middle, and end. It includes myth, realistic fiction, historical fiction, biography, science fiction, fantasy, folktale, and legend.
- Expository writing is informational writing. It includes research reports, scientific investigation, summaries, and explanations of a process.
- Descriptive writing is observational writing that includes details. It has descriptive paragraphs that may be part of narrative or expository writing.
- Poetry writing involves particular attention to word choice and rhythm. Poetry may be free form, ballad, rhyming, or a variety of other forms.
- Personal writing is functional writing to help record ideas, thoughts, or feelings or to communicate with others and may include E-mail, journals, lists, and messages.
- Persuasive writing involves the development of a persuasive argument. It includes posters, persuasive essays, and advertisements.

In ***Open Court Reading*** the first unit of every grade teaches the writing process and traits of writing. Each subsequent unit focuses on a particular genre appropriate for the unit content. Expository and persuasive writing are typically in the units with research themes such as medicine or business; personal, narrative, descriptive, and poetry writing are in units with universal themes, such as friendship and courage. Exemplary models of each form of writing are included either in the literature selection, on the ***Language Arts Transparencies***, or in the ***Language Arts Handbook.***

Each genre has its own form and function. For example:

- A personal narrative is probably best ordered as a straightforward chronological retelling of events. Dialogue may help to tell the story.
- A process description should be told in a step-by-step order. The draft should include as much information as possible; each step must be clear. If the piece needs cutting, the student can always do it later.
- A persuasive piece appeals to feelings. It requires facts as well as expert opinions.
- An interview could be written as a series of questions and answers.
- The order of details in a descriptive piece must be easy to follow—from left to right, top to bottom, or whatever order makes sense.
- A fictional story must include details describing characters, setting, and the characters' actions. Dialogue also helps to tell the story.

The goal is not to develop full-blown novels and compositions, but to experience the structures of different forms of writing.

Structures of Writing

Structures of writing involve the effective development of sentences, paragraphs, and compositions. In ***Open Court Reading*** structures of writing are taught within the context of the Writing Process Strategies activities rather than in isolation, so that students integrate their practice of writing structures as they develop different writing genres.

Writer's Craft

Writer's Craft involves the elements and choices writers make to add drama, suspense, or lightheartedness to a written work. These elements may include foreshadowing, use of figurative language, dialogue, or enhancement of setting or use of description to affect the mood and tone. In ***Open Court Reading,*** along with structures of writing, the writer's craft is pointed out in the literature selection and then taught and practiced within the context of the Writing Process Strategies activities.

Writing Traits

Writing traits are those elements and qualities in a composition that enhance the effectiveness of the writing. These include:

- Ideas/Content. Not only the quality of the idea, but the development, support, and focus of the idea makes a strong composition.

- Organization. In quality writing, the organization develops the central idea. The order and structure move the reader through the text easily. The beginning grabs the reader's attention and the conclusion adds impact.
- Voice. Voice is the overall tone of a piece of writing. Good writers choose a voice appropriate for the topic, purpose, and audience. As students develop writing skills, a unique style begins to emerge. The writing is expressive, engaging, or sincere, demonstrating a strong commitment to the topic.
- Word Choice. In quality writing words convey the intended message in an interesting, precise, and natural way appropriate to audience and purpose.
- Sentence Fluency. Sentence fluency enhances the flow and rhythm of a composition. In good writing sentence patterns are somewhat varied, contributing to ease in oral reading.
- Conventions. Good writers demonstrate consistent use and awareness of English language conventions.
- Presentation. A quality piece of writing includes an impressive presentation with attention to format, style, illustration, and clarity.

In ***Open Court Reading,*** the traits of writing are taught in the first unit and then practiced in every Writing Process Strategies activity as an integral part of the writing process.

The Writing Process

Providing a routine or process for students to follow will help them to learn a systematic approach to writing. By following the steps of the writing process, students will learn to approach everything they write with purpose and thought. They learn that although writing takes time and thought, there are steps they can take to make their writing clear, coherent, and appealing to their audience.

In ***Open Court Reading,*** the first unit of every grade provides an overview and teaching of the writing process, including strategies and examples for getting ideas, determining audience and purpose for writing, organizing writing, drafting, revising, editing, and presenting. The vehicle used to apply this instruction is a student autobiography. The autobiographies can be collected in a school portfolio to assess writing development over the course of the elementary years.

Prewriting

Purpose

Prewriting is that phase of the writing process when students think through an idea they want to write about. To improve their writing, students should think about their ideas, discuss them, and plan how they want readers to respond. It is important for students to take time before writing to plan ahead so that they can proceed from one phase of the writing process to another without spending unnecessary time making decisions that should have been made earlier. Prewriting is the most time-consuming phase of the writing process, but it may be the most important.

The goal is not to develop full-blown novels and compositions, but to familiarize and practice the structures of different forms of writing.

Procedure

Good student writers

- Listen to advice about time requirements and plan time accordingly.
- Spend time choosing, thinking about, and planning the topic.
- Spend time narrowing the topic.
- Determine the purpose for writing.
- Consider the audience and what readers already know about the topic.
- Conduct research, if necessary, before writing.
- Get information from a lot of different sources.
- Use models for different types of writing, but develop individual plans.
- Organize the resource information.
- Make a plan for writing that shows how the ideas will be organized.
- Elaborate on a plan and evaluate and alter ideas as writing proceeds.

Noting Writing Ideas

Students can make notes of writing ideas at any time, with a special time being set aside following the discussion of each reading selection. The writing ideas students get from a discussion might be concerned with the topic of the selection they just read or with an aspect of the author's style. You should keep such a list of writing ideas also, and think aloud occasionally as you make writing idea notes.

Students must make many decisions during the prewriting phase of the writing process. Most students can benefit from talking with a partner or a small group of classmates about these decisions. They may want to discuss some of the following points.

- **Genre** or format of each writing piece. Having decided to use a writing idea such as "a misunderstanding on the first day of school," the student must decide how to use it—for example, as a personal narrative, a realistic fiction story, a poem, a fantasy story, a play, a letter, and so on.
- **Audience**. Although students' writing pieces will be shared with classmates and with you, some may ultimately be intended for other audiences.
- **Writing Purpose**. Each student should write a sentence that tells the purpose of the piece he or she plans to write. The purpose statement should name the intended audience and the effect the writer hopes to have on that audience. For example, a writer may want to describe her first day in school. The intended audience is kindergarten students, and she intends her story to be humorous. Her purpose statement would read, "I want to write a funny story for other students about my first day in kindergarten."
- **Planning**. Some writers may find it helpful to brainstorm with a partner or small group to list words and phrases they might use in a piece of writing. Sometimes this list can be organized into webs of related ideas or details. This kind of prewriting activity might be particularly useful for planning a descriptive piece. For planning a comparison/contrast piece, a writer might use another kind of visual organizer, such as a Venn diagram. Students planning fiction pieces might use a story frame or plot line.

Tips

- Circulate as students make notes on writing ideas or work in small groups on prewriting activities.
- Notice which students are having difficulty coming up with writing ideas. It may help to pair these students with students who have many ideas.
- Do not worry if this phase of the process seems noisy and somewhat chaotic. Students must be allowed to let their imaginations roam in free association and to play around with words and ideas until they hit on something that seems right. They must be permitted to share ideas and help each other.
- Do not worry if, in the early sessions, the class as a whole seems to have few ideas. Through the reading and discussion of selections in the reading anthology, most students will soon have more writing ideas than they can use.

Writing (continued)

Drafting

Purpose

During the drafting phase of the writing process, students shape their planning notes into main ideas and details. They devote their time and effort to getting words down on paper. Whether students are drafting on scrap paper or on computer screens, your role is to encourage each writer to "get it all down." You must also provide a suitable writing environment with the expectation that there will be revision to the draft and to the original plan.

Good Student Writers

- Express all their ideas in the first draft.
- Stop and think about what is being written while drafting.
- Evaluate and alter ideas while drafting.
- Change or elaborate on original plans while drafting.
- Discover that they need more information about certain parts of their writing.
- Learn a lot more about the topic while drafting.

Procedure

Here are some points to share with students before they begin drafting:

- Drafting is putting your ideas down on paper for your own use. Writers do not need to worry about spelling or exact words. They just need to get their ideas down.
- Write on every other line so that you will have room to make revisions.
- Write on only one side of a page so that when you revise you can see all of your draft at once.
- As you draft, keep in mind your purpose for writing this piece and your intended audience.
- Use your plan and your notes from research to add details.

Using Word Processors for Drafting

Many students enjoy drafting on the screen of a computer more than drafting on paper. Once they have mastered the keyboard, they may find it easier to think as they write. Their first attempts look less sloppy, and they are often more willing to make changes and experiment as they draft. They will certainly find it neater to use the delete key on the word processor than to correct their mistakes by crossing out. The Basic Computer Skills instruction in the Language Arts Overview of every lesson provides instruction on using the computer.

Tips

Sometimes the hardest part of drafting is getting the first sentence down on paper. It may help a student even before she or he starts writing to begin a story in the middle or to write the word "Draft" in big letters at the top of the paper.

- If a student feels stuck during drafting, he or she may need to go back and try a different prewriting technique.
- After an initial fifteen or twenty minutes of imposed silence, some students may work better and come up with more ideas if they share as they write.
- You may find that it is difficult to get students to "loosen up" as they draft. Remember, most students have been encouraged to be neat and to erase mistakes when they write. It may help to share some of your own marked-up manuscripts with students.

Revising

Purpose

The purpose of revising is to make sure that a piece of writing expresses the writer's ideas clearly and completely. It has been said that there is no good writing, just good rewriting. A major distinction between good writers and poor writers is the amount of time and effort they put into revision. Poor writers look for spelling and grammatical errors if they do read their work.

Good Student writers

- Evaluate what has been written.
- Read the draft as a reader, not the writer.
- Identify problems with focus, giving enough information, clarity, and order.
- Think of solutions to problems and understand when solutions will and won't work.
- Recognize when and how the text needs to be reorganized.
- Eliminate sentences or paragraphs that don't fit the main idea.
- Identify ideas that need elaboration.
- Do more research if needed to support or add ideas.
- Identify and eliminate unnecessary details.
- Ask for feedback from peer and teacher conferences.
- Take advantage of classroom and outside resources.
- Check the accuracy of facts and details.
- Give credit for any ideas from other people or sources.

Procedure

Model asking questions like the following when revising various kinds of writing:

- About a narrative:
  - ✓ Does my first sentence get my readers' attention?
  - ✓ Are events in the story told in an order that makes sense?
  - ✓ Have I included dialogue to help move the story along?
  - ✓ Does the story have a clear focus?
- About a description:
  - ✓ Have I used details that appeal to the senses?
- About a comparison/contrast piece:
  - ✓ Have I made a separate paragraph for each subject discussed?
- About an explanation:
  - ✓ Will readers understand what I am saying?
  - ✓ Are the steps of the explanation in a clear order?
  - ✓ Have I made effective use of signal words?
  - ✓ Have I included enough information?
- About fiction:
  - ✓ Have I described my characters and setting?
  - ✓ Does the plot include a problem, build to a climax, and then describe the resolution of the problem?
- About persuasive writing:
  - ✓ Have I made my position clear?
  - ✓ Does my evidence support my position?
  - ✓ Have I used opinions as well as facts, and have I said whose opinions I used?
  - ✓ Have I directed my writing to my audience?

Help students understand the value of asking questions such as the following as they revise:

- About each paragraph:
  - ✓ Does each sentence belong in it?
  - ✓ Does each sentence connect smoothly with the next?
  - ✓ Does each sentence say something about the main idea?
- About each sentence:
  - ✓ Do the sentences read smoothly?
  - ✓ Have I combined sentences that were too short?
  - ✓ Have I broken sentences that were too long into two shorter sentences?
  - ✓ Have I varied the beginnings of the sentences?
- About the words:
  - ✓ Have I changed words that were repeated too often?
  - ✓ Do transition words connect ideas?

Tips

- Use the student Writing Folder to review student progress. Check first drafts against revised versions to see how each student is able to apply revision strategies.
- You may find that some students are reluctant to revise. You might then try the following:

✓ If a student doesn't see anything that needs to be changed or doesn't want to change anything, get him or her to do something to the paper—number the details in a description or the steps in a process, circle exact words, underline the best parts of the paper. Once a paper is marked, the student may not be so reluctant to change it.

✓ One reason many students do not like to revise is that they think they must recopy everything. This is not always necessary. Sometimes writers can cut and paste sections that they want to move. Or they can use carets and deletion marks to show additions and subtractions from a piece.

✓ Give an especially reluctant student a deadline by which she or he must revise a piece or lose the chance to publish it.

✓ Students will hopefully be writing in other classes and on a variety of topics. Revision techniques can be used to improve writing in any curriculum area. Stress to students the importance of focusing on their intended audience as they revise.

Proofreading

Purpose

Writing that is free of grammatical, spelling, and technical mistakes is clearer and easier for readers to understand. By proofreading their pieces, students will also notice which errors they make repeatedly and will learn not to make them in the future.

After a piece of writing has been revised for content and style, students must read it carefully line by line to make sure that it contains no errors. This activity, the fourth phase of the writing process, is called proofreading and is a critical step that must occur before a piece of writing can be published. Students can begin proofreading a piece when they feel that it has been sufficiently revised.

Good Student Writers

- Edit the work to allow the reader to understand and enjoy the words.
- Correct most errors in English language conventions.
- Use resources or seek assistance to address any uncertainties in English language conventions.

Procedure

Using What They Have Learned

Students should be expected to proofread at a level appropriate to their grade. Young authors should not be held responsible for skills they have not yet learned. Older students will be able to check for a greater variety of errors than younger students and should be expected to take greater responsibility for their proofreading. For example, students in first grade can be expected to check for and correct omitted capital letters at the beginning of sentences, but they should not necessarily be expected to understand and correct capital letters in proper nouns or in names of organizations. Older students will have mastered many more grammatical, mechanical, usage, and spelling skills and can be expected to perform accordingly. When you spot an error related to a skill beyond a student's level, make clear to the student that you do not expect her or him to be responsible for the mistake, but do explain that the error still needs to be corrected. The following suggestions may be useful as you introduce proofreading to the students and help them develop their proofreading skills.

Proofreading Checklist

Have students use a proofreading checklist similar to the one shown here to help them remember the steps for effective proofreading.

✓ Read each sentence.

✓ Does each sentence begin with a capital letter and end with correct punctuation?

✓ Do you notice any sentence fragments or run-on sentences?

✓ Are words missing from the sentence?

✓ Is any punctuation or capitalization missing from within the sentence?

✓ Do you notice any incorrect grammar or incorrect word usage in the sentence?

✓ Do you notice any misspelled words?

✓ Are the paragraphs indented?

✓ Can very long paragraphs be broken into two paragraphs?

✓ Can very short paragraphs be combined into one paragraph?

Tips

- **Proofreader's Marks** Students should use standard Proofreader's Marks to indicate the changes they wish to make. Explain to students that these marks are a kind of code used to show which alterations to make without a long explanation. Students may also be interested to know that professional writers, editors, and proofreaders use these same marks. You may want to review these marks one by one, illustrating on the board how to use them. For example, they may insert a word or a phrase by using a caret (^). If students wish to insert more text than will fit above the line, they may write in the margin or attach another sheet of paper. It may be a good idea, when such extensive corrections are made, for students to proofread their final copy carefully to make sure they have included all their alterations.
- **Sentence lifting** is a very effective method of showing students how to proofread their own work. Because students are working on their own sentences, they will be more inclined to both pay attention to what is going on and better understand the corrections that are made.

✓ Choose several pieces of student writing and look for common errors.

✓ On an overhead transparency, write several sentences. Include at least one sentence that has no errors.

✓ Tell students that you are going to concentrate on one type of error at a time. For example, first you will concentrate on spelling.

✓ Ask students to read the first sentence and point out any words they feel are spelled incorrectly. Do not erase errors. Cross them out and write the correctly spelled word above the crossed out word.

✓ Next move to a different type of error. Ask students to check for capitalization and punctuation.

✓ Continue in this way, correcting errors as you go through the sample sentences.

- **Using a Word Processor.** If the students are using a word processor to write their pieces, they may wish to run a spell check on their document. Caution them, however, that even the most sophisticated computer cannot catch every spelling error. Misuse of homophones and typographical errors may not be caught by the computer if the misused words appear in the computer's dictionary. For example, if a student types *form* instead of *from*, the computer will not register a mistake because *form* is also a word.

Circulate as students are proofreading on their own or in pairs.

✓ Are students able to check references when they are unsure of a spelling or usage?

✓ Are students criticizing each other's work constructively?

✓ Does a student no longer omit end punctuation because he or she noticed this error repeatedly during proofreading?

✓ Note students who are having difficulty. You may wish to address these difficulties during individual conferences.

PROGRAM APPENDIX

Publishing

Purpose

Publishing is the process of bringing private writing to the reading public. The purpose of writing is to communicate. Unless students are writing in a journal, they will want to present their writing to the public. Such sharing helps students to learn about themselves and others, provides an opportunity for them to take pride in their hard work, and thus motivates them to further writing.

Publishing their work helps motivate students to improve such skills as spelling, grammar, and handwriting. Publishing can be as simple as displaying papers on a bulletin board or as elaborate as creating a class newspaper. Publishing will not—indeed should not—always require large blocks of class time. Students will wish to spend more time elaborately presenting their favorite pieces and less time on other works. If students take an inordinate amount of time to publish their work, you may want to coach them on how to speed up the process.

Good Student Writers

- Present the work in a way that makes it easy to read and understand.
- Consider format, style, illustration, and clarity in the presentation of the work.
- Show pride in the finished work.

Procedure

Preparing the Final Copy

When students feel that they have thoroughly proofread their pieces, they should copy the work onto another sheet of paper, using their best handwriting, or type the work on a computer or typewriter. They should then check this copy against the proofread copy to make sure that they made all the changes correctly and did not introduce any new errors. You may need to proofread and correct students' papers one final time before publishing to make sure that they have caught all errors.

Publishing Choices

In publishing, students need to decide

✓ how to prepare the piece for publication.
✓ what form the published work should take.
✓ whether to illustrate their writing with photographs, drawings, or charts with captions, as necessary.
✓ where to place any art they are using.

Publishing Checklist

The following checklist will help students when they are publishing their work. (Not every question applies to every form of publishing.)

✓ Have I revised my work to make it better?
✓ Have I proofread it carefully?
✓ Have I decided upon my illustrations?
✓ Have I recopied my piece carefully and illustrated it?
✓ Have I numbered the pages?
✓ Have I made a cover that tells the title and my name?

Tips

- Read through the piece, and tell the student if any corrections still need to be made. Also make some suggestions about the best way to publish a piece if a student has trouble coming up with an idea.
- Make suggestions and give criticism as needed, but remember that students must retain ownership of their publishing. Leave final decisions about form and design of their work up to individual students.
- Remind students to think about their intended audience when they are deciding on the form for their published piece. Will the form they have selected present their ideas effectively to the people they want to reach?

Writing Seminar

Purpose

The purpose of Writing Seminar (Levels 1–6) is for students to discuss their work in progress and to share ideas for improving it.

Writing Seminar is one of the activities in which students may choose to participate during Workshop. Students will meet in small groups to read and discuss one another's writing. One student reads a piece in progress. Other students comment on the writing and ask questions about the ideas behind the writing. The student whose work is being critiqued writes down the comments made by his or her classmates and decides how to use these comments to make the writing better.

Procedure

To begin the seminar, have one student writer read his or her revised draft as other students listen carefully. When the student has finished, invite other students to retell the story in their own words. If they have trouble retelling the story, the writer knows that he or she must make some ideas clearer.

Then have listeners who wish to comment raise their hands. The writer calls on each in turn. The listeners ask questions or make comments about the writing, telling, for example, what they like about it or what they might change to make it better. After several comments have been made, the writer notes any information that she or he might use. Another student then reads his or her piece.

Guidelines for Peer Conferencing

In an early session, work with students to establish guidelines for peer conferencing. You might suggest rules such as the following:

✓ Listen quietly while someone else is speaking.
✓ Think carefully before you comment on another person's work.
✓ Make your comments specific.
✓ Comment on something that you like about the piece before you comment on something that needs to be improved.
✓ Discuss your work quietly so as not to disturb the rest of the class.

Modeling Seminar Behavior

You may need to model meaningful comments and questions. For example:

✓ What was your favorite part?
✓ I like the part where (or when)
✓ I like the way you describe
✓ What happened after . . . ?
✓ I'd like to know more about
✓ Why did ________ happen?
✓ What do you think is the most important part?

Teacher Conferencing

During Writing Seminar, you will want to schedule individual conferences with students to help them evaluate their writing so that they can recognize problems and find ways to solve them. Teacher conferences are useful during all phases of the writing process, but they are crucial during the revising phase. Conferences give you an opportunity to observe students as they evaluate their writing, solve problems, make decisions about their work, and take responsibility for the development and completion of their work. The basic procedure for conferences is:

- Have the student read his or her work aloud.
- Review any feedback the student has received so far.
- Identify positive elements of the work.
- Use one or more of these strategies to help the student improve his or her work.
  ✓ Have students explain how they got their ideas.
  ✓ Have students think aloud about how they will address the feedback they have received.
  ✓ Ask students to help you understand any confusion you may have about their writing.
  ✓ Have the student add, delete, or rearrange something in the work and ask how it affects the whole piece.
  ✓ Think aloud while you do a part of what the student was asked to do. Ask the student to compare what you did to what he or she did.
  ✓ Have the student prescribe as if to a younger student how to revise the work.

- Ask two or three questions to guide students through revising (see below).
- Conclude by having the student state a plan for continuing work on the piece.

Writing Conference Questions

Ideas

- Who is your audience?
- What is your purpose for writing?
- How does the reader know the purpose?
- Is there enough information about the topic?
- Do you like one part of your work more than the rest? Why?
- Is your main idea clear?
- Is there a better way to express this idea?
- Is this a good topic sentence?
- Is your introduction engaging?
- Are any important details left out?
- Are any not-so-important details left in?
- Do you use specific details and examples?
- Are your ideas accurate and, if necessary, supported by research?
- Does your conclusion sum up or restate your purpose for writing?
- What might be another way to end the work?

Organization

- Is the writing organized in a way that makes the most sense based on the main idea?
- Is the structure clear for the reader? Is there a clear beginning, middle, and end?
- Are there smooth transitions from one part to the next?
- Are supporting details ordered in the most logical way?
- Can you combine any smaller paragraphs or separate larger ones?

Voice

- Do you sound confident and knowledgeable?
- Does the voice you use reflect the purpose of your writing? Does your writing sound funny or serious when you want it to be?
- Is your voice appropriate for your audience?
- Do you sound interested in the subject?
- Have you confidently stated your opinion? Have you used the pronoun "I" if appropriate?
- Does your writing sound like you?
- Is your voice too formal or informal?
- Will this writing get a strong response from the reader?
- Does your writing make the reader care about your topic?

Word Choice

- Do you use the same word/phrase repeatedly?
- Could you say the same thing with different words?
- Have you defined words your audience may not understand?
- Have you used precise words to describe or explain?
- Is there a better word to express this idea?
- Have you used your own words when summarizing information from another text?
- Do you use time and order words such as *first, next, then,* and *last* to help the reader understand when events take place?

Sentence Fluency

- Are your sentences clear and to the point?
- Have you used different kinds and lengths of sentences to effectively present your ideas?
- Could any of your sentences be combined?
- Is there a rhythm to your sentences?
- Does each sentence introduce a new idea or a new piece of information?
- Do some sentences repeat what has already been stated? If so, cut or change them.
- Have you used transition words such as *in contrast, however,* and *on the other hand* to move smoothly from one subject to the other?
- Have you used transitional phrases, such as *according to, in addition to,* or *at the same time* to link sentences?
- Have you used conjunctions such as *and, but,* and *or* to combine short, choppy sentences?

Tips

- Completed pieces as well as works in progress can be shared during Writing Seminar.
- Concentrate on one phase of the writing process at a time.
- Remember to keep conferences brief and to the point. If you are calling the conference, prepare your comments in advance. Be sure that you confer regularly with every student if only to check that each one is continuing to write, revise, and publish.
- During teacher conferences, you might use the following responses to student writing.
  - ✓ To open communication with the writer:
    - How is the writing going?
    - Tell me about your piece.
    - How did you get your ideas?
  - ✓ To give encouragement:
    - I like the part where . . . .
    - I like the way you open your piece by . . . .
    - I like your description of . . . .
  - ✓ To get the writer to clarify meaning:
    - I wonder about . . . .
    - What happened after . . . .
    - Why did . . . ?
  - ✓ To get the writer to think about direction and about writing strategies:
    - What do you plan to do with your piece?
    - How will you go about doing that?
    - What could I do to help you?
- As you confer with students, also recognize growth—evidence in the text that a student has applied what he or she learned in earlier conferences to another piece of writing.
- Some cues to look for when evaluating a student's growth as a writer include:
  - ✓ The writer identifies problems.
  - ✓ The writer thinks of solutions to a problem.
  - ✓ The writer recognizes when and how the text needs to be reorganized.
  - ✓ The writer identifies ideas in the text that need elaboration.
  - ✓ The writer makes thoughtful changes and pays attention to detail.
  - ✓ The writer takes advantage of peer and teacher conferences, books, and other resources to improve his or her writing.

Teaching Strategies for Writing

The teacher's role in writing instruction is critical. Certain strategies have been shown to be particularly effective in teaching writing.

Teacher Modeling Students learn best when they have good models. Models for the forms of writing appear in the literature selections, ***Language Arts Transparencies,*** and ***Language Arts Handbook.*** The Writing Process Strategies include instruction and models for all phases of the writing process. Teachers can also model the writing process for students every time they write.

Feedback. The most effective writing instruction is the feedback good teachers give to individual student work. Unfortunately many teachers simply mark errors in spelling, grammar, usage, and mechanics. The ***Routine Card*** and the ***Writer's Workbook*** provide questions that teachers can consider to offer constructive and meaningful feedback to students.

Clear Assignments. A well-written assignment makes clear to students what they are supposed to do, how they are supposed to do it, who the students are writing for, and what constitutes a successful response. When students have this information, they can plan, organize, and produce more effective work.

Instruction. Having students write a lot does not make them good writers. Few people become good writers, no matter how much they write. For many, the effect of years of practice is simply to produce increasingly fluent bad writing. Students need specific instruction and practice on different forms of writing and on different phases of the writing process, which they receive with instruction, modeling, practice, and feedback.

Reading (continued)

	Level K	1	2	3	4	5	6
Comprehension Strategies							
Asking Questions/Answering Questions		✔	✔	✔	✔	✔	✔
Making Connections		✔	✔	✔	✔	✔	✔
Monitoring and Clarifying		✔	✔	✔	✔	✔	✔
Monitoring and Adjusting Reading Speed			✔	✔	✔	✔	✔
Predicting/Confirming Predictions	✔	✔	✔	✔	✔	✔	✔
Summarizing		✔	✔	✔	✔	✔	✔
Visualizing		✔	✔	✔	✔	✔	✔
Comprehension Skills							
Author's Point of View			✔	✔	✔	✔	✔
Author's Purpose			✔	✔	✔	✔	✔
Cause and Effect	✔	✔	✔	✔	✔	✔	✔
Classify and Categorize	✔	✔	✔	✔	✔	✔	✔
Compare and Contrast	✔	✔	✔	✔	✔	✔	✔
Drawing Conclusions	✔	✔	✔	✔	✔	✔	✔
Fact and Opinion			✔	✔	✔	✔	✔
Main Idea and Details	✔	✔	✔	✔	✔	✔	✔
Making Inferences		✔	✔	✔	✔	✔	✔
Reality/Fantasy	✔	✔		✔			
Sequence		✔	✔	✔	✔	✔	✔
Vocabulary							
Antonyms	✔	✔	✔	✔	✔	✔	✔
Comparatives/Superlatives		✔	✔	✔	✔	✔	✔
Compound Words	✔	✔	✔	✔	✔	✔	✔
Connecting Words (Transition Words)						✔	✔
Context Clues		✔	✔	✔	✔	✔	✔
Contractions			✔	✔	✔	✔	
Figurative Language				✔		✔	
Greek and Latin Roots				✔	✔		
High-Frequency Words	✔	✔	✔	✔	✔	✔	✔
Homographs			✔	✔	✔	✔	
Homophones/Homonyms		✔	✔	✔	✔	✔	✔
Idioms					✔	✔	✔
Inflectional Endings		✔	✔	✔	✔	✔	✔
Irregular Plurals				✔		✔	✔
Multiple Meaning Words			✔	✔	✔	✔	✔
Multisyllabic Words			✔	✔		✔	
Position Words	✔	✔				✔	
Prefixes			✔	✔	✔	✔	✔
Question Words		✔					
Base or Root Words		✔	✔	✔	✔	✔	✔
Selection Vocabulary	✔	✔	✔	✔	✔	✔	✔
Suffixes		✔	✔	✔	✔	✔	✔
Synonyms		✔	✔	✔	✔	✔	✔
Time and Order Words (Creating Sequence)				✔	✔	✔	✔
Utility Words (Colors, Classroom Objects, etc.)	✔	✔					
Word Families			✔	✔	✔	✔	✔

Inquiry and Research

Study Skills	K	1	2	3	4	5	6
Charts, Graphs, and Diagrams/Visual Aids			✔		✔	✔	✔
Collaborative Inquiry			✔	✔	✔	✔	✔
Communicating Research Progress Results			✔	✔	✔	✔	✔
Compile Notes						✔	✔
Conducting an Interview							✔
Finding Needed Information			✔	✔	✔	✔	✔
Follow Directions	✔			✔			
Formulate Questions for Inquiry and Research			✔			✔	✔
Give Reports					✔	✔	✔
Make Outlines				✔		✔	✔
Making Conjectures			✔	✔	✔	✔	✔
Maps and Globes					✔		✔
Note Taking			✔	✔	✔	✔	✔
Parts of a Book			✔	✔	✔		
Planning Investigation			✔	✔	✔	✔	✔
Recognizing Information Needs			✔	✔	✔	✔	✔
Revising Questions and Conjectures			✔	✔	✔	✔	✔
Summarize and Organize Information					✔	✔	✔
Time Lines					✔	✔	✔
Use Appropriate Resources (Media Source, Reference Books, Experts, Internet)					✔	✔	✔
Using a Dictionary/Glossary		✔	✔	✔	✔	✔	✔
Using a Media Center/Library					✔		✔
Using a Thesaurus			✔	✔	✔	✔	✔
Using an Encyclopedia					✔		✔
Using Newspapers and Magazines					✔		✔
Using Technology							

Skills, strategies, and other teaching opportunities

✔ Formal, progress, or informal testing opportunitie

Language Arts

Writing/Composition

	Level K	1	2	3	4	5	6
Approaches							
Collaborative Writing		✔					
Group Writing							
Process							
Brainstorming/Prewriting	✔	✔		✔	✔	✔	
Drafting	✔	✔		✔	✔	✔	
Revising	✔	✔		✔	✔	✔	
Proofreading	✔	✔		✔	✔	✔	
Publishing	✔	✔		✔	✔	✔	
Forms							
Biography/Autobiography	✔	✔	✔	✔	✔	✔	✔
Business Letter				✔	✔	✔	✔
Describe a Process		✔	✔	✔	✔		✔
Descriptive Writing	✔	✔	✔	✔	✔	✔	✔
Expository/Informational Text	✔	✔	✔	✔	✔	✔	✔
Folklore (Folktales, Fairy Tales, Tall Tales, Legends, Myths)			✔	✔	✔		
Friendly Letter		✔	✔	✔	✔	✔	✔
Historical Fiction						✔	✔
Journal Writing		✔	✔	✔	✔	✔	✔
Narrative		✔	✔	✔	✔	✔	✔
Personal Writing		✔	✔	✔	✔	✔	✔
Persuasive Writing	✔	✔	✔	✔	✔	✔	✔
Play/Dramatization				✔	✔	✔	✔
Poetry		✔	✔	✔	✔	✔	✔
Realistic Story				✔			
Writer's Craft							
Characterization			✔	✔	✔	✔	✔
Descriptive Writing	✔	✔	✔	✔	✔	✔	✔
Dialogue		✔	✔	✔	✔	✔	✔
Effective Beginnings			✔	✔	✔	✔	✔
Effective Endings			✔	✔	✔	✔	✔
Event Sequence		✔	✔	✔	✔	✔	✔
Figurative Language	✔		✔	✔	✔	✔	✔
Identifying Thoughts and Feelings	✔		✔	✔	✔	✔	✔
Mood and Tone				✔	✔	✔	✔
Plot (Problem/Solutions)	✔	✔	✔	✔	✔	✔	✔
Point of View				✔	✔	✔	
Rhyme	✔	✔	✔	✔	✔	✔	
Sensory Details				✔		✔	✔
Sentence Variety				✔		✔	✔
Sentence Elaboration				✔		✔	✔
Setting	✔		✔	✔		✔	✔
Suspense and Surprise			✔	✔	✔	✔	
Topic Sentences			✔	✔	✔	✔	✔
Using Comparisons						✔	
Purposes							
Determining Purposes for Writing	✔	✔				✔	

Scope and Sequence (continued)

Language Arts

Grammar

	Level K	1	2	3	4	5	6
Parts of Speech							
Adjectives	✔	✔	✔	✔	✔	✔	✔
Adverbs			✔	✔	✔	✔	✔
Conjunctions			✔	✔	✔	✔	✔
Nouns	✔	✔	✔	✔	✔	✔	✔
Prepositions	✔			✔	✔	✔	✔
Pronouns	✔	✔	✔	✔	✔	✔	✔
Verbs	✔	✔	✔	✔	✔	✔	✔
Sentences							
Fragments					✔	✔	✔
Parts (Subjects/Predicates)		✔	✔	✔	✔	✔	✔
Subject/Verb Agreement	✔	✔	✔	✔	✔	✔	✔
Structure (Simple, Compound, Complex)				✔	✔	✔	✔
Types (Declarative, Interrogative, Exclamatory, Imperatives)	✔	✔	✔	✔	✔	✔	✔
Verb Tenses	✔	✔	✔	✔	✔	✔	✔
Verbs (Action, Helping, Linking, Regular/Irregular)	✔	✔	✔	✔	✔	✔	✔
Usage							
Adjectives	✔	✔	✔	✔	✔	✔	✔
Adverbs			✔	✔	✔	✔	✔
Articles	✔	✔	✔	✔	✔	✔	✔
Nouns	✔	✔	✔	✔	✔	✔	✔
Pronouns	✔	✔	✔	✔	✔	✔	✔
Verbs	✔	✔	✔	✔	✔	✔	✔
Mechanics							
Capitalization (Sentence, Proper Nouns, Titles, Direct Address, Pronoun "I")	✔	✔	✔	✔	✔	✔	✔
Punctuation (End Punctuation, Comma Use, Quotation Marks, Apostrophe, Colon, Semicolon, Hyphen, Parentheses)	✔	✔	✔	✔	✔	✔	✔

Spelling

	K	1	2	3	4	5	6
Contractions		✔	✔	✔		✔	
Inflectional Endings			✔	✔	✔	✔	
Irregular Plurals			✔	✔	✔	✔	✔
Long Vowel Patterns		✔	✔	✔	✔	✔	✔
Multisyllabic Words			✔	✔		✔	
Phonograms		✔	✔	✔			✔
r-controlled Vowel Spellings		✔	✔	✔	✔	✔	✔
Short Vowel Spellings		✔	✔	✔	✔	✔	✔
Silent Letters				✔			
Sound/Letter Relationships		✔	✔	✔			
Special Spelling Patterns (*-ough, -augh, -all, -al, -alk, -ion,-sion, -tion*)		✔	✔	✔	✔	✔	✔

(shaded box) Skills, strategies, and other teaching opportunities ✔ Formal, progress, or informal testing opportunities

Language Arts (continued)

Listening/Speaking/Viewing

	Level K	1	2	3	4	5	6
Listening/Speaking							
Analyze/Evaluate Intent and Content of Speaker's Message		✔	✔	✔	✔	✔	✔
Ask and Answer Questions	✔	✔	✔	✔	✔	✔	✔
Determine Purposes for Listening			✔	✔	✔		
Follow Directions	✔	✔	✔	✔	✔	✔	✔
Learn about Different Cultures through Discussion					✔	✔	✔
Listen for Poetic Language (Rhythm/Rhyme)	✔	✔	✔	✔			
Participate in Group Discussions		✔	✔	✔	✔	✔	✔
Respond to Speaker	✔	✔	✔	✔	✔	✔	✔
Use Nonverbal Communication Techniques	✔	✔	✔	✔	✔	✔	✔
Speaking							
Describe Ideas and Feelings	✔	✔	✔	✔	✔	✔	✔
Give Directions					✔	✔	✔
Learn about Different Cultures through Discussion				✔	✔	✔	✔
Participate in Group Discussions	✔	✔	✔	✔	✔	✔	✔
Present Oral Reports			✔	✔	✔	✔	✔
Read Fluently with Expression, Phrasing, and Intonation			✔	✔	✔	✔	✔
Read Orally		✔	✔	✔	✔	✔	✔
Share Information	✔	✔	✔	✔	✔	✔	✔
Speak Clearly at Appropriate Volume	✔	✔	✔	✔	✔	✔	✔
Summarize/Retell Stories	✔	✔	✔	✔	✔	✔	✔
Understand Formal and Informal Language	✔	✔	✔	✔	✔	✔	✔
Use Appropriate Vocabulary for Audience		✔	✔	✔	✔	✔	✔
Use Elements of Grammar in Speech				✔	✔	✔	✔
Viewing							
Analyze Purposes and Techniques of the Media				✔	✔	✔	✔
Appreciate/Interpret Artist's Techniques							
Compare Visual and Written Material on the Same Subject	✔				✔		
Gather Information from Visual Images	✔	✔	✔	✔	✔	✔	✔
View Critically		✔	✔	✔	✔	✔	✔
View Culturally Rich Materials	✔	✔	✔		✔	✔	✔
Penmanship							
Cursive Letters			✔	✔	✔	✔	✔
Manuscript Letters	✔	✔	✔				
Numbers	✔	✔	✔	✔			

Unit Themes

PROGRAM APPENDIX

	LEVEL K	LEVEL 1	LEVEL 2
Unit 1	School	Let's Read!	Sharing Stories
Unit 2	Shadows	Animals	Kindness
Unit 3	Finding Friends	Things That Go	Look Again
Unit 4	The Wind	Our Neighborhood at Work	Fossils
Unit 5	Stick to It	Weather	Courage
Unit 6	Red, White, and Blue	Journeys	Our Country and Its People
Unit 7	Teamwork	Keep Trying	
Unit 8	By the Sea	Games	
Unit 9		Being Afraid	
Unit 10		Homes	

LESSON	PHONICS SKILLS	DECODABLE BOOKS
Getting Started		
DAY 1	review /ā/ spellings; review /ē/ spellings	1 Dave the Brave 2 Sleepy Steve
DAY 2	review /ī/ spellings; review /ō/ spellings	3 The Shy Bird's Trick 4 Chinlow of Singboat
DAY 3	review /ū/ spellings; review /aw/ spelled *au_, aw*	5 Mrs. Music 6 Paul, Aunt Maud, and Claude
DAY 4	review /ow/ spelled *ou_, ow;* review /oi/ spelled *oi, _oy*	7 Flower the Cow 8 Toy Store Explorer
DAY 5	review /o͝o/ spelled *oo;* review /o͞o/ spelled *u, u_e, _ew, _ue, oo*	9 A Book for Mr. Hook 10 Root Stew
Unit 1		
LESSON 1	/ī/ spelled *i_e, _y, igh;* endings *-ed, -ing, -s, -ful, -er;* review /a/; review short vowels	11 The Frog Who Wanted to Fly
LESSON 2	plural *–s;* inflectional endings; homographs; comparative and superlative adjectives; /e/ spelled *e;* special spelling pattern /m/ spelled *mb;* /e/ spelled *ea;* review short vowel;cvc – closed syllables	12 Up to Bat
LESSON 3	antonyms; homophones; prefix *re-;* related words; review /i/; /ā/ spelled *a, ai_, a_e, _ay*	13 Baking Princess
LESSON 4	suffixes *-ly, -ed, -ing;* contractions; /ō/; /ē/ spelled *e, ea, e_e, _y, ee, _ie_*	14 City Girl
LESSON 5	suffix *-tion;* prefixes and suffixes; frequently misspelled words; plural forms of nouns that end in *y;* /ū/ spellings; /ī/ spelled *i, _y, i_e, _ie, igh*	15 The Prince's Foolish Wish
LESSON 6	inflectional endings and suffixes added to base words; /k/ spelled *c;* nouns; review short vowels; /ō/ spelled *o, _ow, o_e, oa_, _oe*	16 Rose, the Brave
Unit 2		
LESSON 1	antonyms; synonyms; compound words; suffix *-y;* prefix *un-;* spelling patterns /ar/ and *air;* review /ū/ spelled *u, u_e, _ue, _ew*	17 Hugo Bugle
LESSON 2	compound words; homophones; suffix *-tion;* suffix *-ly;* /er/ spelled *ur* and *ir;* /or/ spelled *or* and *ore;* review long vowels with open syllables	18 Queen Kit
LESSON 3	word families; synonyms; /əl/ spelled *-le;* open syllables with vowel digraphs	19 Dead as a Dodo, Bald as an Eagle
LESSON 4	compound words; related words; vivid verbs; /ow/ spelled *ou_* and *ow;* open syllables - vcv; closed syllables; multisyllabic words with long vowels; /s/ spelled *s, ce, ci_;* special spelling pattern: /s/ spelled *sc*	20 The Lives of Sea Turtles
LESSON 5	contractions; suffixes *-ly, -ing;* prefix *un-;* /oi/ spelled *oi* and *_oy;* multisyllabic words with long and short vowels ending *-le*	21 Nesting and Burrowing Birds
LESSON 6	compound words; suffix *-ed;* antonyms; vivid verbs; /əl/; /ow/; /oi/; /er/; multisyllabic words with long and short vowels	22 Loop and Hook a Dream

Introduction to Sounds (continued)

LEVEL APPENDIX

LESSON	PHONICS SKILLS	DECODABLE BOOKS
Unit 3		
LESSON 1	compound words; homophones; related words; /c/ spelled *s, ce, ci_;* /ā/ spelled *a, a_e, ai_, ay_;* review multisyllabic words with long and short vowels; special spelling patterns /n/ spelled *n, kn_,* and *gn_;* /m/ spelled *mb;* /g/ spelled *gh;* /l/ spelled *sl;* word families with spelling changes	23 Sweet and Sour Soup
LESSON 2	suffixes *-ful, -ly, -ing;* contractions; irregular past tense verbs; /ē/ spelled *ea, ee;* review diphthongs; /r/ spelled *er, ir, ur, ar;* /ə/ spelled *o*	24 No Noise!
LESSON 3	base words with suffixes; compound words; comparatives and superlatives (-er/-est); related words; /ī/ spelled *i_e, igh;* review diphthongs; suffixes *-ing, -ly, -er, -est*	25 Summer Pen Pals
LESSON 4	cardinal and ordinal numbers; suffixes; comparative and superlative endings *-er, -est;* /ō/ spelled *o* and *o_e;* diphthongs; prefixes *un-, re-, pre-, bi-, mis-, dis-*	26 Joyce Writes a Good Story
LESSON 5	prefixes and suffixes; /o͞o/ spelled *u_e, _ew;* diphthongs	27 Little Hare
LESSON 6	suffix *-ed;* comparatives; plural forms of words that end in *f;* homographs; related words; review long vowels; affixes as syllables	28 Ralph, a Bug
Unit 4		
LESSON 1	homophones; base words and suffixes *-ed, -ment, -tion, -sion;* word families; double consonants	29 Kitty and the Nothing Day
LESSON 2	synonyms; base words with suffixes *-ly, -able;* final double consonants	30 Traveling Star
LESSON 3	compound words; /ā/ spelled *a_e, ai_, _ay;* contractions; base words with affixes; base words with suffixes: *-ful, -er, -tation*	31 Whales
LESSON 4	base words with suffixes *-ful, -ly, -ed, -ing;* /ē/ spelled *_ie_, ei*	32 The Stone Wall
LESSON 5	compound words; suffixes *-ed, -ing, -ial;* plural endings *-s* and *-es*	33 Say It in Code
LESSON 6	suffix *-ment;* antonyms; related words; special spelling patterns: *nk,* /t/ spelled *bt,* /n/ spelled *gn;* compound words	34 Peace and Quiet
LESSON 7	compound words; suffixes *-ment, -tion, -sion*	35 School Days Long Ago

Introduction to Sounds (continued)

LESSON	PHONICS SKILLS	DECODABLE BOOKS
Unit 5		
LESSON 1	synonyms; hard *g;* /ā/ spelled *eigh*, consonant blends	
LESSON 2	antonyms; base words with suffixes *-ed*, *-able*, *-ation*, *-ative;* prefix *re-;* spellings *wr_*, *kn_*, *wh*	
LESSON 3	compound words; /wh/ spelled *wh-;* base words and suffix *-ness;* silent *l* in *lf;* /ch/ spelled ■*tch;* silent *g* in *gn*	
LESSON 4	homographs; /k/ spelled *c*, *k*, ■*ck;* base words with suffixes *-tion*, *-sion;* /ə/	
LESSON 5	base words with prefixes and suffixes; /ā/ and /ī/; suffix *-ed;* /ē/ spelled *_ie;* /kw/ spelled *qu*	
LESSON 6	base words with prefix *be-*, *re-;* compound words; /s/ spelled *s* and *ce* and *ci_;* /j/ spelled *ge*	
LESSON 7	base words with suffixes *-ed*, *-ing*, *-y*, *-es;* review spelling patterns	
Unit 6		
LESSON 1	vivid verbs; base words with suffixes *-ible* and *-ness;* irregular plurals	
LESSON 2	short vowel base words ending in *-tch* and the suffix *-ed;* long vowel base words ending in silent *e* with the suffix *-ing;* compound words; double consonants ending with *-y*	
LESSON 3	comparatives and superlatives; vivid verbs and adjectives; homophones; /f/ spelled *lf;* /m/ spelled *lm;* words ending in suffixes *-er*, *-est*	
LESSON 4	compound words; base words with the prefix *auto-;* plural words; Latin roots	
LESSON 5	compound words; prefix *un-;* suffix *-less;* Greek roots	
LESSON 6	compound words; suffix *-est;* prefix *re-;* French, Spanish, and German roots	
LESSON 7	contractions; vivid adjectives; irregular plurals	

High-Frequency Word List

a
about
after
again
all
always
am
an
and
any
are
around
as
ask
at
ate
away
be
because
been
before
best
better
big
black
blue
both
bring
brown
but
buy
by
call
came
can
carry
clean
cold
come
could
cut
did
do
does
done
don't
down
draw
drink
eat
eight
every
fall
far
fast
find
first
five
fly
for
found
four
from
full
funny
gave
get
give
go
goes
going
good
got
green
grow
had
has
have
he
help
her
here
him
his
hold
hot
how
hurt
I
if
in
into
is
it
its
jump
just
keep
kind
know
laugh
let
light
like
little
live
long
look
made
make
many
may
me
much
must
my
myself
never
new
no
not
now
of
off
old
on
once
one
only
open
or
our
out
over
own
pick
play
please
pretty
pull
put
ran
read
red
ride
right
round
run
said
saw
say
see
seven
shall
she
show
sing
sit
six
sleep
small
so
some
soon
start
stop
take
tell
ten
thank
that
the
their
them
then
there
these
they
think
this
those
three
to
today
together
too
try
two
under
up
upon
us
use
very
walk
want
warm
was
wash
we
well
went
were
what
when
where
which
white
who
why
will
wish
with
work
would
write
yellow
yes
you
your

Card 1: /a/ Lamb

I'm Pam the Lamb, I am.

This is how I tell my Mommy where I am: /a/ /a/ /a/ /a/ /a/.

I'm Pam the Lamb, I am.
This is how I tell my Daddy where I am: /a/ /a/ /a/ /a/ /a/.

I'm Pam the Lamb, I am.
That young ram is my brother Sam.
This is how I tell my brother where I am: /a/ /a/ /a/ /a/ /a/.

I'm Pam the Lamb; I'm happy where I am.
Can you help me tell my family where I am? *(Have the children respond.)* /a/ /a/ /a/ /a/ /a/

Card 2: /b/ Ball

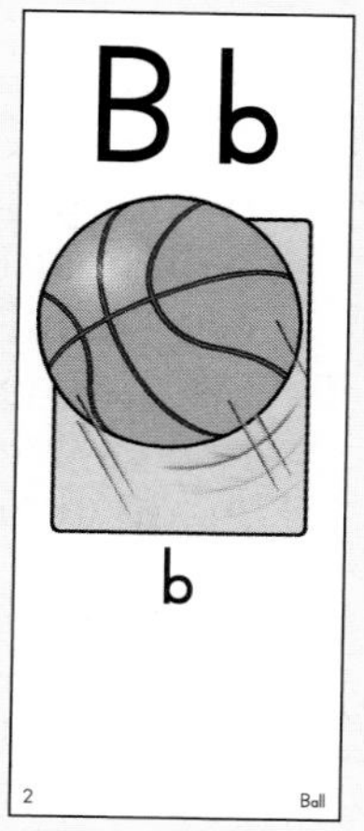

Bobby loved to bounce his basketball.
He bounced it all day long.
This is the sound the ball made: /b/ /b/ /b/ /b/ /b/.

One day, while Bobby was bouncing his basketball,
Bonnie came by on her bike.

Bonnie said, "Hi, Bobby. I have a little bitty ball.
May I bounce my ball with you?"

Bobby said, "Sure!" and Bonnie bounced her little bitty ball.
What sound do you think Bonnie's ball made?
(Encourage a very soft reply.) /b/ /b/ /b/ /b/ /b/

Soon Betsy came by. "Hi, Bobby. Hi, Bonnie," she said.
"I have a great big beach ball. May I bounce my ball with you?"

Bobby and Bonnie said, "Sure!" and Betsy bounced her big beach ball.
What sound do you think the beach ball made?
(Encourage a louder, slower reply.) /b/ /b/ /b/ /b/ /b/

(Designate three groups, one for each ball sound.)
Now when Bobby, Bonnie, and Betsy bounce their balls together, this is the sound you hear:
(Have all three groups make their sounds in a chorus.) /b/ /b/ /b/ /b/ /b/

Card 3: /k/ Camera

Carlos has a new camera. When he takes pictures, his camera makes a clicking sound like this: /k/ /k/ /k/ /k/ /k/.

In the garden, Carlos takes pictures of caterpillars crawling on cabbage: /k/ /k/ /k/ /k/ /k/.
At the zoo, Carlos takes pictures of a camel, a duck, and a kangaroo: /k/ /k/ /k/.
In the park, Carlos takes pictures of his cousin flying a kite: /k/ /k/ /k/ /k/ /k/.
In his room, Carlos takes pictures of his cute kitten, Cozy: /k/ /k/ /k/ /k/ /k/.

Can you help Carlos take pictures with his camera?
(Have the children join in.) /k/ /k/ /k/ /k/ /k/ /k/ /k/

Card 4: /d/ Dinosaur

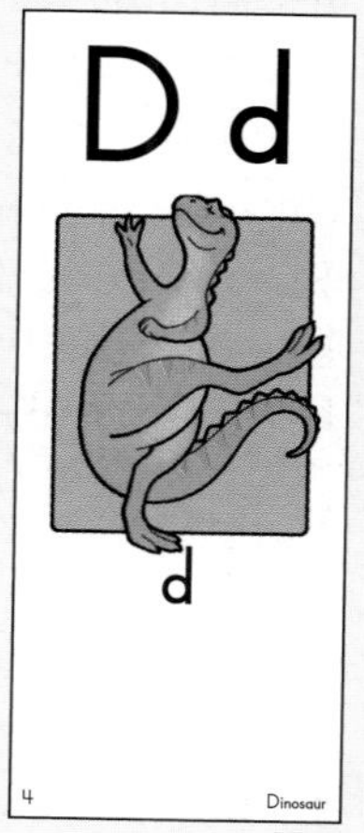

Dinah the Dinosaur loves to dance.
She dances whenever she gets the chance.
Whenever that dinosaur dips and whirls,
This is the sound of her dancing twirls:
/d/ /d/ /d/ /d/ /d/ /d/!

Dinah the Dinosaur dances all day.
From dawn to dark, she dances away.
And when Dinah dances, her dinosaur feet
make a thundering, thudding, extremely loud beat:
(loudly, with an exaggerated rhythm)
/d/ /d/ /d/ /d/ /d/ /d/!

Now if you were a dinosaur just like Dinah,
you would certainly dance just as finely as she.
And if you were a Dino, and you had a chance,
what sound would your feet make when you did a dance?
(Have the children join in.) /d/ /d/ /d/ /d/ /d/ /d/

Sound/Spelling Card Stories (continued)

Card 5: /e/ Hen

Jem's pet hen likes to peck, peck, peck.
She pecks at a speck on the new red deck.
This is how her pecking sounds:
/e/ /e/ /e/ /e/ /e/.

Jem's pet hen pecks at corn in her pen.
She pecks ten kernels, then pecks again.
This is how her pecking sounds:
/e/ /e/ /e/ /e/ /e/.

Jem's hen pecks at a cracked egg shell.
She's helping a chick get out, alive and well.
This is how her pecking sounds:
/e/ /e/ /e/ /e/ /e/.

Can you help Jem's hen peck?
(Have children say:) /e/ /e/ /e/ /e/ /e/.

Card 6: /f/ Fan

/f/ /f/ /f/ /f/ /f/—What's that funny sound?
It's Franny the Fan going round and round,
and this is the sound that old fan makes:
/f/ /f/ /f/ /f/ /f/.

When it gets too hot, you see,
Franny cools the family: /f/ /f/ /f/ /f/ /f/.
She fans Father's face
and Foxy's fur
and Felicity's feet.
Hear the Fan whir: /f/ /f/ /f/ /f/ /f/.

Can you make Franny the Fan go fast?
(Have the children say quickly:)
/f/ /f/ /f/ /f/ /f/.
Faster? /f/ /f/ /f/ /f/ /f/
Fastest? /f/ /f/ /f/ /f/ /f/

Card 7: /g/ Gopher

Gary's a gopher.
He loves to gulp down food.
/g/ /g/ /g/ /g/ /g/, gulps the gopher.

Gary the Gopher gulps down grass
because it tastes so good.
/g/ /g/ /g/ /g/ /g/, gulps the gopher.

Gary the Gopher gulps down grapes—
gobs and gobs of grapes.
/g/ /g/ /g/ /g/ /g/, gulps the gopher.

Gary the Gopher gobbles green beans
and says once more,
/g/ /g/ /g/ /g/ /g/. He's such a hungry gopher!

Gary the Gopher gobbles in the garden
until everything is gone.

What sound does Gary the Gopher make?
(Ask the children to join in.) /g/ /g/ /g/ /g/ /g/

Card 8: /h/ Hound

Harry the Hound dog hurries around.
Can you hear Harry's hurrying hound-
dog sound?
This is the sound Harry's breathing
makes when he hurries:
/h/ /h/ /h/ /h/ /h/ /h/!

When Harry the Hound dog sees a
hare hop by,
he tears down the hill, and his four
feet fly.
Hurry, Harry, hurry! /h/ /h/ /h/ /h/ /h/ /h/!

How Harry the Hound dog loves to hunt
and chase!
He hurls himself from place to place.
Hurry, Harry, hurry! /h/ /h/ /h/ /h/ /h/ /h/!

When Harry the Hound dog sees a big skunk roam,
He howls for help and heads for home.

What sound does Harry make when he hurries?
(Have the children answer.) /h/ /h/ /h/ /h/ /h/ /h/

Card 9: /i/ Pig

This is Pickles the Pig.
If you tickle Pickles, she gets the giggles.
This is the sound of her giggling:
/i/ /i/ /i/ /i/ /i/.

Tickle Pickles the Pig under her chin.
Listen! She's giggling: /i/ /i/ /i/ /i/ /i/.
Wiggle a finger in Pickles' ribs.
Listen! She's giggling: /i/ /i/ /i/ /i/ /i/.

Give Pickles the Pig a wink,
and what do you think? First comes a grin.
Then listen!
She's giggling again: /i/ /i/ /i/ /i/ /i/.

Quick! Tickle Pickles the Pig. What will
she say? *(Have the children join in.)* /i/ /i/ /i/ /i/ /i/

Card 10: /j/ Jump

When Jenny jumps her jump rope,
it sounds like this: /j/ /j/ /j/ /j/ /j/.
When Jackson jumps his jump rope,
it sounds like this: /j/ /j/ /j/ /j/ /j/.

The judges generally agree
that Jenny jumps most rapidly:
(quickly) /j/ /j/ /j/ /j/ /j/.

When Jenny jumps, she jumps to this jingle:
"Jump, jump, jump so quick.
Whenever I jump, I like to kick."
/j/ /j/ /j/ /j/ /j/

The Judges generally agree
that Jackson jumps most quietly:
(quietly) /j/ /j/ /j/ /j/ /j/.

When Jackson jumps, he jumps to this jingle:
"Jump, jump, nice and quiet.
See what happens when you try it." /j/ /j/ /j/ /j/ /j/

(to the children) Jump rope like Jenny.
(quickly) /j/ /j/ /j/ /j/ /j/
(to the children) Jump rope like Jackson.
(quietly) /j/ /j/ /j/ /j/ /j/

Card 11: /k/ Camera

Carlos has a new camera. When he
takes pictures,
His camera makes a clicking sound like this:
/k/ /k/ /k/ /k/ /k/.

In the garden, Carlos takes pictures of
caterpillars crawling on cabbage:
/k/ /k/ /k/ /k/ /k/.
At the zoo, Carlos takes pictures of a camel,
a duck, and a kangaroo:
/k/ /k/ /k/.
In the park, Carlos takes pictures of his
cousin flying a kite: /k/ /k/ /k/ /k/ /k/
In his room, Carlos takes pictures of his
cute kitten, Cozy. /k/ /k/ /k/ /k/ /k/

Can you help Carlos take pictures with his camera?
(Have the children join in.) /k/ /k/ /k/ /k/ /k/ /k/ /k/

Card 12: /l/ Lion

Look! It's Leon the Lion.
Leon loves to lap water from lakes,
and this is the sound the lapping lion
makes: /l/ /l/ /l/ /l/ /l/.

Let's join Leon. Quick!
Take a little lick: /l/ /l/ /l/ /l/ /l/.

Are you a thirsty lass or lad?
Then lap until you don't feel bad:
/l/ /l/ /l/ /l/ /l/.

What sound do you make when you lap
like Leon the Lion?
(Have the children say:) /l/ /l/ /l/ /l/ /l/.

Card 13: /m/ Monkey

For Muzzy the Monkey, bananas
are yummy.
She munches so many, they fill up
her tummy.
When she eats, she says:
/m/ /m/ /m/ /m/ /m/!

Bananas for breakfast, bananas
for lunch.
Mash them up, mush them up,
Munch, munch, munch, munch!
What does Muzzy the Monkey say?
(Have the children say:) /m/ /m/ /m/ /m/ /m/.

Bananas at bedtime? I have a hunch
Muzzy will mash them up, mush them up,
Munch, munch, munch, munch!
Then what will Muzzy the Monkey say?
(Have the children say:) /m/ /m/ /m/ /m/ /m/.

G

H

INDEX

Index (continued)

INDEX

INDEX

M

N

O

Q

R

INDEX

S

INDEX

INDEX

INDEX

W